a 365 day devotional

———

THE DAILY GRACE CO.

DAY 01

New Beginnings

In the beginning God created the heavens and the earth.

GENESIS 1:1

Whether we fear new beginnings or embrace them, it is wise to consider who is the beginning of all things. In the beginning was God, and from Him, all things were created. He created the heavens and the earth with His words. God's creation came *ex nihilo*, a Latin phrase meaning "out of nothing." The creation story is a pertinent reminder that God is very good at making something out of nothing. He is very good at building from the ground up. He is very good at sculpting, molding, making, and shaping us, regardless of the state we are in. When our circumstances leave us staring at a blank slate, feeling as though we are formless materials, we can remember that we are held in the hands of the world's great artist and sculptor.

The hope presented in the first sentence of the Bible is that our beginnings would have never happened apart from the work of God. He is the beginning of all things. Nothing happens outside of His sovereign hand. When God created us, He sovereignly knew every part of us and every course our lives would take. God knew sin would enter into the world, resulting in chaos and disorder. If left to ourselves, God's perfect beginning would result in a sad ending because of our sin. But God the Father sent His Son, Jesus Christ, to purchase the hope of a perfect ending for all who place their faith and trust in Him. Every moment of our lives, every person who has crossed our paths, every trial we have faced, every joy we embrace, every change, has continued the creating, shaping, and sanctifying work of the Creator in our lives.

Every new beginning is an opportunity for God to perfect us into the likeness of Jesus and bring us closer to Himself, even when His work is not clearly visible to us. The Bible brings us to know who God is, what He is capable of, and how He promises to sustain a miraculous work in us to completion (Philippians 1:6). May you rest assured in new beginnings—that God's good work in you began with intention and purpose. He does not erase or rewrite His plan for your life. Every single moment has always been part of your story. God is the perfect author of beginnings and—through salvation in Jesus Christ—secures our triumphant ending.

"NOTHING HAPPENS OUTSIDE OF HIS SOVEREIGN HAND."

DAY 02

Hold Fast to the Faith

For we have become participants in Christ if we hold firmly until the end the reality that we had at the start.

HEBREWS 3:14

If you have ever been hiking, you may know the ping of excitement that you feel as you prepare for your trek. You are ready for the beauty you will see—the pine trees, the budding wildflowers, and, most importantly, the view at the summit.

But the hike is also a little harder than you anticipated. Perhaps a short time into your journey, you notice sweat soaking the lower half of your t-shirt and a blister forming on your ankle. These annoyances feel like simple inconveniences at first, but, over time, they overtake your thoughts. And, before you know it, those wildflowers, fresh from their winter's sleep, do not even get a nod. You forget your initial amazement at the grandeur of the tall pines (as grateful as you are for their silent labor of providing shade from the sun).

As the journey becomes more difficult, the thought presents itself, *Maybe this isn't worth it?* But then you remember why you started. You need to get to the summit. And so you fix your mind on the vision of victory at the top, and you press onward. One step, and then another, and still another, even as your blisters grow. And finally, you begin to see the summit.

And once you reach the pinnacle, sweat dripping and ankles burning, you survey everything below the peak. You see the path you took as well as the one that leads to a dead end. You see the clouds and the way they hang over the valley in the distance. And then, after you breathe in the beauty of the surrounding scene, you sit down to rest and notice, once again, the common grace beside you—a budding flower straining upward in new life.

This, of course, is not just about the summit or that wildflower. This is a simple picture of something better, of something greater. This is about Jesus. It is about hope born on another hillside long ago, where God became flesh and offered Himself in our place as He died upon the cross to give us new life. It is about a garden of the past and a golden city of the future, where all pain and striving cease. So we focus on this glorious future as we take hold of Christ's hand and walk one step, then the next, toward home.

"THIS IS A SIMPLE PICTURE OF SOMETHING BETTER, OF SOMETHING GREATER. THIS IS ABOUT JESUS."

DAY 03
God's Plan All Along

I will put hostility between you and the woman, and between your offspring and her offspring. He will strike your head, and you will strike his heel.

GENESIS 3:15

The first few chapters of the Bible provide some of the most beautiful and heartbreaking scenes in all of Scripture. God's creation unfolds, and He creates man and woman to enjoy His good world with Him. He reigns over them as their loving King, and they enjoy unbroken fellowship with Him. But Adam and Eve rebel against God. They fall into the trap of deception laid by the serpent, and they must leave God's presence because of their sin. Thus, God's creation is marred.

And yet, God declares His plan of redemption. He does not wait to show mercy to Adam and Eve. He shows them immediate mercy. There will be a way of deliverance, and it will come through one of their offspring. God's people await this promised offspring throughout the Old Testament. He is the One who fulfills God's promise to David. He will sit on the throne as King forever. This promised offspring is Jesus. He will strike the head of the serpent and defeat death forever by His perfect life and substitutionary death on the cross. Though the serpent will strike His heel, and He will lay dead in a tomb for three days, He will overcome the serpent's bite in His resurrection. And He will give this same resurrection and eternal life to all who believe in Him.

When we read about the fall of man, we may be overcome with sadness. We are right to mourn sin's entrance into the world, for it has caused brokenness. But it should give us great hope and love for God to see how He immediately responds to our sin. God desires to bring us back to the original fellowship with Him. He wants to commune with us, and He has given us salvation through His Son so we can be His for all of eternity.

We read the gospel for the first time in the book of Genesis, and God foretells His plan of redemption again and again until the arrival of Christ. When the time came, He sent His Son to die so that we could have life, and He seeks to draw us to Himself. What joy and comfort we have knowing that when He returns, sin will be no more, and we will live reunited with Christ.

"GOD DESIRES TO BRING US BACK TO THE ORIGINAL FELLOWSHIP WITH HIM."

DAY 04
Where Wandering Eyes Can Lead You

The woman saw that the tree was good for food and delightful to look at, and that it was desirable for obtaining wisdom. So she took some of its fruit and ate it; she also gave some to her husband, who was with her, and he ate it.

GENESIS 3:6

God told Adam and Eve not to eat from the Tree of Knowledge of Good and Evil. However, Eve was deceived by the serpent and no longer saw the tree as a prohibition. Instead, she perceived it to be the bestower of wisdom. While Eve was attracted to the tree for its delicious-looking fruit and its beauty, she was most attracted to the promise of divine knowledge. The serpent convinced Eve that she would understand all things and be like God if she ate from the tree. Under this false promise, Eve reached toward the branches, bit into the fruit, and shared some with Adam. Their eyes were indeed opened but not because of the tree, for the tree was simply a symbol of obedience. Eve's eyes were opened by her God-given conscience. Through this conviction, the Lord redirected her wandering eyes to her sin and folly.

God desires His people to have true wisdom. Scripture illuminates this desire through the the book of Proverbs. In Proverbs 2:4, the author calls the reader to search for wisdom like one searches for silver or hidden treasure. The Lord wants the eyes of His people to actively seek knowledge and understanding in Him. However, because of our sinful nature, we do not see God's wisdom as a gift. Instead, we wander toward counterfeit wisdom in things apart from Christ, rebelling against God's Word and establishing our own ways. But, through God's grace, verses like Genesis 3:6 and Proverbs 2, expose our wrong. Like Adam and Eve, we stand with the bitten fruit in our hands, aware of our folly and need for a Savior.

Fortunately, the Savior came and possessed the fullness of divine wisdom. God took on flesh in the person of Jesus Christ. Though He knew all things, Jesus perfectly sought knowledge and understanding by depending on the Father. His eyes stayed focused on defeating sin and accomplishing the plan of redemption. Through our faith in Jesus, God gives us wisdom, forgives us of sin, and helps us live by faith according to His Word. Let us seek biblical wisdom with the Lord's help, for the search will always lead us to Jesus.

DAY 05

His Light Overcomes the Darkness

In him was life, and that life was the light of men. That light shines in the darkness, and yet the darkness did not overcome it.

JOHN 1:4–5

When sin entered the world, darkness made its way into everything God created. The world was bright, good, and full of God's presence. Adam and Eve even walked with Him in the garden. But when Adam and Eve disobeyed God, darkness fell like a blanket upon all of creation, destroying everything in its path. Sin spared nothing.

Yet, from the beginning of the redemption story, God promised a deliverer who would save the world from this darkness. He would restore what had been lost. He would redeem those who loved the Lord and save them from their sins. So when this deliverer entered the world in the person of Jesus Christ, He was announced with light—a bright star, unlike any that had ever been seen before, adorned the sky. And as the light shined to announce the birth of the Messiah, it also foreshadowed what was to come because of our Savior's birth.

As Jesus grew up and began His ministry, He carried His light to all who would receive it. His light woke people from their sin, disease, and affliction. It changed the hearts of men. It restored them to how things were meant to be before darkness infected God's creation. Even though darkness tried to overcome Christ's light, He overcame darkness through His death on the cross and resurrection from the grave.

Now Jesus gives His light to us, to those who trust Him as their Savior. We carry it wherever we go, just like He did. And though the darkness tries to swallow us, His light is stronger. One day when Christ returns, darkness will finally be cast out for all of eternity. We will feel the infection of sin no longer, finally free, living in Christ's light. That light will be in us and all around us.

As you go throughout your day and see how the darkness has wounded and broken the world in which you live, remember that it has an expiration date. The light you carry inside of you, the light that was placed there by the Lord, will never run out but overflow to those around you. The light of Christ is stronger than the evil of this world and is a seal of your eternal inheritance to come. So may darkness flee as you shine His light to everyone you meet.

DAY 06
God is Sovereign Over the Times

May the name of God be praised forever and ever, for wisdom and power belong to him. He changes the times and seasons; he removes kings and establishes kings. He gives wisdom to the wise and knowledge to those who have understanding.

DANIEL 2:20–21

Do you ever attempt to control situations? Maybe you try to control by worrying, thinking that if you think through every possible situation you will somehow control the outcome. Or maybe you micromanage others in your home to ensure that things go your way. However, if you have lived any amount of time, you know that despite our best efforts, humans are ultimately not in control of life's outcomes. That said, we can rest easy knowing that we have a sovereign God who is in control of it all.

When Daniel was in Babylon, King Nebuchadnezzar had a dream that troubled him, and he desperately wanted someone to interpret it for him. The king was so desperate that he vowed to kill all of the wise men of his kingdom if they could not tell him what the dream meant. So Daniel and his friends prayed, asking the Lord to reveal Nebuchadnezzar's dream to them. And the Lord revealed it to Daniel. The dream showed the rise and fall of empires through the ages and how the only unshakable kingdom belonged to the Lord. The remaining kingdoms would crumble and fade away, including the kingdom of Babylon.

The verses we read today show Daniel praising God for revealing the dream, but they also teach us that the Lord is in control of time. He sees the past, present, and future. Anyone who is wise and understanding has been gifted these traits from God's hand. All rulers and leaders of the world, like Nebuchadnezzar, are in power because God has allowed it to be so. We often go about our lives as if we are the ones in control of everything, but this simply is not the case. God is the One who is sovereign over all things. We can place our trust in our Heavenly Father, knowing that He works on behalf of those who love Him.

So while none of us will ever understand what it is like to know all time and all things, may we place our hope and trust in this One who does. May we worship God and give Him the honor due His great name.

DAY 07
Surrounded by His Love

"Many pains come to the wicked, but the one who trusts in the Lord will have faithful love surrounding him."

PSALM 32:10

Have you ever been confronted by your own sin? It can be painful to acknowledge when we go wrong. However, it is also essential to our growth as Christians.

In Psalm 32, King David confronts his sin and teaches others to learn from his mistakes and obey God out of love and gratitude. David points the sinner to repentance, for repentance is wisdom for life. He advises that turning from sin and moving toward the Lord brings joy and faithful love. On the other hand, remaining in wickedness is folly and brings pain. David echoes the gladness that comes from a repentant person who is welcomed into the love of God. There in His hand, one finds deep comfort that this is where one was meant to be all along.

Furthermore, in his role as king, David pointed to the true King who came in the person of Jesus Christ. Jesus was the eternal Son of God who proved Himself to be the perfect human. He never needed to repent of any wrong, for He was sinless. Jesus was full of wisdom, yet as He took on and persevered through the world's fallen state, He understood more about the refuge He had in the Father's love. Jesus remained committed to this truth as He was led to the cross. Jesus submitted Himself to pain and wickedness in order to pay the punishment for our sin. In this way, Jesus embodied the faithful love of God.

Let us trust in Jesus's saving work, for God's enduring love surrounds us. Like David, when we remain in our sins, we experience torment, restlessness, and weariness. But, when we come to the Lord in repentance, we experience freedom and peace. Having faith in Jesus as the fulfillment of God's love and clinging to the cross for mercy allows us to truly live as God's children. Through the Holy Spirit, we can walk in God's love now, as we await the fullness of His love that will one day forever erase sin and our need for repentance when He returns to call us home to glory.

"GOD'S ENDURING LOVE SURROUNDS US."

DAY 08
The Unmatchable Help of God

When all our enemies heard this, all the surrounding nations were intimidated and lost their confidence, for they realized that this task had been accomplished by our God.

NEHEMIAH 6:16

We all need safety and protection. In our modern world, we seek safety through the common grace of shelter, clothing, and enacting and following laws.

Likewise, the Israelites sought safety through the rebuilding of Jerusalem as led by Nehemiah. Having suffered from enemy attacks, the city's tall gates and stone structures laid in piles of rubble when Nehemiah arrived. Surrounding nations were upset at Jerusalem's revival. They did not want the exiles to return and establish God's kingdom. Full of fear and rage, the enemies burned the city wall to the ground. With a team of others, Nehemiah set out to rebuild the wall.

Strengthened by the help of God, Nehemiah stayed focused on the work. Enemies plotted his downfall, but threats to his life did not distract Nehemiah from the construction. By God's grace, Nehemiah saw the project to completion. When the enemies heard the wall was finished, they became discouraged, for no scheme of theirs could stop the work of God. Through Nehemiah, God Himself had raised the wall, and He would protect those who trusted in Him.

Walls were significant for ancient cities. They provided security from invasion. In a way, walls acted as armor for the people behind them, providing social resistance in times of danger. But, as the story of Nehemiah shows us, God is the One who is our ultimate defense. He provides safety from sin, the true enemy. The Lord is our unmatchable help. Like the city of Jerusalem, which was vulnerable to enemy attack, we too are vulnerable to the attacks of evil. Satan roams around like a lion waiting to trap us in his grip. He wants to steal us from God's life-giving presence and lead us on the path to destruction.

But God gives us protection that cannot be destroyed. Jesus was mocked, threatened, pursued, and wrongly executed. Despite such suffering, Satan never overcame Him. Jesus remained obedient to the Lord unto death, and through His death, we are freed from sin and freed from Satan's ploys. By the Holy Spirit, Jesus has clothed us in His righteousness. In this impenetrable armor, we are safe. During times of weakness and when darkness is near, let us seek the help of God. Let us trust in His strength and in the accomplished work of Christ, our defender.

DAY 09
His Covenant Cannot Be Shaken

Though the mountains move and the hills shake, my love will not be removed from you and my covenant of peace will not be shaken," says your compassionate Lord.

ISAIAH 54:10

There are moments when our lives feel shaken. In these moments, it feels as if we are placed in a snowglobe, and one quick jostle turns our world upside down, setting everything around us in motion. When everything is shaken, nothing feels secure. If all we know and see is shaken, what do we hold onto for stability?

There is a hope to which we can cling in a shaken world: God and His promises. From the beginning of Scripture, God set forth a covenant with His people. This covenant promised forgiveness from sin, hope of deliverance, and everlasting peace. Not once did God fail to fulfill His covenant. Even when the nation of Israel saw everything around them crumble, they could trust in the promises of their compassionate Lord. For those of us in Christ, we stand today as witnesses to God's unshaken covenant. Through Christ, God's covenant was fulfilled. Because of Jesus, we have forgiveness of sin, the hope of deliverance, and everlasting peace.

God's promises are unshakable because God is unshakeable. He can never be moved, shifted, or changed. Because we are in a relationship with an unshakeable God, we have complete security in this life. Even in the moments we feel shaken, God's promises are unshaken. In fact, holding on to God's promises helps us remain steady. Because of God's unshakeable promises, we do not have to be shaken. In any and every situation, we can hold fast to God's promises, knowing that they are true and everlasting.

And in the moments fear comes and our hope begins to waver, God's promises remind us that our salvation cannot be shaken (John 10:28). Our eternity in heaven cannot be shaken (1 Peter 1:4). Our relationship with Christ cannot be shaken (John 6:37). Our identity in Christ cannot be shaken (Philippians 3:20).

The stability of God's promises helps us walk steadily in this life. Knowing that God's promises have been fulfilled through Christ and will one day be completely fulfilled through Him brings us lasting hope and peace. There will be times when it feels as though your world is falling apart. When these times come, may you cling to the promises of our compassionate Lord. He holds you close and offers His steadfast love and peace.

DAY 10
The Inclusive Grace of God

...I knew that you are a gracious and compassionate God, slow to anger, abounding in faithful love, and one who relents from sending disaster.

JONAH 4:2

God is a God of impartiality. He calls people from different nations, tongues, and tribes. God does not choose to give grace to only those who look or act a certain way. Yet, in the story of Jonah, God's decision to relent from inflicting punishment on the city of Nineveh causes Jonah to become angry. He considers it unfair for God to relent in His punishment, even though Nineveh repented from their sinful ways. In fact, Jonah's belief that Nineveh did not deserve salvation kept him from going to the city in the first place.

Jonah knew that God was merciful, but he did not want God to be merciful to Nineveh. In essence, he did not like this characteristic of God when applied to those he felt were undeserving of such favor. In Jonah's pride, he believed only certain people were worthy of God's grace and forgiveness, and Nineveh was not one of them. Jonah's pride and anger can serve to reveal how we as humans often think we know what is right and best. The sinful hearts of mankind can cause us to pick and choose who we think deserves compassion and mercy. As a result, man's partiality causes others to be shut out and rejected.

Yet God is not like us. Jonah may have thought Nineveh was undeserving of God's grace, but in reality, we are *all* undeserving of God's grace. But still, He gives it freely. An immense display of God's inclusive grace is the cross. Jesus's death on the cross was for people from every tribe, tongue, and nation. In His kindness, God has offered us salvation through Jesus in the present. This gift of grace is extended to anyone who trusts and believes in Jesus—it is an invitation for all mankind.

If the gospel is inclusive, those who believe in the gospel are to be inclusive as well. As believers, let us not follow in Jonah's footsteps by believing only certain people are worthy of God's grace. In response to our merciful God, may we humble our hearts and desire for all people—even those who are difficult or sinful—to experience the grace of Jesus Christ.

"JESUS'S DEATH ON THE CROSS WAS FOR PEOPLE FROM EVERY TRIBE, TONGUE, AND NATION."

DAY 11
Words of Grace

Let your speech always be gracious, seasoned with salt, so that you may know how you should answer each person.
COLOSSIANS 4:6

When you meet people who have gracious speech, you immediately recognize how different they are from the rest of the world. Their words are encouraging, empathetic, and kind. Their words give life rather than destruction. We all probably have a few people in mind who we know speak this way. And because their speech is so gracious, we are drawn to them.

Paul tells us in Colossians that this kind of speech should characterize all believers. When we are first saved, our speech is often one of the clearest areas of change in our lives. And it is typically most recognizable to the people in our families and communities because we speak throughout the majority of our day. Our tongue is one of the most used parts of our bodies. Yet saying thousands of words a day is not always a good thing.

Consider the history of the world and even the last few years of history you have witnessed. Everything is influenced by words. Words are more powerful than any weapon. They can destroy or save. They move the world forward, and they can also bring the world to incredible destruction. Because words are so powerful, believers of Jesus must steward them well.

Our Savior is the ultimate example of how we should use words. Christ used words to teach the gospel, welcome the outcast, rebuke the self-righteous, encourage His disciples, and ultimately, reveal Himself as the Savior of the world. Before He ascended into heaven, Christ commissioned us to go into the world, baptizing His disciples in His name. Our gracious speech will be used by God in the lives of others. And so, as we interact with various people wherever we go, may we remember that our words hold great power, and stewarding them well is an opportunity to serve the Lord and imitate Him. May our speech be like Christ's—gracious and life-giving to every person we meet.

"OUR GRACIOUS SPEECH WILL BE USED BY GOD IN THE LIVES OF OTHERS."

DAY 12
Unwavering Confidence in God's Purposes

Then Job replied to the Lord: I know that you can do anything and no plan of yours can be thwarted.
JOB 42:1-2

Job was a man of great influence. He possessed wealth, a large family, and plenty of livestock. One day, all of that disappeared—he lost everything. Job wrestled with feelings of abandonment and despair. He was a righteous man, always seeking to do good to others and rightly worship the Lord. Instead of comforting him, Job's friends confronted him, assuming that Job must have violated the Law in some way to be experiencing such hardship. However, his suffering was the result of Satan's attacks. Though Job experienced deep anguish, his emotions did not move him to retreat within himself. Though he wanted to give up, by God's grace, Job sought the Lord for answers.

As the book of Job concludes, we read that God responded to his cries. He answered Job's accusations with declarations of His power and majesty. God did not directly give Job an answer as to why his suffering occurred but instead pointed to His sovereignty. God's hand gave Job blessings and allowed those blessings to be taken away, but it would also be God's hand that would later restore. The Lord's supremacy awakened Job and humbled him before the Lord. His repentance began with a confession of his trust in God's purposes. Despite his circumstances, Job realized God was in control and would work everything out for His glory.

Because we live in a fallen world, suffering will not cease. Sometimes, suffering may seem unjustifiable, and our souls will cry out to the Lord as Job did. We might be provoked to challenge God's goodness. But in these difficult times, may we remember Job's actions, recalling how he surrendered to the Lord. We must humble ourselves in awe before Him as we realize that hardships cannot happen unless God allows them. But let us also trust that God allows hardships for His good purposes. One day, those broken parts of our lives will be redeemed and restored when we meet our Father face to face.

We may not be able to see His reasons amidst the pain, but He will work all things out for His glory and our sanctification. He is our good Father. May we allow Him to work in our hearts through the trials that we face, shedding our pride, exposing our sin, and strengthening our dependence on Him as we confidently hope in His good purposes.

DAY 13
The Power of Our Words

Death and life are in the power of the tongue, and those who love it will eat its fruit.

PROVERBS 18:21

Think of a time when someone spoke words to you that you have never forgotten. Maybe it was a name you were called in middle school or a comment a teacher made to you after a failed test. Maybe it was the encouragement of a boss or the life-giving words of a mentor. If there is one thing we find to be true in remembering these things people said to us, it is that our words matter.

Our words to one another hold great impact. We likely see this in conversations with our children, arguments with our spouses, or conflicts with our friends. The words we use bear fruit that will impact those to whom we speak. We face continual opportunities to leave lasting impacts with our words, but the question is whether we use our words to hurt or heal.

Scripture reminds us of the power our words have to build up or tear down. James 3:5 warns us that the tongue, with a small spark, can start a great forest fire. We can hurt people deeply with the things that we say. When we gossip, slander, ridicule, or speak unkindly to others, we ignite small sparks with the potential to burn and scar. Ephesians 4:29 encourages us to only let talk come out of our mouths that is useful for building one another up and giving grace to those who hear. We have the opportunity to spur one another on every day with the way we speak to and about one another. When we encourage, affirm, support, admire, or serve one another with our words, we are able to spur others on in the faith and build them up in their efforts.

As Christians, our words serve as a small glimpse of Christ to those around us. When we speak harshly, unkindly, hurtfully, and disgracefully toward others, we misrepresent who He is and how He longs to communicate Himself to His people. But when we speak graciously, kindly, carefully, generously, and thoughtfully, we reveal the beauty of His redemptive work in our hearts and represent Him more faithfully. Proverbs 18:21 reminds us that our words matter, and they will produce fruit. May our words aim to plant life-giving seeds in the lives of those we speak to, and may we trust in the power of Christ to bring good fruit from them.

DAY 14

Prayers of the Righteous

Therefore, confess your sins to one another and pray for one another, so that you may be healed. The prayer of a righteous person is very powerful in its effect.

JAMES 5:16

A mother faithfully prays for her rebellious daughter. Day and night, she offers up words to Jesus, calling on Him to intercede and open her little girl's eyes to the gospel. She writes her prayers in a journal. Year after year, she records her petitions as her daughter continues a life apart from Christ. In old age, the mother still cannot see the fruit of her prayers, and she dies with a heart still hopeful in the Lord's salvation for her daughter. Later, the daughter stumbles upon her mother's old journal and pages of prayers. She feels Jesus through the faded lettering as the Lord softens her heart. The Holy Spirit convicts her and leads her to pick up a Bible. She meditates on the Lord's words of salvation through Jesus Christ. On her knees, she prays for His help to heal her soul.

James was the half-brother of Jesus and authored a letter to the Christians of the early Church. Mirroring the wisdom literature of the Old Testament, his letter contains moral exhortations to walk one's journey in true faith. He identifies that true faith in Jesus leads to obedience, to a life lived in reverence before Him. Two areas of Christian living James mentions are prayer and confession. Scripture highlights how God uses these disciplines to bring about powerful effects. God heals His people through prayer and confession and brings the prayerful and repentant into His grace.

We may often find ourselves discouraged when it seems as though our prayers have no effect. We forget that the Lord hears our cries—He hears our prayers, He hears our cries of repentance, and is working in our lives and the lives of others, even when we cannot see it, cannot feel it, and cannot understand it. Let us trust that as we prayerfully come to the Lord—in joy, in sadness, in repentance—the righteousness of Christ will sanctify us as we learn to trust His hand in our lives. May we remain faithful in prayer as we fall on our knees, hearts lifted to our heavenly Father.

"GOD HEALS HIS PEOPLE THROUGH PRAYER AND CONFESSION AND BRINGS THE PRAYERFUL AND REPENTANT INTO HIS GRACE."

DAY 15
Not by Our Own Strength

He guards the steps of his faithful ones, but the wicked perish in darkness, for a person does not prevail by his own strength.

1 SAMUEL 2:9

Hannah was childless for years. She deeply desired a child and could not get pregnant. But she took her pleas to the Lord and waited. Eventually, God promised to give her a son as long as she vowed to give him back to the Lord in service. Soon after Samuel was born, Hannah dedicated him to the Lord. She prayed that God would continue to strengthen, equip, and provide for her son in the same way He had provided for her. God answered her prayers and prepared Samuel to be a messenger for the Lord. Just as his mother prayed, not by his own strength, but by God's.

How often do we position ourselves like Hannah did as recipients of God's good gifts? Do we claim them in our own strength? Or do we receive them humbly and return them in glory to the Lord?

We can be tempted to look to our own efforts when things go well and accredit the glory to ourselves. From a worldly point of view, this is expected and normal—the harder you work or the harder you try, the more accomplishments you can attribute to your name. This mentality can trickle into so many areas of life, making the assumption that if you just work hard enough, you can accomplish anything! But not everything can be accomplished by sheer willpower. Truly, some things are just out of our control. Many of us will at some point face trials we did not bring upon ourselves, and some of us will bear those burdens for a lifetime. But even life's greatest challenges can bring us to a greater dependency on the Lord and a greater reliance on His strength over our own.

We are created with different strengths, weaknesses, and different purposes, which are all ordained by God. Indeed nothing can happen outside the sovereign ordinance of God—the good and the bad and everything in between. Every good thing we have is dependent on God bringing it to be. And every good thing He withholds, He withholds for our good and His glory. Allow this to bring comfort to you when God gives and when He takes away. He does so with intention and purpose so that we would find our ultimate hope and strength in Him.

DAY 16
Knowing What God Really Says

Now the serpent was the most cunning of all the wild animals that the Lord God had made. He said to the woman, "Did God really say, 'You can't eat from any tree in the garden'?"

GENESIS 3:1

Our understanding of God's Word is vital to the daily choices we make. It shapes our thoughts about God and what we believe to be true about Him. It shapes our understanding of the commands God gives us as parameters to the ways He calls us to live in this world. If we hold His Word loosely or misinterpret it, we are far more likely to misunderstand God and what He says.

Consider the example of Adam and Eve. When God made Adam, He placed Him in the garden and said, "You are free to eat from any tree of the garden, but you must not eat from the tree of the knowledge of good and evil, for on the day you eat from it, you will certainly die" (Genesis 2:16–17). Then the serpent appeared, tempting Eve with a challenge to God's command, asking, "Did God really say, 'You can't eat from any tree in the garden'?" (Genesis 3:1). Eve's response revealed a misunderstanding of the Lord's instruction. She replied, "We may eat the fruit from the trees in the garden. But about the fruit of the tree in the middle of the garden, God said, 'You must not eat it or touch it, or you will die'" (Genesis 3:2–3). Eve believed the lies of the serpent and disregarded what the Lord had commanded. And, indeed, the moment they ate of the tree, everything changed as sin entered and marred God's creation.

God has revealed Himself, His intentions, and His purposes through His Word. He gives us commands, and He does so because He knows what is good for us. In order to understand God's Word and obey it, we must know what it says—not just parts of Scripture, paraphrases, or generalized quotes that sound like Scripture. We need to know what He says, word for word, for ourselves. At times, internal desires and external temptations may provoke us to sin, yet when our hearts are shaped by God's Word, we are able to fight against it. And as we fight the sin that so easily entangles, may we steady our hearts and minds on things that are true, honorable, just, pure, lovely, and commendable to the Lord (Philippians 4:8) and find victory in Christ!

"GOD HAS REVEALED HIMSELF, HIS INTENTIONS, AND HIS PURPOSES THROUGH HIS WORD."

DAY 17
A Challenging Commission

"But you, son of man, do not be afraid of them and do not be afraid of their words, even though briers and thorns are beside you and you live among scorpions. Don't be afraid of their words or discouraged by the look on their faces, for they are a rebellious house. Speak my words to them whether they listen or refuse to listen, for they are rebellious."

EZEKIEL 2:6–7

The prophet Ezekiel was one of the exiles who was taken out of Judah and brought into Babylon. As he dwelled in the land of his enemies, Ezekiel saw the glory of the Lord come to Him, and God gave him a vision. The Lord commissioned Ezekiel to bring His Word to His people. Though they had wandered far from the Lord and refused to repent, the Lord once again beckoned them to return.

Many of the people who surrounded Ezekiel rejected the Lord. However, Israel had hated and rejected the prophets who came before Ezekiel. Why should he expect anything different? What the Lord asked Ezekiel to do was challenging.

Bringing light into darkness places a spiritual target on your back. God's people had killed His messengers, and many of the prophets struggled under the burden of carrying God's Word to those who refused to listen. These men knew that the end of the people's rejection was spiritual and physical death, and no matter how much they told them what was true, many hearts remained unchanged.

But the Lord instructed Ezekiel to speak His Word anyway. He was not to be afraid, even if God's people refused to listen, even if none of them repented. His only job was to deliver the messages God gave Him, and the people's response was up to them.

We have also been tasked with carrying an important message to the people around us. Jesus's last command to His disciples was to proclaim the gospel and make disciples in His name (Mark 16:15, Matthew 28:19). He does not want us to be afraid of rejection or persecution.

At the end of the day, our fears should not lead us to reject the Lord but instead lead us to the One who has given us His message to deliver. We must obey Jesus. We must know His commands are for our good. The gospel call is challenging, and it always has been, but God is with us. We are never alone when we speak for Him.

DAY 18

He is Faithful

In addition, brothers and sisters, pray for us that the word of the Lord may spread rapidly and be honored, just as it was with you, and that we may be delivered from wicked and evil people, for not all have faith. But the Lord is faithful; he will strengthen and guard you from the evil one.

2 THESSALONIANS 3:1-3

How often do you pause to consider the Lord's faithfulness? When you think back on the course of your life, you can probably point to a considerable number of moments that have revealed God's provision. All of our lives are evidence of this. Each day is a gift from God, but we also have anchoring moments that seem to tie the pieces of our story together, and these moments are likely when God's presence and work in our lives have been clearest to us.

How do you remember what He has done on your behalf? When the Israelites crossed the Jordan river into the land of Canaan—the land God promised their ancestor, Abraham, long ago—they built a memorial of remembrance to the Lord out of stones. This memorial would serve as a reminder that God fulfilled what He promised.

We can follow the Israelites example and set up memorials for ourselves so that we also remember. But these memorials do not need to be strong pillars or towers of stone. They could be words written down in a journal or recorded in a family Bible. You could also grab small stones, write down moments of God's faithfulness on them with permanent markers, and keep them in a well-displayed place in your home. Each time someone asks you about the purpose of your decoration, you can rehearse what God has done, leaving your guest with the encouragement of the Lord's work in our lives.

God's faithfulness will never cease, even when you may feel overwhelmed by evil and the brokenness of this world. He will never abandon you. He will deliver and rescue you. The only thing the world can take from us is our bodies, but our souls are beyond its touch. Our souls are held in the hands of a faithful God who loves and keeps us to the end when He will bring us to a new beginning.

The faithfulness of Christ is what we must remember as we continue through our lives. May we dwell on His faithfulness often and let it comfort us from day to day. His faithfulness will forever remain our stronghold.

DAY 19

Faith under Fire

Whoever does not fall down and worship will be thrown into a furnace of blazing fire.

DANIEL 3:11

King Nebuchadnezzar of Babylon established a centralized religion for his empire and declared that everyone must bow before the idol he built. Whoever refused would be thrown into the fiery furnace. Scripture emphasizes that people of various ethnic groups and languages obeyed Nebuchadnezzar's order and worshiped the idol. In a way, this new centralized religion would be a uniting force, bringing sinners together in their rebellion against God's command to worship Him alone. But, by God's grace, three men refused to bow: Shadrach, Meshach, and Abednego. God was in a covenant relationship with them and called them to be set apart from the world's idolatrous ways. With the Lord's help, they remained faithful and did not join in Babylon's rebellion. However, for their defiance, they faced death.

Because of their faith, the Lord blessed Shadrach, Meshach, and Abednego and proved He was indeed their God. Though bound and cast into the flames, the men were comforted by a holy presence. Some scholars argue that the pre-incarnate Jesus Christ was with them. Regardless, the mysterious fourth person or presence unbound them and kept them unharmed and alive. Amazed, King Nebuchadnezzar opened the furnace to release the men, but the fourth person was gone. Many generations later, the presence of Jesus would come to save all of God's people from perishing in the fire of God's judgment for sin. When he suffered on the cross, He died the death we deserved. And, through our faith in Him, Jesus has unbound our chains to sin and protected us from harm. Like Shadrach, Meshach, and Abednego, we can walk out of the furnace free and alive—when our physical bodies die, those who know Christ will live eternal lives with Him.

Jesus was victorious over sin and death, but our fallen world pressures us to rebel against God. We can look around at what the world seems to demand we worship—money, media, status, attractiveness, entertainment. But, we know the one true God who alone deserves our worship. In Christ, we can find comfort that we too have inherited the promises God made to the Israelite patriarchs. We are God's, and He is ours. He will protect our spirits from harm. Despite persecution to varying degrees, we have a lasting hope that God's kingdom will soon come, and all people will bow before Jesus Christ, the Lord, in true worship.

DAY 20

What is Inside the Heart

"Don't let your beauty consist of outward things like elaborate hairstyles and wearing gold jewelry or fine clothes, but rather what is inside the heart – the imperishable quality of a gentle and quiet spirit, which is of great worth in God's sight."

I PETER 3:3-4

A teenage girl checks her phone, scrolling through social media feeds of influencers wearing the latest trends. She turns on her television to see perfectly sculpted models walk the runway in a fashion show. The young girl is inundated with media that portrays outward appearances as true beauty. But behind the images are lives separated from the flourishing life God desires for His people. God designed us to admire aesthetics. He purposes beautiful clothing and our bodies to be expressions of worship and reflections of His glory, though, in our fallen state, we distort God's design. Nevertheless, the Lord points us back to true beauty through His Word.

Peter's first letter gives insight into what true beauty is in God's eyes. Peter wrote to Christians and declared that despite their different backgrounds, they were a holy people, made righteous through Christ. Peter identified them as a royal priesthood. The Jewish priests adorned themselves in ornate clothing as they served in the temple of God. Because of Jesus's saving work as the True Priest, all believers were now dressed in His radiance. But this beauty would not come from clothing or body shape. True beauty would emanate from the inward dwelling of the Holy Spirit within God's people. Peter called Christians to live in response to this new identity. He wrote to Christian women, encouraging them to be adorned in humility as they display the character of Christ.

Jesus demonstrated this true beauty as He journeyed through life, perfectly humble and servant-hearted. He submitted to God the Father, giving up His life so that we could be redeemed. To imitate Jesus's gentle and quiet spirit, we must have faith in Him. We must trust that He has saved us from sin and death and will continue to refine us into His beautiful image. Let us let go of the fading, outward beauty our culture strives to obtain through impressive clothing and physique. While we should certainly care for the bodies that the Lord has given us, let us first be concerned with the state of our hearts. As His people, we represent a greater and imperishable beauty that gives us a glimpse of eternity.

DAY 21
Our Perfect Intercessor

Now many have become Levitical priests, since they are prevented by death from remaining in office. But because he remains forever, he holds his priesthood permanently. Therefore, he is able to save completely those who come to God through him, since he always lives to intercede for them. For this is the kind of high priest we need: holy, innocent, undefiled, separated from sinners, and exalted above the heavens. He doesn't need to offer sacrifices every day, as high priests do—first for their own sins, then for those of the people. He did this once for all time when he offered himself.

HEBREWS 7:23–27

In the Old Testament, priests were those who interceded between God and man. They offered sin sacrifices to make atonement and offer blessings to God's people. But of all the earthly priests and the incredible role and responsibility they held in the life of God's people, none could escape the reality of death. They could never fulfill the role of priest forever in the life of the people. Even great priests like Aaron could not perfectly meet the requirements necessary to unite God with His people forever.

The writer of Hebrews points us to the One who could accomplish every requirement—Jesus Christ. He accomplished what no other priest could accomplish for God's people. He atoned for the sins of people through His sacrificial death on the cross. Not only did He fulfill the required sacrifice for sin, but He secured a relationship between God and His people forever.

Not only has Jesus made a once-and-for-all sacrifice for God's people, but He continues to intercede on our behalf. Jesus Christ advocates for our righteousness before God the Father. Each day, we stumble and fall into sin. But each time our sin nature is exposed, Jesus goes before the throne of God to advocate for us (1 John 2:1). Long ago, while we were still sinners, He took our every sin and placed them upon Himself as He died on the cross. We are justified. The Father now looks at us and sees His Son, Jesus. Through Jesus, we have access to a relationship with the Father. What a hope we have in Jesus Christ, our eternal Great High Priest. May we come before Him with humility and gratitude for standing in our place.

"JESUS CHRIST ADVOCATES FOR OUR RIGHTEOUSNESS BEFORE GOD THE FATHER."

DAY 22
Every Tear Wiped Away

He will wipe away every tear from their eyes. Death will be no more; grief, crying, and pain will be no more, because the previous things have passed away.

REVELATION 21:4

When was the last time your eyes welled with tears? Was it a painful memory? A deep disappointment? A moment of utter overwhelm? Whatever the reason may have been, tears are a reminder of all of our earthly aches. They fall from our eyes when life is falling apart.

Yet, God promises tears will not always be intertwined with our existence. One day, He will defeat sin and death forever. When Jesus returns to earth at His second coming, He will destroy our enemy, Satan, and rid the earth of his influence. And Christ will reign over a new heaven and earth, where all those who believed in Him will reside with Him in perfect peace. God will dwell with man once again, as He intended in the garden of Eden. But, this time, there will be no evil to tempt or sin to entice. The absence of sin will mean the absence of tears, grief, crying, and pain.

God created us to long for a life that is free of pain. He gave us that part of ourselves that knows injustice, death, and disappointment should not exist. But we do not give up hope, for the Lord promises perfection one day. Until then, we cling to the hope of Jesus through every struggle and hardship. In John 20:11–18, Mary stands outside the tomb of Jesus weeping. She has come to find her Savior, but His body is gone. As she weeps, Jesus comes and asks, "why are you crying? Who is it that you are seeking?" And in a beautifully tender moment, Jesus reveals Himself to Mary as the risen Lord. Mary realizes that Jesus is not gone but that He is alive again. Her tears turn to joy, and she runs to tell the disciples the good news.

How wonderful that Jesus's first resurrected work on the earth was to dry the tears of one who longed for His return? He did this for Mary. And He will wipe away your tears, too. We look forward in hope, knowing that one day He will wipe away our sadness forever.

"THE ABSENCE OF SIN WILL MEAN THE ABSENCE OF TEARS, GRIEF, CRYING, AND PAIN."

DAY 23

A Faithful Friend

But Ruth replied: Don't plead with me to abandon you or to return and not follow you. For wherever you go, I will go, and wherever you live, I will live; your people will be my people, and your God will be my God.

RUTH 1:16

God designed humans for community. That is why loneliness is so incredibly painful for people. And more than being painful, it can at times be dangerous to our health. Loneliness has been associated with high blood pressure, heart disease, and early death. Unfortunately, loneliness is prevalent in some cultures. However, out of painful loneliness, we can recognize godly friendship as a balm to our souls.

This is perhaps why the story of Ruth is so enduring to us. Ruth 1 introduces us to a woman named Naomi. Naomi loses her husband and two sons within a short period of time while living in a foreign country. After sustaining these painful losses, she decides to return to her homeland to live out the rest of her life alone. However, her daughter-in-law, Ruth, refuses to leave her. As much as Naomi tries to push Ruth away, Ruth stays with Naomi and travels with her to live in Naomi's homeland.

Ruth is the example of the friend we all desire—someone who stays with us through thick and thin, refusing to leave us, even when we are at our worst. However, such friends can be hard to find. Thankfully, for us, we have a faithful friend in Jesus, and He will never leave us (Matthew 28:20). More than that, Jesus left His perfect union with God and came to earth to experience our same painful loneliness. He knows what it is to have that gnawing feeling in your stomach—that feeling that we often fill with food, drugs, sex, online shopping, social media, or binges of our favorite shows. He understands our desire to confide in and lean on someone. And what is more, He took on our sin and shame and died on the cross so that we would not have to live in loneliness forever.

If you are in a season of loneliness, know that you are never too much for Jesus. You can share your bitterness, pain, and sorrow with the Lord. He will meet you where you are and comfort you there. He will fulfill the aching feeling in your soul in a way that no one else ever could. May you rest in Jesus, who is our ultimate, faithful friend.

> "IF YOU ARE IN A SEASON OF LONELINESS, KNOW THAT YOU ARE NEVER TOO MUCH FOR JESUS."

DAY 24
Let Justice Flow

But let justice flow like water, and righteousness, like an unfailing stream.
AMOS 5:24

God is a God of justice. As a holy and righteous God, God does not allow sin to run rampant without consequence. He fights for the cause of the oppressed and restores those who are in need. He is also perfect in righteousness. In the Old Testament, the nation of Israel was to reflect the justice and righteousness of God. They were to care for one another, treating one another fairly and rightly. And not only this, but they were to treat those outside Israel with the same respect.

But the nation of Israel rebelled against God over and over again. Instead of worshiping Him as they should, they turned away from Him and worshiped other gods. They became unjust and unrighteous people. Though they brought sacrifices to the Lord, their sacrifices were not genuine or evidence of true worship, and they continued in their rebellious ways. In Amos 5, God calls out Israel for their hypocritical worship. He commands them to remove from Him their sacrifices and instruments of worship. He desired instead for justice and righteousness to flow from them as streams of water, for them to repent of their ways and worship Him rightly once again.

Like Israel, we are to uphold justice and righteousness. As followers of Christ, justice and righteousness should overflow from us and into the world around us. Yet, how often do we neglect to live as the Bible commands? Instead of loving others, we speak lies against them. Instead of giving freely to the poor, we keep our money to ourselves. Instead of confessing our sins, we live in unrepentance. These actions stem from misplaced worship. When we are not worshiping God, we turn away from the One who keeps us walking in holiness. Only by coming to and worshiping our just and righteous God will justice and righteousness flow.

To whom or what do you direct your worship? When we worship God rightly, we cannot help but live rightly. All of what we do flows out of our worship to the Lord. Let us not follow in the footsteps of Israel by worshiping God with only our mouths but with our lives. Let us not hurt our gospel witness by living in a way that does not glorify the character of Christ. May justice and righteousness flow out of us into our broken world, telling others of the love and mercy of our God.

DAY 25
Our Transgressions Removed

As far as the east is from the west, so far has he removed our transgressions from us.

PSALM 103:12

Have you ever taken a trip across the country? Getting from the east coast to the west coast is not a quick trip. In Psalm 103:12, the psalmist paints a picture of just how removed our sins are from us. God has removed our transgressions as far as from the east is from the west. The psalmist's metaphor is meant to communicate immeasurable distance. Christ's sacrifice on the cross has cast our sins so far away they are never seen again. Because of Christ, we are completely forgiven. Every sin is washed away, and every transgression removed.

There are times, however, when we may worry that God holds our sins against us. Perhaps we view God as a father who holds grudges when his children make mistakes. This mentality only keeps us from coming to the Lord. We become afraid to confess our sins to God. However, to question God's attitude toward our sin is to question the very character of God.

God is compassionate, slow to anger, and abounding in steadfast love and mercy. From the very beginning, God put forth a plan so that we could receive forgiveness for our sins. God's forgiveness through Christ was not meant to be temporary but eternal, not partial but complete. On the cross, *all* of our sins were forgiven—past, present, and future. Because of Christ, God looks upon us and does not see us in our sin but His blameless son covered in righteousness. Romans 8:1 tells us there is no condemnation for those in Christ Jesus. On the days when we mess up, we can freely confess our sins, knowing that we are forgiven and loved by the Lord.

But while God will never hold our sins against us, the enemy will. The enemy will try to use our past or present sins to invoke guilt and shame. He will whisper accusations against us to make us question God's forgiveness. In these moments, we must remember Christ's grace. The truth of God's forgiveness overshadows the lies of the enemy. Because of Christ's grace, we live in freedom for the rest of our days, knowing that our sin cannot overtake us. Christ's grace and mercy toward us stretch from east to west—a distance that cannot be measured. We are wholly free from guilt and shame as we rest covered in the blood of Christ.

DAY 26
Eternal God

Before the mountains were born, before you gave birth to the earth and the world, from eternity to eternity, you are God.

PSALM 90:2

Psalm 90 was written by Moses, and it was through Moses that God brought the Israelites out of Egyptian slavery and through the wilderness. The Israelites spent forty years on this journey. Though the terrain was difficult, the people's sinful nature challenged Moses more than anything as they grumbled and rebelled against the Lord. One of the ways they rebelled against God was by building a golden calf to worship in His place. Forgetting the circumstances of their captivity in Egypt, they begged to return to slavery. The Israelites showed a lack of faith and love toward the God who had rescued them. But still, God was faithful and protected His people as they traveled and were without homes of their own for generations.

Moses opens Psalm 90 by proclaiming that God is their refuge. His nearness was their dwelling place. Though the landscape was unfamiliar and likely threatening to them at times, they had a home in the Lord. They were safe because He was in control. The backdrop of the wilderness, even with its unfamiliarity and dangers, led Moses to celebrate God as eternal. Moses looked around at God's surrounding creation and proclaimed that the Lord had been before anything else existed. Though the Israelites would fail to recognize His power and might, the Lord reigned from "eternity to eternity." And He will always be God—the same God who rescued His people and led them through the desert and into the Promised Land.

On a walk or hike through nature, has your heart ever brimmed with wonder at the eternality of the Creator God? Perhaps you have seen changes in nature and praised Him for His constant presence over all creation. Or maybe you have experienced circumstances of life that have seemed as wilderness to you—yet, in that wilderness, God was your refuge along the way. We can reflect on any of these experiences when considering Psalm 90 through a Christ-centered perspective.

When the journey is hard, may we remember to look to the eternal Son of God, who is our refuge. Jesus made His dwelling place among us so that in his life, death, and resurrection, we could be brought out of our sin and into the eternal hope of Christ. We have a Promised Land that awaits us when Christ returns to call us home.

DAY 27
Mustard Seed of Faith

...For truly I tell you, if you have faith the size of a mustard seed, you will tell this mountain, 'Move from here to there,' and it will move. Nothing will be impossible for you.

MATTHEW 17:20

The disciples carried out Jesus's redemptive mission, but their lack of faith challenged them. In Matthew chapter 17, the disciples tried to heal a boy who had uncontrollable seizures. To their surprise, they could not release the boy from his violent tremors, so the boy's father brought him to Jesus for help. Jesus grieved over the faithlessness of His people. He rebuked the demon who possessed the boy and instantly healed him. After the miracle, the disciples approached Jesus to inquire about why they could not rebuke the demon themselves. Jesus pointed to their unbelief, specifically their unbelief in God, though the disciples did have belief in some capacity. They had great faith in their own abilities to perform the miracle. Their expectation was not based on a humble dependence on the Lord's might.

Jesus did not leave the disciples in their discouragement, but He taught them the requirement of true faith in the Lord. He expounded that the size of their faith need not even be large. If they had faith the size of a mustard seed, the Lord would work through them. Jesus uses a hyperbole to describe the great miracle that arises out of a humble believer. A hyperbole is a literary device that uses an exaggeration to convey powerful truth. Bringing the kingdom of God to a broken world would be like moving a mountain. This work would be a supernatural event, only caused and accomplished by God's divine activity.

Jesus demonstrated the fullness of faith, and through that, established His good kingdom. He is God in the flesh, but in His human nature, He prayed and depended on the Father to bring redemption. Like the disciples, we ignore the limitations of our human nature and put false confidence in ourselves. We experience disappointment when we fall short of our expectations. But putting faith in Jesus is our firm foundation. As His redeemed, we should hope in Jesus's righteousness and cultivate the faith we were given. Trusting in Jesus will move mountains; it will produce a supernatural work that points to His eternal kingdom. We should strive to develop our faith in Jesus, but at the same time, we can rest, knowing that even our small faith can bring about the transforming power of Jesus.

DAY 28

We Need Rest

God blessed the seventh day and declared it holy, for on it he rested from all his work of creation.

GENESIS 2:3

Have you ever stopped to consider that God is a God of rest? When God created the world in six days, He rested on the seventh. This does not mean that God rested because He was tired, nor does it mean that God ceased from all activity. God's rest points to the completion and satisfaction of the creation He made. It also points to God's desire to celebrate the works of His hands. The Sabbath is not an ordinary day but a significant day that we should honor. The seventh day is a day of completion and celebration.

What is wonderful about God's rest is that He invites us into it. If we read on in Genesis, we learn that God created mankind to dwell with Him and enjoy the creation He made. His rest is to be our rest. Sadly, the disobedience of Adam and Eve and the entrance of sin disturbed the perfect rest we once had. We experience the ramifications of that now, as we live in bodies that tire with hearts that are prone to restlessness. The restlessness of our hearts speaks to our desire to return back to what once was. Our hearts search for what is missing to make it feel settled. In response, we try to use the things of this world to provide us with rest. We book trips along tranquil beaches. We even fill our time with things that seem "restful," like binge-watching television shows. While those things may provide rest for a moment, they never last.

If you feel restless today, God wants you to find your rest in Him. Because God sent His Son, Jesus, all those who come to faith in Him will find rest for their souls (Matthew 11:28–30). This does not mean that we will never grow tired but that in times of weariness, we have somewhere to go for rest. Because God is a God of rest, His rest is the only rest that truly satisfies. Our hearts no longer have to search aimlessly for rest. In Christ, our hearts find rest. His forgiveness has repaired the rest that was broken between God and us.

"ALL THOSE WHO COME TO FAITH IN JESUS
WILL FIND REST FOR THEIR SOULS."

DAY 29
Like a Little Child

Truly I tell you, whoever does not receive the kingdom of God like a little child will never enter it.

LUKE 18:17

Young kids have the biggest imaginations. How sweet it is to watch a little girl pretend to be a princess of a huge castle. Little boys run around the backyard pretending to be pirates hunting for treasure. Children believe anything is possible. This is also why they can sometimes ask so many questions! Their minds are curious, and they are eager to discover.

Jesus once said that we must be like little children to be a part of the kingdom of God. His reason for saying this is that we tend not to be as faith-filled and expectant as adults. We stop believing that God can work beyond our imaginations. We seek concrete evidence instead of having the blind trust of a child. Perhaps some people have a hard time receiving the gospel because they try so hard to have all the answers. They desire evidence and complete confidence that the Bible is true before they can believe. But this kind of mentality can keep people from ever receiving the gospel. For these people to see things differently, they need to be like a little child again.

To be a little child in faith is to trust without having all the answers. The Bible is trustworthy and true because God is trustworthy and true. God has given us His Word to receive knowledge of who He is and who we are. While there may be some questions we cannot answer, this should not keep us from moving forward in faith. Even though we may not understand every aspect of our faith, we can humbly trust the Lord.

Even if we have been walking with Christ for a long time, we should seek to have childlike faith. When we struggle to trust God with our lives, it often means we need to let go of having all the answers. Having childlike faith brings peace instead of stress, allowing us to regularly keep our hands open to receive what God has for us without question. And when thoughts of doubt arise, we can remember to whom we belong. Our heavenly Father cares for us and invites us as His beloved children to trust Him. May we run to Him like a child, fully trusting and depending on His sovereign hand.

> "TO BE A LITTLE CHILD IN FAITH IS TO TRUST WITHOUT HAVING ALL THE ANSWERS."

DAY 30

Power of the Holy Spirit

He said to them, "It is not for you to know times or periods that the Father has set by his own authority. But you will receive power when the Holy Spirit has come on you, and you will be my witnesses in Jerusalem, in all Judea and Samaria, and to the end of the earth."

ACTS 1:7–8

These two verses contain the last known words Jesus spoke to His disciples before He ascended to heaven. Jesus knew the exact words that His disciples needed to hear before His ascension. And these words were not only for those who heard them first hand, but they are also for all believers throughout history, including you and me.

In Jesus's final words, He gives us a job and explains how to fulfill that job. To fully understand the job He is giving us, we need to jump back one verse to Acts 1:6 for context. In verse 6, the disciples asked Jesus when He was going to restore the kingdom of Israel. For centuries, God had promised the Israelite people that He would make them into a flourishing nation, free from the rule of outsiders. But, at that time, Jerusalem was being occupied and terrorized by the Roman empire.

The disciples wanted Jesus to throw the Romans out and establish peace in Israel. However, this was not Jesus's plan. He told the disciples that it was not the time for military conquests. God would only fulfill the promise of Israel's freedom in the perfect time and period He had set.

Now was the time for the disciples to build a different kind of kingdom—a spiritual kingdom. This kingdom would not be made of cities but of people from across the world who believed in Jesus. The disciples were to tell everyone they knew about Jesus's life, death, and resurrection and invite them to join in the spiritual kingdom. They were to start in Jerusalem, then expand their efforts until eventually, they were witnesses for Jesus to the entire world.

This was a daunting task! Therefore, Jesus sent the Holy Spirit who would empower them to do the work of building God's kingdom. In the same way, the Holy Spirit empowers us today to be witnesses for Jesus. You have the ability to tell people about Jesus through the power of the Holy Spirit. And because you have the ability, it is now time to use it to build the kingdom of God! Who will you tell about Jesus today?

DAY 31

Even When You Cannot See

For we walk by faith, not by sight.

2 CORINTHIANS 5:7

Walking by faith is what God has required of His people from the very beginning. When the Lord first called Abraham, the forefather of all of God's people, Abraham had to choose to believe and trust that the Lord would do what He promised. Abraham could not see the Lord. He could only hear His voice. His family members must have thought he was crazy. They all worshiped man-made idols set up in their homes. They could see their gods as they worshiped, for they fashioned them themselves. But Abraham knew that the God He worshiped was the one true God, and though Abraham did not see the fulfillment of all of the promises God made to him, he walked by faith.

This theme of walking by faith continues throughout the Old Testament. Character after character in God's story faces fears and worries, and then God shows that He is present and will deliver them. He orchestrates His plan of redemption while His people wait. Many of them fall away from believing in Him because they are more consumed with their present circumstances, but there is a faithful remnant of people who choose to have faith and trust in what God has said.

Even though we can see the general scope of God's plan of redemption from beginning to end in Scripture, we are also told to have faith. We know that Jesus was once here on the earth, moving and walking about and proclaiming the gospel to all who would hear. But now, He has ascended to the Father and is no longer physically with us. So we have faith as we wait for His return. We cannot see His face, but we have faith that He is with us. And we have faith that one day, we will see Him and be reunited with Him. He will be close enough to embrace. Many of us may not be alive when He returns, yet we have faith that He will do what He has promised, and when we close our eyes and pass from this life to the next, we will awake to His glorious splendor. We are on this journey with the Lord for the long haul, and we are commanded to walk by faith through every season of life. Someday our faith will become sight, and what we could not see before will become the greatest reality we have ever beheld.

"SOMEDAY OUR FAITH WILL BECOME SIGHT."

DAY 32
Wisdom in the Fear of the Lord

He said to mankind, "The fear of the Lord —that is wisdom. And to turn from evil is understanding."

JOB 28:28

In the midst of Job's trials, he wrestled with the question, "If God is just, why am I enduring such terrible suffering?" Job's friends were quick to say that his affliction must have been because he had committed wrongdoing, but Job declared his innocence. While Job knew he was a sinner and that no one was righteous before God, he also knew he had followed God faithfully. Job struggled with God's justice in light of this. Maybe God was not who Job thought He was.

But as Job wrestled with his questions and frustration with his situation, he was also quick to point out the truth about God. Job's back and forth emotions are a comfort to us because they display the reality of what it is like to endure suffering. One moment we are anchored in the Word of God, knowing it is our only means of survival. In the next moment, we are angrily questioning whether or not God is good. However, God allows us to struggle in our suffering, and as we experience these troubling emotions and thoughts, He will always bring us back to the truth of who He is.

In the midst of one of Job's responses to his friends, he includes a hymn regarding the wisdom of God. He says that God's wisdom is a rare treasure, greater than hidden jewels and precious stones. But just as miners dig painstakingly for gold, so we must also carefully labor to discover wisdom. It is not readily available in the world around us. It can only be found in God. And while many people are blind to God's wisdom because they have rejected Him, He gives His wisdom freely to those who fear Him. God loves when we seek Him in humility and place all of our trust and confidence in who He is. When we turn from our sin and look to Him, we finally understand.

Even while we suffer and struggle with questions about God that both confuse us and frustrate us, we know that He is the source of all wisdom. He will not lead us into confusion. God will give us peace, even on the darkest of days.

"GOD WILL GIVE US PEACE, EVEN ON THE DARKEST OF DAYS."

DAY 33

A Chosen People

But you are a chosen race, a royal priesthood, a holy nation, a people for his possession, so that you may proclaim the praises of the one who called you out of darkness into his marvelous light.

1 PETER 2:9

One of the greatest feelings is the feeling of being chosen. Whether you are picked to be on a sports team, take the lead on an important presentation, or receive a marriage proposal, how gratifying it is to be chosen! Yet, there are times when we are not chosen, and someone else receives the desired opportunity.

We often attribute being chosen as a measure of our worth and identity. If we are chosen for something, we believe that there is something in us worth choosing. So when the opposite happens, and we are not chosen, we can feel as if something about us is flawed or unloveable. Even though others may not choose us, as followers of Christ, God has chosen us. Yet God does not choose people based on their strengths, abilities, or appearances. We are chosen people because of His grace.

Being chosen by God holds far greater weight than being chosen by man because of the purpose of our choosing. We were chosen not only to be God's people but also to be used by Him to proclaim the gospel. Before Christ, we were wandering in darkness, lost because of our sin. When Christ saved us, He rescued us from our bondage to sin, bringing us out of darkness and into His marvelous light. As followers of Christ, we have a testimony of Christ's saving grace to share with others. In response to Christ's deliverance, we proclaim the praises of the One who saved us and gave us new life.

When others overlook or reject us, may we find our worth and confidence in knowing who we are in Christ. We belong to the God of the universe, and nothing can remove us from that position. The fact that God chose us despite our sin should also give us great joy and gratitude. We did not deserve to be chosen by God, but He chose us anyway. By His great grace, we live as a set-apart people, used by God to declare His glory and power. God chose us for an eternal position and purpose, so let us proclaim the praises of our great God!

"WHEN CHRIST SAVED US, HE RESCUED US FROM OUR BONDAGE TO SIN."

DAY 34

The Mountain of the Lord

In the last days the mountain of the Lord's house will be established at the top of the mountains and will be raised above the hills. Peoples will stream to it, and many nations will come and say, "Come, let us go up to the mountain of the Lord, to the house of the God of Jacob. He will teach us about his ways so we may walk in his paths." For instruction will go out of Zion and the word of the Lord from Jerusalem.

MICAH 4:1-2

Sometimes, life seems to fall apart, and we have no one to blame but ourselves. We made the decisions. We disregarded wise advice. The mess is seemingly our fault. Can we then find hope in the ruins of destruction?

Throughout the book of Micah, God spoke of Jerusalem's coming judgment (Micah 1–3). The people had rebelled against God, and destruction was coming. But even though Jerusalem would fall, God would not abandon His people. He would not only rebuild His city, but He would bring it to even greater heights than before (Micah 4:1). In this future time of prosperity, people from every nation, country, and land would come to worship the Lord (Micah 4:2). There would be peace, restoration, provision, and rest.

Like the Israelites, we experience the consequences of our sin. In the end, our sin always leads to our ruin, despair, and death. Like the Israelites in the book of Micah, we sit in the mess of our own making. Yet, even then, God has not forsaken us. One day He will come to fully restore what has been broken. God will rescue His people and cover us in His perfect peace, as He does so even now. There is a day coming when His kingdom will reign over the whole earth, and we will see Him face to face.

So, in seasons of destruction, we hold fast to His promises. Christ paved the way for us to be clean through His perfect righteousness. He founded a kingdom of peace built upon the gospel. And He is coming again to bring us to our eternal home in heaven. There, he will restore us to an existence without fear, war, or sorrow. Though destruction may be present in our lives today, a future glory is coming. In response to this promise of restoration, let us follow, love, and obey Him today.

> "SO, IN SEASONS OF DESTRUCTION, WE HOLD
> FAST TO HIS PROMISES."

DAY 35
For Everything There is a Season

There is an occasion for everything, and a time for every activity under heaven: a time to give birth and a time to die; a time to plant and a time to uproot; a time to kill and a time to heal; a time to tear down and a time to build; a time to weep and a time to laugh; a time to mourn and a time to dance.

ECCLESIASTES 3:1-4

Each year, we witness the same four seasons coming and going. Winter turns to spring. Spring turns to summer. Summer turns to fall. Fall turns to winter. And the cycle repeats. Babies are born, but then they and their children grow. A relationship ends, and another blossoms. Nothing remains permanent in our lives. Even those we hold dear will leave us at some point. Like the seasons, our lives will always shift and change. No matter how much we try, we cannot make time stand still. But in the midst of an ever-changing world, we have a God who never changes.

We can rest contentedly in the seasons of our lives because God is the creator and sustainer of seasons. By His hand, He brings us into seasons that are slow and seem never to end. By His hand, He brings us into seasons that quickly move. Just as every season in nature is necessary, every season of our lives is necessary as God grows us and works in our hearts to make us more like Himself. How kind is the Lord to use all things in every season to shape us, forming us into who He created us to be as His children. And when we embrace God's work of sanctification in our lives, we will be able to embrace every season He gives us.

Even in difficult seasons, we can cling to our God, who is ever constant. When we have a hard time letting go of things that have changed, we can find rest in the God who never changes. In moments that shift, we can trust in Jesus, who is the same yesterday, today, and forever (Hebrews 13:8). There is a time for everything, and we can trust the Creator of time, for all things are in His hands. May we open our hands and embrace His great work of making us more and more like Himself each day.

"WE CAN REST CONTENTEDLY IN THE SEASONS OF OUR LIVES BECAUSE GOD IS THE CREATOR AND SUSTAINER OF SEASONS."

DAY 36

His Love Endures Forever

Give thanks to the Lord, for he is good; his faithful love endures forever.

1 CHRONICLES 16:34

Through all of eternity, God's love endures. It never runs dry or disappears. We serve a God whose faithful love is part of His nature. This means that if God's faithful love ceased, God would cease to be God.

God's faithful love is like a thread woven throughout every page of Scripture. God built the world in His faithful love. He set forth a plan of redemption after the fall in His faithful love. He led the people of Israel and formed a covenant with them in His faithful love. And this love was manifested fully through the life, death, and resurrection of Jesus Christ. Now, for those who belong to God, His love will never be removed.

When we sin, we can forget this truth. We become afraid to come before God, confess our sins, and be honest with Him about our shortcomings. If God's faithful love has always endured, though, why would it not remain when we sin? In our sin and weaknesses, God surrounds us with His faithful love. He gives us grace and forgiveness through the salvation we have received in Christ.

Romans 8:38–39 tells us that nothing can separate us from the love of God that is in Christ Jesus our Lord. Even when we fall short, His faithful love endures. Even when we fail to obey, His faithful love endures. Even when we struggle to put sin to death, His faithful love endures. What a comfort it is to know that there is nothing we can do to remove God's love from us. We can walk boldly in confidence with our heavenly Father, freely worshiping and praising Him for His steadfast and unwavering love and faithfulness.

On the hard days, we have the sure promise that God's faithful love is carrying us. We live in this broken world now, but one day, we will experience the fullness of God's love and glory forever. He will remove all sin and brokenness and restore everlasting peace and rest. From eternity to eternity, God's love endures. His love will never fail.

"WE SERVE A GOD WHOSE FAITHFUL LOVE
IS PART OF HIS NATURE."

DAY 37
What Does God Require?

Mankind, he has told each of you what is good and what it is the Lord requires of you: to act justly, to love faithfulness, and to walk humbly with your God.

MICAH 6:8

Micah was a prophet in the Old Testament. In chapter 6 of Micah's prophecy, the Judeans sat in the defendant's chair as the Lord acted as both judge and plaintiff. God listed the ways He was faithful to His people. The people could not give a defense. They were guilty of all the allegations. Instead of justifying their actions, they asked for a ritual to satisfy God's righteous anger. *Will a burnt offering of a young calf work? How about the presentation of thousands of rams and tens of thousands of oil rivers? Will the Lord take the sacrifice of my firstborn to pay for Judah's sin?*

Micah depicted an escalation of absurdity with each question. He highlighted the people's reliance on empty rituals rather than on obedience to the Lord. God did not desire the sacrifice of a bunch of rams, oil, or a firstborn child. He ultimately required justice, a faithful heart, and humility. The people's desperation for divine favor showed their fundamental misunderstanding of salvation.

The Lord's requirements are clear to mankind. His requirements cover three aspects: relationships with others, inner devotion, and a life centered on intimacy with God. But, we fail in every area. Furthermore, when we are caught in our sin, we easily forget God's unmerited favor and search for works to appease Him like the people of Judah. However, in the Lord's heavenly court, there is nothing we can bring to the stand that will clear our crimes and treason. We are in the defendant's chair, awaiting our deserved punishment for sin. But, thankfully, God did not leave us to suffer that end. As judge and plaintiff, He became our defense attorney too. In the person of Jesus Christ, God presents His justice, His faithfulness, and His humility to cover our wrongs. Jesus's righteous record met the requirements in full.

In our guilt, let us not look around for the next empty act we can perform to satisfy our debts. We need to sit in the defendant's chair to recognize our deep sin and corruption despite anything that we do. And, we must plead the name of our great mediator, Jesus, and trust that His accomplishments will credit us with justice, faith, and humility. It is through Christ alone that we are saved and washed clean!

"JESUS'S RIGHTEOUS RECORD MET THE REQUIREMENTS IN FULL."

DAY 38
A Strong Tower

The name of the Lord is a strong tower; the righteous run to it and are protected.

PROVERBS 18:10

A proverb is a concise saying that reflects a general truth and gives practical wisdom for life. When we read a proverb, we should consider whether its principles reinforce and confront our worldview and the worldviews of our culture today. At times, a proverb may not seem true in our fallen reality. However, we should study the saying through an eternal lens and through the saving work of Jesus Christ. For example, Proverbs 18:10 challenges us and our culture. We value self-reliance and finding strength within ourselves to protect ourselves from harm. We do not seek the Lord's protection. As sinners, we do not see Him as a strong tower. Instead, we consider God to be like a prison, keeping us from the freedom we desire.

Proverbs 18:10 is not always true in our fallen reality. The faithful followers of God are not always physically protected. Many Christians have suffered from the hands of persecution and injustice. Therefore, we know this verse points to a greater, spiritual reality. If we look at this verse through the lens of the gospel, we see its eternal truth. Those who are declared righteous in Jesus Christ are protected from the eternal consequences of sin. Indeed, *Yahweh*, God's name as given in Exodus 3, is their strong tower who has redeemed them from the hands of the enemy and brought them into His kingdom.

Jesus Christ bears the eternal name of God (John 8:58). In Him, we see how God is our strong tower. Through His life, death, and resurrection, Jesus shielded us in His perfection. He took on the weight of sin and died to pay our debts. We can enter the holy presence of God. There, we can rest in God's abounding care and love. Do you believe Jesus has protected you from sin and death? If so, will you run to the tower that is the Lord? Run to the cross of Christ, and receive the wisdom of His Word. Though hardship will persist in our fallen world, we can have joy and peace. We have victory over our greatest threat: sin. We can cling to this proverb's promise until all threats are defeated. At that time, the Lord's eternal tower will descend from heaven in the new creation.

"RUN TO THE CROSS OF CHRIST, AND RECEIVE THE WISDOM OF HIS WORD."

DAY 39

Appealing on the Basis of Love

For this reason, although I have great boldness in Christ to command you to do what is right, I appeal to you, instead, on the basis of love. I, Paul, as an elderly man and now also as a prisoner of Christ Jesus, appeal to you...

PHILEMON 8-10

An eye for an eye. A tooth for a tooth. When someone harms us, we desire restitution and repayment. But, God often asks us to drop charges against our adversaries and respond in grace. We can watch how this idea plays out in the story of Paul, Philemon, and Onesimus.

Philemon, a Christian and friend of Paul, had a bondservant (a servant who worked for an agreed-upon period of time to pay a debt) named Onesimus, who had most likely stolen from Philemon and run away. Onesimus fled to Rome in an attempt to create a new life away from Philemon. But, by the ever-sovereign hand of God, while in Rome, Onesimus had befriended Paul. Paul shared the gospel with him, and Onesimus believed in Christ and was saved. He served Paul during his especially burdensome imprisonment in Rome, taking letters to churches and probably conducting other gospel business on behalf of Paul who was bound in chains.

Now, Paul was sending Onesimus back to Philemon. A culturally typical response from Philemon would have been harsh backlash and an increased length of servitude demanded from the runaway servant. But Paul appeals to Philemon to have grace on Onesimus.

He asks Philemon to receive Onesimus as not only a bondservant but a beloved brother. Paul says, "receive him as you would receive me." And then, astonishingly, because he is a poor and imprisoned man, he offers to pay for any loss Philemon has incurred due to Onesimus. Paul demonstrates first the brotherly love he is asking Philemon to give Onesimus by taking care of any debts owed. Some scholars even suggest he was asking for Onesimus's freedom from servanthood.

This would have been wildly countercultural but perfectly in line with the way Jesus called His followers to live. When we encounter someone who has wronged us, let us too consider not only what is due to them, but on the basis of love, let us consider how we might treat people who wrong us, in light of God's great and glorious grace toward us.

DAY 40
Well Guarded Heart

Guard your heart above all else, for it is the source of life.
PROVERBS 4:23

Most of us have heard the phrase, "guard your heart." This phrase is typically used to warn friends in a romantic relationship not to let their emotions control them. Friends warn others not to get swept up in the romance while failing to be wise. This phrase shows an understanding of how powerful our hearts are. If there is nothing protecting our hearts, our hearts can seize the driver's seat and take hold of the steering wheel. Where it turns, we turn. If we are not careful, our hearts can lead us down roads that lead to sin, heartache, and disappointment.

What makes our hearts so important is that the heart is the source of life. Physically, it keeps the blood pumping through our veins, but it is also the source of spiritual life. When Scripture uses the word "heart," it often describes the whole inner being of a person. Therefore, to guard our heart goes beyond our physical heart but to all of who we are. We read in God's Word that we should protect our hearts, "for everything you do flows from it" (NIV). Jesus expands on this truth in Mark 7:20 when He says, "What comes out of a person is what defiles him." What our heart focuses on shapes who we are. Our outward actions reveal our inward attitudes. Just as the condition of our heart affects our physical health, so does the condition of our heart affect our spiritual health.

If you want to gauge your spiritual health, take a look at your actions. We must also gauge what we allow ourselves to take in. What makes our hearts healthy are the nutrients we take in, but our hearts become unhealthy when we feed it the wrong things. The best way to keep our hearts guarded is by spending time meditating on God's Word. When God's Word continues to come in and flow through our minds, we will find our hearts well guarded. As God's Word remains in the driver's seat, we will continue down roads of spiritual vitality. As believers, may we be vigilant in keeping our hearts well protected. Let us not put our guard down and become susceptible to sin. God's Word is our indestructible guard.

"WHAT OUR HEART FOCUSES ON SHAPES WHO WE ARE."

DAY 41
Filled with Good Desires

In view of this, we always pray for you that our God will make you worthy of his calling, and by his power fulfill your every desire to do good and your work produced by faith, so that the name of our Lord Jesus will be glorified by you, and you by him, according to the grace of our God and the Lord Jesus Christ.

2 THESSALONIANS 1:11-12

Every one of us desires something. We desire happiness, love, comfort, and more. Most of the things we desire are good desires. Yet, sometimes our good desires can lead us to make wrong or harmful decisions. A desire to feel loved can cause us to choose a relationship that leads us astray. A desire to feel comfort can lead us to become isolated from the community. When we fail to evaluate our desires and their outcomes, we can form habits of sin that we overlook in ourselves.

As believers, God wants us to have and live out those good desires. But what happens when we realize wrong desires within us? Paul writes in 2 Thessalonians 1:11–12 that it is God's power that fulfills our desire to do good. Prayer and being in God's Word fill us with good desires. Not only this, but God's Word and the Holy Spirit help us live out good desires. When we saturate ourselves with the truth of God's Word and rely on the Holy Spirit, we will know how to live out our desires wisely.

Paul also writes in 2 Thessalonians 1:11–12 that through our good desires and faithful work, the name of Christ is glorified. Good desires carried out with holy intentions lead to Christlike actions. The opposite occurs when we intend to seek our own glory and happiness. Good desires, with the intention of pleasing ourselves and others, often only perpetuates sin in our lives. Our sole motivation as believers should be to bring glory to Christ in all that we think, say, and do.

As we continue to live for Christ and His glory, resting in the power and wisdom of the Spirit, we will walk in faithfulness. But let us not forget that Christ's grace and power help us live holy lives. It is Christ who equips us by the Spirit to walk in faithfulness. May we continue to rely on and rest in Him to live lives of holiness and full of a great desire to glorify Him.

"IT IS CHRIST WHO EQUIPS US BY THE SPIRIT TO WALK IN FAITHFULNESS."

DAY 42
Careless Indulgences

> *Now this was the iniquity of your sister Sodom: She and her daughters had pride, plenty of food, and comfortable security, but didn't support the poor and needy. They were haughty and did detestable acts before me, so I removed them when I saw this.*
>
> EZEKIEL 16:49–50

How prone we are to place much above and before our heavenly Father. We indulge in beauty, the latest trends, newer cars, bigger houses, and self. And certainly, the list could go on. Whatever the indulgence might be, we tend to want more. And when we place the importance of these things above our Lord and Savior, we create an idol that can never fill the void we have. Do we so easily forget that these things are fleeting—that they are ever-changing and cannot satisfy? We give so much of ourselves to indulgences of earthly pleasures that we somehow manage to forget there is only One who fully satisfies. There is only One who is unchanging and who loves us still, even as we turn away from Him. In our carelessness, we lower our guards to believe the lie that God is not enough—that to be happy, enough, and worthy, we must have that which we do not have yet.

In Ezekiel 16:49–50, we read of Sodom, a city that was so overtaken by pride it succumbed to its evil indulgences, wholly turning from the Lord and worshiping other things instead. The people's pride—their elevation of self above all else—seemingly blinded them of their need for God. And indeed, this brought about their downfall, as we see in verse 50. Though God loves His creation, He cannot bless that which is dishonoring to Him. Time and time again and grace upon grace, He allowed them to turn from sin and back to Him, yet their hearts were hardened against Him.

When we fail to chase after Christ and let careless indulgences have their way in our hearts, we find ourselves just as the city of Sodom as it crumbled beneath the weight of its pride and the sin that so entangled it. How easily we too chase after that which can never truly satisfy our deepest longing, which is our heavenly Father. As we go about our days, let us instead cling to the truth of who God is. May we pour our time, service, and love into knowing Christ and growing in our knowledge of who He is and how much He loves us.

"AS WE GO ABOUT OUR DAYS, LET US INSTEAD CLING TO THE TRUTH OF WHO GOD IS."

DAY 43

In God's Time

The least will become a thousand, the smallest a mighty nation. I am the Lord; I will accomplish it quickly in its time.

ISAIAH 60:22

Impatience is a common struggle most of us share. Our fast-paced culture has conditioned us to want things fast, but when things come slowly, impatience begins to show itself in our thoughts, words, and actions. If the line is too long at the store, we hop on self-checkout in hopes of moving more quickly. We order takeout for meals so we can grab it and go on with our to-do list. Yet, one of the most frustrating but humbling realities is that we cannot control God's timing. Whether we like it or not, God moves and works as He so wills, sometimes fast and sometimes slow.

The nation of Israel had to learn to trust God's timing. Whether He provided manna to eat or parted the Red Sea, the Israelites knew that time was in God's hands. Yet as they wandered the wilderness, the hope of their restoration likely often felt slim. Nevertheless, God promised them that He would deliver them and restore them back to a thriving nation—not in their timing but in His perfect timing.

We, too, must learn to trust God's perfect timing. Yet trusting the Lord's timing can be difficult as believers. We may say to the Lord that we trust His timing then feel ourselves growing impatient when He seems to be working slowly. When we have prayed for something for a long time, it can be disheartening when it seems God has not acted. Israel's situation gives us hope because we know the end of their story. Even though they had to wait, God did deliver them from their exile. And later, He would bring about a deliverance far beyond their post-exile restoration through Jesus's sacrifice on the cross.

God's timing can be trusted because He is a faithful God. He does not withhold maliciously but purposely and lovingly. As we wait on the Lord, we can do so joyfully, knowing that His plans are for our good. Knowing that God works all things for our good encourages us to leave our lives in His hands. Instead of trying to seize control, we must place our trust in the God who is in control. Every season of our lives has been divinely orchestrated through God's perfect timing. He has been faithful before, and He will be faithful again.

"GOD'S TIMING CAN BE TRUSTED BECAUSE HE IS A FAITHFUL GOD."

DAY 44
God's Gracious Pardon

The Lord is slow to anger and abounding in faithful love, forgiving iniquity and rebellion. But he will not leave the guilty unpunished, bringing the consequences of the fathers' iniquity on the children to the third and fourth generation. Please pardon the iniquity of this people, in keeping with the greatness of your faithful love, just as you have forgiven them from Egypt until now.

NUMBERS 14:18–19

The nature of God can be difficult for us to comprehend. He is both gracious and just, forgiving and a righteous judge. The way that these seemingly opposite characteristics are balanced in perfect harmony makes little sense in human wisdom. For some, we see Him show gracious compassion and, for others, execute swift judgment. This passage in Numbers helps us understand more about the complex and flawless character of God.

In Numbers 14, Moses converses with the Lord regarding the waywardness of the Israelites. Despite God's miraculously delivering them from Egypt and His constant care and provision, the people still feel things are not as good as they should be. The desert is hot without reprieve, and water is scarce. They fear that everyone will die. But, instead of trusting God to get them through, they turn away from God and make known their desires to live in Egypt once again.

God is rightfully angered by their betrayal. Fear is not a good reason to forgo wholehearted devotion to the Lord, and He threatens to destroy the unbelieving nation. The Lord tells Moses He will bring upon the Israelites the just consequence for their sin. But Moses pleads, knowing that the Lord's compassion is great, and the Lord gives them another chance. God does love those wayward people. Oh, how He loves them, and He waits eagerly for their return to Him. However, because sin cannot go unpunished, the wayward generation cannot enter the Promised Land. God has spared their lives but will keep them from experiencing the promise fulfilled.

God is faithful, kind, and loving, while He is also just and righteous. Jesus has paid the price for our sins, and our eternity is secure in Him. Yet, God still justly deals with our sins. They do not condemn us but can create distance between us and the will of God. What should be our response to our sin and the Lord? Reverence and repentance. While we can rest in the faithful forgiveness of our loving Lord, we also should strive to be holy as He is holy (1 Peter 1:16).

DAY 45
Nothing Without Love

If I speak human or angelic tongues but do not have love, I am a noisy gong or a clanging cymbal. If I have the gift of prophecy and understand all mysteries and all knowledge, and if I have all faith so that I can move mountains but do not have love, I am nothing. And if I give away all my possessions, and if I give over my body in order to boast but do not have love, I gain nothing.

1 CORINTHIANS 13:1-3

God gives His people gifts through the Holy Spirit. Paul, one of the leaders of the early Church, identified these gifts in his letters to believers. Paul acknowledged the diversity of gifts in the Church and deemed them important for contributing to the gospel mission. But, in his letter to the Corinthian church, Paul addresses how the people were abusing their gifts.

The believers of Corinth used spiritual gifts to create a false measure of superiority. The Corinthians did not strive to magnify God's glory through their gifting. Paul confronted them in this area and urged them to see the futility of gifts without love for God and others. In other words, they could not use their gifts to spread the gospel mission if they did not come from a place of humility.

Spiritual gifts assessments are popular in our current church culture. These tests are beneficial as they help identify areas of skill to point others to Jesus. However, we must examine ourselves to see if we are using them to create a false measure of superiority like the Corinthian believers. Though we are redeemed believers, we still wrestle with our selfish natures. We have Holy Spirit-generated desires to use our gifts for God's kingdom, but if we do not actively fight sin, our witness to Christ may be challenged by our desires for self-glory.

At times of self-examination, we must recall Paul's exhortation to love above all. Love, in the biblical sense, does not mean romance or a fleeting feeling. Instead, biblical love conveys sacrifice and caring for another's well-being. On the basis of biblical love, our spiritual gifts can truly operate in the way they were intended. But we cannot live out this type of love in our own will. We need the saving work of Jesus Christ to equip us to love as He loved us. In gratitude, let us always reflect Jesus's humility and sacrificial love by giving our gifts back to Him in service.

DAY 46

Our Purchased Peace

But he was pierced because of our rebellion, crushed because of our iniquities; punishment for our peace was on him, and we are healed by his wounds.

ISAIAH 53:5

Our world is filled with division—politically, economically, racially. Global crises, injustices, and calamities cause grief, anxiety, and unrest. Our world is far from peaceful. But it was not always that way. When God created the world, there was perfect harmony between God, man, and creation. Creation lived in praise and worship of the Lord as they were created to do. But this perfect harmony was lost when Adam and Eve sinned in the garden. The cost of sin was a broken relationship with God and a broken peace on earth.

But God knew all along that sin would cause disunity and division. In His sovereignty, He was already preparing a way to restore us back to Himself and by extension, give us peace. The book of Isaiah prophetically looks forward to the One whom God would send to save us from our sin—His own Son. He would be pierced for our rebellion. He would be crushed for our iniquities. He would be wounded so that we could find healing. And He would be punished so that we could have peace through a relationship with God. The Lord would exchange His life for ours so that we could be united to Christ again through His Spirit and in eternity to come.

In the last hours of Jesus's life, He assured His people, "Peace I leave with you. My peace I give to you. I do not give to you as the world gives. Don't let your heart be troubled or fearful" (John 14:27). He gives us His perfect peace—a peace that pierces through the darkness and calms our every fear. These words speak of the hope we can cling to in life's hardest moments. Jesus Christ purchased peace for us with His life so that we could be assured at every moment, through every circumstance, that there is hope beyond what we face now. That hope is the promise for all to be right in the world when Jesus returns–when there will be no more cause for division, no more tears, no more pain, and no more sorrows. When Jesus returns, He will unite all the saints in harmony in the presence of God and fully restore peace on earth. May His presence secure our peace until that great day!

"JESUS CHRIST PURCHASED PEACE FOR US WITH HIS LIFE."

DAY 47
Renewed Day by Day

Therefore we do not give up. Even though our outer person is being destroyed, our inner person is being renewed day by day.

2 CORINTHIANS 4:16

Do you ever feel overwhelmed by our broken bodies? Do you struggle with illness or injuries? If so, you are not alone. However, we have this encouragement that while our outward bodies are breaking down, God is renewing our spirit day by day.

In fact, Paul proclaimed that God brings glory to Himself through human limitations. In chapter 4, he wrote about his troubles in preaching the truth of Jesus Christ. Because of this message, he experienced much persecution and oppression. The gospel was not attractive in a fallen world, and unbelievers reacted violently against Paul. Though his body was wasting away through the trials of his journey, Paul knew the Holy Spirit was renewing his soul each day. The Holy Spirit was transforming Paul's inner person into the image of Jesus. As his body was abused and beaten, Paul remained hopeful and joyous in Christ. He embraced suffering as a way to mirror the death of Jesus on the outside while, on the inside, radiating the life of Jesus.

The soul of the believer remains whole, even while the body suffers, but through Christ, we know that the body does not vanish forever like the dust in the wind. God cares for our bodies as His creation and sent Jesus to restore them from moral corruption. As the God-Man, Jesus encountered the utmost suffering on His redemptive mission. He was falsely accused and punished for His message. Though His body weakened, He was without sin. His light continued to shine from the fullness of God dwelling inside Him. After Jesus died on the cross for our sins, He arose from the grave three days later, His body restored.

Through our faith in Jesus, our entire beings share in the suffering of Christ and will be restored with Him. While we perish on the outside, on the inside, He transforms us into the beauty of our Savior. We do not have to be discouraged when people hurt or oppress us. With the indwelling Holy Spirit, we can display the love of Jesus as we boast in His renewing power. Let us embrace this renewal by pushing forward, even in life's hard circumstances. Our day by day sanctification is a foretaste of the full glorification we will experience when Jesus raises us from the grave. May this truth give us hope!

"GOD IS RENEWING OUR SPIRIT DAY BY DAY."

DAY 48
The Greatest Commission

Go, therefore, and make disciples of all nations, baptizing them in the name of the Father and of the Son and of the Holy Spirit

MATTHEW 28:19

We were designed to want to share life with one another. As believers in Christ, we are all part of something far greater than these experiences. Before He ascended into heaven, Jesus commissioned His disciples to spread the gospel. A commission is an instruction or command given to a group of people. Our commission as believers is to make disciples by sharing the good news of the gospel. This is not a one man job. The Great Commission is a mission that we all share together as the body of Christ.

This commission from Christ should fill us with excitement. Jesus has chosen *us* to make His name known among the nations. What an incredible honor it is to be used by the Lord for such a mission. We are on a mission to change hearts and change lives through the power of the Holy Spirit. We should not be satisfied in keeping the gospel to ourselves. As Christ's disciples, we are to make more disciples. As disciple-makers we share the good news of Jesus and help shape the faith of those who come to know Jesus. As we do so, we encourage the disciples we make to make disciples of their own. As we are faithful disciple-makers, we teach others to be faithful disciple-makers. As a result, lives are changed, and God is glorified.

The Great Commission is ongoing. We do not make one disciple and place a checkmark next to Jesus's command. It is our life pursuit as the body of Christ to make disciples of Jesus Christ. We are to make disciples until our last breath. Why? Because we want the body of Christ to grow! While the motivation of the Great Commission should not be numbers, we should find encouragement when the body of Christ grows. One new disciple means one new person in the family of God. We cannot read Jesus's command and assume it is only a command for other believers. This command is for you, dear reader. May these words from Christ challenge you to grow as a disciple-maker for Him. May the good news of gospel spur you on to share with those around you. Take up the Great Commission and go.

"JESUS HAS CHOSEN US TO MAKE HIS NAME KNOWN AMONG THE NATIONS."

DAY 49
Love in Action

Let love be without hypocrisy. Detest evil; cling to what is good. Love one another deeply as brothers and sisters. Outdo one another in showing honor.

ROMANS 12:9–10

When we are in Christ, we move from spiritual death into spiritual life. Before Christ, our hearts are inclined toward ourselves, but when the Lord changes our hearts and helps us see the truth of the gospel, we are made completely new. The Lord gives us the Holy Spirit as our guide—He puts His own Spirit inside of us. And as we live out the rest of our days on earth, He sanctifies us to be more like Him. We grow out of darkness into His glorious light and life.

All believers become active reflections of the Lord's love wherever they go. And this love is to be displayed through our actions. Jesus's love is not hypocritical. It loves purely and sincerely. It detests evil, helping us cling to what is good. It unites all believers as the family of God and helps us honor one another. His love changes us. So when we do not walk in love and choose instead to walk in our own desires, we act as we did before we were saved.

But because of Christ's love and our salvation in the gospel, we are safe and secure. When we are hypocritical or choose evil over good, the Lord does not forsake us, though there are certainly consequences for our actions. We hurt those around us. We do not honor one another. Our sin leads to pain and suffering in the body of Christ. But because of our position in Christ, His love leads us to repentance. Choosing to glorify God in all that we say and do serves not to tear down but to build up the body of Christ.

Each day presents different challenges and situations with plenty of opportunities to obey or disobey God's Word, and there will be times we fail to display Christ's love. But because we have the Holy Spirit, we are able to call on the Lord for help. He will give us the strength we need to carry out His love in the world. He showers us with His love and provides us with the means to let His love overflow through us to others that they may know Him too.

"THE LORD DOES NOT FORSAKE US."

DAY 50
Life in Christ

I have been crucified with Christ, and I no longer live, but Christ lives in me. The life I now live in the body, I live by faith in the Son of God, who loved me and gave himself for me.

GALATIANS 2:20

When we come to faith in Jesus, our lives are forever changed. Through Christ's saving work within us, we are transformed into a new person. In essence, who we were before Christ has died and has been replaced with a new person, redeemed and forgiven by Jesus. Our salvation through Christ gives our lives new meaning. Before coming to Christ, we lived for ourselves. We chased our own desires and pursued what made us happy. But when we come to know Christ, the orientation of our hearts shifts. Out of deep love and gratitude for Jesus's sacrifice, we live for Him.

Not only this, but we no longer live on our own. When we experience salvation, we are gifted with the Holy Spirit. The presence of God comes to make His home within us. The indwelling of the Spirit allows us to walk with God daily and depend on Him in all things. The Spirit aids us as we live for Christ, strengthening us and empowering us to walk in obedience. What an incredible joy to have the One we love living inside of us.

1 Corinthians 6:19–20 tells us, "Don't you know that your body is a temple of the Holy Spirit who is in you, whom you have from God? You are not your own, for you were bought at a price. So glorify God with your body." Dear reader, you are not your own. Yet sometimes we forget this truth and seek to live for ourselves instead of Christ. Rather than thinking first about pleasing and obeying Christ, we think about pleasing ourselves. Perhaps you feel tension within but choose to ignore the Spirit's prompting to turn back to Him. In those moments, may our hearts be nudged to repentance, for continuing in disobedience will leave us restless and unsatisfied.

In what ways are you seeking to follow your own desires instead of following Christ? In the moments you find yourself tempted to gratify your flesh, remember the price Jesus paid. Christ loves you and gave Himself for you. He has given you new life and resides within you to lead, guide, and help you. It should be our greatest joy to live for the One who saved us.

"WHAT AN INCREDIBLE JOY TO HAVE THE ONE WE LOVE LIVING INSIDE OF US."

DAY 51
Words that Build

No foul language should come from your mouth, but only what is good for building up someone in need, so that it gives grace to those who hear.

EPHESIANS 4:29

One of the most misunderstood truths about the words that we say is that foul language goes beyond curse words and innuendos. While we do not want this type of language to be on our lips, we sometimes overlook that speech with the appearance of innocence can be even more deadly than an inappropriate word. Words are tools the Lord has given us to build each other up. But while they can be fragrant and sweet to others, they can also be poisonous and deadly.

The book of Proverbs speaks again and again about the weight of what we say. Some of the wise sayings even caution us to "keep silent" at times because it is so easy to let destructive words flow from our lips (Proverbs 17:28). But Paul says in his letter to the Ephesians that our words can be used to build up the body of Christ, especially those who are in need.

When Christ comes into our lives, He shows us how to speak. Changing how we speak can be difficult for us to do, but it can also be one of the simplest ways to share the gospel with another person. People notice how you speak, and they take note if your speech is full of words that build up or tear down. When we speak life with our words, we represent Christ to others wherever we go. Our words can be used as a healing balm to soothe those who are hurting and in pain. They can create joy in the heart of their hearer. They can inspire another to keep going. They can remind our brothers and sisters in Christ of the truth of the gospel.

But, so often, we do not think of our words as having this kind of power. We flippantly speak them and forget that if we are intentional with what we say, we can contribute to building up others in the kingdom of God. Let us focus on how our words may shape those around us. We should see our words as the tools that they are, using them with care and diligence. And as we speak in love, we are better able to advance the gospel of Christ to a world who longs to hear.

"WHEN CHRIST COMES INTO OUR LIVES,
HE SHOWS US HOW TO SPEAK."

DAY 52
Our Tears are Temporary

For his anger lasts only a moment, but his favor, a lifetime. Weeping may stay overnight, but there is joy in the morning.

PSALM 30:5

Inevitably the tears will flow. Because we live in a fallen world, heartache surrounds us. We hear about it, we read about it, we tell about it, and we experience it. Sometimes it may seem as though the tears will never stop flowing. We read in Psalm 30 that weeping may endure for the night, but joy will certainly come in the morning. David explains here that our weeping is temporary. Though trial after trial may come in this life, and the tears may continue, there will surely be a day when they are no more.

Revelation 21:4 tells us that when we get to heaven, God "will wipe away every tear . . . Death will be no more; grief, crying, and pain will be no more, because the previous things have passed away." What incredible tenderness we see here as we read that when the Lord calls us home to heaven, He will not be taken aback by our tears and broken places—the betrayals, losses, heartbreaks—in fact, He knows them better than anyone else, and He longs to wipe them away and make us new. Although we may never understand the pain and sadness we experience on earth, and we may never have the closure or answers we so desire, we cling still to the hope of Christ and the redemption He will bring to our mourning, our sadness, our anger, our weakness.

But what do we do with our tears until that day? Is God not able to take away our suffering now? We look to His Word and the gospel where we can find comfort in our present circumstances. And we allow God to use us to comfort others in their pain. As the Lord extends kindness and mercy to us, let us do so for others who are hurting—sharing with them our reason for hope in the pain. Yes, the tears will flow right now, but we await a great joy of being with Christ for all of eternity. In place of our tears will be joy, in place of our crying will be praise.

"WE ALLOW GOD TO USE US TO COMFORT OTHERS IN THEIR PAIN."

DAY 53
God's Plans are Protected

They will fight against you but never prevail over you, since I am with you to rescue you." This is the Lord's declaration.

JEREMIAH 1:19

"Why me, God?" When Jeremiah was called by God to be a prophet to the people, he had all kinds of objections. He was too young and afraid. But, God equips those He calls. He gave Jeremiah the words needed to become a prophet to the Israelites. And despite the difficult task of preaching a message of destruction to the people, Jeremiah was faithful to the Lord. God protected His people and His plan.

Jeremiah's ministry would not be an easy one, though. In fact, Jeremiah was known as the weeping prophet. To modern-day pastors, the phrase "a Jeremiah ministry" connotes years of hardship, hardness, and pain. This makes the promise God gave Jeremiah especially interesting. God promised to fight for Jeremiah and that the people would never prevail over him. But as expected, the people were not happy with Jeremiah's warnings of destruction. They tried to kill him, and at one point, even beat him and put him in the stocks. Later, they threw him in a mud pit, and they often plotted to destroy him. Even then, God protected Jeremiah against their murderous schemes. While God's promise to protect Jeremiah did not ensure a painless ministry, He was with Jeremiah every step of the way.

Faithfulness to the Lord does not mean that we escape pain. Rather, it means that He will be with us in the midst of it. When we surrender our lives to Christ, we follow our Savior wherever He leads us. Sometimes, it will be a dark night of the soul or to grief unimaginable. Sometimes, it will be into rivers of blessing and joy. In either case, God promises to be with us and fight for us.

Like Jeremiah, we may face trouble in this life because we follow God. But even when we are rejected, we can remember that these are momentary trials. Jeremiah's faithfulness is now being rewarded before the King of kings for all of eternity. Though the people fought against Jeremiah, they did not prevail. God rescued Jeremiah from this fallen world, into the kingdom of eternal pleasure and joy. We can be confident that He will do the same for us.

"GOD PROMISES TO BE WITH US AND FIGHT FOR US."

DAY 54
Light Out of Darkness

Now the earth was formless and empty, darkness covered the surface of the watery depths, and the Spirit of God was hovering over the surface of the waters. Then God said, "Let there be light," and there was light.

GENESIS 1:2–3

In Genesis 1, there was no light, no sun, and no moon, but when God spoke, He made the light out of nothing. With a word, God brought light into being, letting it shine brilliantly in a dark world. This light pierced through the darkness as God readied the world for His image-bearers. But today, the world can often feel dark. Although we have a physical sun to light our days, our emotional and spiritual lives may feel dim. Evil seems to have won. Darkness appears to prevail. God feels far, and the world looks bleak. What hope is there for our souls?

Thankfully, God did not leave us in the darkness. Instead, He came in person to pierce through the black night and dwell among us. He lived perfectly, as light to a dark world, and loved perfectly, dying on the cross for our sins. Not only this, He rose again from the dead, securing our victory over death and darkness (1 Corinthians 15:20–28). Because of this, on the days when life feels dark, we can remember that we are not alone. Christ is the light of our lives (John 8:12), and He has sent His Spirit to live within us (John 14:16). He promises that whoever walks with Him will not walk in darkness but have the light of life.

God has given us His Word to guide us. Scripture refers to the Bible in this same "light" imagery, calling it a lamp to our feet and a light to our path (Psalm 119:105). In this life, Scripture becomes our guide, our lantern, and our truth. Though we may feel like we dwell in darkness, He has given us a beacon to light the way. Until we see Him again, we use His Word, our lamp, to guide our paths.

One day, we will be united with the Giver of light. We will not need to worry about the sun any longer, because God will be our light (Revelation 21:23). Every darkness, sorrow, and pain will cease. God is and will be our radiance and joy. As we eagerly wait for that day, we rejoice in the One who has secured our victory and our eternal life with Him.

"GOD DID NOT LEAVE US IN THE DARKNESS."

DAY 55
A House of Worship

But if it doesn't please you to worship the Lord, choose for yourselves today: Which will you worship—the gods your fathers worshiped beyond the Euphrates River or the gods of the Amorites in whose land you are living? As for me and my family, we will worship the Lord.

JOSHUA 24:15

Some non-Christians claim that Christians believe what we believe because society or our parents made us accept the Christian doctrine. But coercion of belief is not how Christianity works. Belief in the gospel involves an inward longing of the heart; this disposition cannot be something we are forced to possess. Furthermore, Scripture tells us that all humans have a sinful nature. In other words, we have a natural inclination to reject God. We freely act on the disastrous desires of our hearts, and we seek idols that destroy.

We see this type of freedom expressed in Scripture. Joshua, an Israelite man who led the nation of Israel in securing the Promised Land, presented the Israelites with a freedom of choice in worship. At the end of his time as leader, Joshua gave a convicting speech to the Israelites. They had watched God defeat their Egyptian oppressors and their enemies in Canaan. Even though the Israelites had received God's undeserved grace, they still filled their homes with idol statues. Earlier, in the book of Deuteronomy, God told them to fill their houses with His Word and Law so that they would remember and obey. But, with rebellious hearts, they rejected the Lord's commands.

Joshua called the people to renew their vow of loyalty to God. But then, he told them if worshiping the true God was not what they desired, they could choose to go back to the gods of their ancestors or the surrounding pagan nations. Despite the Israelites' wayward desires, God was on a redemptive mission and was going to send the Savior. The Savior would save God's people from their corrupt desires so that they could obey.

By God's grace, Joshua had the faith to pursue correct worship. But, he too was a sinner and not the Savior. Rather, Joshua pointed to Jesus, the Commander of the Lord's armies. Through His life, death, and resurrection, our Savior, Jesus, not only defeated our enemy, spiritual evil, but He also saved us from our sinful selves. God gave us the indwelling Holy Spirit who renewed our hearts. Day by day, God transforms us into the image of Christ and makes us into His own house of worship.

DAY 56

This is God's Will

But now Timothy has come to us from you and brought us good news about your faith and love. He reported that you always have good memories of us and that you long to see us, as we also long to see you. Therefore, brothers and sisters, in all our distress and affliction, we were encouraged about you through your faith. For now we live, if you stand firm in the Lord.

1 THESSALONIANS 3:6–8

Very little about the way God's kingdom functions seems logical to us. If God is all-powerful, then would He not use His power to keep us safe? And if God is perfectly just, should He not use His strong arm of justice to cause only what is right to happen? These conclusions seem logical, but they do not align with Scripture. If we cling to them as gospel truth, we will find confusion, and our faith will feel fragmented.

In these verses, Paul was writing to the Christians in Thessalonica about the trial and tribulations they were experiencing. We know that they were facing intense persecution (Acts 17:5–8) and he worried that continued anger against the new Christians would tempt them to desert their faith. But it did not! And their steadfast devotion comforts Paul.

He reminds them that as for persecution, "we are appointed to this." Opposition to our faith does not mean God is not present or at work. It means that Satan is at work opposing the things God seeks to accomplish. Even Jesus Himself tells us that we will face persecution: "Remember the word I spoke to you: 'A servant is not greater than his master.' If they persecuted me, they will also persecute you. If they kept my word, they will also keep yours" (John 15:20).

Paul is relieved to hear from Timothy that the extenuating circumstances the Thessalonian believers faced have not caused them to depart from the faith. He warns them to hold fast to the true gospel—that the call of a Christian is often toward temporal death, but all the while, God is moving them toward eternal life.

From Paul's warning to the Thessalonians, we can learn to embrace trials, persecution, and hatred as a result of our faith in Christ and the will of God. We know that when we face these hardships, our faith is being perfected in us (James 1:4). We are never promised comfort in this life, but we are promised eternal peace, joy, and rest in the next.

DAY 57
All-Consuming Worship

Love the Lord your God with all your heart, with all your soul, and with all your strength. These words that I am giving you today are to be in your heart. Repeat them to your children. Talk about them when you sit in your house and when you walk along the road, when you lie down and when you get up. Bind them as a sign on your hand and let them be a symbol on your forehead. Write them on the doorposts of your house and on your city gates.

DEUTERONOMY 6:5–9

When we want to remember something, we likely write it down. Today we do things like setting phone reminders, writing on sticky notes, or even taping index cards to mirrors or doors so that we do not forget what is important. For the people of Israel, God gave them the Law to remind them how to obey Him. The Law was meant to grow the hearts of the people in love and worship to the Lord as they obeyed Him. The words of the Law helped the people love the Lord wholeheartedly. But these words needed to be regularly repeated lest they forget.

God desires for our whole hearts to love Him. However, God knows that this does not come naturally for us. On our own, our hearts are not bent toward Him but to the things we want and desire. If we were honest, we might admit that it is hard to love the Lord with all of who we are. But God desires us to be in all-consuming worship to Him. For us to do this, our hearts must be fully devoted to Him. Since God knows this is difficult for us, He has given us His Word. Through reading and meditating on God's Word, His words remain in our minds and hearts.

If your heart is struggling in devotion to the Lord, there is grace. God's love for you is not determined by your amount of love for Him. Allow His great love and grace to encourage you to come to Him in all-consuming praise. Ask the Holy Spirit to keep your heart stayed in worship to God above all else. Fix your eyes on His Word, and meditate on the truth of the gospel. Remember what He has done, and rejoice in the God of your salvation!

"GOD DESIRES FOR OUR WHOLE HEARTS TO LOVE HIM."

DAY 58

Our Prayers Reveal Our Theology

Therefore, you should pray like this: Our Father in heaven, your name be honored as holy. Your kingdom come. Your will be done on earth as it is in heaven. Give us today our daily bread. And forgive us our debts, as we also have forgiven our debtors. And do not bring us into temptation, but deliver us from the evil one.

MATTHEW 6:9–13

Our prayer lives reflect a great deal about our theology. Prayer is an overflow from what comes to mind when we think about God and what we believe in our hearts to be true about Him. As we approach God in prayer, the ways in which we do so say much about who we think He is. Do we praise and thank Him for who He is and what He has done, or do we simply jump right into prayer by listing all that He can do for us?

When we lift our praises and requests to the Lord, we show our daily need for Him. As we pray for God's help, we reveal an understanding of His power and authority. If we repent of our sin, we recognize Him as the One who made a way for forgiveness and righteousness. To approach Him with our burdens, we acknowledge His capability to carry the weight of them all. All that we pray speaks to our fundamental knowledge of God.

Prayer also reveals how we view ourselves in relation to God. We often show the trust we can too easily place in ourselves when we neglect to pray for certain things. And we learn about what we value most, for we pray about the things that matter most to us. Consider your most frequented prayer requests and what they might tell you about your priorities. We may be tempted to think only of ourselves and our own needs in prayer. But, when we are prayerful for God's people, we participate in God's kingdom work. Not only do we encourage one another by praying for one another, but we participate in the privilege of prayer together, and we more clearly see the fruit of God's faithfulness in the lives of one another. May our prayer lives exude great love and reverence for God, a declaration of our great need, and a genuine care for the lives of others.

"WHEN WE ARE PRAYERFUL FOR GOD'S PEOPLE, WE PARTICIPATE IN GOD'S KINGDOM WORK."

DAY 59

The Radience of God's Glory

Long ago God spoke to the ancestors by the prophets at different times and in different ways. In these last days, he has spoken to us by his Son. God has appointed him heir of all things and made the universe through him. The Son is the radiance of God's glory and the exact expression of his nature, sustaining all things by his powerful word.

HEBREWS 1:1-3A

God delights in dwelling with His people. Though He reigns high in the heavens, God comes near to His creation. When we go to the pages of Scripture, we learn how God used to walk with the people He created. The entrance of sin prevented God from dwelling with His creation in such an intimate way, but this did not keep God from being connected to His people. By His grace, God spoke to and through people throughout the Old Testament so His people could hear from Him. He also used the temple and tabernacle to manifest His glorious presence. However, God took one step further in His efforts to dwell with man: He sent His Son. In coming to earth, Jesus was the manifestation of the divine revelation of God (John 1:14).

Jesus is the radiance of God's glory. Jesus reflects the glory of God because He is God. Those who spoke with Him spoke directly with God and witnessed the power of God within Him. Throughout His ministry, Jesus reflected and declared the glory of God to all who saw Him. But God's glory was also displayed through the death and resurrection of Jesus. By dying on the cross and rising triumphantly from the grave, Jesus proclaimed the power and glory of the Lord. As followers of Christ, we are witnesses to the glory of God. How? Because we know Jesus.

We read in 2 Corinthians 4:6, "For God who said, 'Let light shine out of darkness,' has shone in our hearts to give the light of the knowledge of God's glory in the face of Jesus Christ." By knowing and believing in Jesus, we behold the glory of God. Everyday, we have the opportunity to behold the glory of God by reflecting and rejoicing over the gospel. And, when Christ returns, we will spend eternity dwelling with God. But, for now, let us praise God that we can behold His glory through His Son, Jesus.

"BY KNOWING AND BELIEVING IN JESUS, WE BEHOLD THE GLORY OF GOD."

DAY 60
Godly Contentment

But godliness with contentment is great gain.

1 TIMOTHY 6:6

What keeps you from being content? Contentment can be difficult as circumstances often determine our level of contentment. When all is well, is it easy for us to feel content, but when circumstances go awry, our contentment can change. In 1 Timothy 6:6, Paul encouraged Timothy to teach sound doctrine—teaching that brings about godliness in the lives of believers. The reason for this encouragement was that Paul knew there were people who did not listen to sound doctrine and listened to false teaching instead. They had a skewed thinking of godliness as the means to obtain material wealth. Yet Paul says that true godliness is contentment, no matter our financial situation. Godliness with contentment brings a gain that far surpasses material gain.

Godly contentment trusts that God will provide. Even in trying circumstances, we can remain content knowing that God takes care of us. Our contentment should not be contingent upon the number in our bank accounts. The more we surrender every area of our lives to the Lord, including our finances, the more we will grow in Christlikeness. Ceasing to worry about money and possessions frees us to focus on growing in our walks with the Lord, for we will then focus on what matters instead of growing fearful or prideful over our wealth.

Finding full contentment in Christ also declares that He is all we need. Christ is the key to contentment (Philippians 4:12). Even if our situation changes, whether for good or bad, our relationships with Christ remain. We do not need any material wealth for satisfaction, for our relationships with Christ eternally satisfy. Our love for Christ and gratitude for our relationships with Him encourage us to grow in godliness. And because we know that God will provide and that Christ is all we need, we can be content as we grow in godliness. No earthly riches compare to the gain of knowing Christ and growing in Christlikeness. May the true motivation of godliness bring us full contentment, no matter what circumstances arise.

"GODLY CONTENTMENT TRUSTS THAT GOD WILL PROVIDE."

DAY 61
God is Greater than Our Hearts

This is how we will know that we belong to the truth and will reassure our hearts before him whenever our hearts condemn us; for God is greater than our hearts, and he knows all things.

1 JOHN 3:19–20

We all hear the voice of condemnation from time to time. And, when our voices condemn us, our culture's solution is self-love. "Self-love" is a term that expresses regard for one's own wellbeing and happiness. Most times, self-love focuses on pampering oneself, improving confidence, and boasting in one's good qualities. Outside the biblical context, our culture's definition of self-love only covers up inner problems. This definition disregards our fallen nature, sin, and our need for a Savior. But, truly loving ourselves and silencing the condemnations of our hearts can only be realized in Jesus Christ. God does not desire for us to wallow in our shame when Jesus laid down His life to make us new. The Lord wants us to enjoy who we are in Him.

We can go to Scripture for the basis of biblical self-love. John's first epistle is filled with the theme of love in general. In chapter 3, John explains that the way of true believers is loving one another through forgiveness, patience, and gentleness. As God's children, we can love someone else in this way because Jesus showed this love toward us. John urged his audience to show others compassion and mercy. John also expanded the ethic of loving one another to loving oneself (1 John 3:19–20). Though redeemed, believers still wrestle with persistent sins and the shame of their pasts. It takes time for the heart to rest fully in the Lord's love.

When you sin, do you dwell on your shortcomings? Do you continue to replay past mistakes? If our hearts condemn us, we join the false accusation that claims the power of the cross was not sufficient. But God's great work of salvation is complete. We can be sure that the Lord will remind us of His sufficient love. Let us allow His Word to restore our hearts. In Scripture reading and prayer, we see that God's words prevail over our condemning thoughts. The Holy Spirit will remind us that God does not condemn us who have placed our faith in Jesus. As children of God, we can show forgiveness, patience, and gentleness toward ourselves because God Himself has done so. We can look forward to eternity with Jesus when our hearts will be full of God's love.

"GOD'S GREAT WORK OF SALVATION IS COMPLETE."

DAY 62

The Path of Purity

How can a young man keep his way pure?
By keeping your word.

PSALM 119:9

Psalm 119 is the longest psalm in the book of Psalms, and it is an expression of the psalmist's love for God's Word. While the author desires to keep the Law, he also recognizes his limitations. He knows he is not the example of perfect obedience. He, like all others, has failed to keep God's Word perfectly because of impure desires of the heart.

The word "pure" describes something that is without contamination. A pure substance is wholly composed of one element and is not tainted with anything else. The psalmist desired to have a pure heart. However, because he was human, he was also likely corrupted by his desire to sin. Like the psalmist, we have the same problem. Because of our sin nature, our ways are not pure. We do not have a love for God's law and desire to obey it. Instead, we attempt to satisfy our own desires.

Psalm 119 points to Jesus Christ. Jesus deeply desired to keep the law, and He was always obedient to it. Because He was God, Jesus was the only One pure in heart, not possessing any corrupt intentions. In His humanity, Jesus remained pure as He held on to the Father's Word to direct His path. Jesus kept the Law perfectly on our behalf. His accomplishment frees us to trust in Him and see His Word, the Bible, as a guiding light for our journeys. In humble gratitude for God's salvation, we can remain on the path of purity by clinging to Jesus and cherishing His truth and wisdom, not out of obligation but out of a desire to enter into His place of peace.

"WE CAN REMAIN ON THE PATH OF PURITY BY CLINGING TO JESUS AND CHERISHING HIS TRUTH AND WISDOM."

DAY 63
He Gives More Grace

But he gives greater grace. Therefore he says: God resists the proud, but gives grace to the humble.

JAMES 4:6

The New Testament has its own wisdom literature. While it reads differently than the Old Testament book of wisdom, Proverbs, the book of James is full of instruction and encouragement for those who follow Christ. At the time when it was written, the church was new. James, the brother of Jesus and prominent leader of the early church, wrote this book to challenge believers in Christ with how they were living in light of the gospel they had received.

Although this book's wisdom is rich and precious, many of the statements James makes can be hard to receive. He covers a variety of difficult topics like doubting the faith, the purpose of trials, the sin of partiality, and even the danger of our words. James shows us how to live holy lives and war against the world. However, while reading all of these challenges and instructions, we may become discouraged. We are so prone to wander from the wisdom of God and instead listen to the wisdom of the world. But James 6:4–5 tells us that when we pursue friendship with the world, we are at the same time showing hostility toward the Lord. We cannot love both the things of the world and the things of God.

Now, we can nod along in agreement with James as we read this passage, but putting what he says into practice is difficult. We live in the world and interact with people, entertainment, and belief systems that are completely opposed to the truth of the gospel. Until we reach eternity, we will never be free from the presence of sin. But as we pursue Christ and the wisdom of God, we grow to love the things of God more than the things of the world. And even on days where we fail miserably and choose friendship with the world over friendship with God, He gives us grace upon grace. He disciplines us through the wrong choices we make, but He does so for our restoration. So, when we fail in our interactions with the things of this world, we can humbly come to God for forgiveness, knowing that His grace is neverending. May we not take advantage of this grace but rather, be overwhelmed by the Lord's great mercy and compassion for us as His children.

"WE CANNOT LOVE BOTH THE THINGS OF THE WORLD AND THE THINGS OF GOD."

DAY 64
Gifted What We Could Never Earn

For the wages of sin is death, but the gift of God is eternal life in Christ Jesus our Lord.

ROMANS 6:23

Romans 6:23 is one of the most well known verses in the Bible, yet every time we break it apart and meditate on its meaning, the glorious truth of the gospel is revealed. The first phrase tells us that "the wages of sin is death." The Greek word Paul uses here would have referred to a soldier's pay or allowance for his service. The idea Paul is communicating is that the allowance or payment for sin is death. Every human being is born into sin. Because of this, we are spiritually dead and apart from Christ.

But Paul continues on in this verse and immediately contrasts the hopelessness of the first phrase with the word "gift." And this is no ordinary gift, for it is a gift from God. A gift is something bestowed on another, not earned or paid for or traded. It is a gift freely given. And this gift comes from the Lord. Consider how important you might feel in receiving a gift from the president of a country or another important person. We have been given a gift by the One who holds all things. And it is not a small gift but a gift of eternal life through Christ.

Our original wages for sin was death, and this sin separated us from God because He is holy and perfectly good. Our sin reveals our rejection and rebellion against God. But still He offers us eternal life, and what a true gift it is—one that we could never earn. It was a gift that had to be given by the One who could provide it. And in order to provide it, God sacrificed His Son, Jesus, so that our original wages of sin could be taken away, and we could be given new life.

When you fall into the temptation of thinking that your works earn God's favor, remember that you have already been given the gift of eternal life. It is not a gift He holds hesitantly in His hands to see if you will perform well in order to receive it. And it is not a gift He will take back upon your first big failure or mistake. The gift of salvation is entirely based upon what He has already done in the gospel. Know this, and rest in Christ's accomplished work for you on the cross.

"THE GIFT OF SALVATION IS ENTIRELY BASED UPON WHAT HE HAS ALREADY DONE IN THE GOSPEL."

DAY 65
Uprooting Bitterness

Make sure that no one falls short of the grace of God and that no root of bitterness springs up, causing trouble and defiling many.

HEBREWS 12:15

Bitterness is a settled anger. Someone has wronged you, and you are angry about it. Maybe the perpetrator has even repented to you, and you said you forgave them. But you cannot seem to move on from the issue. You do not want to be around the person, and you speak with passive-aggressive comments toward them. Your anger has not gone away. Instead it has hidden itself beneath the surface as it yet grows more intense.

As Christians, we are called to forgive as God forgave us. Because of the gospel, we have been shown grace beyond measure. While we were God's enemies, Christ died for us. He did not hold our sins against us but loved us while we were stuck in our sins. When we do not forgive those who wrong us, we show that we do not fully understand the grace we have received. To be clear, forgiveness does not mean excusing, minimizing, or justifying someone's wrong behaviors. At times, even as we forgive someone, we may need to hold them accountable to their actions or slowly rebuild trust. If we loan someone money and they have not paid us back, for example, forgiving does not necessarily mean you loan out more money or that you cancel any outstanding balances owed. Instead, forgiveness is a disposition of freeing the person from the judgment of wrongs committed.

We are only able to forgive others in this way because Christ forgave us. While we were God's enemies—dead in sin—He forgave us. And now, as God's children, we entrust our lives to Him, knowing that whenever someone sins against us, it is not just toward us that he or she sins. They primarily sin against a holy God. This God will one day right every wrong, and He sees it all. He knows where you have been wronged and cheated, and He will restore every misdeed. We can trust Him to make things right.

So, if you are struggling with bitterness today, ask the Lord to remind you of His grace toward you, and ask Him for help to forgive. Forgiveness does not justify the sin of another but frees you from the burden and poison of bitterness.

"WHILE WE WERE GOD'S ENEMIES—DEAD IN SIN—HE FORGAVE US."

DAY 66

A God of Justice

The Rock—his work is perfect; all his ways are just. A faithful God, without bias, he is righteous and true.

DEUTERONOMY 32:4

We all crave fairness and equity. Justice is a natural yearning, given to us by a just God. However, God's justice looks different than we expect. We see this truth played out in Deuteronomy 32, when Moses was at the end of his life, reflecting and making provisions for the future. He reminded the Israelites of the goodness of God through a song. This song was not joyous, however. Its words rang with a negative tone as Moses described the Israelte's sin and rebellion against God. He reminded the people of the faithfulness and goodness of God and how they did not measure up to His standards because of their rebellious hearts.

As Moses sang, he told the people about God's steadfast and just nature. This God knew every sinful word, deed, and thought of the Israelites. He knew that the rebellion of the people stemmed from unbelief and a lack of fear of Him (Exodus 17:7, Exodus 32:2–10). He knew that they did not deserve mercy, and yet, time and time again, God was merciful toward His people, giving them time to repent and turn back to Him.

Just as our God loves justice (Psalm 37:28), He is also faithful, righteous, and true. When God judges mankind, He does not look at popularity or image to influence His favor. He has no bias toward money or power. Instead, He looks at the heart and will perfectly judge the world (Matthew 25:31–46). This is great news for us when others sin against us, for we know that God will avenge every wrong. We do not need to take vengeance into our own hands because vengeance is the Lord's, and He will repay (Hebrews 10:30).

This is also an encouragement to press into the grace of Christ. Justice demands payment for our sins, and the penalty for sin is death (Romans 6:23). To overlook sin would be unfair and unjust. But God made a way so that we can be at peace with Him. By sending His Son, Jesus, who lived the perfect life and died the death we deserve, He made a way for our sins to be paid in full. When Jesus died on the cross, He nailed our sins to it with Him. The penalty was paid, and we stand forever forgiven.

"HE IS ALSO FAITHFUL, RIGHTEOUS, AND TRUE."

DAY 67
A Way in the Wilderness

Look, I am about to do something new; even now it is coming. Do you not see it? Indeed, I will make a way in the wilderness, rivers in the desert.

ISAIAH 43:19

As Isaiah delivered words of judgment to Israel from the Lord because of their rejection of God, the prophet also gave the people words of hope. Because of the judgment they were about to face, they would one day experience the Lord's deliverance. The Lord would not abandon them. He would allow them to be exiled to Babylon, but He would also bring them back home. And all the while, His faithful remnant would never stop being His.

The Lord was doing a new thing in His people. While they had experienced His deliverance before, He would bring about a deliverance that was final and complete. He would provide a way for their transgressions to be completely forgiven and wiped away. He was going to send His Son, Jesus, to save them. Their exile and return home was just a piece of the story. It was part of His great work of redemption.

We have also experienced this "new thing" from the Lord. We have received new life in Christ, and we will someday witness Christ's return and the beginning of a new world where Christ will reign forever. We can often become just like the Israelites. We forget the promises we have been given, and we turn to things that do not offer us life. But God will use our wandering to accomplish new things within us. God has been faithful before, and He will be faithful again.

If you are in the midst of trial and difficulty, or even if you are stuck in your sin, know that the Lord is with you. And if you have accepted Christ, you are safe in His salvation. The sin that causes you to stumble or the difficult situation that weighs on your heart is no match for Him, and He will help you. As you endure in this season, He will do a new thing within you as He continues working in your heart. He will use what you are experiencing to draw you closer to Him and make you more like His Son. He will give you a way in the wilderness and water in the desert—He will help you in those hard days as you rest and lean on Him—because you are His.

"GOD HAS BEEN FAITHFUL BEFORE, AND HE WILL BE FAITHFUL AGAIN."

DAY 68
Alert to Deception

Be on your guard against false prophets who come to you in sheep's clothing but inwardly are ravaging wolves.

MATTHEW 7:15

In Matthew 7:15, Jesus warns believers to be alert to these people and not fall prey to their schemes. Sadly, a lot of people in our world today get swept up in following false teachers. There are some who speak in the name of Jesus, but their words and lives do not reflect the gospel of Jesus. The reason why many people follow false teachers is because they lack a strong biblical foundation. Without knowing the Bible well, they believe an ideology that sounds biblical but has no biblical basis.

Furthermore, people fall into the trap of false teaching because false teaching can resonate with their deepest desires. Paul speaks of this in 2 Timothy 4:3 by saying, "For the time will come when people will not tolerate sound doctrine, but according to their own desires, will multiply teachers for themselves because they have an itch to hear what they want to hear." False teaching can appeal to people because they want to experience a life devoid of suffering. Or a self-help version of the gospel can appeal to those who do not want to depend on someone else. However, false teaching fails to uphold its promised results. This teaching only leads people further into sin and away from Jesus.

If we are not careful, we too can easily buy into teaching that is anti-gospel. As we read and listen to biblical teaching, let us be critical thinkers. We should ask ourselves what is being said about Jesus. We should consider what the teaching encourages us to do and if it aligns with God's Word. The more we grow in our knowledge and understanding of Scripture, the more we are guarded against false teaching. Instead of abandoning sound doctrine, we need to stand on sound doctrine. As believers, we should also help others be on guard, lovingly pointing them back to God's Word.

As the body of Christ, we must stand together and remain committed to the truth of God's Word. Let us seek to know our Bibles well and test the teaching of others by holding what they say against Scripture. In a world that seeks to pursue its own truth, let us remain grounded in the truth of God's Word. May we hold fast to the gospel and resist anything contrary to the gospel of Christ.

DAY 69

Our Weakness Displays His Power

> *But he said to me, "My grace is sufficient for you, for my power is perfected in weakness." Therefore, I will most gladly boast all the more about my weaknesses, so that Christ's power may reside in me.*
>
> 2 CORINTHIANS 12:9

There is nothing instinctual about boasting about our weaknesses. Imagine posting a picture of your home on social media with the caption, "I'm having a really hard time being content here because I'm jealous of the pictures other people post of their houses!" Or what if you posted a picture of you with a friend and said, "I'm feeling bitter toward this person right now. I'm working on it, but she really upset me." Yikes! Those are things we rarely ever speak about in such a public setting—which is probably a good thing!

But God does tell us there is an appropriate time to boast in our failures, and that is when we use those weaknesses to display His power. For the believer in Christ, there is an amazing inner work that takes place when our strength runs out. God fills the gaps our weaknesses leave with His strength. He enables us to find contentment in any circumstance (Philippians 4:12), forgive when it feels impossible (Ephesians 1:7), persist in trials (James 1:2–4), and avoid temptations to sin (1 Corinthians 10:13). And the bigger the gaps our weaknesses leave, the more strength He imparts to us and the more Christ's power resides in us. Our weakness displays His mighty power. The weaker we are, the more we see and experience His strength within us.

Just a few chapters earlier in 2 Corinthians 4:7–8, Paul gives another description of how God's power invades our fragile frames. He likens us to something that would have been available in every home at the time—a clay jar. Clay jars were brittle and breakable, hardly fit to carry anything of value. We are like those clay jars. Yet, God chooses to put the treasure of His power and presence into our frail selves. Imagine how a handful of gold coins would gleam all the more when found inside of a dull, earthy clay pot. In the same way, how much more glorious does God's strength appear when it is housed in our weakness!

What would change if we began to look at our weaknesses as spaces for God to enter our lives and work powerfully through us rather than as mistakes that are beyond repair? There is no weakness we have that Christ is not sufficient to overcome.

DAY 70
Judgment of Every Hidden Thing

For God will bring every act to judgment, including every hidden thing, whether good or evil.

ECCLESIASTES 12:14

When little kids play on the playground, they size one another up. They voicelessly determine who will be the leader of the group and who will be the followers. There can even be some childhood teasing as the strongest kids mock, bully, or make fun of the weakest ones. Small acts of bullying can seem to go unnoticed by chatting grown-ups, and a little one may wonder, *Who will stand up for me? Who will right these wrongs? Where is help when I need it?*

But imagine if a child's parent is watching nearby—a loving father who observes every interaction and is close by to protect his child. In his wisdom, the father lets his child play and scuff his knees. He does not act as a helicopter parent, but he is near, always watching, always protecting. All his child needs to do is say the word, "Dad, help!" and his dad comes running. He was there all along, and he would make things right in the end.

Today's verse reminds us of the perfect presence of God. He is the mighty judge who will make all things right in the end. He sees all, from the first thoughts we had this morning to our deepest, darkest fears. He knows every hidden thing. He knows every hurt that you have endured and all of the pain that you have inflicted on others. According to His perfect wisdom, He may allow injustices to last for a moment. But in the end, He will have the final say. He will bring every action to judgment. Every good deed, every act of kindness, every sacrifice will be rewarded. Conversely, He will judge every evil deed.

Before a holy God, we are sinners who deserved death (Romans 3:23). Our hidden deeds condemned us before the perfect King, and we stood guilty, condemned, and dirty. But praise be to God, He provided a way for our sins to be forgiven through the blood of His Son. When Jesus died on the cross and paid our penalty, He gave us His righteous covering. Because of the cross, our sins are forgiven. We are protected, known, and loved. We are no longer condemned but shielded by the grace and perfection of Christ. Justice has been served through His righteous blood, and we are set free by His grace.

DAY 71

Impartial God

For there is no favoritism with God.

ROMANS 2:11

Did you know that in many countries, policemen intentionally take bribes at traffic stops? They eye foreigners and purposely target them for bribes. They notice the kind of car you drive, your clothing, and your language ability to impulsively determine the requested bribe amount. To make matters worse, this corruption often reaches further than just traffic stops, even court cases wait in limbo until bribes are paid.

Consider if God were to work in this way. What if we could not receive His promises until we paid Him our dues? What if He preferred one profession or personality or hair color over another? What if He treated us differently based on upbringing, car type, or race? Our God is more powerful than a policeman because He holds the world in His hands. He is the all-powerful King, a consuming fire (Hebrew 12:29). If God were malicious or bribeable, we as His creation would be in a very precarious condition. We would be unstable and dependent on our own ability to make Him happy.

Thankfully, God does not play favorites. He is impartial. He does not show preference to one person over another because that person is smarter, richer, or more beautiful. He does not withhold His favor until we earn His good will. He loves us. He is kind. He is patient with all, not wanting any to perish but all to come to repentance (2 Peter 3:9). It is God's kindness, not His abuse of authority, that leads us to repentance (Romans 2:4).

God is the impartial, righteous judge. He will repay us according to our works, regardless of our income or social status (Romans 2:6). He sees the heart and judges us perfectly. He is not like a corrupt police officer, trying to selfishly benefit Himself. He is a perfect Savior, a wise King, and a loving Father.

While God is perfectly impartial, He is also gracious. Thanks be to God, we have not been treated as our sins deserve. When we trust in Jesus as our Savior, we are covered by the blood of Christ, and God counts our sins against us no more. He loves us and approves of us perfectly through Christ. His favor toward us is secure because of the cross. We are accepted, loved, and made righteous through the perfection of His Son.

"WHILE GOD IS PERFECTLY IMPARTIAL, HE IS ALSO GRACIOUS."

DAY 72

Nothing Can Separate Us from God's Love

For I am persuaded that neither death nor life, nor angels nor rulers, nor things present nor things to come, nor powers, nor height nor depth, nor any other created thing will be able to separate us from the love of God that is in Christ Jesus our Lord.

ROMANS 8:38–39

Many of us have broken relationships with loved ones. Perhaps even now you stand in the wake of losing a relationship with someone you care deeply about. Because we live in a broken world, everyone who walks this earth is a sinner, and because of that brokenness, relationships will fail. While some may be restored through forgiveness, other times they will break, never to be put back together, at least on this side of eternity. And for many of us, this may be a great fear—a fear of losing the cherished love of the people who are closest to us. Yet we read in Romans that nothing—absolutely nothing—can ever separate us from the love of Christ.

When Adam and Eve sinned in the garden, sin entered the world. We no longer had the same kind of communion with God that Adam and Eve experienced before the fall—daily walking with Him. We became separated from Christ and would forever be unless there was atonement for our sins. That is why God sent His Son to save us—so that we could one day be wholly restored and redeemed to new lives in Christ. Because of His great sacrifice for us, we are able to commune with Him, and His Spirit lives inside of us if we have accepted Him as our Savior. We can come to Him in prayer, knowing that He hears our cries—cries of sadness, of repentance, of thanksgiving—and accepts and loves us as we are. Praise be to God that He made a way!

We do not have to fear being separated from His love. When Satan attacks us with lies that we are not good enough or have made too big of a mistake to keep God's love, may we remember God's promise: Never will He leave us or forsake us (Hebrews 13:5). When we become fearful that surely His love cannot endure our circumstances, let us return the truth of His Word. May we rest in knowing that though earthly love may fail, the love of our Lord, our Heavenly Father, will endure forevermore.

"BECAUSE OF HIS GREAT SACRIFICE FOR US, WE ARE ABLE TO COMMUNE WITH HIM."

DAY 73

Disgraced for Jesus's Sake

Then they went out from the presence of the Sanhedrin, rejoicing that they were counted worthy to be treated shamefully on behalf of the Name.

ACTS 5:41

When Jesus ascended into heaven, the apostles were tasked with fulfilling the commission He had given them. They were to take the gospel into all of the world, and they were to make disciples and baptize them in the name of Jesus. But just because Christ was who He said He was and rose from the dead did not make this task easier. The world hated Jesus and those who followed Him. Christ is the source of all light, and the world is full of darkness.

When the apostles began to teach about Jesus, they faced serious opposition, specifically from the religious rulers of their day. These rulers did not want them to preach the gospel, and when the apostles did, the rulers took action against them. They imprisoned them, beat them, publicly ridiculed them, and then instructed them not to preach the gospel. But the apostles could not comply because what they were asking went directly against what Jesus had asked them to do. And unfortunately for the religious rulers, the apostles did not see being disgraced as a burden or shame. They counted themselves blessed to suffer for Christ. Their persecution was an honor. It created the opposite reaction to what the religious rulers wanted.

We also will face suffering and persecution for the gospel. And even though we may be disgraced by people in our lives for the name of Jesus, we are not disgraced by our Savior. As foreign as it may be to us today, especially since we are able to worship freely, there will be times we are persecuted for the name of Jesus. But this suffering is a gift. It draws us closer to our Savior as we experience what He did, and it can encourage us as we see the world actively coming against our faith because it reminds us that Jesus's warning is true. The world hates the light, but it will never be able to destroy it.

So, as we live our lives, may we not run from persecution or suffering. When we experience it, may we run to Christ, the One who understands and empathizes with our hardship. And may we be like the apostles, who counted their suffering for their own joy, as it produced godly perseverance and steadfastness. Our suffering makes us more like Christ. If our Savior suffered, why would we think that we will not?

"SUFFERING IS A GIFT."

DAY 74
The Lord's Fire Fell

Then the Lord's fire fell and consumed the burnt offering, the wood, the stones, and the dust, and it licked up the water that was in the trench.

1 KINGS 18:38

God rescued, led, and provided for the Israelites, yet they often worshiped other gods. In particular, they chose to worship Baal, the god of storms and rain, and Asherah, the god of fertility. Worshiping these gods meant engaging in sinful acts and breaking God's laws.

Elijah called the nation of Israel back to a wholehearted, faithful commitment to God in 1 Kings 18:21 when he said, "How long will you waver between two opinions? If the Lord is God, follow Him. But if Baal, follow him." The people had no answer. They were fickle, worshiping the Lord when it was convenient and worshiping Baal when it pleased them. Elijah wanted to prove God's supremacy over Baal once and for all, so he challenged the prophets of Baal.

On Mount Carmel, both Elijah and the prophets of Baal would prepare a bull for sacrifice, yet neither would set fire to the burnt offering. They would call upon their god to send down fire from heaven. Baal's prophets first set the bull on the altar and cried out to him to send fire. When he did not respond, they slashed their bodies and danced around the altar in hopes of gaining his attention.

This is an odd scene to imagine. Yet we all cry out to false gods at times. We chase success, intellect, relationships, or health, believing they will bring us salvation and peace. Sometimes, we even pursue things that we know ultimately harm us. We, like the prophets of Baal, would sometimes rather suffer harm than admit we were wrong. Baal never answered his raving prophets. Likewise, the false gods we serve do not provide the fulfillment we desire.

When Elijah asked God to send fire upon the bull he placed on the altar, the Lord responded immediately. God sent fire from heaven, and the fire consumed the bull that had been soaked in water. Baal remained silent. God sent a powerful, consuming fire. What if you stopped pursuing anything other than God for fulfillment and instead cried out to the Lord? How applicable Elijah's challenge to the nation of Israel is for us today. If the Lord is God, and He is, then follow Him. May we be faithful to Him alone!

DAY 75
Near the Brokenhearted

The Lord is near the brokenhearted; he saves those crushed in spirit.

PSALM 34:18

Do you feel alone in your troubles? Does your heart feel disfigured, broken, or unrepairable? If you identify with any of these thoughts, find hope in today's verse. Jesus came to save sinners, not the righteous. He came to save the brokenhearted and those crushed in spirit. The Lord is near.

Though you may feel abandoned in your seasons of hardship, you are never truly alone. God is with you—the Good Shepherd, the Great King, the Almighty God is near. He has not left you to figure out life on your own. When tears blur your vision, and you cannot breathe because of your anxiety, He is near. He is near in the midst of a scary health diagnosis or in the uncertainties of unemployment. He is with you in the midst of the stinging betrayal of your spouse or in the aches of chronic pain. No matter the source of your brokenness or discouragement, He is near.

Not only this, God *saves* those who are crushed in spirit. He does not leave us in our brokenness and despair, but He binds up our wounds. He is healing and restoring our broken hearts. He does not recoil at our pain but presses into it. When the Good Shepherd sees His sheep struggling and hurting, He does not run away. He runs toward them. He rushes to their aid, bringing tools for their soothing care. He does the same for us today.

Christ has never abandoned us. He loved us so much that He bore all the weight of our sin and death, the penalty that we deserve. He chose us as His adopted children and promises us an eternal inheritance. He bears our sorrows. He also leads us to local churches to be His hands and feet in the midst of our pain. He has also left us the truth and wisdom of the Bible, which is his very Word. No, He has not left us alone, and He has provided all that we need until He returns.

One day, God will heal our hearts once and for all. There will be no more brokenness or pain. We will see Him face to face. He will rescue us from our troubles and make everything new. Until then, we wait with eager expectation and lean into the loving arms of our Father, who saves us in our brokenness and brings healing to our pain.

"GOD SAVES THOSE WHO ARE CRUSHED IN SPIRIT."

DAY 76
Faithful to Forgive

If we say, "We have no sin," we are deceiving ourselves, and the truth is not in us. If we confess our sins, he is faithful and righteous to forgive us our sins and to cleanse us from all unrighteousness.

1 JOHN 1:8–9

Sin. It is an uncomfortable and sometimes unwelcome topic. We do not enjoy recounting the mistakes we have made or the ways we have sinned against God. We want instead to focus on the forgiveness of God and how it frees us from our shame. How uncomfortable it can be to revisit an argument with our parents or friends, knowing we were wrong. How uncomfortable is the regret of refusing to stand up for what is right, choosing rather to go along with the crowd. How unbearable the shame of knowingly living in sin, ignoring the Spirit's gentle prompting to live in light of the gospel. We often find ourselves in these places, living beneath the weight of our every shortcoming. We too quickly forget the forgiveness of our heavenly Father who welcomes us back with open arms, His grace poured out over and over again upon His children.

The author of 1 John shows us in chapter 1, verses 8–9 that admitting sin is the first step to being forgiven of our sin. Perhaps for many, this is difficult, not readily wanting to humble ourselves in repentance. Yet Jesus humbled himself for us to the greatest extent upon the cross where He died to save us. Although Christ's death has atoned for our sins once and for all (Hebrews 10:14), we are not sinless. We must still be mindful of our sinful ways and confess them before God. Colossians 3:3–5 says it this way, "For you died, and your life is hidden with Christ in God . . . Therefore, put to death what belongs to your earthly nature: sexual immorality, impurity, lust, evil desire, and greed, which is idolatry."

When we are hidden in Christ—when we have accepted Him as our Savior and are forgiven and covered by Him—we must continue to put to death the things in us that are sinful. And as we are faithful to confess our sin to God, He is faithful to forgive. As Christians, we revel in this forgiveness, acutely aware of the ways we *continually need* His grace in our confession. We only must admit our sin to Him and confess, for He will always wipe clean and renew.

"AS WE ARE FAITHFUL TO CONFESS OUR SIN TO GOD,
HE IS FAITHFUL TO FORGIVE."

DAY 77

Expectant Prayers

Therefore I tell you, everything you pray and ask for—believe that you have received it and it will be yours.

MARK 11:24

One of the sweetest gifts of being a believer is prayer. The ability to have complete and unhindered access to God is a blessing given to us through Christ. Yet prayer can sometimes be frustrating for us as believers. Not only can it be hard to form the words to pray, but we do not always receive what we ask for in prayer. This can lead us to doubt God, and, if we are not careful, our doubt can harm our prayer lives. Without the correct perspective, we can grow discouraged and even give up on prayer altogether.

In Mark 11:24, Jesus challenges His disciples to trust in the Lord instead of doubting Him. Trust fuels prayer life. This is why Jesus speaks these words right after His disciples see Jesus curse the fig tree. This was a visual representation of the power of prayer. Jesus used His words to invoke a curse, and His words proved effective as the tree withered. The disciples marvelled at Christ's power, but Jesus wants the disciples to see that they possess this power as well. Our words in prayer are effective and powerful.

When we doubt our prayers, we do not believe the power they hold. Yet James 5:16 says the prayers of the righteous are powerful and effective, for God works through our prayers. In a beautifully mysterious way, God uses our prayers to sovereignly carry out His will. But when we doubt that which we pray, we fail to believe God is who He says He is. Knowing that God is good, faithful, and sovereign encourages our hearts to trust Him. The more we trust Him, the stronger our prayers will be. We will pray boldly and expectantly, knowing that God will carry out His will through us.

Knowing that God carries out His will through our prayers encourages us to pray according to His will. This means that our prayers should be primarily shaped by wanting God's will to be accomplished rather than our desires met. The more we pray for God's will to be done, the more our desires align with God's desires. As a result, our faithful prayers are answered through God's perfect sovereignty. May we lift up our prayers with great boldness and expectancy for all that Christ will accomplish.

"KNOWING THAT GOD IS GOOD, FAITHFUL, AND SOVEREIGN ENCOURAGES OUR HEARTS TO TRUST HIM."

DAY 78
Wait for the Lord

I wait for the Lord; I wait and put my hope in his word. I wait for the Lord more than watchmen for the morning—more than watchmen for the morning.

PSALM 130:5–6

In our fast-paced world, we often want things quickly, so when we must wait, we can grow frustrated. Waiting on the Lord can also be a frustrating task. We cannot always see how God is working, and He often operates in timing that is different than we desire. Yet the Bible encourages us to wait for the Lord.

In Psalm 130, the writer speaks of waiting for God's redemption. It is likely that this psalm was written when Israel was in exile, and the people were waiting to be redeemed from their painful circumstances. But even in trying times, this psalmist places his hope in the Lord, and he calls Israel to do the same. He teaches us how we can wait on the Lord because we know God is a faithful God who always keeps His Word.

It is interesting to note that the psalmist also compares himself to watchmen. It is not known from these verses what kind of watchmen the writer is speaking about. Whether he is comparing himself to a military guard who was waiting for the morning light to see trouble or a priest who was waiting for the morning to begin sacrifices, the psalmist reveals how he is like someone who waits for the morning. His words demonstrate how he knows the morning will come even though he has to wait for it to arrive. In the same way, the psalmist knows God will enact His redemption even though He must wait for this time to come.

We, too, can be like this psalmist. We can wait expectantly for the Lord, even if God's timing seems slow to us, trusting that He will come through. And in the moments we struggle to trust, we can remember God's past works of faithfulness. We can remember that although the Israelites waited for redemption from exile, God was ultimately bringing redemption through Jesus. Though they had to wait many years for His arrival, God sent Jesus, whose sacrifice on the cross frees us from our sin. Scripture teaches how we never wait in vain when we wait for God.

Whatever it is that you are waiting for the Lord to do, you can wait with confident hope. He has shown Himself faithful in and through Jesus, and He will show Himself faithful still.

DAY 79
Imitate Wisely

Dear friend, do not imitate what is evil, but what is good. The one who does good is of God; the one who does evil has not seen God.

3 JOHN 11

We become what we imitate. The more we imitate something, the more that particular thing shapes our lives. We see this idea played out in movies and television shows. A young girl wants to be like the popular girls, so she imitates everything about them—their clothes, their hair, their speech. But soon, she finds herself adopting the popular girl's bad habits. She ignores her friends, picks on other students, and becomes prideful about her looks. Her imitation led her to adopt sinful habits. If we want to walk in holiness and wisdom, we must imitate what is good and not evil.

Living in a sinful world makes it hard to imitate what is good. Social media floods us with posts and pictures that make it seem like we need to look a certain way or have a particular thing in order to be happy. This mentality can easily persuade us to imitate what we see on our phones, leading us to make poor decisions and develop unhealthy habits. As believers, we are to imitate Jesus Christ. He is the One to whom we look to shape our lives. After all, as followers of Christ, we are to grow into the image of Christ. Instead of growing into the images on our phones, we are to grow into the image of the God who saved us.

Paul says in 1 Corinthians 11:1, "Imitate me, as I also imitate Christ." Paul understood the goal of believers to imitate Jesus Christ. Jesus is the epitome of goodness and perfection. As we imitate Christ, we become like Christ. We will love as Jesus loves, serve as Jesus serves, and give mercy like Jesus gives mercy.

Every day, we have the choice to imitate the things of this world or of Jesus. To fight against worldly imitation, we must continue to go to God's Word. We must be rooted in the truth of Scripture that teaches us how to walk in godliness. By reading God's Word, we learn how to imitate Jesus as Scripture shows us who He is. Our greatest desire as believers should be to look like our Savior above the fading things of this world. May we be shaped by nothing else but Jesus Christ.

"JESUS IS THE EPITOME OF GOODNESS AND PERFECTION. AS WE IMITATE CHRIST, WE BECOME LIKE CHRIST."

DAY 80
The Greatness of God

This is why you are great, Lord God. There is no one like you, and there is no God besides you, as all we have heard confirms.

2 SAMUEL 7:22

When was the last time you stood in awe? Awe strikes us when we behold a majestic scene in nature, cradle a newborn baby, or witness an inspiring story of human courage. In 2 Samuel 7:22, David stood in amazement, not of something he saw but something he heard—God's words from the prophet Nathan. David wanted to build a temple for the Lord, but God spoke through the prophet Nathan, telling David not to build a temple for Him. Instead, He wanted to build something for David.

Through Nathan, God made a covenant with David to preserve His family forever and bring from his line a Son who would bring salvation to all. David may not have understood this at the time, but that Son was not his physical son, Solomon, but a distant descendant—Jesus. And this covenant was not simply a blessing for David's lineage but a blessing for the entire world.

Still, David was completely awed by God's promise to him and responded with the words of 2 Samuel 7:22. Did David speak these words to the Lord because he realized how blessed he was to have the Lord make this promise to him? Maybe. But his response was so much more than that. David remembered how sinful he had been. He remembered the times he had forsaken God. He knew how he had disobeyed Him and how many mistakes he had made as Israel's king. Yet, in light of that, he saw how faithful God had been. He had remained with him, sustaining the nation of Israel and upholding David through it all. And now, after decades of reigning as an imperfect king, God promises David that he would forever have a place in the redemptive work He was doing in the world through Israel.

Even more incredible than this promise to David is that those who believe in Christ and are saved also get to enter into a covenant relationship with God. Believers sin, make mistakes, and mess up, yet God promises to never forsake us. God will remain steadfast and is committed to allowing His children to be a part of His redemptive plan for the world!

"GOD PROMISES TO NEVER FORSAKE US."

DAY 81
The Lord Looks at the Heart

But the Lord said to Samuel, "Do not look at his appearance or his stature because I have rejected him. Humans do not see what the Lord sees, for humans see what is visible, but the Lord sees the heart."

1 SAMUEL 16:7

How quickly and how easily we look first to outward appearances. We so easily decide what we think we know based on what we see with our eyes. Maybe we choose friends this way. Maybe we choose who we speak to this way. Or maybe we choose our social media following this way. Yet, we read in Scripture that when the Lord looks at us, He looks at our hearts. His ways are not our ways (Isaiah 55:8–9). Our heavenly Father is not concerned with outward appearances. It is the person with a heart for the Lord who is worthy of praise.

This principle is one we see clearly illustrated in 1 Samuel. In chapter 16, Samuel travels to Bethlehem to anoint a new king from among Jesse's sons. When Samuel sees Eliab, one of the sons, he feels certain that he must be the one whom God has chosen. Perhaps Eliab looked of a decent age and appeared strong and handsome as many might picture a future king to be. Perhaps it looked as though he would play this part well. But Eliab was not the man God had chosen for anointing, and God explains to Samuel that "humans see what is visible, but the Lord sees the heart" (1 Samuel 16:7). Later in the chapter, we see David chosen as the anointed one—the youngest of the brothers and a shepherd boy. The Lord selected David to become king, for He looked not at David's outer appearance but at His heart for the Lord. David was a man after God's own heart (1 Samuel 13:14). This is the man God chose to become king and from whose line the Savior of the world would come.

The Lord desires to use those who are fully committed to Him. Though it is certainly good to take care of the earthly bodies God has given us, our focus should remain on what is within. May we tend our hearts—growing to become more like Christ through the time we spend in His Word, in prayer, and in serving others. Let us grow our hearts so we can be worthy of our Savior's praise.

"THE LORD DESIRES TO USE THOSE WHO ARE
FULLY COMMITTED TO HIM."

DAY 82

Our Cornerstone

But he looked at them and said, "Then what is the meaning of this Scripture: The stone that the builders rejected has become the cornerstone? Everyone who falls on that stone will be broken to pieces, but on whomever it falls, it will shatter him."

LUKE 20:17–18

In Luke 20:9–18, Jesus tells a parable to reveal to others their rejection of Him as Messiah. Jesus foretells His own death as He draws a connection to Himself and the vineyard owner's beloved son. The people are aghast at hearing of the innocent son's murder, yet they will soon do the same to Jesus when they nail Him to a cross. Even as Jesus exposes their sin to them, they do not see the error of their ways.

Jesus also uses this parable to reveal how the people's rejection will not prevent God's will from being accomplished. Jesus quotes Psalm 118:22 to teach how He is a stone that builders have rejected, but God, the ultimate builder, has made Him the cornerstone. A cornerstone is a stone placed at a corner of a foundation to help the building stand correctly. Without this stone, a building will not hold together. Jesus Christ is the cornerstone of our faith. This means that our entire lives as believers are connected and built upon the life, death, and resurrection of Christ.

The fate of those who ultimately reject Jesus is eternity without Him, but those who trust in Jesus receive Him as their cornerstone forever. Jesus builds believers into something beautiful. 1 Peter 2:4–5 tell us, "As you come to him, a living stone—rejected by people but chosen and honored by God—you yourselves, as living stones, a spiritual house, are being built to be a holy priesthood to offer spiritual sacrifices acceptable to God through Jesus Christ." The body of Christ is built upon Jesus, our cornerstone, to be a spiritual house dedicated to God. As living stones, we reflect Him as our great cornerstone. And as believers, we too will be rejected by others, yet like Jesus, we are chosen and honored by God. Even if others reject us, we are eternally accepted by God.

Because Jesus is our cornerstone, we will never be let down. He is our sure foundation who keeps our faith steady. He is our source of strength when storms come and trust and obedience are difficult. Jesus, our cornerstone, keeps us forever strong and secure forever in Him.

DAY 83

Not Exiled Forever

The king of Babylon put them to death at Riblah in the land of Hamath. So Judah went into exile from its land.

2 KINGS 25:21

We all long for home, a place where we can rest, be ourselves, be in relationship with those we love. But, for many of us, home is a fleeting reality. Seasons of life are always changing, and hardships continually occur. Though we may find somewhere to settle, this place is not guaranteed a permanent home. Ultimately, we are always searching for a place where our souls can be forever still. An everlasting home is what we truly desire.

The theme of "home" is evident in Scripture. The Israelites, God's people, had a kingdom they called home. The Lord kept His covenant promise to the Israelites, and He preserved a place called the Promised Land for them. After God rescued the people from slavery and brought them through the wilderness, the Promised Land was theirs. Surrounding enemy nations were not a threat, nor were famine and plagues. Because of the Lord's love and protection, the land remained fruitful and in their possession.

God wanted to make His home among His people and abide with them forever. The Israelites built a kingdom, and the temple of God was in the center. But, unfortunately, led by their wicked kings, the people disregarded their Lord and engaged in idolatry. Because of the corruption, the Lord gave the Israelites over to their enemies and the spiritual darkness they desired. Nebuchadnezzar and his Babylonian army besieged Jerusalem, the temple city. Thousands were captured, and God's people became exiles, dragged away from the land the Lord had graciously gifted them. The Israelites mourned in Babylon and prayed for the Lord to restore them. In the midst of their grief, God promised to draw those exiled in sin back to Himself. He would raise a King whose kingdom would be eternal.

Jesus is this Promised King. We were exiles, oppressed in captivity to sin. But, through His saving work, Jesus made a way for the displaced to return home in the holy place of God. We no longer live on our own destructive paths. God has reclaimed us and exchanged our ruined clothing for Jesus's perfection. We are granted peace in relationship with Him and are called to an eternal resting place. Now belonging to Christ, we look to Jesus's second coming when He will fully reveal His kingdom, end all evil, and give us abundant joy in God's presence.

DAY 84
God-Breathed Scripture

All Scripture is inspired by God and is profitable for teaching, for rebuking, for correcting, for training in righteousness, so that the man of God may be complete, equipped for every good work.

2 TIMOTHY 3:16–17

Taking Scripture and misinterpreting, twisting, or omitting pieces of it is a modern-day problem that plagued the early church as well. And Paul, writing to Timothy, addresses this issue in 2 Timothy.

Paul explains that God inspires all Scripture. We cannot remove anything from its pages. When we find ourselves with questions or upset with what we read, we must study to understand and resolve the conflict we feel with God's Word rather than trying to change it.

Paul describes Scripture as God-breathed. And maybe the image of God breathing His breath of life into the pages of His Word is the image we need to realize the level of care His Word deserves. When we see gleaming oceans before us or soak in colorful sunsets and highest mountain peaks, we likely do not question their glory, their beauty. We marvel at the maker who thought to make something so perfectly complex and brilliantly beautiful. So it should be with God's Word.

God's Word leads us from untruth to righteousness as it teaches, rebukes, corrects, and trains. And as it does so, with malleable hearts, we become aware of how we have not obeyed His commands, and we course correct. Through this process, God makes us like Him, and we are therefore equipped for every good work as we accept the whole counsel of Scripture and allow *it* to change *us*.

Just as Paul admonishes Timothy in verse 14 of chapter 3, so you are admonished today, "But as for you, continue in what you have learned and firmly believed." Do not stray. Do not change or reimagine the Word. It is God-breathed and needs nothing added or taken away—God's Word is perfect.

"GOD'S WORD LEADS US FROM UNTRUTH TO RIGHTEOUSNESS AS IT TEACHES, REBUKES, CORRECTS, AND TRAINS."

DAY 85

Persistent in Prayer

Pray at all times in the Spirit with every prayer and request, and stay alert with all perseverance and intercession for all the saints.

EPHESIANS 6:18

Short news briefs fill our television screens as we change from station to station. Social media stories consume our brains in fifteen-second increments. Inadvertently, as Christians, we have been conditioned to expect prayer to have the same rapid expediency. We pray quick prayers and expect instant results. When our prayers are not immediately answered, we give up or focus our attention elsewhere. But Scripture calls us to more.

In Ephesians 6, Paul reminds the believers at Ephesus about spiritual warfare. He speaks of the need for spiritual armor to protect ourselves from the schemes of the enemy. We are to put on the belt of truth and breastplate of righteousness and take up the shield of faith. We are to stay alert by remaining in the Word and communing with the Father in prayer. Paul says that we are to pray as an act of spiritual battle.

There are many ways to pray. We can pray on behalf of others or for ourselves. We can pray aloud or silently. We can pray on our knees or while driving a car. We can pray the words of Scripture or freely pray about the concerns in our hearts. Lest we get caught up in a search for perfect words, we must remember that God knows everything. He knows our every thought, anxiety, and stress. He does not judge us if our words are not poetic enough. He wants us to come and present all of our requests before Him, for He uses our prayers to accomplish His grand purposes.

Because of the cross, we can talk directly to the King of the universe and know that He hears us. We are accepted as sons and daughters of the King, and He bends His ear to our cries and pleas. We can pray with perseverance, even when we do not see the results right away, because we know that He is in control. He is good, powerful, steadfast, and true, and He hears our prayers.

Ignoring life's spiritual battle does not make it disappear; it makes us more vulnerable. As our act of spiritual warfare, let us engage with God in daily prayer. Let us pray with perseverance, defy the desire for instant gratification, and trust in the sovereign King of heaven and earth.

"WE MUST REMEMBER THAT GOD KNOWS EVERYTHING."

DAY 86
Glimpses of God's Glory

The appearance of the brilliant light all around was like that of a rainbow in a cloud on a rainy day. This was the appearance of the likeness of the Lord's glory. When I saw it, I fell facedown and heard a voice speaking.

EZEKIEL 1:28

The most glorious canyons, sunsets, and waterfalls pale in comparison to the glory of God. In the book of Ezekiel, Ezekiel experienced an astounding vision of the throne room of God. A brilliant light surrounds God, and Ezekiel compares the site to a rainbow on a rainy day. While it is not possible to capture the glory of God with words, Ezekiel's description helps us visualize how great His glory is.

We, too, can witness glimpses of God's glory, even if we cannot see Him face to face. First, we see glimpses of Him through creation. Psalm 19:1 says, "The heavens declare the glory of God, and the expanse proclaims the work of his hands." God designed creation to point to Himself. We are meant to see the beauty of nature as a display of God's glory. When we step outside, we have the opportunity to see glimpses of God's glory. But we must take the time to notice. Instead of rushing from one thing to the next, what if you stopped to look up at the sky? What if you took a moment to breathe in the air or noticed a flower growing nearby? Let the beauty of nature whisper the glory of God to you, and respond to God in praise.

We also receive glimpses of God's glory in His Word. While God reveals Himself to us in nature, we need His Word in order for us to know Him intimately. Through God's Word, we learn about God's character and His works. We read stories from the past about how He revealed His glory to mankind, such as this account from Ezekiel. But we also see God's glory displayed through the gospel. We see God's power and holiness through Christ's death and resurrection. And one day, we will see the fullness of God's glory when He returns and calls us home to eternal life with Him.

"THROUGH GOD'S WORD, WE LEARN ABOUT GOD'S CHARACTER AND HIS WORKS."

DAY 87
Never Alone

Haven't I commanded you: be strong and courageous? Do not be afraid or discouraged, for the Lord your God is with you wherever you go.

JOSHUA 1:9

Many of us have struggled with feelings of loneliness or confusion. In those times, may we remember that the steadfast love of our Father in heaven never ceases. And as we read the words of Joshua 1:9, we also consider Psalm 27:10, which tells us that even if everyone else abandons us, God is always with us. We do not need to fear, for we are never alone. Even if our fathers or mothers forsake us, the Lord will draw us ever closer.

These beautiful words from Joshua were originally spoken to him when he assumed his new leadership role as Moses's successor. Joshua was about to bring God's people into the Promised Land. Such a huge task was before him, and he had big shoes to fill. Would he succeed? Would God be with him? Would he be enough? The Lord knew Joshua's every thought, and as Joshua ventured out into the unknown, God spoke these words of promise to him (Joshua 1:2–9). Notice how the Lord did not point Joshua to himself, to how smart or strong he was. Instead, God reminded Joshua of His presence. He commanded Him, "Don't be afraid, because I am with you."

In the same way, we do not need to be afraid as we venture into the unknowns of tomorrow. The Lord is with us. He has secured our futures and leads us in paths of righteousness (Psalm 23:3). We can laugh without fear of the future (Proverbs 31:25) because we know the One who controls our tomorrows. This truth can also help us in our troubles, for we know that God is with us in the midst of them. Even though trials will undoubtedly come, He will work them all for our good and the glory of His name (Romans 8:28). The God of angel armies is the One who protects us, fights for us, and loves us. We need not fear—He is with us always, wherever we may go.

"THE LORD IS WITH US. HE HAS SECURED OUR FUTURES AND LEADS US IN PATHS OF RIGHTEOUSNESS."

DAY 88
Seeking to Save

"Today salvation has come to this house," Jesus told him, "because he too is a son of Abraham. For the Son of Man has come to seek and to save the lost.

LUKE 19:9–10

A wealthy tax collector named Zacchaeus heard that Jesus was in Jericho and sought to find Him. Zacchaeus knew that Jesus was the Messiah, the anointed Savior for God's people. But, while Zacchaeus sought to find Jesus, Jesus was looking for Zacchaeus. Scripture says that Jesus came to Jericho and was passing through the city. Though it may have seemed like a casual visit, Jesus was the Good Shepherd focused on finding His lost sheep.

A crowd surrounded Jesus as He was walking, so Zacchaeus climbed a tree to see Jesus as He passed by. Jesus looked up and called Zacchaeus's name, requesting that He stay in his house that day. Though Zacchaeus was a despised tax collector, seen as a traitor of the Jewish people, Jesus wanted to fellowship with him. The crowd grumbled, misunderstanding the Old Testament prophecies of the Messiah. The prophets had not prophesied about a revolutionary political figure but a servant and the Savior. God had promised to give Abraham's descendants a place in His presence. And through His saving work, Jesus would fulfill that mission. So, Jesus did not reject Zacchaeus but rescued him.

We see that Jesus took the initiative in building a relationship with Zacchaeus and gave him the faith he needed. Scripture proves Zacchaeus's faith by his admission that he would give half of his riches to the poor and pay back anyone he cheated in a greater amount than required. Through faith, Zacchaeus became a true child of Abraham and would dwell in the presence of God when Jesus stayed at his home. That moment would be only a taste of dwelling in eternity with God.

As He sought Zacchaeus, Jesus has sought us as well. Jesus knew our names before He set time in motion. We were His lost sheep, wandering apart from Christ as captives to sin. But Jesus rescued us from the hand of the enemy. He gave Himself to the judgment and wrath of God so that we could be forgiven and redeemed. We receive the covenant blessings because of Jesus's obedience and sacrifice on the cross. May we, with great joy, accept God's invitation and take comfort that we have been found by our Shepherd, who welcomes us into His presence.

DAY 89
Powerful Provision

So she left. After she had shut the door behind her and her sons, they kept bringing her containers, and she kept pouring. When they were full, she said to her son, "Bring me another container." But he replied, "There aren't any more." Then the oil stopped.

2 KINGS 4:5–6

Under Levitical law, widows were to be supported and cared for. But they were often cast aside and ignored because supporting them meant giving generously with no expectation of repayment. Because women could not make an honest wage for themselves, this overlooking of Levitical law left many widows destitute. We meet one such widow in this passage.

The widow has become so indebted that she may have to give her children as slaves to repay what she owed. Her husband has already been taken, and now she faces losing her children as well. In despair, she comes to Elisha to ask for help, for her husband had been part of a company of prophets, and Elisha was their leader. If anyone had access to ask God for help, it would be Elisha.

When she first brings her request, Elisha is unsure. He cannot revive her husband. He does not have money to pay her debts. However, God *can* meet all her needs, and He does so through Elisha. Elisha instructs her to pour from her one jar of oil into a collection of several other jars and containers. Miraculously, she pours until she has a house full of oil jars. When she came to Elisha, she told him a little oil was her only possession. Now, God has multiplied that oil to be the answer to her prayers.

She sells the oil, pays her debts, secures the safety of her children, and still has oil left to sell for income. God has powerfully provided for her needs! She was not rich or powerful. She was the least and the poorest. But she was not unseen by God. He saw her need, and He met it.

God took into His own hands the matter of providing for the widow. God saw her need, and He did not overlook her as others did. When Jesus arrives centuries later, He acts in the same way. Jesus goes to the unwanted, the hurting, the outcasts, and the unclean. And to them, He offers both physical and spiritual healing. So today, be encouraged. You are not overlooked. Even when others may abandon you, God sees your needs. He cares, and He will provide.

DAY 90
The Sovereignty of God

The Lord brings death and gives life; he sends some down to Sheol, and he raises others up. The Lord brings poverty and gives wealth; he humbles and he exalts.

1 SAMUEL 2:6-7

The Lord's sovereignty can be hard for us to grasp. Our minds do not possess knowledge to understand how God works the way He does. Yet, we can worship Him for it. Without God's sovereign hand, the world would have no order. Events would be random instead of divinely orchestrated. But because God is in control, we can confidently trust Him in all areas of our lives. There is purpose in every moment, for Christ orchestrates each one.

God controls both life and death. He can bring people low and raise them up. He allows for some to be poor and others to be rich. In our human understanding, we might not like that God gives and takes in such a way. We may view these acts as unloving. Yet, in light of Romans 8:28, when we recognize that God uses everything for good, we can trust the way He acts and know that He is loving. Every sovereign act of God works to accomplish His eternal purposes. In all circumstances, believers can trust that God uses all things to accomplish His work of salvation in us. When we do not understand what God could possibly be doing, we can rest in the comfort of His sovereignty. Even in the hardest places and seasons of our lives, we can cling to hope that God is purposefully working.

When we struggle to understand how even death is purposeful, we must fix our gaze upon Christ. In God's sovereignty, God gave His Son to die on the cross. Though Jesus died, it was His death and resurrection that gave us life. For those who trust in Him, we have a living hope that can never be taken away. We can rejoice in the sovereignty of the Lord that has bought our salvation. Even in the day-to-day, may we rejoice as God uses everything around us and in our own lives to bring us closer to Him if we will allow Him. Let us rest in knowing that our mistakes and shortcomings cannot thwart God's plans. Like a conductor of an orchestra, God takes the notes we play, even the ones that seem off key, and moves them into a symphony of His great design.

> "THERE IS PURPOSE IN EVERY MOMENT, FOR CHRIST ORCHESTRATES EACH ONE."

DAY 91

Loving God With All Our Heart, Soul, and Strength

Love the Lord your God with all your heart, with all your soul, and with all your strength.

DEUTERONOMY 6:5

At the beginning of Deuteronomy, Moses gives a series of opening speeches to a new generation of Israelites who are learning how to participate in the covenantal relationship between themselves and God. Moses is re-giving the Law in this last book of the Torah, and he is encouraging the people to obey the Lord. At the center of these opening speeches lies Deuteronomy 6, and we see the greatest commandment of Scripture: "Love the Lord your God with all your heart, with all your soul, and with all your mind." Jesus repeats this commandment in the gospels along with the second greatest commandment, which is, "Love your neighbor as yourself" (Matthew 22:39). He says that all of the Law and the Prophets depend upon these two commandments.

When Moses says we must love the Lord with all of our heart, soul, and strength, he communicates that our love for God should consume all of who we are. Everything we do should flow out of our love for the Lord. This commandment is central to who we are as followers of Christ, especially because we can only love God in this way due to the new hearts He places within us to see the truth of the gospel. He enables us to love Him. And because He gives us new hearts, we can love God and others.

Jesus says that all of the Law and Prophets depend upon loving God and loving our neighbors because if we always followed these commands, we would not need to hear from the Law and Prophets. But we are unable to love God and our neighbors on our own, which is why Jesus came to atone for the sins of the world, bringing us into new life. So as you read this commandment today and ponder how you might better love the Lord with all of your being, remember that He is the One who enables you to do so in the first place. Our entire lives represent the sanctifying process of us learning to love Christ more and more. And as you learn to love Him with all of your heart, all of your soul, and all of your mind, you will see all of life through the lens of who He is and how He changes everything.

"EVERYTHING WE DO SHOULD FLOW OUT OF OUR LOVE FOR THE LORD."

DAY 92
God and His Kingdom Will Stand

Saviors will ascend Mount Zion to rule over the hill country of Esau, but the kingdom will be the Lord's.

OBADIAH 1:21

Do you feel like the darkness of this world is heavy? Do you feel as if evil always seems to win? Our world is desperately broken, and the sinfulness of mankind can make it seem as if brokenness, injustice, and evil will reign forever. Sadly, the wickedness we see today has been apparent since the fall. We see a piece of evidence in the Old Testament as Israel has to continually combat enemies and resist those who seek to persecute them. One of Israel's neighbors, Edom, stood against Israel and even stood idly by when Israel was being attacked.

God did not turn a blind eye to the persecution of Israel and the passivity of Edom. Through a prophecy given to the prophet Obadiah, God declared how He was going to bring judgment upon Edom and give justice to the people of Israel. God would remove all the Edomite enemies, and God's people and the kingdom of Israel would remain. Israel did not deserve such grace from God, but God chose to extend His grace willingly. This act of grace and justice points us to Jesus, who would triumph over evil through His death and resurrection, offering those who believe in Him deliverance from the enemy of sin and death.

The deliverance Christ provides also points us to the future deliverance that is to come. Just as God enacted justice by removing the evil people of Edom from the land, so will God enact justice by removing all evil from our world when He returns. The injustice we see in our world will be punished, and every wrong will be made right. The hope that the Israelites had in God's future deliverance is the same hope we have today. Our hope as the people of God is the promise of God's eternal kingdom. The world we live in today will not remain overcome by evil. By His grace and power, Jesus, our Savior, will return to rule over the earth and will wipe away all wickedness and evil.

On days when the world feels heavy, let us remind ourselves of the victory to come in Christ. Let us grieve the brokenness of this world yet with hope, knowing that God will mend every broken part of our world. God's kingdom is coming, and it will stand forever.

DAY 93

Humble Before a Holy God

and [if] my people, who bear my name, humble themselves, pray and seek my face, and turn from their evil ways, then I will hear from heaven, forgive their sin, and heal their land.

2 CHRONICLES 7:14

In 2 Chronicles, God calls for the obedience of the people of Israel and warns that destruction will come if Solomon and the people do not remain obedient to Him. Sadly, the nation of Israel brings this destruction upon themselves as they turn away from the Lord to idols. Our hearts can become idol factories in our own lives when we set our eyes on worldly gain, placing those pursuits above our pursuit of Christ. In our sin, we become prideful in believing we can operate without the Lord. It is not until we discover the emptiness of what this world has to offer that we realize that only God can fill our emptiness and our need.

If we want to remain obedient to the Lord, we must remain humble, and this is hard. Pride is an easy trap, though, with discipline, it is possible to stay humble before God. We must humble ourselves by surrendering our desires. Worshiping the Lord means that we remain open-handed before Him. If we operate our day-to-day lives with closed fists, our pride keeps us from submitting to the Lord. We must also turn from empty pursuits toward the face of God. It is one thing to hold on to selfish desires without actively pursuing them, but it is another to turn away from them completely and toward the Lord as we seek His face.

In this posture of humility, we turn from our idols and repent. However, repentance can be hard for us. Sometimes we fear coming before the Lord when we are disobedient, perhaps viewing Him as a cruel God who pours out His wrath upon us in our sin. However, God's wrath has already been poured out upon Jesus. Because Jesus took the punishment for our sins when He died on the cross, those in Christ will never receive God's wrath, though we certainly experience consequences for our sin on earth. But we rejoice in the words of 1 John 1:9, which encourages us by saying, "If we confess our sins, He is faithful and righteous to forgive us our sins and to cleanse us from all unrighteousness." Our repentance is always met by God's forgiveness.

"WE MUST HUMBLE OURSELVES BY SURRENDERING OUR DESIRES."

DAY 94

The Fruit of the Spirit

But the fruit of the Spirit is love, joy, peace, patience, kindness, goodness, faithfulness, gentleness, and self-control. The law is not against such things. Now those who belong to Christ Jesus have crucified the flesh with its passions and desires. If we live by the Spirit, let us also keep in step with the Spirit.

GALATIANS 5:22–25

One of the simplest ways to observe your spiritual growth is by looking at the fruit you produce. "Fruit" in this sense is not literal fruit that is growing on trees or bushes. It is the "fruit" of your life. What fruit is revealed through your words and action? Do you plant seeds of laziness or jealousy, the fruit of which might be a lack of consistency in your quiet time with the Lord or ongoing discontentment that leaves you bitter?

However, if you plant seeds of faithfulness to God's Word, prayer, and serving His church, you will see the fruit of the Spirit. Love, joy, peace, patience, kindness, goodness, faithfulness, and self-control will begin to be yours. These are the characteristics of our Savior, and as we grow closer to Him, we begin to display them in our lives.

Yet there are times that we still bear bad fruit. While our flesh has been crucified at the cross, we still live in our flesh on earth. This means that the power of the flesh has died: Our passions and desires do not rule us, and we no longer are subject to spiritual death. But while we are still on this earth, our bodies have yet to be made perfect, so we still feel the desire for sin and may produce bad fruit, though sin is no longer our master.

As we journey toward heaven, we are constantly at war with our flesh, but God equips us and gives us strength to walk in His Spirit. He puts His Spirit inside of us, and He helps us become more and more like Him. Our entire lives are a process of this sanctification, and as we walk in His ways, He produces His fruit in us. As He produces that fruit in us, may we let others see so that they too may come to know Christ through the way we live.

"GOD EQUIPS US AND GIVES US STRENGTH TO WALK IN HIS SPIRIT. HE PUTS HIS SPIRIT INSIDE OF US, AND HE HELPS US BECOME MORE AND MORE LIKE HIM."

DAY 95

He Meets Us in Our Grief

I called on your name, Lord, from the depths of the pit. You heard my plea: Do not ignore my cry for relief. You came near whenever I called you; you said, "Do not be afraid."

LAMENTATIONS 3:55–57

Throughout our lives, there are seasons when it may feel as though God is far away. It may feel like we have been left alone in a pit of despair. Yet, we are not alone in these seasons of suffering. God does not stand at a distance but is with us in our grief.

When we cry out to God, He always hears. He never ignores the cries of His children, and not only does He listen to us, but He responds to us. When we cry out to Him in despair, His gentle voice encourages us not to fear. In seasons of suffering, we find peace in the presence of the Lord. He meets us in our pain and comforts our souls. When we cry out for relief, God gives it to us, if only by His very presence. He is a light in the darkness, a beacon of hope when all seems grim.

God meets us perfectly in our grief because He, too, knows grief. He knows what it is like for a friend to die. He knows betrayal and rejection. And He knows the pain of sacrifice, for He gave His one and only Son to die for the sins of many so that we could know an end to suffering and pain. So, while we are in an intimate relationship with One who knows suffering well, we are also in an intimate relationship with the One who delivers us from suffering. Through Jesus's sacrifice, He brings relief to sinners by rescuing them from death and raising them to new life.

Because of Christ, we can echo the words of Job: "He redeemed my soul from going down to the Pit, and I will continue to see the light" (Job 33:28). In suffering, may we fix our gaze on His light. The Lord eases our fears as He reminds us that He has already overcome them. He has rescued us from the pit of death, and as we wait for His full deliverance when He returns, we rest confidently in His love and presence through every season of grief.

"WHEN WE CRY OUT FOR RELIEF, GOD GIVES IT TO US, IF ONLY BY HIS VERY PRESENCE."

DAY 96

Life-Changing Transformation

We all, with unveiled faces, are looking as in a mirror at the glory of the Lord and are being transformed into the same image from glory to glory; this is from the Lord who is the Spirit.

2 CORINTHIANS 3:18

On the top of Mount Sinai, Moses received the Law from God. There, he also saw a partial viewing of the Lord's glory. Though Moses hid so as to not be consumed by the Lord's holiness, the encounter transformed him. His weary face became radiant, appearing to shine like a bright star. With this new appearance, Moses came down from Mount Sinai, holding the Ten Commandments, a written sign of the covenant relationship between God and His people. When the Israelites saw Moses coming, they were awestruck by his light. So Moses covered the waning radiance with a veil.

The Apostle Paul harkened back to this Old Testament event in his second letter to the Corinthian church. He wrote about the new covenant that Jesus Christ established through His saving work on the cross and how it replaced the old covenant of the Law. The Law guided the Israelites toward righteous living so that they could radiate God's light to the world. But their rebellious natures prevented them from obeying the Lord. So the old covenant did not erase the looming curse of death for sin. But the old covenant pointed to the coming Savior, Jesus, who would reverse the curse and give life through His death. In the new covenant, the old was fulfilled. Jesus met the requirements of the Law on our behalf. The new covenant is a spiritual sign, sealed by the Holy Spirit. We who are covered in Christ's righteousness through faith bear this sign in our hearts as we receive the never-fading glory of Christ.

Moses saw the partial splendor of God on the mountain, but we can see God's full majesty when we gaze upon Christ. Moses put on a veil to cover the fading radiance, but in Christ, the veil is set aside because the Holy Spirit inside us always reflects the wonder of the Lord. Day by day, we are being transformed into Jesus's brilliant image, and with His light, we can stand unashamedly before the world. We can put off our past shame and sins. We can exchange our weariness for restoration. Let us be confident in the work of Christ to transform our lives and help us to be light-bearers for His glory.

"WE CAN EXCHANGE OUR WEARINESS FOR RESTORATION."

DAY 97
He Is Worthy of It All

Our Lord and God, you are worthy to receive glory and honor and power, because you have created all things, and by your will they exist and were created.

REVELATION 4:11

The book of Revelation awakens believers to the majesty of Christ and propels us to worship. The symbols in Revelation draw upon Old Testament signs to create the ultimate drama between good and evil. The signs warn believers of complacency and encourage them to remain steadfast in faith. Revelation is a difficult book to understand, but as God's redeemed, we can remember that the aim of Scripture is the proclamation of Christ's supremacy. Revelation points to Jesus's sovereignty and Kingship as the Creator who is due our worship.

The disciple John wrote his vision of God's heavenly throne. There, the Lord appeared like precious jewels. Elders wearing crowns sat around the throne. In the Old Testament, the elders advised the king and priests. Their crowns indicated authority, but their authority did not match the One before them. Seven flames hovered around the Lord, and a sea of sparkling crystal flowed from His feet. Four angelic beings with faces of powerful creatures stood on all sides of the throne. Though the beings looked intimidating, they knew their position was to worship God. At their lead, the elders bowed and casted their crowns to the throne, demonstrating that God was the Only One worthy of receiving glory.

Jesus joined the Lord's place of sovereign power. He was the perfect Man and Eternal Son of God in flesh. With the Father and Spirit, Jesus is Creator of heaven and earth, and He entered His creation to restore it from sin. As the obedient Son, Jesus was resurrected and honored for His righteousness. Now, He sits and reigns by the throne at the center of the elders and angelic beings. He waits for the appointed time to defeat sin and death for good. The captivating images of Revelation evoke us to worship in the way we were created. Let us cast our eyes on Jesus's majesty. When we gaze upon His life, His cross, and His ascension to heaven, we need not fear judgment. Jesus welcomes us into His love. We can bow in reverence before His throne in prayer, for He is great and worthy of praise. One day, we too will witness what the elders and angelic beings see, and we will rejoice in His presence forever.

"JESUS WELCOMES US INTO HIS LOVE."

DAY 98

The Riches of Redemption

In him we have redemption through his blood, the forgiveness of our trespasses, according to the riches of his grace that he richly poured out on us with all wisdom and understanding.

EPHESIANS 1:7-8

What indelible grace the Lord has bestowed upon His children that we may receive the riches of His redemption. For even while we were still sinners, Christ sent His Son to die on the cross to save us from our sins. Because He died, we receive life through His Son when we trust Him as our Savior—our lives that are broken by sin on this earth will be redeemed—wholly saved or freed from sin—when the Lord calls us home to eternity with Him.

Because Jesus was perfect in every way, because He lived a sinless life and was pure in His thoughts, words, and actions, His life was the only one worthy of sacrifice to pay for the sins of the world. Stricken by sin, no man or woman would have been or could be worthy of taking His place. He loved us so much that He gave everything—He poured out His blood so that we could stand redeemed before Him, no longer captive to the bondage of sin and death.

And in that atonement or payment for our sins, we have forgiveness of the very sins that He died to cast away as far as the east is from the west. When we have accepted Him as our Lord and Savior, He looks upon us and sees not our trespasses and failures but His beloved Son. As the blood was wiped over the doorposts in Egypt as a sign for God to pass over, so as believers, He marks us with the blood of His Son so that instead of the death we deserve, we receive life everlasting in Him.

May we fall to our knees in worship as we consider this grace that the Lord lavishes upon His children—we who are so undeserving, we who fail Him each day, we who fall short time and time again. We do not have to live in a state of failure because we cannot measure up to His perfect standard, for He sent the One who did. Jesus paid the price that we never could. So we set our minds on what is ahead, we hope in the riches of His redemption that we have received, and we sing with joy in thankfulness of His amazing grace!

"JESUS PAID THE PRICE THAT WE NEVER COULD."

DAY 99

Boundary Lines

Lord, you are my portion and my cup of blessing; you hold my future. The boundary lines have fallen for me in pleasant places; indeed, I have a beautiful inheritance.

PSALM 16:5-6

We complete one task, only to pick up another. Running to-do lists flood our minds, likely on a regular basis. We wonder when we will have time to ourselves or if there will ever be days that do not feel so scheduled. It can feel like the walls are closing in on us, and we have nowhere to go. Perhaps we are tempted to envy the lives of those with more freedom, or maybe we look for some kind of escape. But instead, we should allow God's Word to comfort us. For there, we will find the protective and purposeful truth of God.

We all experience seasons when we feel as though we have nothing left to give. Maybe we feel like we moved from wide-open meadows to gated pastures. But what peace we have knowing God determines our boundary lines in every season. He intentionally limits us for our good and His glory. He intentionally brings the fence line in to protect us from moving outside of our necessary roles and responsibilities. Relationships may change, schedules may change, ministry may change, the way we do life may change. But God is our portion in every season. What a gift that God protects us from wandering and running away from the joy that we can find right where we are. In our limitations, He brings us close to Himself. He helps us to pour out where the need is present. Close to Him, we can remain faithful in the places He calls us to in these seasons.

Wherever God has placed your boundary lines for this season, can you say that God is your portion? Do you notice the pleasant places within your boundary lines? God is always purposeful and present. The small faithfulness of today, no matter where the Lord has us, is being rooted by God to bring the bloom of a beautiful inheritance. May we trust in Him with all that we have and find our greatest delight and joy in Him.

"WHAT A GIFT THAT GOD PROTECTS US FROM WANDERING AND RUNNING AWAY FROM THE JOY THAT WE CAN FIND RIGHT WHERE WE ARE."

DAY 100

No Longer Condemned

Therefore, there is now no condemnation for those in Christ Jesus, because the law of the Spirit of life in Christ Jesus has set you free from the law of sin and death.

ROMANS 8:1-2

How mightily the weight of our sin bears down upon us. Our shame overwhelms us. We cannot seem to escape the deep thoughts of regret, feeling as though we have failed, we are not enough, we are past the point of forgiveness. But then we remember Christ. We remember His death on the cross so that our sins could be forgiven. We remember His loving-kindness that draws us to Himself and restores what has been broken. No longer must we live in a constant struggle to escape the heaviness that comes from every place of failure. For indeed He came to save us, and indeed those in Christ no longer stand condemned but are freed from the weight of sin and death.

What a sweet reminder of this truth we find in Romans 8:1 as Paul writes, "there is now no condemnation" for those whose hope is in the Lord. All of us are sinners, inevitably falling short of who God has called us to be. And while we should be broken and grieved over our sin, we rejoice, and we have hope because God has already paid its penalty by sending Jesus in our stead. Though He too is broken over the effects of sin, and some consequences come in our failure to obey His Word, He does not condemn us to the eternal death we deserve but offers us life through the gift of His grace.

When we sin and find ourselves drowning in thoughts and feelings of guilt, let us run to Jesus because it is in Him that we find forgiveness and a heavenly Father who calls us to bring our worries and shame and lay them at His feet. We need not carry them, for they have already been nailed to the cross, offering us life in place of death. What joy, what blessing, what grace that our Lord looks upon His children with love and forgiveness that extends for all of eternity.

"INDEED HE CAME TO SAVE US, AND INDEED THOSE IN CHRIST NO LONGER STAND CONDEMNED BUT ARE FREED FROM THE WEIGHT OF SIN AND DEATH."

DAY 101
The Marvel of His Mindfulness

When I observe your heavens, the work of your fingers, the moon and the stars, which you set in place, what is a human being that you remember him, a son of man that you look after him?

PSALM 8:3–4

The brilliance of a sunrise. The joyful songs of a bird. The majestic mountains rolling softly in the distance. God's creativity bursts forth in creation. He gave the butterfly its wings, each with such a delicate design. He formed the stars in the galaxy, each with varying brilliance. When we stop to observe the heavens and the earth—to mindfully take it in—it provokes us to worship.

But of all the animals and plants that God created, one stands apart. Only one of God's creations was made in His image. When God made man and woman, He made them *imago Dei*, or in the image of God. He granted us the ability to think, pray, make decisions, and speak. He gave us dominion over the plants and animals. He gave us complex emotions and the ability to learn and grow. He gave us the capacity to know Him to understand His revealed Word. He protects us, prays for us, and reveals Himself to us. What did we do to earn such incredible favor?

The beauty is that we have done nothing to earn this favor. Solely because of His grace, God designed us in His image. He made us for His glory, and as His children, we respond to God's mighty blessing with joyful worship. In response to God's power and grace, we give our whole lives to Him. We respond with emotions, actions, words, and thoughts that celebrate our great Maker.

Because of the gospel, we have been reunited with the Creator. Through Christ's perfect life, death, and resurrection, we are forgiven. We are able to live out the fullness of our existence in a life that is made right with God. We are restored and reconciled to our Maker. We are reunified with a God who remembers us and looks after us. He is the creative designer of this world, and we stand amazed at His mighty works, knowing that His eye is always upon us. By His grace, He has made us His own.

"SOLELY BECAUSE OF HIS GRACE, GOD DESIGNED US IN HIS IMAGE."

DAY 102
This Little Light of Mine

You are the light of the world. A city situated on a hill cannot be hidden.
MATTHEW 5:14

Have you ever known someone who lights up a room? All that person has to do is smile and begin a conversation, and immediately the room becomes more exciting and lively. The joy is contagious. In a similar way, when we accept the Lord, His Spirit comes to live in us, and we are filled with the joy and light of Christ. He changes everything about us, and we become more and more like Him. His light cannot be contained. When we interact with people and have conversations with them, they experience His light and peace through us. And His joy is the best kind a person could have.

The world we live in does not love Christ, and it often rejects His light. The world is full of darkness and may try to cover the light it sees. Sometimes those who delight in darkness will hate the light of Christ as it shines on their sin and exposes what is in their hearts. Because of this, there are many people who will attempt to dispel this light and make it seem as though it is wrong. How easy it is to live in our world and feel the pressure to cover up our light. We sometimes want to ignore the gift of salvation we have been given or put it away for a time in order to feel comfortable or accepted by those who walk in darkness.

Christ's light inside us is not meant to be hidden. It is meant to be shared with everyone we know and meet. The world is full of spiritual death, and the light of Christ is the means by which God shares His love with the world. We will be faced with the darkness of the world at times, and the darkness may try to overcome us, but the light inside us is stronger than any darkness of the world.

So, as you interact with neighbors, family, and those you work with, remember the light of Christ inside you. Let it shine that God's glory will be displayed for everyone you know. While you may receive backlash or angry words for sharing Christ, remember that because we are carriers of His light in a world of darkness, some may hate us for the hope we have. Press on and know that His light cannot be overcome.

"WHEN WE ACCEPT THE LORD, HIS SPIRIT COMES TO LIVE IN US, AND WE ARE FILLED WITH THE JOY AND LIGHT OF CHRIST."

DAY 103
From Infinite to Infant

Today in the city of David a Savior was born for you, who is the Messiah, the Lord. This will be the sign for you: You will find a baby wrapped tightly in cloth and lying in a manger.

LUKE 2:11–12

Most of us sometimes find ourselves wishing in one way or another that we were not bound by our human capacities. This desire to be freed of limitations is why it is important to understand Jesus's infinite nature before He came to earth. Jesus's infinite nature means that space, time, and human limitations do not bind Him. Instead, He exists with no restraints. In addition to being infinite, Jesus also lived in perfect community with boundless love and peace in the Trinity—the Father, Son, and Holy Spirit. In fact, Scripture tells us that Jesus was with God when God hung the stars in the sky and formed man from dust (John 1:1–3).

Yet, when man fell from perfection, God put into action His plan to restore His people to Himself through Jesus Christ. All of the Old Testament points to His coming. We even see the preincarnate Jesus (before He was born of man) appear to Abraham, Jacob, and Joshua (Genesis 18:1–3, Genesis 32:24–30, Joshua 5:13–15). However, though we see Jesus make appearances in the Old Testament, Scripture tells us that He lived in glory with God His Father and the Holy Spirit (Philippians 2:6–7).

Even still, Jesus chose to leave His boundless nature and take on human flesh with all its limitations. He did not choose to come as a full-grown man but as a tiny infant—a completely helpless baby, wholly dependent on His parents to feed Him and take care of Him. And Jesus took it a step further still. He humbled Himself and took on our inability to obey God's commands. He kept the Law perfectly, then died in our place so that we could be restored and redeemed to God.

When we wish for our limitations to change, we must remember that our constraints point us to our need for a limitless God. And thankfully, because of His boundless love, Jesus abandoned His infinite nature to become an infant, live a perfect life, and die in our place. Because He loves us, those who accept Him as their Lord and Savior experience the presence of our infinite God for all of eternity.

"JESUS CHOSE TO LEAVE HIS BOUNDLESS NATURE AND TAKE ON HUMAN FLESH WITH ALL ITS LIMITATIONS."

DAY 104

God Will Accomplish His Purposes

But the Lord replied to Moses, "Now you will see what I will do to Pharaoh: because of a strong hand he will let them go, and because of a strong hand he will drive them from his land." Then God spoke to Moses, telling him, "I am the Lord."

EXODUS 6:1–2

God's promise to Moses that He would set the Israelites free from slavery in Egypt seemed bleak in the midst of their situation. Yet, God's strong hand delivered them. Their journey out of Egypt and through the wilderness reminds us that God always accomplishes His purposes, no matter the circumstances. Yet, in our difficulty, it can be hard to trust the Lord. Even as we read how God was faithful to Israel, we doubt His faithfulness to us.

Our hesitancy to trust the Lord often lies in a failure to believe God is who He says He is. We can think, *Maybe He did that for Israel, but He won't do that for me.* But God's words to Moses are the same to us in our doubts: "I am the Lord." Earlier in Exodus, Moses asks God what name he should reference when people ask. God says, "I AM WHO I AM" (Exodus 3:14–15). By this name, Yahweh, God declares His character. He declares that He is a God like no other. He stands alone, depending on no one. He is the sovereign Lord over all.

By God's very nature, He asserts Himself as One who can be trusted. In our own lives, we can wait in faith as God reveals His faithfulness, just as He did for Moses. But His past works also attest to His faithfulness. He says to us, "See what I have done!" God has shown us His character through His Son, Jesus. We do not have to wonder if God will accomplish His purposes; He has already accomplished them through Christ.

God is our deliverer, the One who delivered the Israelites from slavery and delivers sinners from their slavery to sin. We can view every one of His purposes as trustworthy just by looking back through history. Yet we must also learn to trust His character and not just His acts. As we go to God's Word, the more we grow in our understanding of who the Lord is and the more we will trust Him. Let us trust with confidence that He will accomplish His every purpose, for He is the Lord, and He loves us so!

"BY GOD'S VERY NATURE, HE ASSERTS HIMSELF AS ONE WHO CAN BE TRUSTED."

DAY 105
It is Finished

A jar full of sour wine was sitting there; so they fixed a sponge full of sour wine on a hyssop branch and held it up to his mouth. When Jesus had received the sour wine, he said, "It is finished." Then bowing his head, he gave up his spirit.

JOHN 19:29–30

From the very beginning, God put forth a plan to redeem His people. Even though mankind would reject Him and rebel against God, God promised to see this plan through. As we read through the Old and New Testaments, we see the story of redemption unfold as God faithfully abides by His covenantal promise to save His people. Just like a twist in a story, the story of redemption reveals how God's plan to save His people involves His Son. It is God Himself who will see this work of redemption through to the end.

God's plan of redemption led Jesus to be nailed to the cross, where our sin and shame were placed on Jesus's shoulders. He took our place by offering Himself as a sacrifice for our sins. As Jesus took His final breath, He breathed three words that would change everything: "It is finished" (John 19:30). His death was complete and so was our salvation.

For God's work of redemption to be finished means that our salvation through Jesus is secure. There is nothing that we need to do for our salvation—it was all accomplished on the cross. When the enemy whispers the lie that we are not truly saved, as believers, we must remember that it is finished. When we feel the impulse to work for our salvation, we must remember that we are His, and indeed it is finished. When we feel like our sin is too great for God's forgiveness, we must remember that it is finished. If you are in Christ, your salvation is complete. While we are being sanctified daily by the Spirit and have yet to experience the full removal of sin, Christ's sacrifice has fully satisfied our debt. We can walk in freedom with complete confidence, knowing that the work of redemption has been finished. For all of eternity, we have the sure promise of Christ's forgiveness.

May the security of our salvation move us in gratitude for the grace of God. May the sure reminder that the work is complete wash over our fears and doubts. It is finished and so is our striving.

"IF YOU ARE IN CHRIST, YOUR SALVATION IS COMPLETE."

DAY 106

The Splendor of God

Ascribe to the Lord the glory of his name; bring an offering and come before him. Worship the Lord in the splendor of his holiness.

1 CHRONICLES 16:29

We were made to worship. All creation breathes God's glorious splendor. In Psalm 19:1, we read that the "heavens declare the glory of God, and the expanse proclaims the work of his hands." Creation speaks of His glory and might through each and every marvel. He called into being the deepest caverns of the ocean to the furthest reaches of the galaxies. By His hands, the highest mountain tops and tiniest grains of sand have taken their places on the earth; the flowers blossom in magnificent arrays of beauty; the mighty rivers rush, bringing life through each coursing stream. And by His hands, He created us in His image to bring glory to His name—to worship our Creator God as we come before Him in awe of who He is.

In 1 Chronicles 16, David recognizes God's splendor and majesty in a joyous song of thanksgiving. The ark of the covenant, God's earthly dwelling place, had been brought to Jerusalem as a continued sign of God's faithfulness—a reminder of the covenant God made to Abraham that from him would come many nations and a King who would be the Savior of the world. What rejoicing overflows from David's heart, for as he reigns as king for a defined place and time, he considers the greater kingship of Christ: "the Lord made the heavens. Splendor and majesty are before him; strength and joy are in his place" (1 Chronicles 16:26b–27). Unlike David, the Lord reigns as the true King over every tribe and nation for eternity.

As David found delight in this truth and in "the splendor of [God's] holiness," so we should today. When we consider David's rejoicing and praise through his psalm, we know that this was but a momentary celebration that would come to an end, as would David's reign as king. But David's temporary kingship would make way for the true King who would come, not in a manner of worldly glory and splendor but in the form of a humble baby who would one day give His life on the cross for the sins of many. It was His death that made our life everlasting with Him possible. Someday, those who believe in Him will forever stand in the presence of His glorious, heavenly splendor, worshiping Him in celebration that has no end.

"ALL CREATION BREATHES GOD'S GLORIOUS SPLENDOR."

DAY 107

Hope in God's Outcome

"Go and assemble all the Jews who can be found in Susa and fast for me. Don't eat or drink for three days, night or day. I and my female servants will also fast in the same way. After that, I will go to the king even if it is against the law. If I perish, I perish."

ESTHER 4:16

When Esther spoke these words to her cousin, Mordecai, she was preparing to go before her husband, the King Xerxes of Persia, on behalf of Israel. The people were in terrible danger as Haman, an Agagite and official of the king, planned to have the Jews killed. When King Xerxes elevated Haman to be one of his highest officials, he ordered all the royal staff to bow down to him, but Mordecai did not comply. He would not worship anyone but the Lord. This refusal so angered Haman that he convinced the king to eliminate all of the Jews.

Mordecai approached his cousin, Esther, out of desperation. If anyone could save the Jews, she could, for the king had chosen her as his queen. However, Esther knew that, even still, approaching the king without being summoned was forbidden and could result in a penalty of death. But Esther knew she must go before him and asked Mordecai to assemble all the Jews in the city and fast for her. She and her servants would do the same. Then she would go to the king.

Esther knew that, ultimately, her fate was in the Lord's hands, yet she had much to fear. Her husband did not know she was Jewish. But Esther would be heard by the king who extended his scepter to her, an invitation for her to present her request before him. The Lord would save His people through her brave intercession on their behalf.

Esther's response should encourage us as we face difficult situations. While we may never encounter a life-threatening circumstance in the way that Esther did, we will certainly face suffering and hardship. In every circumstance, we can approach the Lord in earnest prayer and trust that He is sovereign over all things. Even when things do not go our way, God is still in control, and He works all things according to His divine wisdom. He is trustworthy, and we can confidently rest in His sovereignty.

"WE CAN APPROACH THE LORD IN EARNEST PRAYER AND TRUST THAT HE IS SOVEREIGN OVER ALL THINGS."

DAY 108

Chosen

Blessed is the God and Father of our Lord Jesus Christ, who has blessed us with every spiritual blessing in the heavens in Christ. For he chose us in him, before the foundation of the world, to be holy and blameless in love before him. He predestined us to be adopted as sons through Jesus Christ for himself, according to the good pleasure of his will, to the praise of his glorious grace that he lavished on us in the Beloved One.

EPHESIANS 1:3–6

From the first moments of creation, as God brought beautiful order out of darkness and chaos, He knew you. He knew your name and that one day you would be His. God has delighted in His children since the beginning of the world, desiring to pour spiritual blessing upon them.

Even when Adam and Eve sinned against God in the garden, putting themselves and all their descendants in broken fellowship with the Lord, He still made us! And not only that, He saw our sin and knew that our future was better because He was going to make a way for us to be holy and blameless. He chose this sacrifice because He loves us.

He sent Christ on our behalf into the world to live a perfect and holy life and die the death we deserved. His death paid the penalty for our sins, and we received His righteousness. Jesus's status before the Lord became ours, so we are chosen sons and daughters of the most high King. Paul says Christ made this sacrifice "according to the good pleasure of His will." What grace, what mercy, what joy, that the Creator of the world was well pleased to save His children.

That we are united to our Savior is the believer's identity in Christ. And as we grow to know the depths of who Jesus is, we experience more of Him and become more like Him. We see the riches of the blessings God has given us, and we bask in His grace and kindness. There is no self-care or motivational speech that will succeed in guiding our hearts back to truth. So we place our trust in God and His Word, knowing that we are chosen and beloved children of our Savior and King.

"AS WE GROW TO KNOW THE DEPTHS OF WHO JESUS IS, WE EXPERIENCE MORE OF HIM AND BECOME MORE LIKE HIM."

DAY 109
Resurrection Life

But God, who is rich in mercy, because of his great love that he had for us, made us alive with Christ even though we were dead in trespasses. You are saved by grace!

EPHESIANS 2:4–5

When Jesus rose from the dead and left His tomb, He gave us a picture of the life He invites us to live. Though Christ took on our spiritual death as He died on the cross, He would not stay dead. Christ overcame death and brought His people new life—one the world had never known.

This life begins right after we accept Christ as our Savior. We cannot see it, but our old selves pass away. We are no longer held prisoner to sin and death. We are given new hearts, and thus we begin new lives. This transformation should be evident to all who interact with us because we have gone from spiritual death to spiritual life.

Stop and think about this for a moment. What Christ has accomplished for you on the cross is incredible. You were like a dying man or woman who had no hope of survival. You were only waiting for your ultimate demise, and then Christ came and saved you. And Christ not only kept you from dying, but He also gave you a new heart and identity. You are now part of the family of God. You were saved from death, and you were given abundant life in Him.

This transformation is also a picture of how Christ overcomes our physical death. While we, as believers, walk in new life now with Christ, we will also experience new life after our physical death. We are all going to die, but we also will all be raised from the dead. And when we experience this resurrection, we will be more alive than we ever were before. Christ gives us His resurrection life, and He uses it to bring His people into fellowship with Him—now and forever.

Do you live like you are no longer spiritually dead? Do you realize the great gift you have been given and how it changes every decision you make? You have been saved from eternal death and separation from God, and you now have His life within you. And someday, when your life on earth runs out, and you confront death, you will have no reason to fear. You will have the promise of His resurrection, and He will be there to welcome you home into the most beautiful life you have ever known.

DAY 110
The Fruit of Our Faithfulness

If you follow my statutes and faithfully observe my commands, I will give you rain at the right time, and the land will yield its produce, and the trees of the field will bear their fruit.

LEVITICUS 26:3-4

In ancient covenants, it was common to include a list of blessings for adherence and a list of curses for disobedience. Since God entered into a covenant relationship with His people, He did the same for them. He made His requirements clear and explained what they could expect if they followed His way or broke His commands. God was making a way for His people to enjoy fellowship with Him. The onlooking world would watch Israel and see what it looked like to follow the Lord and live for Him. Their very obedience would draw others to God. However, Israel often rebelled against these commandments just like their ancestors, Adam and Eve. They became like all the other nations, and they missed out on the fruit of obeying God.

While we are under a new covenant in Christ, we are still called to follow the Lord in obedience. However, our salvation is not dependent on good works. Rather, our good works are the fruit of the heart God has renewed within us. When we obey God and love Him, He pours out His blessing upon us, giving us more and more fellowship with Him, the greatest blessing we can receive. Each moment is an opportunity to show love for Christ and become more like Him. Our small steps of obedience contribute to our sanctification as we journey toward eternity. As we grow in holiness and obedience, our lives beckon others to the gospel, just as the lives of the Israelites were meant to call other nations to worship God.

We should not be surprised when sin hurts our relationship with God and brings consequences into our lives. While Christ defeated the power of sin, sin is still present in the world. Its effects linger. God wants to help us live free from sin's destructiveness, even while living in a broken world. When we inevitably reject God's commandments, He will not reject us. He will faithfully restore us when we call to Him and use the natural consequences we receive from sin as means to bring us into a stronger relationship with Him. May we take this to heart. Let us remember that the fruit of our faithfulness to the Lord is His glory and joyful fellowship with Him.

"HE WILL FAITHFULLY RESTORE US WHEN WE CALL TO HIM.

DAY III
God's People — A Precious Possession

Now this is what the Lord says—the one who created you, Jacob, and the one who formed you, Israel—"Do not fear, for I have redeemed you; I have called you by your name; you are mine."

ISAIAH 43:1

Through Isaiah, God reminded the Israelites of His covenant promise that He first made in Genesis 17. The Lord declared to Abraham that there would be an everlasting relationship between Him and Abraham's descendants. God would be theirs, and they would be His possession. Though Abraham and his wife, Sarah, had no children due to their old age, the Lord formed a son in Sarah's womb. And with each new generation, Abraham became the patriarch of a great nation who had received covenant commitment from the Lord, for it was God Himself who formed and preserved them. But the nation of Israel was rebellious and faced judgment for their wickedness. Those with Abraham's faith were Abraham's descendants. Those who trusted in God as their Lord and Savior received the blessing of being called God's precious possession, and they received the blessing of an eternal relationship with Him. Despite their sin, God preserved the Israelites, which was a picture of His work to come.

God supplied His people with the faith they needed. The Old Testament saints trusted in the coming Savior for redemption from sin. This Savior was Jesus. He was proof that God sought to preserve a people for His own. By His saving work, He brings us into this intimacy through our faith in Him. In Jesus, our sins are forgiven, and our relationship with the Lord is restored.

If we are in Christ, we can trust that we are children of God. The Lord calls us to Him. We are fully known, yet God does not reject us or change His affections. We belong to Him, and because we are His, we are loved. Before the foundation of the world, He planned to form us and send His Son to die in order to redeem us. Though we were sinners deserving judgment, God preserved us by sending the Holy Spirit to open our eyes to the truth of the gospel. When we fall short, we may feel that God begrudgingly loves us or will no longer claim us, but that is not true. In these moments, may we cling to the cross. There, we see God's great love, which covers our shortcomings and secures our identity in Him alone.

"BY HIS SAVING WORK, HE BRINGS US INTO THIS INTIMACY THROUGH OUR FAITH IN HIM."

DAY 112
He is Risen!

"Why are you looking for the living among the dead?" asked the men. "He is not here, but he has risen!"

LUKE 24:5B–6A

After His crucifixion, Jesus was wrapped in linen and laid in the tomb on a Friday. According to Jewish religious tradition, this day was called the Day of Preparation. People had to finish the last tasks of the week before the Sabbath rest came on Friday evening. The women who went to the tomb saw that Jesus's body needed further care, so they returned home and gathered spices and oil, which were used to cover a dead body and prevent the smell of decay. They assembled the materials but rested when the Sabbath came. On that Friday evening, gloom and darkness were in the air. The women must have sat in their homes, reflecting on Jesus's broken body. They must have eagerly awaited Saturday evening when the Sabbath concluded so they could tend to their Lord.

At dawn on Sunday, the faithful women assembled the spices and oil and headed to the tomb. When they arrived, two angels met them there and exposed the women's hopelessness behind their act of devotion. The women knew the Old Testament prophecies that predicted the resurrection of the anointed Son. They had even heard Jesus foretelling His resurrection from the grave. The angels reminded them there was still hope. Their Savior, Jesus, indeed was alive!

What motivates our acts of devotion to the Lord? If we examine our hearts, we may see that our efforts for the church and ministry come from a place of hopelessness. We may think that it is all up to us to serve God. We forget to consider the hope and rest Jesus has accomplished for us. Our perfect service to God is not required, but faith in Jesus's perfect service is. Through His sacrifice on the cross, our loving Savior served us in every way. There is nothing left to be done. May we not allow our past efforts or sorrows to keep us from seeing the joy of the resurrection today. Christ has fulfilled God's promises and has given us new life in Him. Because Jesus is alive, we can take hold of the enduring hope and rest that carry us into eternity.

"MAY WE NOT ALLOW OUR PAST EFFORTS OR SORROWS TO KEEP US FROM SEEING THE JOY OF THE RESURRECTION TODAY."

DAY 113
Atonement from Our Sins

"This is to be a permanent statute for you, to make atonement for the Israelites once a year because of all their sins." And all this was done as the Lord commanded Moses.

LEVITICUS 16:34

"Atonement" is not a word we often use today, but it was a way of life for the people of Israel. In the Old Testament, the people of Israel received forgiveness for their sins by sacrificing spotless animals in the place of the people. The animal's death pardoned the punishment for the people's sin. But this atonement had to happen repeatedly for their sins to be forgiven so they could have a right relationship with the Lord.

What joy that in God's great grace, He has secured for us permanent atonement. Through His death on the cross, Jesus sacrificed Himself in our place. Because Jesus is sinless, His sacrifice makes atonement possible once and for all. His permanent sacrifice replaces the permanent statute. Hebrews 10:11–14 says, "Every priest stands day after day ministering and offering the same sacrifices time after time, which can never take away sins. But this man, after offering one sacrifice for sins forever, sat down at the right hand of God . . . For by one offering he has perfected forever those who are sanctified." Because Jesus's sacrifice is sufficient, we will never need another sacrifice to maintain the forgiveness of our sins.

But many of us still live as though we must maintain our salvation through our works for God to truly forgive us. We must not forget that Jesus Christ has broken us out of that cycle of continual sacrifice. How freeing it is to know that believers stand forgiven and redeemed because of Christ and His death on the cross for our sins! As we go about our daily lives, may we never take what Jesus has done for us for granted. May we dedicate our lives to living in response to the atonement we have received. His grace has covered our sins, so let us serve Him with ever-grateful hearts.

"BECAUSE JESUS'S SACRIFICE IS SUFFICIENT, WE WILL NEVER NEED ANOTHER SACRIFICE TO MAINTAIN THE FORGIVENESS OF OUR SINS."

DAY 114
What is Unknown to Us is Known by God

"The hidden things belong to the Lord our God, but the revealed things belong to us and our children forever, so that we may follow all the words of this law."

DEUTERONOMY 29:29

The will of God is all that He has sovereignly ordained to happen. And God works all things in accordance with His will (Ephesians 1:11). He even works through the evil of this world to continue accomplishing His purposes for our good and His glory (Romans 8:28). The Bible indicates that God's will is both hidden and revealed to us. In this passage, Moses tells the Israelites that some things are known only by God. Yet, He sent God's Son, Jesus Christ, to reveal His necessary truths about His character and plan of redemption. So, though some things remain hidden and unknown to us, God reveals what is essential for life and godliness in pursuit of His good and sovereign will.

But we are not left guessing answers to those big questions. God calls us to seek Him in all things (Philippians 4:6), which places God at the forefront of our hearts and minds, making our choices less about us and more about Him. Much of what God asks of us is clear in His Word. But sometimes, the Bible does not give a clear answer, and we are exhorted to trust in the Lord and acknowledge Him so that He can shape our paths (Proverbs 3:5–6). We find comfort and safety in God's Word. If we seek Him and desire to obey His Word, He brings fruit to our faithfulness. When we hope in His sovereign plan for our lives, we can make choices, fully trusting that He will fulfill what He plans for our lives (Psalm 115:3). Likewise, God encourages us to seek wisdom from other believers (Proverbs 11:14).

What a gift that God has revealed so much of Himself to us. Yet if God made everything known to us, how would we be prompted to trust Him and walk forward in faith? He takes advantage of every opportunity to lead us to lean on Him. May we be humbled to the point of walking forward in faith and trusting in the sovereign knowledge of God instead of worrying over what we do not know in the circumstances we confront. Even when we face the unknown, we can rest in confident assurance that God fully knows everything.

"WHAT A GIFT THAT GOD HAS REVEALED SO MUCH OF HIMSELF TO US."

DAY 115
Our Coming and Going

The Lord will protect your coming and going both now and forever.
PSALM 121:8

Psalm 121 is a song of ascents, typically sung as the people of God traveled to Jerusalem for the annual feasts. The song comforted and reminded the travelers to put their trust in the Lord. The author of the psalm starts with a declaration that he will lift his eyes toward the holy mountain where Jerusalem sits, relying on the Spirit to carry him to the destination. The psalmist sings that the Lord is a protector who will not let his foot slip. He will watch over the pilgrim day and night, for God never slumbers or grows weary. He will shelter His people from the harsh conditions, and He will be with them when struggles come. What great hope that God's protection is not just for this journey, but it is an eternal promise. Nothing will separate us from the Lord's protection as we journey through this life.

Though people of the Old Testament traveled to Jerusalem, their hearts remained far from the Lord. Because of their rebellion, they could never enter the temple. Still, the pilgrim and the pilgrimage were pictures of Jesus Christ. Jesus perfectly relied on God for protection. He grew up in Nazareth, so He, too, made the journey to Jerusalem every year. However, Jesus was the only One to travel with a heart completely dependent on the Father. Jesus was the true temple of God. He possessed the fullness of God in embodied form. His saving work tore the veil of the Holy of Holies, which separated us from the Lord's presence (Matthew 27:51). Jesus granted us access through His righteousness and fulfilled God's promise of protection. Christ protected us from sin and eternal death through His death on the cross, securing us in the Father's hand.

Just as the Israelites, we are still on a pilgrimage of our own. This life is not the end. We are not yet home. We journey toward eternal life guaranteed in Jesus. We journey toward fully reflecting the image of Christ when He returns, and our bodies are made new. As we walk, we can be confident that the Lord will protect us as we come and go. Though threats surround us, we can rest in the safety of His guiding hand. He will bring us to eternal life, joy everlasting, so let us sing praises to Him in our journey.

"NOTHING WILL SEPARATE US FROM THE LORD'S PROTECTION AS WE JOURNEY THROUGH THIS LIFE."

DAY 116

He Will Equip Us For His Purposes

*Then the Lord reached out his hand, touched my mouth, and told me:
I have now filled your mouth with my words.*

JEREMIAH 1:9

When Jeremiah heard these words from the Lord, he faced a daunting task. The Lord was sending him to speak His judgment over the people of Judah. They were caught up in their sin and had become enamored with the ways of the world. Jeremiah's words would not be well received. God's people were infamous for persecuting the prophets. Many of us might understand if Jeremiah wanted to run from what God had asked him to do, especially since God called him at a young age. But God came to Jeremiah and touched him on the mouth. He showed the prophet that He was the One who equipped him to perform the task He had given him. Jeremiah did not have to summon extra strength and ability. He had to remember that He was fully dependent on the Lord.

There are so many tasks God calls us to that seem daunting or unattainable. We look at what has been asked of us and want to find every excuse that we cannot meet the task. But our inability should not be why we do not say yes to something He has given us to do. Our inability can push us to rely on God's wisdom and strength. Inability is a gift, for it reminds us that we are limited and finite. But we serve a God who can do all things, and through His power, we will be able to complete the tasks He has prepared for us.

These tasks are not always grand. Each day, there is work to do. There are ways God has called us to be faithful, and He does not leave us to figure out these things on our own. He is with us, and He equips us because His Spirit is inside of us. So as you speak to your neighbors about the gospel, as you love your friends and family when they are not easy to love, when you face an unexpected challenge or frustration and want to hide from the day, know that He has equipped you for the task. The Lord is sovereign over your life and sanctification. How comforting it is to know that He does not leave you empty-handed as you walk through this life. He will be with you every step of the way.

"OUR INABILITY CAN PUSH US TO RELY ON
GOD'S WISDOM AND STRENGTH."

DAY 117
The Profitable Good

This saying is trustworthy. I want you to insist on these things, so that those who have believed God might be careful to devote themselves to good works. These are good and profitable for everyone.

TITUS 3:8

Imagine two hikers at a crossroads. One hiker insists that they go to the left, while the other insists they go to the right. The second hiker knows that the left path leads to a dead-end, but the first hiker insists that the left is the correct way, and he keeps trying to lead the second hiker down that path. This picture represents what false teachers were trying to do in the book of Titus. Paul warned Titus and many other believers to be careful of false teachers who seek to lead others away from the gospel, a path that leads to destruction. To combat these teachers, Paul encouraged believers to remain dedicated to the truth he presented to them throughout His letter thus far—the truth of the gospel.

We, too, should heed Paul's encouragement in our own lives. Many teachers today preach a message that is more aligned with their own subjective truth rather than the truth of God's Word. Instead of being led away by these teachers, we must remain grounded in the gospel. We must not veer off the path Christ has set us on in His grace, turning toward teaching that leads us away from Him. As believers, we should be careful to devote ourselves to the gospel and to respond to the gospel by walking in obedience and faithfulness to Christ, for He bought our life by giving up His own. We should also remain devoted to God's Word, seeking to hold teaching against Scripture to discern whether it aligns or deviates from the truth of God's Word.

If we do stumble upon teaching that deviates from Scripture, we must continue to insist on the truth of God's Word, clinging to the gospel of Christ. Remaining devoted to the gospel and God's Word keeps us from veering off the path of righteousness. As we respond to the gospel and walk in light of Scripture, we will produce good works that glorify God and encourage others in the faith. The gospel is our profitable good, so may we walk in its truth each day as we journey toward our eternity with Christ.

"REMAINING DEVOTED TO THE GOSPEL AND GOD'S WORD KEEPS US FROM VEERING OFF THE PATH OF RIGHTEOUSNESS."

DAY 118

Putting On

Therefore, as God's chosen ones, holy and dearly loved, put on compassion, kindness, humility, gentleness, and patience, bearing with one another and forgiving one another if anyone has a grievance against another.

COLOSSIANS 3:12–13A

In the New Testament, the Greek word *endyō* is used to describe the act of settling into a garment or putting on clothing. The Apostle Paul used this word to show how believers should live in light of Jesus's redemption. Paul wrote to the church in Colossae about this topic and explained that as one clothes himself, the people of God must clothe themselves in Christ's righteousness.

At the time of Paul's letter, the Colossian church dealt with a heresy that denied the sufficiency of Christ. Some claimed that a person must adhere to certain philosophies, observe specific festivals, and practice an ascetic lifestyle to obtain salvation. But Paul declared that Christ was God in the flesh, holding all authority and power, so His saving work alone was perfect. Believers died with Jesus on the cross and rose with Him as He walked out of the grave. Paul claimed that through faith, their old flesh was no more, and they now could rest in their identity in Christ. As we read Paul's letter, we learn the necessity of our union with Christ for salvation. The obedience and glory of our Savior covered us, His love fully encompassing us to give us a new identity in Him. When God looks at us, He sees His Son.

Union with Christ is the basis for obedience as well. When we are in Christ, we must put on His nature. This statement may seem counterintuitive. Why do we have to clothe ourselves in Christ if we already bear His image? We live in a fallen world, still affected by sin that lingers in our hearts. We must actively fight sin by walking in Jesus's ways. We need to sink into the nature of Christ and put on the fruits of His indwelling Spirit: compassion, kindness, humility, gentleness, and patience, for in those attributes, we will find true peace and confidence as we grow in Him. And as the Holy Spirit grows us and works in us, we can look forward to Christ's second coming when we will finally exchange rags for fine, white linen and bow before the glorious Son of God (Revelation 19:8).

"UNION WITH CHRIST IS THE BASIS FOR OBEDIENCE."

DAY 119
Rescued from Running

I called to the Lord in my distress, and he answered me. I cried out for help from deep inside Sheol; you heard my voice.

JONAH 2:2

Imagine how Jonah must have felt as he sank into the ocean after being thrown overboard by the sailors on his escape vessel. The water below was not bright or beautiful, welcoming him back to the surface to take another breath. The stormy ocean was a dark abyss with water like the night. The Lord had instructed Jonah to go to Nineveh and preach His words so that the people might repent. But Jonah did not listen and fled from God's presence. It was not until a violent storm began to brew at sea and the sailors panicked that he realized the storm was from the Lord's hand. He knew he was to blame for the distress of the sailors and others on the boat.

When Jonah had been thrown overboard and remembered what he had done, the Lord intervened. In the dark depths of the water, a great fish came and swallowed him. However, this was not the end of Jonah's life. Jonah lived and pondered his sin and how God rescued him in the belly of a fish. The Lord worked on Jonah's behalf. He made him stop running, and He gave him another chance. He had no other choice, and the fact that he was alive was evidence of God's mercy.

We, too, often run from God as Jonah did. When we are faced with a choice to choose sin over the Lord, it is easy to choose the sin. But even in our running and faithlessness, God is still faithful. He intervenes for us and guides us on the right path as we look to Him to guide us and trust Him with His plan. He opens our eyes to see how we have wronged Him. He causes us to grieve our sin and desire repentance. And He restores us and pursues us when we run away. He is our faithful Shepherd. God knows His flock, and He is willing to come after all who belong to Him.

"EVEN IN OUR RUNNING AND FAITHLESSNESS,
GOD IS STILL FAITHFUL."

DAY 120

The Exaltation of Humility

He sets the lowly on high, and mourners are lifted to safety. – Job 5:11
Blessed are those who mourn, for they will be comforted. Blessed are the humble, for they will inherit the earth. – Matthew 5:4–5

What makes the gospel so powerful is that it is a message for the lowly. It is a message for those who mourn and are humble in heart. When Christ came to the earth, He did not come in a display of glory but humility. He did not serve the proud but the humble. While He shared His table with all kinds of people, His guests primarily included tax collectors and outcasts. He healed the sick and comforted the oppressed. Jesus says in Matthew 9:12–13, "It is not those who are well who need a doctor, but those who are sick . . . for I didn't come to call the righteous, but sinners."

The kingdom of God is an upside-down kingdom. The Jews thought the Messiah they awaited would come in splendor and might. But Jesus came as a servant, gentle and lowly in heart. The gospel speaks to the humble because they know what it is like to be brought low. They know what it is like to hit rock bottom and live in the valleys of life. They recognize their need for salvation. But the proud do not. Those on the mountaintop have a more difficult time accepting the gospel message. They believe that they are fine on their own and have what they need. But in God's kingdom, the lowly are exalted. Even if we feel as if we are in the valley now, as believers in Christ, we will one day experience the fullness of God's kingdom forever. No more will we be in the valley, for we will be exalted with our Savior forever.

What a comfort it is for our souls to know that God cares for the lowly. He is not a God who overlooks those who are needy and grieving. He is not a partial God who offers the proud and rich salvation while withholding salvation to the humble and poor. Meekness is not a weakness in the kingdom of God. The gospel is a call for the proud to humble themselves. It is a call for the humble to lift their hands to the God who lifts them up. Though you may find yourself in the valley, your position with Christ means that you are seated at the right hand of the Father.

"NO MORE WILL WE BE IN THE VALLEY, FOR WE WILL BE EXALTED WITH OUR SAVIOR FOREVER."

DAY 121
Our Shelter in the Storm

The Lord is my shepherd; I have what I need. He lets me lie down in green pastures; he leads me beside quiet waters. He renews my life; he leads me along the right paths for his name's sake. Even when I go through the darkest valley, I fear no danger, for you are with me; your rod and your staff—they comfort me. You prepare a table before me in the presence of my enemies; you anoint my head with oil; my cup overflows. Only goodness and faithful love will pursue me all the days of my life, and I will dwell in the house of the Lord as long as I live.

PSALM 23:1-6

The Bible often refers to God's people as sheep, meaning we are prone to wander. On our own, we are helpless and aimless, falling easily into harm. We need someone to guide us in the way of protection, care, and safety. Sheep require a good shepherd who watches over, cares for, and guides them. And we need a Good Shepherd who will do the same for us as His children.

The chaos and disorder of this world sometimes leave us wondering what to do. We need direction, shelter, and solace from what surrounds us. We need to know that we are not alone. But we have a God who reminds us through His Word that we are never alone. He is an ever-present help in trouble, and He protects and provides for us with His power and presence.

David, the author of Psalm 23, knew God's personal care and protection well. God strengthened and upheld him through difficult circumstances. David wrote of the Good Shepherd, who longs to be our shelter, caretaker, guide, and comforter. Our Shepherd longs to bring us peace. He longs to invite us into His safety, carry our burdens, and offer us true rest.

David likely composed this Psalm while reflecting on a time when his enemies surrounded him. David feared for his life, questioning if God would deliver him. However, the promise of God's presence allowed him to speak truth to his own soul: "Even when I go through the darkest valley, I fear no danger, for you are with me; your rod and your staff—they comfort me" (Psalm 23:4). When we are in harm's way or filled with anxiety, what comfort and help we find in the truth and shelter of God's presence as He guides us through our days.

"WE HAVE A GOD WHO REMINDS US THROUGH HIS WORD THAT WE ARE NEVER ALONE."

DAY 122
From Rags to Riches

All of us have become like something unclean, and all our righteous acts are like a polluted garment; all of us wither like a leaf, and our iniquities carry us away like the wind. — Isaiah 64:6

I rejoice greatly in the Lord, I exult in my God; for he has clothed me with the garments of salvation and wrapped me in a robe of righteousness, as a groom wears a turban and as a bride adorns herself with her jewels. — Isaiah 61:10

The prophet Isaiah echoed the cries of the Israelites after their kingdom fell to pagan nations. In his prayer, he highlighted that the issue was not political defeat but spiritual defeat. The Israelites were overcome and taken into captivity, and their kingdom was destroyed. But this circumstance was a picture of something more serious. The Israelites were overcome by their pride and taken into sin's captivity. Their place in God's presence was compromised. The Israelites had become so unclean that even their good works were like dirty cloths, reflective of a soiled heart. The Israelites wasted away because of their sin, weakened by unrighteousness and pride.

But the Lord also gave Isaiah a message of hope through the coming Messiah, the One to save God's people from sin. Isaiah spoke of His work in healing the brokenhearted, releasing the captives, and comforting the sorrowful. Because the Messiah would accomplish His redeeming work on the cross, there would be a celebration, like a wedding feast where the Lord will give His guests, believers, new garments of salvation and jewels of honor. They will bear the clean, enduring, and beautiful clothing of the Messiah Himself, leaving behind their shame.

This story of God's people is our story too. The Messiah came in the person of Jesus. He healed the sick, fed the hungry, and raised the dead. He preached life, truth, and freedom through Him. Though Jesus's outward clothing was modest, He possessed the riches of God. Though He was dirtied and torn because of our sin, He rose from the grave with a restored body and garments of glory because of His obedience. Through His work, we exchange our shame for His righteousness. When we trust Jesus, we are washed clean and mended together. When we look in the mirror, remembering our mistakes, failures, and guilt, may we call on the name of Jesus, remember His salvation, and marvel at His abundant grace.

> "WHEN WE TRUST JESUS, WE ARE WASHED CLEAN AND MENDED TOGETHER."

Day 123
Deception of the Heart

The heart is more deceitful than anything else, and incurable—who can understand it?

JEREMIAH 17:9

"Listen to your heart" is a popular phrase spoken in love songs or movies as encouragement. Yet this phrase can do more harm than good. We all have a sinful nature, which means our hearts are naturally sinful. Without God's grace, our hearts tend toward the desires of our flesh. When we listen to our sinful hearts, they often lead us to sin, for they are deceitful. They trick us into thinking we can follow our own desires for the best results. Too many times, our hearts lead us to instant gratification that slowly fades and leaves us hopeless.

However, there is hope for our wayward hearts! Jeremiah 17:9 asks who can understand our hearts. God designed us, which means He knows our hearts intimately. He understands their natural propensity to move toward sin and act impulsively. He knows what our hearts need to be cured—Himself. In His great plan of redemption, God provided a way for our hearts to be cleansed from sin. Jesus's sacrifice on the cross washes our hearts clean, and we are given new hearts in place of the old.

While we still struggle with our sin nature, believers have new hearts that desire to obey and follow the Lord. Not only this, but God has given us His Word and Spirit to give us guidance and wisdom. When we find ourselves experiencing temptation, we have the conviction and help of the Spirit inside to provide us with strength in those times. God's Word also helps us examine and understand our heart's desires. Not every desire of the heart is wrong, but we can still act upon a desire in the wrong way. God's Word instructs us in evaluating our desires and teaches us the right way to respond.

In every situation we face, we should turn first to God's Word. This requires daily discipline, as our sinful flesh wants to listen to our own desires. But God fights alongside us as we face these battles and pray to Him for wisdom and guidance. We can ask the Holy Spirit to give us patience and discipline, faithfully take in God's Word, and grow in wisdom. So let us not follow the world's advice but allow the truth of God's Word to guide us in all that we say and do.

"GOD'S WORD ALSO HELPS US EXAMINE AND UNDERSTAND OUR HEART'S DESIRES."

DAY 124
Foolish Priorities

The Lord of Armies says this: "Think carefully about your ways. Go up into the hills, bring down lumber, and build the house; and I will be pleased with it and be glorified," says the Lord.

HAGGAI 1:7-8

The places our hearts focus on reveal our priorities. A common issue for us as believers is that we do not often stop to examine these priorities or think critically about our ways. We simply act on impulse. As believers, our priority in life is to glorify the Lord. We were created to worship Him alone. All of our ways should be set on bringing Him honor and glory. Since we do not do this well on our own, we need God's Word to guide us.

But unless we are in God's Word and in communion with Him, our priorities will probably not be in the right place. Without the wisdom and guidance of the Lord, our actions will not bring honor and glory to Him. God's Word teaches us how to worship the Lord and examine our ways. We are more likely to think carefully about our ways when we hold them against the truth of Scripture. When we compare our ways to His Word, we can ask if what we are pursuing gives God glory or if the action leads us to worship Him or ourselves. When we remain immersed in God's Word and prayer, our priorities will be in their proper place.

Deep heart work comes with priority change. Our hearts are quick to chase after our own ways and pursue our own desires. Daily, we will fight to lay down our foolish priorities and pick up the wise ways of the Lord. In these moments, it is comforting to know the heart work—as hard as it may be—is worth it. As we continue to pursue priorities of worship to the Lord, He will lead us on paths of righteousness. When we stay in God's Word, we will find our ways aligning with God's ways. His priorities become our priorities. As you go about your days, may your heart's desire be to worship God above all else. While our ways lead to destruction, God's ways lead to life everlasting in Him.

"WHEN WE STAY IN GOD'S WORD, WE WILL FIND OUR WAYS ALIGNING WITH GOD'S WAYS. HIS PRIORITIES BECOME OUR PRIORITIES."

DAY 125

Leading with Humility

Remember me favorably, my God, for all that I have done for this people.
NEHEMIAH 5:19

Nehemiah had once been the king of Persia's cupbearer, but the Lord brought Nehemiah back to Jerusalem to help rebuild the city walls. Nehemiah lived after many of the people of Israel had returned from exile in Babylon. They had been trying to piece their lives back together for a few years already. Their city and temple would never look like what they had once been, but nonetheless, the Lord allowed His people to seek restoration and come home.

However, under Nehemiah's supervision, there were plenty of problems between the people who threatened the rebuilding of the city walls. Though the people worked on them together, they were taking advantage of one another. Greed among them was causing unrest. In chapter 5, when Nehemiah gives an account of how he has led the people, he notes how he has not let greed overtake him. He has lived in humility and generosity, though he had access to immense material wealth from the king of Persia. We may look at this account and think Nehemiah is bragging, but many commentators believe that this part of the book was probably never intended for the eyes of others. We are likely getting a glimpse into Nehemiah's diary in these verses, and his appeal is not to be remembered by man but by God.

How we lead where God has placed us—in our families, schools, churches, workplaces—can bring others close to the gospel or away from it. If we lead with a deep concern for the welfare of others, people will notice and wonder why we act the way we do. This interest will allow us to speak of Christ and how He has changed our lives. Leading in humility is the call for every Christian leader, for we are imitating Christ. Christ is our ultimate example of humility. He became nothing so that we could have everything through Him (Philippians 2). Our humility, generosity, and service to the people we are responsible for are an opportunity to imitate Christ's genuine compassion and sacrifice for His people. What a beautiful privilege! May our motivation to lead be like Nehemiah's—to be remembered not by man but by God.

"LEADING IN HUMILITY IS THE CALL FOR EVERY CHRISTIAN LEADER, FOR WE ARE IMITATING CHRIST."

DAY 126

The Lord is My Portion

I say, "The Lord is my portion, therefore I will put my hope in him."

LAMENTATIONS 3:24

So often, it can seem to come as second nature that we look at our circumstances and wish for more, for better, for different. We gaze at what we have been given and feel as if God has given us the wrong lot in life. Maybe we feel as though He is not enough as we look for love, acceptance, peace, and strength in every other place and person but Christ. But may we remember that our heavenly Father *is* our portion. In Him alone should we place our trust, for He provides all that we need. He is enough.

In Lamentations, Jeremiah says, "The Lord is my portion." Jeremiah realizes that satisfaction is found only in Christ—in Him, we find our portion that no amount of money or knowledge or status can or ever will provide. Jeremiah realizes and trusts that all he needs is found in His Lord and Savior: rest, strength, comfort, joy. The reason Jeremiah can hope in Christ is that He knows the Lord is all He needs—that the Lord will provide for His needs for as many days as He has numbered for Him. In the book of Job, Job loses his family, possessions, wealth, and health. He cries out to the Lord in raw honesty, asking why the Lord has allowed him such a portion in life, yet he always comes back to what he knows is true—that His hope remains in God who gives and who takes away (Job 1:21).

May we, too, place our hope in God, who will forever be our portion. While this does not mean that we will never fear or have questions or doubt His goodness in our lives, we can know that no matter what life holds for each of us, Christ will fill us, He will make us whole. And those broken parts of our lives where it seems that we do not have enough to keep going, that we are not enough to keep going, He will walk with us through those places, and on the day He calls us home, those places will be fully restored and redeemed in Him because of what He did for us on the cross. So let us look at our circumstances, not wishing for more, for better, for different, but hoping in the One offering us fullness in the portion that only He is.

"WE CAN KNOW THAT NO MATTER WHAT LIFE HOLDS FOR EACH OF US, CHRIST WILL FILL US, HE WILL MAKE US WHOLE."

DAY 127
Grieving with Hope

We do not want you to be uninformed, brothers and sisters, concerning those who are asleep, so that you will not grieve like the rest, who have no hope.

1 THESSALONIANS 4:13

An empty chair at the table. The words not spoken. The deep sorrow of loss. We live in a fallen world where death and decay surround us. Cancer interrupts our lives. Car accidents devastate our futures. Miscarriages ravage our hearts. Because of the fall, we all lose things that we hold dear.

The Apostle Paul speaks of a kind of grief that believers can experience in the midst of death. He calls it grieving with hope. Admittedly, this phrase may seem confusing to you in your sadness. But the mystery of our living faith is that for a moment on this earth, we will live within the tension of two realities. We will experience suffering, tragedy, and brokenness now, but those things will not last forever. We will see death and decay but understand that they are temporary. We can mourn openly, yet with hope, knowing that God uses these trials for His glory and our good.

Before we knew Christ, we were heading for an eternal death. But because of Jesus's finished work on the cross, we are set free and reunited with Him. Those who trust in Jesus do not need to fear eternity. When we enter eternity with our Savior, there will be only rejoicing and fullness as we are reunited with Him.

We often want to ignore the reality of death. But the Bible calls us to be sobered by its reality and live in light of eternity. We are to "grieve with hope" the loss of loved ones who knew Christ, knowing that they are alive with God in heaven. We are to share the gospel, knowing that heaven and hell are real, and Christ is the only One who saves and brings eternal life. The promise of Scripture is this: one day, there will be no more death, decay, or disease. But more than that, we will finally see our Savior who loved us enough to die for our sins to save us. We can grieve with hope, because Jesus has defeated death. He is alive, and though we die in this life, we will live forever with Him.

> "WE WILL FINALLY SEE OUR SAVIOR WHO LOVED US ENOUGH TO DIE FOR OUR SINS TO SAVE US."

DAY 128
God Keeps His Promise

When the Lord smelled the pleasing aroma, he said to himself, "I will never again curse the ground because of human beings, even though the inclination of the human heart is evil from youth onward. And I will never again strike down every living thing as I have done."

GENESIS 8:21

When we turn in the book of Genesis, we find the story of Noah. In obedience to the Lord, he built a boat where he would remain for more than forty days and forty nights as God's judgment fell upon His creation in the form of a flood. We can only imagine what that time must have been like for Noah and his family. They did not see land for weeks, and everyone they knew died in the flood—friends, neighbors, all others who walked the earth. As thankful as Noah and his family may have been that their own lives were spared, their grief and confusion must have been overwhelming at times as they considered the reality of their circumstances.

After the floodwaters had come and gone and eventually disappeared, Noah left the boat and made a sacrifice to God to praise Him. Noah knew his life was spared only by the Lord's grace, so he worshiped Him. God made a covenant to Noah, placing a rainbow in the sky as a sign of the promise that He would never again flood the earth. And God would keep this promise as He does in every promise He makes, for God does not lie or change (Numbers 23:19, Malachi 3:6).

Because God sent His Son to the cross to bear the weight of our sins, we too are given a promise—one of eternal life. When Christ returns, we will be united with our Savior if we have placed our trust in Him. He will cover us with His love and perfect peace, saving us from pain and sin and death. In Him, tears and suffering will one day be no more (Revelation 21:4), sin will lose its grip on us, and death will have no final say. We praise our Savior, who keeps every promise He makes.

"WHEN CHRIST RETURNS, WE WILL BE UNITED WITH OUR SAVIOR IF WE HAVE PLACED OUR TRUST IN HIM. HE WILL COVER US WITH HIS LOVE AND PERFECT PEACE."

DAY 129
Lost and Found

What man among you, who has a hundred sheep and loses one of them, does not leave the ninety-nine in the open field and go after the lost one until he finds it? When he has found it, he joyfully puts it on his shoulders, and coming home, he calls his friends and neighbors together, saying to them, "Rejoice with me, because I have found my lost sheep!"

LUKE 15:4–6

Religious leaders of Jesus's day criticized Him for spending time with sinners. These men and women the Pharisees talked about were those blatantly living in opposition to God's law. While the Pharisees chose to turn away in disbelief at the truth Jesus spoke, others like prostitutes and tax collectors did decide to listen to Him. There were those too who had obvious physical defects and disabilities, and the culture during this time believed these physical ailments and deformities were the result of sin.

Jesus gave the leaders a parable to demonstrate why He chose to eat with these people. He wanted to demonstrate how the Pharisees deceived themselves about their position before the Lord. Jesus came like a shepherd to take care of His sheep, which meant going after those who went astray. Jesus knew that all people were lost sheep without Him, and He had come to deliver them. Jesus's heart was for the lowly and the outcasts of society. Every human being is lost, broken, and helpless without Him, but the humble best understood their need for Him.

The Pharisees were just as sinful as the people who sat before Christ, but they could not see it. They were so caught up in their own works of righteousness that they did not realize their broken spiritual condition. They knew much about God's laws. But when He came to them in the flesh, they did not want His message of salvation.

We have all been the lost sheep, in spiritual danger, and in need of a Savior. But Jesus rescued us because we could not rescue ourselves. Our spiritual inheritance is found in Christ alone because of His life He gave on the cross. We can now have eternal life with Him, though not as a result of our own works but the grace He so freely gives. Indeed we were lost, but praise be to the Lord that we have now been found!

"JESUS'S HEART WAS FOR THE LOWLY AND
THE OUTCASTS OF SOCIETY."

DAY 130
The High Priestly Prayer

"I made your name known to them and will continue to make it known, so that the love you have loved me with may be in them and I may be in them."

JOHN 17:26

Some of the most precious words in Scripture are found in John 17. Jesus lifts up all believers to the Lord before He goes to the cross for their sins. In the chapters that follow, Jesus is betrayed, arrested, and put on trial. His prayer for His disciples is the last thing He gives before the most excruciating days of His life. Even when He is about to endure death, Jesus demonstrated a humble heart that considered others before Himself.

His prayer was not just for His disciples at the time of His death. It is for all who have chosen to believe in Him. Jesus prayed this for you. At the beginning of His prayer, Jesus states that He is about to fulfill the purpose for which He had been sent. Through Jesus's death, He would give life to all of God's chosen people. He asks the Lord to glorify Him so He could, in turn, glorify the Lord. Jesus knows He is soon about to share in the glory of being in God's presence once again.

And then He prays for us because we are not yet with Him. We are in a world that hates God and hates those who love God. He prayed for our unity, and He asked the Lord to protect us. We will not be lost because we are His, but the world will hate us, and the enemy of God, Satan, will try and destroy us. Jesus knows we will experience much of the same suffering He did and has compassion on us.

As we read this prayer, we catch a glimpse of what Christ has done on our behalf. This prayer shows His heart. He continues to intercede for us before the Father. He prays for and has compassion on us. This prayer is called the "High Priestly Prayer" because our Great High Priest prays it. Jesus is our intercessor before the Lord and has made atonement for our sins. He stands before the Father on our behalf, and we are welcomed into God's presence as He looks on us and sees the righteousness of His Son. May we read this prayer, confident in what Christ has accomplished and in awe of what we now possess because of His sacrifice.

"THROUGH JESUS'S DEATH, HE WOULD GIVE LIFE
TO ALL OF GOD'S CHOSEN PEOPLE."

DAY 131

The Lord is There

The perimeter of the city will be six miles, and the name of the city from that day on will be, The Lord Is There.

EZEKIEL 48:35

The prophet Ezekiel was called to preach a difficult message to the people. The Israelites had rebelled against God, and God was going to bring destruction to their city of Jerusalem. God gave Ezekiel visions and symbols to share with the people, but they did not believe him. Yet, embedded within this message of destruction was a glimmer of hope. God promised to keep His chosen remnant and to give them new hearts. God would give His people living water and make them holy. He promised to restore the land of Israel.

The Lord would not abandon His people. The name of the new promised city in Ezekiel 48 reflects this promise: "The Lord is There." God will always be there. He has not abandoned His people, as dark as the night may seem. He will not forsake His children. Though the world continues in its sinfulness, calling what is wrong, right, and what is right, wrong, God is still King. He is here. He is not far off. He knows and sees it all. And He will one day restore His people, redeeming His chosen remnant. He will enact vengeance for every injustice. He will return and restore the city of God, where believers will live for all of eternity. On this day, people from every tribe, tongue, and nation will come to worship before His throne. There will be no more division, hatred, sin, or death. He will right every wrong and dwell with His people again.

As God's children, we too are promised an inheritance secured for us through Christ (1 Peter 1:4–6). This inheritance will never perish, fade, or spoil. Christ secures it for us in heaven. When we believe in the gospel, God gives us His Spirit as a guarantee of our salvation, holding us fast until we see Him again (Ephesians 1:14). And, oh, what a glorious day that will be! On this day, God will bestow on us all of the treasures of heaven. But more than this, we will see Him face to face, the greatest treasure of all. We will behold the fullness of His glory. But until that day comes, we lift our voices in praise, for surely God is with us now.

"GOD WILL ALWAYS BE THERE. HE HAS NOT ABANDONED HIS PEOPLE, AS DARK AS THE NIGHT MAY SEEM."

DAY 132

What We Cannot Perceive

"For my thoughts are not your thoughts, and your ways are not my ways."

ISAIAH 55:8A

We can think we know what we are going to do and when we are going to do it. But we are often faced with the fact that our plans and thoughts do not happen how we thought they would. We could stumble around in frustration because of this, or we could acknowledge that we are not in control. The Lord alone is sovereign over our days. We do not have perfect foresight to understand exactly what we need and when we need it. Omniscience, knowing everything, is a characteristic that only the Lord possesses. Our desires and ways are usually focused on us, but the Lord's ways and desires are for His glory and our good.

Trusting the Lord and His promises has always been difficult for His people. Throughout the Old Testament, the Lord promised that a Messiah would come. He would save the people of Israel, giving them true salvation. But the people expected a Messiah who would be a mighty warrior and conquer their enemies. Yet, when Jesus came to earth in the form of a baby and years later began His public ministry as a humble teacher, He was not what they expected. The Lord's plan was better. Jesus was the mightiest of warriors, and He conquered death, the greatest enemy of all.

Every day we have a choice of whether or not we are going to relinquish the idea that we are in control and trust that the Lord's plans for us are better. The more we practice remembering His sovereignty, the more we will rest and trust Him. And we will also begin to look for ways the Lord provides for us, sustains us, protects us, cares for us, and loves us. We miss so many moments of experiencing His loving kindness toward us because we are consumed with trying to keep our lives together. It is a task we could never accomplish.

So today, remember that the Lord is doing things in your life that are beyond your comprehension. He is outside of space and time, and He sees your life from its beginning to its end. Trust that each part of your journey is a part of His good work and will toward you, and rest.

"THE MORE WE PRACTICE REMEMBERING HIS SOVEREIGNTY, THE MORE WE WILL REST AND TRUST HIM."

DAY 133
Storing Up Eternal Treasure

But store up for yourselves treasures in heaven, where neither moth nor rust destroys, and where thieves don't break in and steal. For where your treasure is, there your heart will be also.

MATTHEW 6:20–21

Everything that breaks or rusts reminds us that we cannot place our hope in material things, for they do not last. They cannot provide the satisfaction for which we long. When we store up earthly treasure, we lose sight of the fact that nothing we own in this life will be able to come with us into the next. It all will pass away.

Jesus calls us to store up treasure in heaven, in our eternal home. When we reach eternity, there will be no more broken cars or house appliances to frustrate us or empty our bank accounts. We will not have to worry about how to keep up our homes to be just as nice as the neighbor down the street. There will be no urge to have the nicest, latest gadget. All of our affection will be perfectly set on Christ. You will not feel the itch of discontentment because your heart will finally be at rest. What joy awaits us!

In our day-to-day lives, it is easy to forget our future in eternity. It is easy to get caught up in rusty trinkets. But we must instead think of our heavenly home. We remember that our greatest treasure is Christ Himself, the One who gave His life for ours, and we will soon meet Him face to face. As we live our lives, we should invest more in what matters for our eternal home rather than worrying about all that will provide temporary comfort in the present.

We are to enjoy our time in this life, following the Lord, glorifying Him in all things, and loving the people He has given us. May we remember that any possession or wealth we have in this life will soon fade away. Yet, we look back to what Christ did and the cross while focusing our gaze forward in hope toward eternity with Christ. We wait eagerly for the day we enter heaven's gates to behold the Lord and the blessing of His eternal treasure.

"JESUS CALLS US TO STORE UP TREASURE IN HEAVEN, IN OUR ETERNAL HOME."

DAY 134
The Living Temple

"The final glory of this house will be greater than the first," says the Lord of Armies. "I will provide peace in this place"—this is the declaration of the Lord of Armies.

HAGGAI 2:9

The once glorious temple lay in ruin. Israel's enemies had torn down its walls of gold, leaving the place of worship destroyed. But God would not leave His house in ruins. In the book of Haggai, God commands the people of Israel to work to rebuild the temple. However, the Israelites begin building with sadness, for this temple would pale in comparison to the first one Solomon had made that was a sight to behold. God encourages the Israelites by promising the glory of this new temple. Though it did not seem like it, this temple would be far more glorious, one of great glory and peace.

This promise likely motivated the Israelites to build, knowing the joy to come. They found excitement and hope as they began placing stones on top of each other, resurrecting the house of God. Destruction was in Israel's past, but restoration and peace were in their future.

The glory of this temple points us to the ultimate temple of Christ, the new heavens and earth. When Christ returns, God will come to dwell permanently and fully with His creation, making His dwelling place extend to all the corners of the earth. The removal of sin and the presence of God will make the dwelling place of God brilliant and glorious. This eternal temple will be far greater than the earthly temple, for God's presence will dwell among His people forever. With all brokenness, death, and sin removed, our home with God will be a place of everlasting peace.

Just like the Israelites, the promise of this future reality fuels our hope and perseverance in the present. As citizens of heaven, believers have a role in building the kingdom of God. We contribute to the kingdom of God here on earth by spreading the message of the gospel, advocating for the poor and oppressed, and taking care of the creation around us. Without the promise of what is to come, our work in the present would lack purpose. But the promised kingdom to come reminds us that our work is not in vain. Restoration and peace await us, so may we press on with excitement and hope, using our time in the present to build the glorious kingdom to come.

"AS CITIZENS OF HEAVENS, BELIEVERS HAVE A ROLE IN BUILDING THE KINGDOM OF GOD."

DAY 135

Blessed

Blessed are the poor in spirit, for the kingdom of heaven is theirs. Blessed are those who mourn, for they will be comforted. Blessed are the humble, for they will inherit the earth. Blessed are those who hunger and thirst for righteousness, for they will be filled. Blessed are the merciful, for they will be shown mercy. Blessed are the pure in heart, for they will see God. Blessed are the peacemakers, for they will be called sons of God. Blessed are those who are persecuted because of righteousness, for the kingdom of heaven is theirs.

MATTHEW 5:3–10

A beautiful family, a nice home, a well-paying job, and a happy life are certainly good gifts and blessings from God. But those things are not necessary to be blessed. Our society views blessings differently than God. We find a biblical understanding of what it means to be blessed in the Beatitudes found nestled in the book of Matthew.

The Sermon on the Mount was a lesson Jesus gave to uproot cultural and ritualistic practices of the day and address the hearts of those who claimed to follow Him. The Beatitudes, which are part of the Sermon on the Mount, follow a list of "Blessed are..." statements. This list is likely not one you might imagine to be qualifications for being blessed. But notice that these blessings are not external adornments or gifts. They are postures of the heart.

The position of our hearts reveals a foundational understanding of who we are and what we have been given in Jesus Christ. To be poor in spirit acknowledges that no hope lies in ourselves but only in God. To mourn reveals true grief over our sin and the desire to seek repentance. To hunger and thirst for righteousness is to pursue holiness and sanctification. The merciful have an understanding of the mercy shown by God and a willingness to show it to others. Purity of heart serves as the basis for all of life and worship. Peacemaking pushes us forward to share the gospel message of hope and peace in a broken world. The persecuted are willing to endure anything for the sake of Christ and for the joy set before us. The gospel at work in our hearts is how we are truly blessed. May we look to the Beatitudes—to God's Word—to examine our hearts and guide our prayers to receive and live in light of the Lord's true blessings.

"THE GOSPEL AT WORK IN OUR HEARTS IS HOW
WE ARE TRULY BLESSED."

DAY 136
Take Every Thought Captive

...since the weapons of our warfare are not of the flesh, but are powerful through God for the demolition of strongholds. We demolish arguments and every proud thing that is raised up against the knowledge of God, and we take every thought captive to obey Christ.

2 CORINTHIANS 10:4-5

As followers of Christ, we fight a spiritual battle. This is not simply a metaphorical fight. Paul explains in Ephesians 6:12 that our fight "is not against flesh and blood, but against the rulers, against the authorities, against the cosmic powers of this darkness, against evil, spiritual forces in the heavens." One of the ways the enemy uses his powers of darkness is by clouding people's minds with lies. He causes them to oppose the truth of the gospel and form arguments against the truth.

We live in a world full of anti-gospel thoughts and arguments. We, as believers, must be vigilant when it comes to teaching the truth. We must be wise to remove strongholds by speaking the truth of the gospel. These strongholds are things that contradict the truth of who God is and what His Word tells us. Let us use Scripture to break down arguments that attempt to dispel the gospel.

As believers, we also need to be vigilant in taking in the truth. When we are not grounded in God's Word, we are more susceptible to becoming swept away by false truths. If we are to guide people to what is true, we need to be people of truth. But the only way we can recognize and detect false teaching is to know God's Word. The enemy not only wages war by deceiving those who do not Jesus, but he also wages war by trying to deceive us. He whispers lies to us and seeks to lead us away from the truth of God's Word. Let us be active in recognizing and refuting the lies the enemy speaks to us and replacing them with the truth of the gospel.

As followers of Christ, we are to speak the truth in love (Ephesians 4:15). In this way, the love of Christ is to be displayed through our words and actions. While it may seem daunting to combat the arguments and thoughts that arise, the most loving thing we can do is share the gospel with others. May our every thought be set on what is above and grounded in Christ and the redemption and restoration He gives.

"LET US BE ACTIVE IN RECOGNIZING AND REFUTING THE LIES THE ENEMY SPEAKS TO US AND REPLACING THEM WITH THE TRUTH OF THE GOSPEL."

DAY 137
For the Sake of David

For the sake of his servant David, the Lord was unwilling to destroy Judah, since he had promised to give a lamp to David and his sons forever.

2 KINGS 8:19

One Old Testament king, in particular, may hold a memorable place in your mind—King David. From playing music for King Saul in the royal courts, slaying the great Philistine warrior Goliath, to His abuse of power and affair with Bathsheba and the murder of Uriah the Hittite, he had great triumphs and great falls. Yet, despite his flaws, Scripture remembers King David as a man after God's own heart. His life was ultimately shaped by His repentant heart before the Lord. His reign and rule had a great impact on the nation of Israel, and he became the standard by which every Judean King would be measured.

From the reign of David to each following succession, the history of Israel's kings represented a downward spiral of idolatry and disobedience, with only a handful of faithful ones who desired to please the Lord. It may lead us to wonder how God showed mercy to Israel for so long. A theme woven through the book of 2 Kings is God's mercy being shown to his people "for the sake of David." Though David was indeed a sinner, God remembered him as a faithful servant who honored the Lord. What a merciful God! Even with all that God could have held against David, God chose not to remember his sins, for he had sought the Lord with a heart of repentance.

Of course, David's faithfulness was imperfect and insufficient to sustain the Lord's mercy on His people. But, David merely pointed toward a true and perfect King who would be faithful through the ages. The New Testament reveals that the obedience and faithfulness of Jesus Christ were perfect and complete. He is our true and perfect King. Jesus Christ bore the sinful weight of His people in a way that every king failed to do. He would open the floodgates of God's grace on undeserving sinners who turned to Him. Because of Jesus, those who put their faith and hope in Him can stand before the Lord with confidence as one approved. What grace that God then looks on us and bestows His endless mercy upon us for all time.

"JESUS CHRIST BORE THE SINFUL WEIGHT OF HIS PEOPLE IN A WAY THAT EVERY KING FAILED TO DO."

DAY 138
Unashamed for the Gospel

For I am not ashamed of the gospel, because it is the power of God for salvation to everyone who believes, first to the Jew, and also to the Greek.
ROMANS 1:16

What keeps you from sharing the gospel? As believers, we tend to avoid sharing parts of ourselves out of fear of rejection or receiving another negative response. We can withhold the truth from others because we fear that revealing the truth will lead to rejection. We are ashamed to share things, so instead of saying them, we bury them inside. Many times, we do the same thing when it comes to sharing the gospel.

In those moments, we feel embarrassed to share the gospel. Perhaps, we have forgotten its power. When we hide and withhold the gospel, we prevent others from experiencing God's powerful work of salvation. The Apostle Paul, who wrote the book of Romans, experienced much ridicule for sharing the gospel. He was opposed by others and persecuted many times because of his faith. Even still, Paul never backed down from sharing the gospel. He never let the reactions of others keep him from sharing the good news of Christ. Paul's actions should encourage us in our own evangelism. There is nothing shameful about the gospel message. In fact, the gospel covers people's shame. Though parts of the gospel may offend—that we are sinful and deserving of punishment for our sin—people need to hear about this reality that points to our need for God's grace. His gift of redemption covers our guilt and shame.

If we want to live unashamed for the gospel as Paul did, we must learn to accept any response we receive for sharing the gospel. We need to care more about a person's salvation than our reputation. Even if we are rejected for sharing the gospel, may we rejoice that the gospel message is heard. As believers, we have experienced the power of God within us that has wiped our sins clean. There are people around us who need to experience God's powerful work of salvation. God has given us His Spirit to embolden us and empower us to share the gospel's message with these people. Let us allow the power of the gospel to propel us forward in faith and courage. Let us live unashamed of the good news of Jesus Christ, for we have a message of great hope to share!

"LET US ALLOW THE POWER OF THE GOSPEL TO PROPEL US FORWARD IN FAITH AND COURAGE."

DAY 139
Repentance and Renewal

God, create a clean heart for me and renew a steadfast spirit within me.
PSALM 51:10

In Psalm 51:10, David cries out in repentance to the Lord after the prophet Nathan confronts him about his adultery and murder. David stayed home from battle (2 Samuel 11:1), and while in his palace, he saw a beautiful woman bathing. David knew who she was and that she was married, but this did not matter to him at that moment. He took Bathsheba and slept with her. David not only committed adultery but abused his power as king to have Bathsheba sleep with him. But while David seemed to think this was something he could do in secret, Bathsheba became pregnant.

Bathsheba's husband, Uriah, was one of David's warriors. While David stayed home when he should have been in battle alongside his men, Uriah faithfully served the Lord and the king. To cover his wrongdoing, David called Uriah home so that he could sleep with Bathsheba. Uriah and all of Jerusalem would think the child in Bathsheba's womb was rightfully Uriah's. But Uriah refused to enjoy the comforts of home while others were out fighting. Uriah was doing everything David should have done. He had gone to battle and continued in faithfulness when he came home. However, Uriah would die at David's command in hopes that he could hide his sins.

When the Lord confronts David through the prophet Nathan, David seeks the Lord in repentance. In Psalm 51, David sheds light on the problem that every person faces. We are born in sin (Psalm 51:5)—there has never been a moment we have not fallen under the penalty of the curse. David considered his sinful acts before he committed them. He knew he was a sinner deep in transgression and needed God's restoration.

David faced the consequences of his sin for the rest of his life. But God did not strip his salvation from him. God used David's wrongdoing to draw the broken king to Himself and does the same for us. Let us come before the Lord humbly, asking Him to do what He alone can do. He will cleanse our hearts and renew our desire to follow Him. We have this gift of grace because of Christ's sacrifice for us on the cross. God has washed us through the blood of Jesus. He has given us His righteousness, and He alone can take our sinful hearts and make them clean (Psalm 51:7).

"HE WILL CLEANSE OUR HEARTS AND RENEW OUR DESIRE TO FOLLOW HIM."

DAY 140
Wisdom in Silence

A fool gives full vent to his anger, but a wise person holds it in check.
PROVERBS 29:11

All of us experience anger. Situations and circumstances arise that do not go our way. Those close to us say things that rub us the wrong way. Our plans are interrupted by the needs of others. And as these circumstances worsen or become more frequent, frustration grows. Anger festers, and at one wrong word from a family member or friend, we lose our cool. And out comes all of our emotions. Our tongues throw darts, flames, knives with no telling when or where they will stop. As a result, those we love end up feeling hurt, and we probably feel no better than we did before we lost our tempers.

Proverbs 29:11 gives us a key to work through these situations. When we feel anger and want to unleash it on someone else, we must ask the Spirit of God for strength. Go to Him in prayer. We take our emotions and lay them at His feet. We allow the Lord to help us respond in a way that glorifies His name.

This act of silence is an act of humility. The world will often tell us that we must defend ourselves no matter what—that we deserve to be heard. Yet the Lord tells us that we will experience much more freedom, joy, and wisdom in not saying a word—being slow to speak. However, there are situations when healthy and loving confrontation is important. The restoration process involves kind and understanding words being spoken between people, not silence or disregarding what has been done. But in that process of restoration, we should listen openly to the thoughts and feelings of others, giving grace where we too have received grace in our lives from our Father in heaven.

Jesus, our perfect Savior, did not speak in self-defense or anger against those who wrongly accused Him—those who sought to kill Him. In quiet and humble submission to the Father, Jesus accomplished the task He was sent from heaven to do, taking His place upon the cross so that we could be saved. May we follow His beautiful example of quiet humility—being slow to speak—allowing our emotions and silence to reflect His strength and power at work within us.

"THIS ACT OF SILENCE IS AN ACT OF HUMILITY."

DAY 141
Rejoice with Hope

You rejoice in this, even though now for a short time, if necessary, you suffer grief in various trials so that the proven character of your faith—more valuable than gold which, though perishable, is refined by fire—may result in praise, glory, and honor at the revelation of Jesus Christ.

1 PETER 1:6–7

Consider raw gold, which is naturally beautiful, yet it is not pure gold. Raw gold has other elements mixed with it. These other elements are called impurities, and for gold to be purified, someone must place it in the fire for refining. During this process, raw gold is placed in a crucible, a small container that holds the gold. The crucible is then placed in the fire. There, the gold melts, and the impurities rise to the top so they can be removed. The gold is now pure and ready to be sold.

The Christian faith mirrors this refining process. We were made in the image of God, but due to the fall, we are naturally marred with impurities. However, after we become Christians, God begins the sanctification process, which means to grow in Christlikeness. Even the crucible mirrors our walk with Christ. A crucible is not only a container in which gold is purified but is also defined as "a severe trial that leads to the creation of something new."

We see the crucible when Christ suffered on the cross so that He could give His righteousness to us, restoring us to God. The cross was the crucible God used to create something new—a new life in Christ for us and the coming of a new heaven and earth. Likewise, the crucible is the reason for our suffering—it is one of the ways God sanctifies us and turns us into new creations. We lay down our old selves and our wants and desires to have things our way, and God turns us into something that looks more like Christ.

Sometimes our sufferings are small—like lost keys, a long day with a cranky toddler, or a season when you and your husband struggle to connect. Sometimes the sufferings are big—like a lost loved one, infertility, or infidelity. But it is all refining fire. It is the crucible in which we are placed, and through it all, God makes us into someone who perfectly reflects Him. At the end of all things, our sufferings are also our hope and our reason to rejoice—our pain is temporary, but our redemption and restoration through Christ are eternal.

DAY 142

Prepare to Meet Your God

Therefore, Israel, that is what I will do to you, and since I will do that to you, Israel, prepare to meet your God! He is here: the one who forms the mountains, creates the wind, and reveals his thoughts to man, the one who makes the dawn out of darkness and strides on the heights of the earth. The Lord, the God of Armies, is his name.

AMOS 4:12-13

Amos was a prophet who spoke the words of God to the Israelites. The book of Amos is unique because, during Amos's life, the Israelites were experiencing peace and prosperity. They believed this tranquil time was a blessing from God because of their obedience. But, this was a misguided belief as they were living in incredible disobedience to God's laws. They just refused to see it. Here, Amos calls the wayward Israelites back to reality by reminding them of the judgment God promised to send if they disobeyed (Deuteronomy 28:15–68). God's judgment and wrath were not things to brush off as inconsequential. They included promises that those who did not keep God's laws would be cursed (Deuteronomy 28:15–18). And that was just the beginning.

Amos reminds us that God creates and sustains the world, and surely He will be able to execute these curses against those who live contrary to His ways. Unfortunately, the Israelites did not repent, and God did send His wrath upon them. Israel was overtaken and all but destroyed only twenty years after this prophetic word from Amos.

Amos's somber discourse regarding God's wrath is a reminder that God does not treat sin lightly. It points us toward Christ, who bears the weight of God's wrath for those who are in Him. And what sweet relief it is, for no human can perfectly keep the law of God. Yet, Jesus did live perfectly according to the law! And by grace through faith, we receive His forgiveness from the wrath we deserve (Romans 5:8–10).

While the Israelites rightly received the wrath of God, those who are in Christ graciously receive the mercy of God. Let this truth move you to praise the Lord for the incredible gift that is salvation through Jesus!

> "WHILE THE ISRAELITES RIGHTLY RECEIVED THE WRATH OF GOD, THOSE WHO ARE IN CHRIST GRACIOUSLY RECEIVE THE MERCY OF GOD."

DAY 143
Payback with Blessing

Finally, all of you be like-minded and sympathetic, love one another, and be compassionate and humble, not paying back evil for evil or insult for insult but, on the contrary, giving a blessing, since you were called for this, so that you may inherit a blessing.

1 PETER 3:8-9

When someone hurts us, we often want to hurt them back. But Scripture calls us to something better. When Jesus was reviled, insulted, and mocked, He did not respond in kind. He did not open His mouth in anger. Instead, He entrusted Himself to God and went willingly to the cross. He was killed for sins He did not commit and falsely accused of heresy. In His trials, He remained firm in His trust in God, responding to their evil with blessing. He rose above their evil words and actions and was obedient to the Father unto death.

Because Jesus responded this way, we, too, can do the same. When others mock, insult, or speak to us with evil intent, we can trust that God sees it all, and He will make all things right one day. This does not mean that you should willingly submit yourself to abuse. Additionally, there are certainly times you may need to involve your local pastor or seek outside help. However, your aim in these actions should not be to hurt the person causing you pain. It is not loving to passively allow someone to stay in their repetitive sins of abuse or manipulation. Yet, in all circumstances, we entrust ourselves to God, the ultimate judge who will one day right every wrong.

In the gospel, we are free. We do not seek revenge for the injustices committed against us. We do not repay evil for evil because we trust that God sees all. Scripture reminds us that our King is coming again—a King who knows all, sees all, and will have justice over all. When we trust in Him, we are blessed. So instead of responding in hate to those who hurt us, we respond in love, even if that is tough love. We bless. We are gentle, humble, and compassionate. And in doing so, we reap the reward of eternal blessings in Christ.

"WHEN OTHERS MOCK, INSULT, OR SPEAK TO US WITH EVIL INTENT, WE CAN TRUST THAT GOD SEES IT ALL, AND HE WILL MAKE ALL THINGS RIGHT ONE DAY."

Our Great Mediator

For there is one God and one mediator between God and humanity, the man Christ Jesus, who gave himself as a ransom for all, a testimony at the proper time.

1 TIMOTHY 2:5–6

A mediator is someone who reconciles two parties. They help resolve a conflict and restore peace. We are born sinners, separated from God because we have inherited the sin that plagues the earth and the people who live in it. We need restoration, but we have no power to reconcile ourselves before God on our own. How could we? He is utterly holy and perfectly righteous.

In the Old Testament, the people of God were reconciled to Him through the work of priests. The priests would go before the presence of the Lord, in the holiest place of the tabernacle or temple, and they would offer atonement for all of the people's sins. Their offering to the Lord for the sins of the people would also be for their own sins, for though religious leaders, they too were sinners. There was never one perfect mediator or priest, and each of them passed away. When one priest died, another took his place.

From the very beginning, the Lord knew that for reconciliation to happen once and for all, He must come and restore us to Himself. So Jesus, God in flesh, came to earth to make peace between God and man. Jesus, though faced with the same temptations and struggles that we face, never sinned. His perfect life made it possible for us to be made holy because He gave up His life for us on the cross. He took our sin and gave us His holiness, His righteousness, bridging the gap between God and His creation that had existed from the moment of the first sin.

Jesus was the only One who could conquer the problem of sin. In love, He offered Himself as the last and final sacrifice. Though Jesus died on the cross, He resurrected from the dead three days later. Jesus overcame death. No more sacrifices were required. And in His resurrection, He created for us a path for salvation. And not only that, we can come before His throne in prayer, confessing our sins, thanking Him, praising His great name. We can rest in the finished work of Christ, for we are now welcome in God's presence, His Spirit inside us. Jesus's sacrifice covers us. His work is enough.

DAY 145
Advocacy for the Unspoken

Speak up for those who have no voice, for the justice of all who are dispossessed.

PROVERBS 31:8

Scripture calls the privileged and the powerful to advocate for the oppressed and needy. Proverbs 31:8, specifically, states such a duty belongs to a king. In biblical times, a king had the greatest authority yet had the most responsibility. His utmost task was to uphold justice in the kingdom. God appointed him to prosecute wrongdoing and protect the vulnerable. A king needed to be reminded of his duties to prevent falling from the Lord's righteous standards. In earlier verses of chapter 31, a mother's voice provides this remembrance to her son, King Lemuel. She explains the oppressed become drunk to numb the pains of life, but for a king, drunkenness will only distract from seeing suffering and providing relief.

In our modern context, we do not have the same kinds of kings who possess sole power and responsibility. But, we do have politicians, supervisors, and advocacy groups who pursue justice in their spheres of influence. Like the kings of Scripture, people in high positions today fall short of God's standards. Sinners, none of us "rule" as God has decreed. We often give ourselves over to fleshly desires to ignore the injustice and pain in our neighborhoods, homes, and even ourselves. Proverbs 31:8 exposes our shortcomings while pointing to fulfillment in Jesus, the King of kings who took the form of a servant. Though He had eternal riches, He was born into poverty and carried the weight of our sin to the cross. Jesus was oppressed by evil's injustice while, like the true King, having His mind fixed on satisfying the justice of God.

Jesus's saving work overcame evil and forgave us of our injustice. With a new identity in Him, God commissioned us to proclaim the kingdom of God throughout our spheres of influence. We can advocate for those who have been silenced and oppressed, remembering that Jesus continues to advocate for us in heaven's court. If we suffer by the hand of evil that lingers in this fallen world, we can remember the Lord's victory and His second coming that will destroy Satan for good. We do not have to succumb to counterfeit pleasures to numb our pain. In Jesus, we are strong and free from the sting of suffering. We can confront the world's injustice while pointing with great confidence to the restorative hope of the gospel.

DAY 146
Hearts and Minds Set on Christ

So if you have been raised with Christ, seek the things above, where Christ is, seated at the right hand of God. Set your minds on things above, not on earthly things. For you died, and your life is hidden with Christ in God.

COLOSSIANS 3:1-3

Our minds and hearts focus on what matters to us most. As followers of Christ, we should set our minds and hearts on the kingdom of God. Through Christ's sacrifice, we have been brought into God's kingdom, which means we live for His kingdom rather than the kingdom of this world. It is as if our earthly citizenship was replaced with a heavenly citizenship when we came to know Christ. Even though our passports say we belong to a certain country, we ultimately belong to the kingdom of God.

Yet, we can still find ourselves living for this world when we are meant to live for God's kingdom. Instead of seeking His kingdom, we become consumed with the kingdom of this world. We get easily wrapped up in matters and desires that are temporary rather than eternal. When we pursue the things of this earth, we forget our position with Christ. As believers, our minds and hearts are meant to match our heavenly position. If we are seated with Christ above, then we should set our minds and hearts on the things above.

To have a heart and mind set on things above is to have a heart and mind set on Christ. When we are focused on Christ, we will live for Christ alone and will not be distracted or consumed by earthly matters. Even if earthly things disappoint us, they will not crush us. We can hold the things of this world loosely, knowing that they are not necessary for our joy, security, and identity.

When you find yourself anxious or upset, ask yourself what you are focusing on most. Is this thing temporary or eternal? Will this matter in the kingdom to come? Is this something that brings honor to Christ? We can ask ourselves these questions on a daily basis. We will find that as we continue to set our minds and hearts upon Christ, we will continue to live out the gospel. We will be committed to seeing the kingdom of God flourish here on earth as it is in heaven.

"IF WE ARE SEATED WITH CHRIST ABOVE, THEN WE SHOULD SET OUR MINDS AND HEARTS ON THE THINGS ABOVE."

DAY 147
Strength in Contentment

I know both how to make do with little, and I know how to make do with a lot. In any and all circumstances I have learned the secret of being content — whether well fed or hungry, whether in abundance or in need. I am able to do all things through him who strengthens me.

PHILIPPIANS 4:12–13

Paul, one of the New Testament authors and leaders in the early church, wrote about contentment in his letter to the Philippian church. At the time, Paul was unjustly imprisoned. Though he experienced terrible circumstances, he chose to rejoice in the gospel. Trusting in Christ's salvation brought him contentment to strengthen him through his suffering. The Holy Spirit gave Paul delight and thanksgiving in Christ so that he could persevere in his faith. Paul, in turn, encouraged the Philippian church to discover the contented life as one that holds grief and joy together.

Paul conformed his life to the way of Christ, who had utmost contentment. Jesus experienced a level of suffering that no human ever had. He faced the full wrath of God on the cross and died to pay the debt for our sin. Knowing that He would experience such spiritual deprivation and separation from the Father, Jesus remembered the joy before Him (Hebrews 12:2). This joy was grounded in His divinity, for He was the eternal Son of God. Jesus would have victory over death and accomplish the plan of redemption. Jesus hung on the cross with peace and contentment, knowing that glory would come.

True contentment does not necessarily mean that one is without any need. As we see in Paul and our Savior, both were content through abuse and rejection. Biblical contentment is a deep satisfaction in God's faithfulness and does not depend on circumstances but on the sure promises of God. We cannot create true contentment within ourselves. This perspective is a product of the Holy Spirit working in us. We can pray that God will reveal to us the secret of contentment that Paul discusses. In times of plenty, let us give our gifts back to God in service. In times of lack, let us lean on God for provision. In all seasons, let us see the Lord as the supplier of our needs. We can look forward to one day being free of any need when Jesus will be with us. We will have eternal life with God, and He will fully satisfy us.

> "JESUS HUNG ON THE CROSS WITH PEACE AND CONTENTMENT, KNOWING THAT GLORY WOULD COME."

DAY 148

The Joy of God's Presence

You reveal the path of life to me; in your presence is abundant joy; at your right hand are eternal pleasures.

PSALM 16:11

Because God is an invisible God, we can often take God's presence for granted. In the presence of a dear friend, we feel joyful and at ease. There is no greater joy to be in the presence of an all-loving and Holy God—the One who made us and has a relationship with us. In the book of Psalms, psalmists such as David rejoiced over being in God's temple. In the temple was where God's manifested His presence. For people like David, it was a gift to be in the same presence of the Almighty God. And we should also find great joy being in God's presence.

Because of Jesus's sacrifice on the cross, God restores those who believe in Christ to Him. God also gives believers the gift of the Holy Spirit, who dwells within them forever. Wherever we go, God's presence is with us, reminding us of the gift of our salvation. By God's grace, He opened our eyes to the truth of the gospel and revealed the path of everlasting life to us. Jesus's sacrifice has secured for us an eternal kingdom that can never be shaken. This should cause us to burst into praise over the goodness of the Lord.

In God's presence is not just joy but *abundant* joy. His presence fuels in us a joy that is overflowing and plentiful. We all struggle to maintain our joy at times through the struggles that come and go through seasons of life. To refill our joy, we must go to the One who gives joy abundantly. We must open God's Word and soak in time in His presence. We must come to Him in prayer, asking for His presence to fill us with joy once again. For the believer in Christ, there should be no deficiency of this abundant joy. For He will never leave us, and that is a reason to rejoice!

"WHEREVER WE GO, GOD'S PRESENCE IS WITH US, REMINDING US OF THE GIFT OF OUR SALVATION. BY GOD'S GRACE, HE OPENED OUR EYES TO THE TRUTH OF THE GOSPEL AND REVEALED THE PATH OF EVERLASTING LIFE TO US."

DAY 149
A New Heart

I will give them integrity of heart and put a new spirit within them; I will remove their heart of stone from their bodies and give them a heart of flesh, so that they will follow my statutes, keep my ordinances, and practice them. They will be my people, and I will be their God.

EZEKIEL 11:19-20

Whatever your season of life, you likely experience plenty of daily frustrations. It can be challenging to follow God's instructions during these moments of frustration. We may be tempted to curse, explode in anger, or act unkindly to those around us. As daily frustrations mount, it is also easy to feel as though we are right to react in these ways.

Thankfully, we have a God who looks at us in our frustrations and has compassion on us still. He knew we would struggle to follow His commands, so He paved a way to send us a helper. God sent His only Son into the world to experience earthly frustrations and temptations, keep the Law that we could not, and die on a cross in our place so that we could be united to Him. Then, as if that was not enough, He sent the Holy Spirit to be with all believers so they would have someone to remind them of His instructions (John 14:16, 26).

When we come to know the Lord, turning to Him in faith, He immediately turns our hearts from stone to flesh. But He also turns our hearts to flesh through sanctification, which is the lifelong process of becoming like Christ. Though sanctification is a lifelong process, it is also something that happens daily. As we experience daily frustrations, God comes to us through the Holy Spirit, our helper, to soften our hearts and enable us to follow His commands.

When we feel our hearts hardening from daily frustrations, we can turn to the Lord. He is good, and He does not leave us to figure out our frustrations on our own. Instead, God gave us the Holy Spirit, who will remind us of His instructions and help us live them out, even when life feels as though it is too much. In moments of frustration, may you turn to the Lord who stands ready to help and strengthen you as you seek to walk in His ways.

"WE HAVE A GOD WHO LOOKS AT US IN OUR FRUSTRATIONS AND HAS COMPASSION ON US STILL."

DAY 150
Watching and Waiting

But I will look to the Lord; I will wait for the God of my salvation. My God will hear me.

MICAH 7:7

Pain. Suffering. Evil. Sin. It is easy to feel overwhelmed by all of the anguish and affliction in the world. The news headlines never stop but seem only to become more frequent and more sorrow-filled. When it feels like corruption and calamity have the upper hand, we can learn what to do from Micah's response in today's verse.

Micah was a prophet who lived in Jerusalem when the people and kings of Israel were corrupt. They ignored God's commands, abused His faithfulness to them by exploiting the land He had given them for wickedness, and openly worshiped idols. As a result, there was rampant chaos and evil in Israel.

God sent Micah to rebuke the people's sins and the leaders, but they rejected his words and refused to return to the Lord. In Micah 7:2, he cries, "Faithful people have vanished from the land; there is no one upright among the people. All of them wait in ambush to shed blood; they hunt each other with a net." This circumstance may sound familiar to the world in which we live. There can be the feeling that everyone is out to harm each other as we look over our shoulders, wondering if evil is right around the corner.

In the face of such peril, Micah does not fall into despair but speaks hope. Instead of watching over his shoulder, he chooses to watch for the Lord. Instead of waiting for harm to befall him, he steadies his gaze upon the God who will save him. Like a deep, long exhale that expels all worry and fear, Micah's trust in the Lord is rejuvenating and refreshing. He knows that God will not leave Israel to their own devices forever. He believed God heard his plea for help and intended to save Israel from themselves. And that He did!

Jesus is the salvation Micah was awaiting. Because of His great sacrifice for our sins, He covers our sin with His righteousness when we trust in Him. Jesus delivers us from evil, promises eternal joy and peace, and redeems every evil we experience for His glory and our good. And, one day, He will return to vanquish all evil forever! Today, may you choose to watch for, wait on, and rest in the Lord's salvation.

"JESUS IS THE SALVATION MICAH WAS AWAITING."

DAY 151
For Such a Time as This

Mordecai told the messenger to reply to Esther, "Don't think that you will escape the fate of all the Jews because you are in the king's palace. If you keep silent at this time, relief and deliverance will come to the Jewish people from another place, but you and your father's family will be destroyed. Who knows, perhaps you have come to your royal position for such a time as this."

ESTHER 4:13–14

High-risk jobs are not usually the business of queens. However, this was not the case for Queen Esther. A Jewish exile, Esther became the wife of King Ahasuerus, who had summoned women from each province to choose a queen. Esther was most favored, and King Ahasuerus placed a crown on her head. Later, Esther's cousin, Mordecai, found himself in trouble with Haman, a leading official in King Ahasuerus's court. Mordecai would not bow to Haman, so Haman decreed that all Jews be murdered. Mordecai sent word to Esther, telling her to intercede on behalf of the Jews, but Esther knew that anyone who went before the king could be put to death. Mordecai explained that God would ultimately save His people, with or without her, but perhaps this was something the Lord had called her to "for such a time as this."

Esther responded with resolve, seeking the Lord through fasting before she approached the king. Esther's risk was based upon knowing God's character. She knew that regardless of the outcome, God would save His people. Her statement, "If I perish, I perish" (Esther 4:16), was not hopelessness but trust in the covenant promises of God who would remain committed to His people, preserving them through Haman's edict, even if Esther failed. For His plan of redemption, God would bring the promised Savior, Jesus Christ, through the Jews. The risk was in Esther's favor, for she had already received the favor of God.

When we face our own life-threatening decisions, we too can approach such decisions with confident hope. We can be sure that what the Lord calls us to, He will also provide us the strength to accomplish. God uses us where we are, in the positions He has placed us, to carry out His perfect plan. And as we allow Him to use us, hands open to what He has for our lives, we can rest in the surety of His hand to guide us and use us in His greater story of redemption.

"THE RISK WAS IN ESTHER'S FAVOR, FOR SHE HAD ALREADY RECEIVED THE FAVOR OF GOD."

DAY 152

The Blessing in Our Testing

Blessed is the one who endures trials, because when he has stood the test he will receive the crown of life that God has promised to those who love him.

JAMES 1:12

When we experience trials, it can feel like anything but a blessing. Our trials can make us walk through pain, grief, and heartache. We can feel overwhelmed and afflicted rather than feel blessed. The weight of our trials can lead us to ask ourselves, How can blessings be found in such suffering? God does not test us and place us within trials without purpose. He is not a malicious God who allows us to experience suffering with no gain or goal.

A helpful way we can view our trials is by visualizing a race. The run itself is not easy. But once runners cross the finish line, they receive a prize for their run and look back with joy on what they accomplished. Like a race, our trials not only have an end but have a glorious reward at the end. Yet we must endure our trials by persevering to the end. We persevere as we continue to step forward in faith and cling to God's strength and power. However, we can hinder the purpose of our trials when we step back rather than step forward. We can stunt the growth God has for us when we give up and allow our trials to overwhelm us. Our trials may be difficult, but God has equipped us with His presence to persevere. He blesses us in our trials by extending to us His strength and power. As we trust in Him and rest in His strength, we will find ourselves with the ability to stand the test.

Jesus persevered in the trial of the cross by setting His focus on what was ahead. Like Christ, we too can persevere in our trials as we set our gaze on the joy to come. We can abound in hope, knowing one day we will receive the crown of life, the reward of eternity with Christ. As we stand the test, we grow in Christlikeness. The blessing in our trials is not only future salvation but sanctification in the present. As we move forward in faith, our tests and trials will shape us into the image of Christ. Growth in Christlikeness makes trials worth enduring. May we abound in faith in our trials and cling to the blessing found within trials and at the end.

"OUR TRIALS MAY BE DIFFICULT, BUT GOD HAS EQUIPPED US WITH HIS PRESENCE TO PERSEVERE."

DAY 153
A Gentle Answer

A gentle answer turns away anger, but a harsh word stirs up wrath.
PROVERBS 15:1

We all have desires, and when we do not get them, we fight (James 4:1–3). We want respect, affirmation, and to prove our value. We look to others to satisfy us, and when they fail, we become angry. Or conversely, when we fail the expectations of others, they become angry with us. Arguments often begin as minor transgressions and quickly turn into an exploding landmine. Conversation grows heated, and harsh words fly as quickly as the steam pours from our ears.

Reflecting on your past experience, when someone speaks to you harshly, how have you responded? Does getting angry help you in those moments? Does it help you to fight fire with fire, responding to someone's wrath with a matching accusatory word? Often the answer is "no."

Admittedly, it can be very tempting to respond to fire with fire in an argument. When someone yells at us or falsely accuses us, we want to fight back. We want to justify ourselves and throw at them what they have thrown at us. But this is not the Christian way. When Christ was reviled, mocked, and falsely accused, He did not revile in return (1 Peter 2:23). When they hurled insults at Him, He made no threats. Instead, He trusted in God, who judges justly. Jesus, the only human who was ever perfect, was yelled at, abused, and mistreated. He is the only one who could have justly defended every perfect action. But He did not do this. When reviled, He trusted the Father.

Because of the gospel, we can respond with a gentle answer during an argument. We have a God who will bring justice to every wrong, and we can trust in His perfect wisdom. We can gently respond to the harsh words of others because we have a Great High Priest who has treated us with gentleness and care. In light of the grace we have received, we can now show grace to others.

> "BECAUSE OF THE GOSPEL, WE CAN RESPOND WITH A GENTLE ANSWER DURING AN ARGUMENT. WE HAVE A GOD WHO WILL BRING JUSTICE TO EVERY WRONG, AND WE CAN TRUST IN HIS PERFECT WISDOM."

DAY 154
The Barren Places

Though the fig tree does not bud and there is no fruit on the vines, though the olive crop fails and the fields produce no food, though the flocks disappear from the pen and there are no herds in the stalls, yet I will celebrate in the Lord; I will rejoice in the God of my salvation! The Lord my Lord is my strength; he makes my feet like those of a deer and enables me to walk on mountain heights!

HABAKKUK 3:17–19

We can find joy and hope in the barren places of our lives. We see this in the short story of the prophet Habakkuk. When God's people rebelled against Him, Habakkuk cries out to the Lord, asking why He would not intercede. God responds, saying that He will bring the Babylonians to enslave them. Habakkuk is broken that the Lord must use such an evil nation as Babylon to bring judgment to His people.

We, too, can look around at the evil around us in this world so broken by sin. But we take heart, and we have hope. Psalm 55:22 reminds us that the Lord will not allow the righteous to be shaken. While this does not mean that bad things will never happen or that we will never see the effects of evil around us, we can take comfort in knowing that we find our security in Christ, our refuge and stronghold in times of trouble.

The Lord tells Habakkuk that the righteous live by faith and reminds the prophet that He can be trusted, though Habakkuk may not be able to see how God is working. Evil seemed to be taking the victory, but evil will not ultimately win, for Christ made a way when He conquered the grave. One day, the earth will be filled not with evil but the fullness of God's glory. As the book closes, Habakkuk says he will rejoice in the God of His salvation. Surely, the Lord is his strength, and He is our strength as well.

As we go through life and come to barren places where it seems God is wholly removed, let us remember that He is present and loves us. He is working in ways that we cannot see, in places we may never see redeemed and restored until He returns. Though we may not understand His plan and all seems hopeless, our God is ever the same. Even in seemingly empty places, God is victorious.

"EVEN IN SEEMINGLY EMPTY PLACES, GOD IS VICTORIOUS."

DAY 155
All for Him

> *He is the image of the invisible God, the firstborn over all creation. For everything was created by him, in heaven and on earth, the visible and the invisible, whether thrones or dominions or rulers or authorities—all things have been created through him and for him. He is before all things, and by him all things hold together. He is also the head of the body, the church; he is the beginning, the firstborn from the dead, so that he might come to have first place in everything. For God was pleased to have all his fullness dwell in him, and through him to reconcile everything to himself, whether things on earth or things in heaven, by making peace through his blood, shed on the cross.*
>
> COLOSSIANS 1:15–20

Jesus's name is likely familiar to all of us. We have heard it, read it, and thought it countless times. But sometimes, the more familiar something becomes, the less spectacular it seems.

In this passage, Paul and Timothy are writing to the Christians at Colossae who doubted Jesus's divinity. Paul and Timothy intended to put those doubts to rest through the contents of this letter. They explain that Jesus is God in the flesh. He is the actual, physical incarnation of God. Jesus created the world alongside the Father (John 1:3). He created the physical earth, the invisible heavenly realms, physical beings.

Jesus existed before anything else, and He sustains the existence of everything. He was human but was not merely a man. Jesus is also the head of the Church. While He created all things, He personally leads and nourishes the body of Christ. He arose from the dead and is supreme in every way. He has first place in everything. And Jesus's preeminence, priority, and supremeness meant that God was happy to fill His humanly body to the full with His presence. Like the tabernacle in the Old Testament held the presence of God, Jesus held the full and holy presence of God while He walked the earth.

Jesus made pure and lasting peace between God and man when He shed His blood on the cross for the sins of the world. All things were created through Him and for Him. And He gave His life so that we could be reconciled to Himself. The name of Jesus is not a commonplace name. Jesus stands alone as supreme. Let the wonder of His name wash over you afresh today.

DAY 156

Blessing in Suffering

Dear friends, don't be surprised when the fiery ordeal comes among you to test you, as if something unusual were happening to you. Instead, rejoice as you share in the sufferings of Christ, so that you may also rejoice with great joy when his glory is revealed. If you are ridiculed for the name of Christ, you are blessed, because the Spirit of glory and of God rests on you.

1 PETER 4:12–14

Have you ever experienced traveling somewhere unfamiliar to you? While the idea of experiencing an unfamiliar place might seem exciting, sometimes the experience can be jarring. Everything from the language to food to the rhythms of daily life can be different. Excitement can give way to discomfort. And discomfort causes a longing for home.

In a way, believers also experience homesickness while living in the world. We have an inner sense that things should be different. We know that God made us to experience perfect love, peace, and joy. Yet, in our daily lives, our experiences are far from this. We instead encounter pain, suffering, chaos, and sorrow. And all of this hardship makes us ache for heaven.

Homesickness is a heart-wrenching feeling. If you have felt it, then you know this well. And heavenly homesickness is something all believers will have for all of their earthly lives. This world is not our home, and our souls know it.

When our suffering makes us ache for the perfection of heaven, we can rejoice, not in our pain but in the fact that we ache as Christ ached. We suffer as He suffered. When we feel the pain of grief, persecution, or adversity, Christ stands before us, reminding us that He, too, has felt this pain.

We also rejoice in anything that detaches us from the comforts of this world and fixes our gaze on heaven. Our pain has a way of turning us toward Christ, and that is why we can embrace it.

But just as we share in His pain, we will also one day rejoice with Him in glory when suffering ends. Even while we suffer, the Spirit of God rests on us. We are not alone in our temporary pain and will not suffer forever. Our homesickness will one day fade as we enter into eternal joy in Christ. Are you craving the comfort of your eternal home in heaven today? Look to Christ. Remember God's Spirit rests on you. This feeling is momentary. Your joy will be eternal.

DAY 157
A Testimony of Grace

This saying is trustworthy and deserving of full acceptance: "Christ Jesus came into the world to save sinners" – and I am the worst of them. But I received mercy for this reason, so that in me, the worst of them, Christ Jesus might demonstrate his extraordinary patience as an example to those who would believe in him for eternal life.

1 TIMOTHY 1:15–16

Paul. A Pharisee. A persecutor of Christians. Reviler of the Christian faith. On the road to Damascus, Paul encountered Jesus Christ, and his life was changed forever. By the grace of Jesus, Paul became a testimony for the gospel he previously scorned. He became a part of the people he once persecuted. Paul's former life led Paul to believe that he was the worst of sinners. He had spent his life rejecting and opposing Christianity. Yet, Paul recognized that his former life was purposeful for his testimony. Paul was a witness of the mercy of Jesus, who can save even the worst of sinners.

Every testimony is a testimony of grace. Regardless of what your life was like before Christ, your life has been changed. Jesus has brought you from death to life, saved you from the punishment of your sin, and given you freedom. He has established you as forgiven, redeemed, adopted, and beloved. You are not who you once were. Your testimony is powerful because it declares the power of Christ within you. Through your testimony, others can learn how they too can receive the mercy and grace of Christ, no matter who they are or what they have done.

Paul's testimony declares that no one is too sinful to come to Christ. No one has a past too heavy for Christ to forgive. If Jesus can save and transform Paul, He can save and transform anyone. Like Paul, we may feel as though we are the worst of sinners, but Christ stands ready to pour His grace upon us. Christ's work on the cross declares His heart for sinners. He loves sinners so much that He was willing to die for them. Jesus came into the world to save sinners, to save you.

Grace marks every page of our testimonies. Now, we have the opportunity to hold out our stories for all to hear and see. We have the opportunity to joyfully declare Christ's work of mercy in our lives. As believers, we stand as witnesses to the transforming grace of Jesus Christ.

DAY 158
Made in God's Image

So God created man in his own image; he created him in the image of God; he created them male and female.

GENESIS 1:27

What binds every human being together is that we are made in the image of God. Every person we pass in the street and every person we see on television is made in God's image. The implications of being made in the image of God are wondrous, but we likely do not think of them often. It is easy for us to read Genesis 1:27 and fail to grasp what it truly means to be God's image-bearers. If we cannot grasp it, how can we live out what it means to be an image-bearer of Christ?

Bearing God's image means that all people are created like Him and reflect Him. God has molded His creation to share His qualities, though we cannot possess those qualities that only He can like perfect knowledge and power. We do, however imperfectly, possess qualities of God like His love, mercy, and wisdom. As image-bearers, we reflect Him through our actions. But the presence of sin has marred us as if there is a crack on our reflection. We are broken image-bearers, unable to fully reflect the glory of God because of our sin. This is why we need Jesus.

Through Jesus's sacrifice on the cross, those who believe and trust in Him have their image redeemed. Because of Christ, believers can "put on the new self, the one created according to God's likeness in righteousness and purity of the truth" (Ephesians 4:24). For those of us in Christ, our lives are opportunities to reflect God's glory and the gospel truth. As we put on our new selves, we show who God is by the power of the Holy Spirit. We have an opportunity to reflect the glory of God in the way we live. Knowing this, how often do we truly live this way? How often do we live for God's glory alone? How often do we hurt the image of God by mistreating other image-bearers? How we live impacts how others see Jesus. Every day, we must ask ourselves whether or not we reflect the truth of who God is by the way we live. May we glorify the Lord and declare the beauty of the gospel in everything we say and do.

"BEARING GOD'S IMAGE MEANS THAT ALL PEOPLE ARE CREATED LIKE HIM AND REFLECT HIM."

DAY 159
Is My Life Pleasing to the Lord?

May the words of my mouth and the meditation of my heart be acceptable to you, Lord, my rock and my Redeemer.

PSALM 19:14

Psalm 19 contains a cry of David's worship to God. The shepherd boy, who is the king of Israel, declares that God's majesty and glory are all around us. The heavens and skies above testify to who He is and what He has done. Their message about the Lord has reached every person and nation; no one is excluded from seeing God's glory.

David offers a series of statements that further describe the Lord's work. His instruction is perfect, and His testimony is trustworthy (Psalm 19:7). His precepts are right, and His commands are radiant (Psalm 19:8). We are to revere Him, and we can trust all of His decisions and judgments. In fact, David tells us we are to desire His counsel more than gold, and the Lord's wisdom is sweeter than the sweetest honey.

In light of who the Lord is, David realizes everything he is not. David knows he cannot be described as perfect or trustworthy. He says in verse 19 that there are sins that men do not even realize they commit. Sin has so infected us and the world we live in that we do not see all the ways we grieve the Lord. In his fallenness, David turns to the Lord for help. He knows the Lord is the only One who can cleanse him from sin. David has a posture of humility before God, and he asks that his words and the meditations of his heart be pleasing to the Lord.

David wonderfully exemplifies what it means to seek God. He begins with praise and adoration, realizing how sinful he is in light of God's majesty. He seeks the Lord for help so he can resist sin and be pleasing to Him. We are only able to seek God because He has given us a new heart through the gospel. David's request to the Lord was most certainly not a one-time event. We need the Lord's help in pleasing Him every day. And this is a request He loves, for it is done out of honor and love for Him. As we grow in our walks with the Lord and realize the depth of our sinfulness, He is ever-present, helping us to follow Him in the way we live our lives.

"WE ARE ONLY ABLE TO SEEK GOD BECAUSE HE HAS GIVEN US A NEW HEART THROUGH THE GOSPEL."

DAY 160
Pride Goes Before the Fall

Pride comes before destruction, and an arrogant spirit before a fall.
PROVERBS 16:18

Do you remember times in your life when your chest swelled with pride over a great accomplishment or victory? Maybe you had overcome something really difficult, or you had demonstrated a particular talent that others found praiseworthy. Maybe you made a really great meal for your family, or maybe you finally were able to keep your plants alive all summer! It is certainly not wrong to feel happy or proud of success or an accomplishment, but when our pride consumes us in a way that leads to arrogance, things can become disastrous.

When we experience those moments of victory, there can be moments of failure coming quickly upon us. Unfortunately, our success can often make us rely too much on ourselves. We get so caught up in what we have done that we begin to think we can do it all. And that is simply not the case. To think you can do all things is to claim a characteristic that does not belong to you. The Lord is the only One who is omnipotent, "having unlimited power" or "able to do anything."

Out of the Lord's kindness and mercy toward us, He does not let us go very long believing that we can do all things on our own. And when we pause and think about this behavior, we realize that by believing this, we are elevating ourselves to be equal to God. Incredibly, He gives us more grace! He lets us fall, and when we are on the floor, spinning from our misstep, we are able to wake up from the illusion that we are "all that." We return to the Lord in repentance and humility, and when we do, we can experience the opposite of this verse. Humility before the Lord does not lead to destruction but to life. And a humble spirit leads to being firmly planted in Christ.

When you are excited about an accomplishment, victory, or success and you can feel pride taking too much of a hold in your heart, pause for a moment, and remember that you are weak in your own strength. Thank the Lord that He has allowed you to experience blessing, and ask Him to help you remember your dependence on Him. He is enough for you, and His omnipotence enables you to rest and cease from striving.

"A HUMBLE SPIRIT LEADS TO BEING FIRMLY PLANTED IN CHRIST."

DAY 161
Open Our Eyes, Lord

Open my eyes so that I may contemplate wondrous things from your instruction.
PSALM 119:18

Often when we read God's Word, we jump into the text without giving a thought to the Lord's presence with us. We hunker down and begin with no prayer for understanding or wisdom. Many of us have limited time, or the day has hit us over the head with responsibilities and tasks. We feel the pressure to get going, feeling our time slip away from us.

The problem with rushing into our quiet times without a thought about the Lord is that we only add to our incorrect sense of self-sufficiency. When we try to read our Bibles and learn from the text without seeking the author of its words, we communicate to the Lord that we do not need Him. Yet, we need Him desperately. He is the One who calls us to read His Word, but He is also the One who equips us to learn as we do. He does not leave us on our own as we seek to know Him. He guides us and teaches us.

He shows us wondrous things. He gives us His very own instruction. And every time we open His Word, He opens our eyes and lets us see more and more of His truth. We will never know everything about Him, and Scripture will always have more to show us. This can seem frustrating, but it keeps us dependent on God. We need Him every moment of our lives.

So when we approach the Lord in His Word, may we come with humility and reverence. May we pause before Him and acknowledge that He is the One who gives us understanding. And may we remember that on our own, we can do nothing without Him—we would not have a hope without His coming into the world to save us from our sin. And when we trust Him as our Savior, His Spirit comes to live inside us, guiding us and helping us to grow. This truth should lead us to wait on His help each day. And as we learn truth and instruction from His Word, we will taste more of His goodness. Praise God that He opened our eyes to the truth of the gospel, and He continues to open our eyes to how the gospel changes everything about us.

"WE NEED HIM EVERY MOMENT OF OUR LIVES."

DAY 162
In All of Life, Fear God

When all has been heard, the conclusion of the matter is this: fear God and keep his commands, because this is for all humanity.

ECCLESIASTES 12:13

The Bible talks about a reverent fear for God that leads us to honor and worship God in light of His holiness. This is a godly expression of fear, stemming from the belief that God is perfect and mighty and will accomplish His purposes. Psalm 111:10 says, "The fear of the Lord is the beginning of wisdom; all of those who follow his instructions have good insight. His praises endure forever." As we learn more about God, we grow in healthy and reverent fear of who He is. We are not afraid of Him but understand the magnitude of His character in a way that leads us to obey, serve, and worship Him. This understanding postures our hearts in awe of who He is.

God is worthy of our obedience and praise. And we are called to worship Him with a reverent fear of His worthiness. However, because of the fall, we are tempted to fear the troubles of this world. The fall is tragic with far-reaching effects. But it could never deter God's plan of redemption. Jesus Christ came to the world in human form to live in reverent fear of the Lord, modeling a life of worship and doing all things to the glory of God's name. In doing so, Jesus's death crushed our sins on the cross so that through salvation, our sin could never crush us. Freedom from sin also means freedom from our fears. We are no longer enslaved by fear because Jesus has purchased for us a peace that surpasses all understanding. He has purchased a promise that He will carry us all the way to glory where the only fear that remains is awe-struck, wonder-filled, worshipful, and reverent fear of the Lord.

A deeper fear of the Lord overshadows every fear of the world, impacting every part of our lives. We cultivate a deeper fear of the Lord by meditating on the truth of God's Word and the truth of God's character by keeping His commands, repenting of our pride and tendency toward self-sufficiency, and preaching to ourselves the good news of the gospel. A fear of the Lord is essential to life and brings us to wisely and joyfully trust and obey Him in all things.

"GOD IS WORTHY OF OUR OBEDIENCE AND PRAISE."

DAY 163
Armor Up

Put on the full armor of God so that you can stand against the schemes of the devil.

EPHESIANS 6:11

The Armor of God serves as a prominent passage in the New Testament. It follows the metaphor of a battle, but the armor of God is drawn from the very nature of God. He has not simply asked us to put on the armor, but He has worn it for Himself as shown in the Old Testament, by acting as a great warrior, our Redeemer, to execute justice against the enemies of Israel (Isaiah 59:17). God set out to redeem and reclaim His people from the spiritual enemies of this world. What God set forth in Israel's exodus and rescue, He continued through the redemptive work of His Son, Jesus, on the cross. Now, through salvation, His armor is imparted to us so that we may walk in His ways and reflect His presence in this world.

Engaging in a spiritual battle takes supernatural help outside of ourselves, and we find a hearty defense in the Armor of God. The Armor of God includes: the belt of truth, armor of righteousness, sandals fitted in the gospel of peace, shield of faith, helmet of salvation, and sword of the Spirit. We lack everything apart from Christ but lack no good thing with Him. Everything He provides for us serves a specific purpose in the fight we face each day. Each piece of armor serves us intentionally and purposefully to accomplish God's will.

The Armor of God requires dependence on the Lord for strength and provision, a readiness to take action, and a willingness to do so. We cannot passively take up the Armor of God, but instead, we must actively lean into the protection God has provided for us through that armor, for we cannot fight this battle alone. We need God's Armor, and as we armor up, we can be assured that we have protection. Yet, wearing His armor does not mean we will never suffer—after all, even our great Redeemer with perfect access to the armor suffered. Therefore, we must remember that though evil battles us at every corner, God ultimately wins the war. Jesus can equip us, rightfully, because He knows what is required to defeat evil once and for all.

"WE MUST ACTIVELY LEAN INTO THE PROTECTION GOD HAS PROVIDED FOR US THROUGH THAT ARMOR, FOR WE CANNOT FIGHT THIS BATTLE ALONE."

DAY 164
Render to Caesar

"Show me a denarius. Whose image and inscription does it have?" "Caesar's," they said. "Well then," he told them, "give to Caesar the things that are Caesar's, and to God the things that are God's."

LUKE 20:24-25

We all feel the tension of navigating the world as God's redeemed image-bearers. Sometimes we can become legalistic, defining the Christian faith outside the saving work of Christ. However, in dealing with culture, we must avoid allowing our personal and generational worldviews to dictate how we respond to social and political issues. Instead, we should seek wisdom in Scripture. Through God's Word, we can trust that our Savior will give us the grace and truth needed to apply in every cultural scenario.

Jerusalem's religious authorities were enraged at Jesus's popularity among the people. They sent spies to ask Jesus if it was lawful to pay taxes to Caesar. This question addressed a controversial topic of the time. The Jewish people were oppressed under Roman rule through heavy tax requirements. If Jesus answered "yes," the people might have interpreted that as Him not being the Messiah, predicted to be the Anointed Savior for God's people. If Jesus answered "no," the Roman authority might assume Jesus was trying to overthrow Caesar. But Jesus answered in such a way that He could be accused of neither. He asked whose image was on their coin, and they identified the image as Caesar's. Jesus responded that the coin should then be given to Caesar. But, because God's image was on the people, they should be given to God. In His wisdom, Jesus identified that there were obligations to both governments and to God.

As Christ's ambassadors, we should be law-abiding citizens of the state and recognize that we submit to a higher authority because we are God's image-bearers. Sin distorted that image. Yet, through faith in the person and work of Jesus Christ, we are redeemed from our fallen nature. The blood of Christ bought us from the hand of evil and brought us into a relationship with God. Now, as citizens of heaven, we have an eternal hope that enables us to submit to government authority as worship unto the Lord. Even if we suffer under an oppressive regime, we can trust that God will help us to persevere in our faith in Christ, and He will come again to fully manifest His kingdom on earth.

"JESUS IDENTIFIED THAT THERE WERE OBLIGATIONS TO BOTH GOVERNMENTS AND TO GOD."

DAY 165
A Generational Testimony

Hear this, you elders; listen, all you inhabitants of the land. Has anything like this ever happened in your days or in the days of your ancestors? Tell your children about it, and let your children tell their children, and their children the next generation.

JOEL 1:2–3

In the past, passing down stories was common. Telling stories to younger generations was a way to pass down history. While it may be more enjoyable to hear a happy story, a realistic story often includes both the good and the bad. And to receive a full understanding of the past, it is helpful to hear the highs and the lows.

In the book of Joel, the nation of Israel was experiencing punishment due to their rebellion against God. Because of their sin, God allowed other nations to take over Israel and send them into exile. Through the prophet Joel, God commanded that the Israelites share this occurrence with their children to pass down their history. Without reading the book of Joel, it might seem confusing to us that God would want such a painful part of Israel's history to be shared. Yet, as the book unfolds, we learn that even though exile would come upon Israel, God would deliver and restore them once again.

The passing down of this story to the next generations was a testimony of God's grace. Those who heard of God's deliverance and restoration of Israel were taught how God is a faithful God. As followers of Christ, Israel's story is our story. Through Christ's sacrifice on the cross, we are brought into the family of God. But unlike Israel, we have seen how God's deliverance and restoration were ultimately filled through Jesus Christ. Exile in the Old Testament foreshadows what would take place in the New Testament when God would come to deliver mankind.

As believers, we have a generational testimony to share. We have the good news of the gospel to tell those around us. Like Israel, this testimony includes brokenness but also redemption and restoration. We have the opportunity to open God's Word and tell stories of God's great faithfulness and be honest about the reality of sin and the hope of our Savior who saved us from that sin. Prayerfully, those we tell will remember this testimony and be shaped by it to come to know the Lord. May we proclaim God's deliverance so that generations to come may place their faith and trust in Him.

DAY 166
To Him Who is Able

Now to him who is able to protect you from stumbling and to make you stand in the presence of his glory, without blemish and with great joy, to the only God our Savior, through Jesus Christ our Lord, be glory, majesty, power, and authority before all time, now and forever. Amen.

JUDE 24-25

No matter how hard we try, we are not limitless people. We fall short, we fail, we tire, and we sin. We do not possess enough power and wisdom to make the right choice every time. In the moments we feel weak and powerless, there is a truth to which we can cling: Christ is able. He is able to give us His strength when we tire, forgiveness when we sin, grace when we fall short. Christ is able to give us all that we need to walk through this life and into the life to come.

Though some seasons of life will be hard, and there will certainly be times we mess up, Christ gives us His steady hand to help us step confidently forward in the plans He has for us. He is there, able to steady us as we are tempted to sin, and while we will certainly mess up sometimes—even as we follow Him—He doesn't remove His hand from our lives. Jesus remains at our side, ready and able to help us walk in holiness as we depend on Him.

Christ is also able to present us blameless before the Lord. Through salvation, we receive Christ's forgiveness, which washes away the debt of our sin. We can stand before God, innocent because of the blood of Jesus. We were unable to make ourselves clean, but Christ was able. His grace and forgiveness allow for us to be blameless in the eyes of the Father. We do not have to fear condemnation when we go before the Lord one day. We can instead have full confidence right now, knowing that we are truly forgiven.

In every place of life where we are unable, Christ is able. May we depend on Him in all things. Let us cling to Him in every area of our lives. To Him be the glory, majesty, power, and authority, now and forever.

"JESUS REMAINS AT OUR SIDE, READY AND ABLE TO HELP US WALK IN HOLINESS AS WE DEPEND ON HIM."

DAY 167

A God Who Cares

You clothed me with skin and flesh, and wove me together with bones and tendons. You gave me life and faithful love, and your care has guarded my life.

JOB 10:11–12

To be cared for is a natural, human desire. Knowing someone cares for us can make us feel loved and secure, but perhaps that love and security is something you struggle to find. What a comfort that even if others fail to care for us, we have a God who does—the One who knit us together with His hands and breathed life into our bodies.

As a loving creator, God never abandons His creation. He has not created us to fend for ourselves. God is both our Creator and Father who loves and takes care of His children, and even in moments of struggle, God never removes His protective hand from our lives. He is like an earthly father who refuses to leave his child's side. He never relinquishes His faithful love for us. Unlike human love, it is everlasting. As flawed people, we can fail to care for others consistently. It is easy for us to become selfish and care only for ourselves. But God never stops caring for us.

When difficulties come, we may find ourselves asking the Lord if He even cares about us. In a time of immense pain and grief, Job, too, questioned God's care for him. In his position of suffering, Job felt as though God had abandoned him. Later on, in the book of Job, God answers Job's questions by affirming His character. As the creator of all things, God asserts that all things are in His hands. He creates, protects, provides, and takes. His providential hand exemplifies His great care. We can rest secure in every moment of our lives, knowing we have a God who sovereignly cares for us. He has demonstrated His care for us by sending us His Son, and in His grace, He will take care of us for the rest of our lives. Because He has given us life, He sustains us. In the caring hands of our Creator, we are forever held.

"AS A LOVING CREATOR, GOD NEVER ABANDONS HIS CREATION. HE HAS NOT CREATED US TO FEND FOR OURSELVES."

DAY 168
Hidden Faithfulness

Be careful not to practice your righteousness in front of others to be seen by them. Otherwise, you have no reward with your Father in heaven.

MATTHEW 6:1

Matthew 6:1 is a segment of Jesus's Sermon on the Mount. As He details the ethics of God's kingdom, scholars note how the sermon mirrors the commands the Lord gave Moses in the Old Testament. On Mount Sinai, Moses received the Law that identified the Israelites as God's chosen people. But, the Israelites and their descendants failed to keep the Law, and those who did keep it did so for outward show. Now, Jesus reveals the true intent for those laws: to love God and others. Jesus shows the nature of true obedience, one that is centered on the heart's attitude. Jesus called His followers and calls us now to glorify God by pursuing kingdom ethics as a reflection of His character and gratitude for salvation. Ultimately, the Law is fulfilled in Jesus. The Law presents a high standard that is too much for a human to bear in his or her own capacity. Sinners, we cannot live up to the call for such inner purity. Instead, we would be tempted to feign obedience when our hearts are far from God.

Jesus began this verse with a warning, giving us a clue into the waywardness of our hearts. He warns against doing good works to be seen by others. Jesus called these people hypocrites, those who say one thing and believe another. These people did not love God and others but sought their own glory. The hypocrites deceived themselves, for they thought they were storing up merit to enter into the kingdom and receive the gift of eternal life. But, Jesus said they would have no reward with God in heaven. Our good works are like filthy rags; our best deeds cannot outweigh the cosmic treason and covenant violations we have committed against the Lord. We must instead cling to the perfect work of Christ.

We need the Holy Spirit to help us obtain kingdom ethics and cultivate a hidden faithfulness. In our secret places, our heavenly Father always sees us. He has approved of us in Christ. Even while we were sinners, He proved His love by dying for us. Let us guard our hearts against prideful attitudes and haughty actions. We can pray that God will give us an inner faith that shows itself in outward humility and gratitude.

"EVEN WHILE WE WERE SINNERS, HE PROVED HIS LOVE BY DYING FOR US."

DAY 169
My Sheep Hear My Voice

My sheep hear my voice, I know them, and they follow me. I give them eternal life, and they will never perish. No one will snatch them out of my hand. My Father, who has given them to me, is greater than all. No one is able to snatch them out of the Father's hand.

JOHN 10:27–29

There are times when God feels close, and we are sure He is moving in our lives. And there are times when He feels distant, and we wonder if He is as near to us as we thought He was. John 10:27–29 gives us a promise to hold tightly to in the times we feel far from God.

It is simply this: God, in His unlimited power, securely keeps all those who know Him and follow Him. Believers are secure in their relationship with God because He is a trustworthy shepherd.

The sheep and shepherd analogy is often used in the Bible to describe the relationship between God and believers. Shepherds fed, watered, protected, and provided for their sheep. But Jesus was the Good Shepherd. He not only did these things, but He also laid down His life for His sheep so that they might find eternal life in Him (John 10:11).

A mere human shepherd was limited in the protection they provided their sheep. They needed to sleep and eat. Their strength and wisdom were finite. But, Jesus, the Good Shepherd, eternally saves, protects, and holds His sheep. He never overlooks or loses track of His flock. His sheep are safe and secure for eternity.

Even more than that, Jesus's sheep hear His voice and follow Him. This does not mean we will hear Jesus audibly every day but, rather, that we have His words readily available at all times to us through the Bible. And when we read His words, we hear His voice, and the Holy Spirit in us moves us to follow His words.

We follow Him as He holds tightly to us. We are His flock. He is our Shepherd. Those who belong to Christ are always firmly and securely in the Father's hands. They know Christ, follow Christ, have eternal life, and will never perish. There is no inner feeling or outer situation strong enough to take them out of God's hands. No, nothing can snatch them away.

"JESUS'S SHEEP HEAR HIS VOICE AND FOLLOW HIM."

DAY 170
The Pursuit of Holiness

"Speak to the entire Israelite community and tell them: Be holy because I, the Lord your God, am holy."

LEVITICUS 19:2

We see words like "holy" and "holiness" throughout Scripture. The Bible shows how holiness is directly tied to God's nature—it is one of His attributes. When we say "God is holy," we mean He is different from us. The Lord is set apart as Creator of all. He is infinite, all-knowing, and all-powerful. There is no other like God. He deserves all of our reverence. An example of His holiness is seen when He appears in the burning bush to meet with Moses (Exodus 3). God's presence there made the land a sacred and pure environment. A sinner, Moses could not enter the place carelessly, and God commanded him to remove his shoes and humbly approach the presence of God.

While God is holy in every way, sin has corrupted us, and we are disobedient to God. Like Adam and Eve, we have a fallen nature that cannot stand in the presence of God. But, as we see in redemptive history throughout Scripture, God desires to be in a relationship with His people. He provided a way to draw near to sinners. In Leviticus, God gives the Israelites laws for living as His redeemed people. After saving them from slavery, God called the Israelites to exercise faith in obedience to His commands. By adhering to the Law, the Israelites loved God and their neighbors. As a result, the Israelites would become a holy people, set apart from other nations.

If we continue reading through the Old Testament, we see that the Israelites did not live up to God's commands but disobeyed time and time again. Yet while they continued in the Law, they waited for the Savior who would fulfill the Law. The Savior came in the person of Jesus Christ. He was the perfect Son of God who was obedient and holy. We are covered in Jesus's righteousness and called to reflect His holiness through our belief in His saving work. When believers today read Leviticus 19:2, we may feel discouraged in our pursuit of holiness. But, while the Lord does call us to holiness, He never leaves us to achieve holiness on our own. The Holy Spirit will continue to perfect us into the image of Christ as we seek Him. May we look to the Lord to continue His work in us as we become more and more like Him—images of His perfect holiness.

> "WHILE THE LORD DOES CALL US TO HOLINESS, HE NEVER LEAVES US TO ACHIEVE HOLINESS ON OUR OWN."

DAY 171
The Self-Guided Way

There is a way that seems right to a person, but its end is the way to death.

PROVERBS 14:12

If you have ever been in a maze before, you know how getting lost is easy. You feel like you are going the right way, only to find yourself at a dead end. Without a map, you find yourself going around in circles or taking you further from the exit. Something similar occurs in our own lives when we try to go our way. We like to think that we are wise people—that we have enough sense to make our own plans and lead ourselves down the right paths. But, without the Lord, we are set on the wrong path. Like being in a maze, we lead ourselves away from the way to life and instead go toward destruction.

If we have come to know Jesus as our Savior, we have been rescued from eternal destruction. By God's grace, He has led us to His Son, who is the way, the truth, and the life (John 14:6). But sometimes we still choose our own way. In our pride, we believe we know what is right for ourselves, rejecting the wisdom of God. Our foolishness may not lead to an eternal place of destruction, but it can lead us into temporary places of destruction in our lives. In these moments, we do not need to be moved to despair. God does not watch us hit a dead end and leave us to our own devices. In His grace and kindness, He calls us back to Himself. Like the prodigal son who went his own way, God welcomes us back with open arms.

God has equipped us with His Word and His Spirit to help guide us in His ways. Daily, we must surrender our self-sufficiency and humble ourselves under God's Word. Scripture is like a map in a maze as its words direct us to the Lord. Let us not wander off this path by pursuing destinations that lead to destruction. His way may be a narrow path, but it leads to everlasting life (Matthew 7:14).

"DAILY, WE MUST SURRENDER OUR SELF-SUFFICIENCY AND HUMBLE OURSELVES UNDER GOD'S WORD. SCRIPTURE IS LIKE A MAP IN A MAZE AS ITS WORDS DIRECT US TO THE LORD."

Day 172
Time to Seek the Lord

Sow righteousness for yourselves and reap faithful love; break up your unplowed ground. It is time to seek the Lord until he comes and sends righteousness on you like the rain.

HOSEA 10:12

You cannot grow plants without first working the soil, removing weeds, and fertilizing the ground. A farmer must plow his fields, preparing for the crops he will plant. Otherwise, it will be impossible for his plants to grow. The book of Hosea compares Israel to an unfaithful wife due to the people's rebellion against God. The people of Israel abandoned their covenant with God, causing sin to infiltrate every area of the nation, just as thorns take over a field left untended.

As a punishment, God prophesied that He would send Israel into exile. The once flourishing nation of Israel will be a desolate land. Even in light of this punishment, God calls for Israel to repent. Using gardening and farming language, God commands Israel to sow righteousness instead of seeds of unrighteousness, reap faithful love instead of unfaithful love, and begin plowing their unplowed ground. God wanted Israel to experience spiritual renewal. Yet, the only way they could experience this renewal was by seeking the Lord. Like an adulterer who realizes their ways and seeks their spouse, it was time for Israel to seek the Lord.

As believers, we too struggle with our obedience to the Lord, just as Israel did by seeking satisfaction apart from Christ. By neglecting the Lord, we cause our spiritual life to shrivel and grow barren. Our once-flourishing faith becomes overgrown with thorns of sin and misplaced worship. But we do not have to stay this way. Just like Israel, God wants us to flourish in our relationship with Him. He wants us to sow righteousness and reap faithful love. He wants us to tend the neglected parts of our walk with Him. We can only do this by seeking the Lord and turning away from what hinders our relationship with Him.

On our own, we cannot be righteous and cannot faithfully love the Lord as we ought. Knowing our dilemma, God sent His Son to purchase our salvation. On the cross, Christ's perfect righteousness poured out over us like rain. His faithful love covered our unfaithful love. God sacrificed His Son so that we could experience forgiveness and everlasting life. Even in the times we fail in obedience, the grace of Christ beckons us to seek Him once again.

DAY 173

God Hears

This is the confidence we have before him: If we ask anything according to his will, he hears us.

1 JOHN 5:14

We may have heard or read the encouragement that God hears our prayers but struggle to believe this is true. At times, it may feel as though our prayers hit the ceiling or that God only listens to the prayers of others and not our own. However, Scripture makes it known that God does hear our prayers. Throughout the psalms, we read of how God listens to the prayers of His people as we see in the following verses:

> *Know that the Lord has set apart the faithful for himself; the Lord will hear when I call to him.* — Psalm 4:3

> *...I cried to my God for help. From his temple he heard my voice, and my cry to him reached his ears.* — Psalm 18:6

> *God has listened; he has paid attention to the sound of my prayer.* — Psalm 66:19

Be cheered today, dear reader, for God hears your voice. We do not serve a God who shuts His ears to the cries of His people. He bends His ear to listen to all who pray to Him. Even if we feel God has not answered our prayers, this does not mean that God does not listen to us. God always listens and responds to our prayers. Yet sometimes He responds in ways we may not understand or expect. He might tell us "no" to show He has something better, and He might tell us "yes" in a way that surprises us. Or He might tell us to wait as He asks you to trust Him in the present. God is sovereign, and He answers our prayers according to His perfect will.

The truth that God listens should encourage us to come confidently to Him in prayer and cry out to Him when we need help or are afraid. So lift your voice in prayer to the Lord who hears your voice. Our God is a loving and compassionate Father who loves to listen to His children.

"GOD IS SOVEREIGN, AND HE ANSWERS OUR PRAYERS ACCORDING TO HIS PERFECT WILL."

DAY 174

Unworthy Servants

In the same way, when you have done all that you were commanded, you should say, "We are worthless servants; we've only done our duty."

LUKE 17:10

One of the main arguments between the disciples was who among them was the greatest. They even bickered about this before Jesus went to the cross at the Passover meal they shared with Him. And in response, Jesus washed their feet to show them the better way—the way of a servant.

In a parable given to His disciples, Jesus shows His students how silly it would be for a servant to do what he has been commanded and then to demand something more from his master. We would likely never go to our jobs at work, perform our everyday duty, and then waltz into our boss's office demanding a raise. Yet this was essentially what the disciples were doing with Christ. They were following what He commanded, but the heart behind their obedience was for their own glory rather than His.

We are not promised fame, success, or comfortable lives in Christ's service. We are promised that He is ours forever, and that should be enough. However, so many times we fail to search for satisfaction in Him alone.

When we follow Christ, our mindsets should not be to think of what Christ "owes us" for obedience. We do not deserve any riches or treasure from Christ. Rather, we deserve His judgment for our sin and rebellion against Him. But in His kindness, He has given us the opposite. We should stand in awe of Him and the way of salvation accomplished on our behalf.

The more we understand the gospel, the more we realize how unworthy we are. Everything that could fill our hearts and satisfy our deepest longings has already been given to us in Christ. So, as we follow Jesus and learn from Him, may we see our unworthiness and worship Him all the more. May our view of ourselves pale in light of His greatness and glory. No one compares to Him, and we deserve nothing from Him, yet He has given us everything. Praise be to our Savior who is ever worthy!

"THE MORE WE UNDERSTAND THE GOSPEL, THE MORE
WE REALIZE HOW UNWORTHY WE ARE."

DAY 175
God Cares for the Details

You must make it according to all that I show you—the pattern of the tabernacle as well as the pattern of all its furnishings.

EXODUS 25:9

Many of us have tried "build-it-yourself" furniture. After receiving a box of parts in the mail, you unpackaged everything and sorted through the various pieces. Gazing at the instructions, however, you became overwhelmed. The steps were not overly complicated, but there were more than you cared to read. Your excitement dimmed as you considered the tediousness of this project, having to adhere to one step after another. The project ended up taking days to assemble, and when it was finally completed, you realized you had attached one major piece incorrectly. Though frustrated, you likely learned the lesson that being patient and obedient in the details is what leads to excellent results.

We also see this lesson play out in biblical history. During their wilderness journey, the Israelites received a message from the Lord that they were to build a tabernacle, a portable tent structure. This tabernacle would be God's dwelling place and the center of their worship. Materials and furnishings would consist of ornate gold altars, beautifully colored fabrics, and angelic symbols. The inside of the tabernacle would represent the Lord's heavenly throne and stir up reverence for Him. God gave Moses, the Israelites' leader, necessary instructions for the tabernacle. When the project was complete, Moses saw how his patience and obedience to the Lord's instruction produced excellent and God-glorifying work.

God blesses the simple and mundane tasks, but we often rush through details to obtain the final product. In a culture that correlates efficiency with worth, we often tie our identities to the end results. But, with our eyes too focused on the end, we miss the blessing of the journey with God. God cares for the details; through them, He teaches us and shows us His character. He wants to walk with us through every step of life.

We are not capable of producing excellence on our own. We complain, grow lazy, and become irritated over small things. Thankfully, God has given us a Savior, Jesus, whose redemption sets us free from sin and enables us to exercise patience and obedience. As we depend on the Lord moment by moment, we will eventually become Christ's completed works, reflecting the excellence and glory of Jesus.

DAY 176
Transformed By God

Look, the days are coming"—this is the Lord's declaration—"when I will make a new covenant with the house of Israel and with the house of Judah. This one will not be like the covenant I made with their ancestors on the day I took them by the hand to lead them out of the land of Egypt—my covenant that they broke even though I am their master"—the Lord's declaration. "Instead, this is the covenant I will make with the house of Israel after those days"—the Lord's declaration. "I will put my teaching within them and write it on their hearts. I will be their God, and they will be my people."

JEREMIAH 31:31-33

Without Christ, all of us need a heart transplant, so to speak. We are sinful people with misplaced worship. Our hearts naturally move toward things apart from our Creator. But God does not leave us in our sinful states.

Before Christ came, God put forth a covenant that would change everything. This new covenant explained in Jeremiah 31 shows us God's desire to make broken people whole. The nation of Israel, chosen by God, constantly rebelled against Him, worshiping things apart from Christ. Yet God remained faithful. Those who God brought into this new covenant receive an intimacy with Him that is constant. His people can know Him and understand His Word through their relationship with Christ. Misaligned worship is transformed into true worship as the new hearts of believers desire faithfulness to the Lord above all else.

The new covenant finds its fulfillment in Christ. By sending His Son, God made a way for our sins to be forgiven and for us to be made new. On the night of His betrayal, Jesus broke bread and drank wine with his disciples, symbolizing His sacrifice to come. He says in Luke 22:20, "This cup is the new covenant in my blood, which is poured out for you." Through these words, Jesus reveals how His sacrifice on the cross institutes the new covenant. His blood poured out satisfies God's wrath and forgives our iniquities as we repent and trust in Him.

Christ's forgiveness through the new covenant transforms us. We are restored to our relationship with God that was lost because of the fall in Genesis. We are given conviction and an understanding of God's Word. We have the Spirit who enables us to walk in obedience and worship of the Lord. Because of Jesus, we are God's people forever.

DAY 177
Eternity Set in Our Hearts

He has made everything appropriate in its time. He has also put eternity in their hearts, but no one can discover the work God has done from beginning to end.

ECCLESIASTES 3:11

The restlessness of our world shows the human heart as a longing heart. As humans, we find that there is a void in us we long to fill. Our mind seeks to grasp what is beyond our knowledge and understanding, desiring answers to our questions about our futures and existence. Our minds and hearts reveal how God created us with the ability to reason. He created our minds to think and discover, but they are limited. We do not have all the answers despite how much we study. But our inability to understand everything is perhaps a good thing, for it humbles us and makes us recognize our need for something greater.

Many people do not realize that Christ is the only One who can fill the void they seek to fill with things of this world. God created our hearts for Him. The longing each of us feels is the longing to be reconciled with our Creator. This is why God has set eternity in each of our hearts. It is a way to bring us to Himself. However, sin gets in the way, and without the Lord, we are left like blind people wandering and searching for light. Yet God has not left us with an eternal longing we cannot satisfy. In His grace, He opens the eyes of the blind to understand the truth of the gospel. Through faith in Jesus, believers can see God's plan for eternity. We understand how God set forth a plan of redemption to rescue His people and bring them to Himself. We understand how God will one day return, bringing restoration, and we will enjoy the new creation with Him forever.

While we can look to Scripture and see this redemptive plan broadly from beginning to end, we cannot see the details. Yet, God has not withheld knowledge to frustrate us but to encourage us to trust Him. If we knew everything, there would be no need to trust God. His ways are higher than our ways, and His thoughts are greater than our thoughts (Isaiah 55:8–9). We can rest in knowing our future without having to know all the details. Through Christ, the eternal longing of our hearts is satisfied, and that is enough indeed.

"GOD CREATED OUR HEARTS FOR HIM."

DAY 178
All for You, Lord

Yours, Lord, is the greatness and the power and the glory and the splendor and the majesty, for everything in the heavens and on earth belongs to you. Yours, Lord, is the kingdom, and you are exalted as head over all.

1 CHRONICLES 29:11

King David, the author of this prayer in 1 Chronicles, attributed none of his successes to himself. The early church shared this humble sentiment by using this passage as a closing line in reciting the Lord's Prayer. The words were used as a benediction, meant to position hearts away from ourselves and toward the kingdom, power, and glory of our wonderful Savior.

The word "benediction" means "a good word or the pronouncing of a blessing." This practice originated in the Old Testament when the Lord commanded Aaron, the high priest, to bless the people with the words found in Numbers 6:24–26: "May the Lord bless you and protect you; may the Lord make His face shine on you and be gracious to you; may the Lord look with favor on you and give you peace." In the New Testament, benedictions were often given at the close of a service or written at the end of a letter and were usually biblical passages written as blessings or encouragement. An example can be found in Ephesians 6:23–24 when Paul wrote, "Peace to the brothers and sisters, and love with faith, from God the Father and the Lord Jesus Christ. Grace be with all who have an undying love for our Lord Jesus Christ." Another example is Paul's invocation of God's love and full Trinitarian work in 2 Corinthians 13:13: "The grace of the Lord Jesus Christ, and the love of God, and the fellowship of the Holy Spirit be with you all."

Each benediction reference is placed at the end of a teaching or prayer to reorient our hearts from what we speak to the One to whom we speak. Benedictions are intended to offer up a final, all-encompassing blessing. This benediction reminds us that whether in word or thought, our prayers and lives should be shaped by this same principle. Benedictions allow a response that draws attention to all God is and all He has done. David's words reflect a heart, mind, and soul that pour out praise and adoration for the Lord. May our hearts, minds, and souls reflect the same.

DAY 179
No More Shame

Those who look to him are radiant with joy; their faces will never be ashamed.

PSALM 34:5

We all feel shame at some point. Perhaps we feel it in our dreams or real life. In that shame, we feel like we are not good enough, and we fear that others will discover our insufficiencies. Maybe you feel ashamed of your family or your upbringing. Perhaps you feel ashamed because of the choices you have made in your past, constantly beating yourself up for your mistakes, an internal dialogue condemning your every action. Or maybe you feel shame because of injustices against you.

When we feel shame, we are likely to try to find ways to cover it up. Sometimes we try distracting ourselves. We dive into our work or relationships, focusing our attention on serving others. Other times, we use positive mantras to make us think that we are okay, though, on the inside, we are crumbling. But at the end of the day, the feelings of shame remain. We feel exposed, flawed, unworthy.

God has provided a better way for our shame to be removed. When Jesus came, He was perfect, holy, and pure. Jesus did not push away from sinners because of His holiness; He pressed into their lives. He loved, ate, and drank with sinners just like us. And when He died on the cross for us, Jesus took our shame upon Himself and destroyed it forever. Jesus removed the condemnation of our shame and clothed us with His righteousness.

Through Christ, we are no longer unacceptable or unworthy. He has given us His perfect record and loves us with unconditional love. He has forgiven every sin and covered every flaw. He has declared, "It is finished," and He is enough (John 19:30). When we look to God, we do not find a judgmental judge, brows-furrowed and ready to condemn. We discover a loving Father who invites us in and makes us clean. We are made clean, not because of anything that we have done but because of His Son. He makes us radiant with joy, our faces never to be ashamed (Psalm 34:5).

"JESUS REMOVED THE CONDEMNATION OF OUR SHAME AND CLOTHED US WITH HIS RIGHTEOUSNESS."

DAY 180
Salvation in No Other Name

There is salvation in no one else, for there is no other name under heaven given to people by which we must be saved.

ACTS 4:12

The world offers us many people, places, and things in which to hope: *If you elect this political candidate, everything will get better. If you use this weight loss product, all of your problems will vanish. If you can travel to this destination, your heart will finally be satisfied.*

We could list out many of these empty promises because we likely face them to some capacity each day. How do we know what and who to trust? We must compare the world's promises to the truth of Scripture. Acts 4:12 tells us that there is no salvation available outside of Christ. He is the only name able to save humanity from their sin.

Some may claim the ability to complete, fulfill, or satisfy you, but they cannot. We must trust that Christ is our greatest satisfaction. He is the only One who can complete us and make us new. He is the fulfillment of all of our every longing and desire. And He satisfies us in a way no person or material item can.

Knowing that our hope is in Christ alone offers believers rest. We cannot achieve salvation in our own names, and we cannot be given salvation by anyone other than Christ. This puts our souls at ease and helps us see what is error and what is true. No one else can save us besides Christ, for we put our hope in His accomplished work on the cross. As we journey through this life, we are sanctified by Him more and more each day.

Even while the world may tell us there is more to do or to achieve, that there is more to hope for on this earth, we know that we have found the true source of hope. That hope is an eternal one, sealed for us in the Lord. Nothing else can save us. And it is this truth we offer in response to false messages of salvation. Christ is the ultimate One for whom we are searching and in whom we find salvation, life everlasting.

"NO ONE ELSE CAN SAVE US BESIDES CHRIST, FOR WE PUT OUR HOPE IN HIS ACCOMPLISHED WORK ON THE CROSS. AS WE JOURNEY THROUGH THIS LIFE, WE ARE SANCTIFIED BY HIM MORE AND MORE EACH DAY."

DAY 181
Living Sacrifice

Therefore, brothers and sisters, in view of the mercies of God, I urge you to present your bodies as a living sacrifice, holy and pleasing to God; this is your true worship. Do not be conformed to this age, but be transformed by the renewing of your mind, so that you may discern what is the good, pleasing, and perfect will of God.

ROMANS 12:1–2

In the book of Romans, Paul provides a theological framework for the gospel. The beautiful book reveals glorious truths about our salvation, and as Paul finishes a hymn of praise at the end of chapter 11 that gives glory to the Lord for all He has done, he beckons a response.

Paul urges us to present ourselves as living sacrifices to the Lord. In one sense, the sacrificial system has been obliterated because of Christ's work on the cross. He is the last and final sacrifice for the atonement of sins, and we no longer offer dead animals on altars to the Lord each time we sin. Christ's blood covers our sins: past, present, and future. However, the heart behind the sacrificial system has not been obliterated. When God required sacrifices from His people for their sin, His greatest pleasure was not the killing of the animal, but the "broken and humbled" heart of the person standing before Him, offering a sacrifice of a broken and contrite heart (Psalm 51:16–17). This heart posture is one that the Lord desires from His people still today.

In light of God's abundant mercy for us, we give ourselves to Him as living sacrifices. We come, broken and humbled, before Him for our sin, and we joyfully give Him our entire lives. We owe everything to Him, and there is no one better to give our lives and worship to each and every day. Paul encourages us to not be conformed to this world but to renew our minds according to what is pleasing to the Lord.

Tell the Lord today that your life is His, and offer it to Him as a sacrifice. Ask Him to help you have a renewed mind, conformed to what He loves. God gives us our salvation through the gospel, but He also provides us with the means to live it out. May we die to ourselves each day as we walk in the newness of life with Christ.

"WE OWE EVERYTHING TO HIM, AND THERE IS NO ONE BETTER TO GIVE OUR LIVES AND WORSHIP TO EACH AND EVERY DAY."

DAY 182
A Legacy of Faith

These all died in faith, although they had not received the things that were promised. But they saw them from a distance, greeted them, and confessed that they were foreigners and temporary residents on the earth. Now those who say such things make it clear that they are seeking a homeland. If they were thinking about where they came from, they would have had an opportunity to return. But they now desire a better place—a heavenly one. Therefore, God is not ashamed to be called their God, for he has prepared a city for them.

HEBREWS 11:13-16

The Bible lists numerous people who walked with God in faith and trusted His calling in their lives. Because God created us for Himself and to give Him glory, our lives are not about our legacies but His legacy through us. In Hebrews 11, we see a people who looked beyond the present to the future. The people's faith was remarkable, trusting God beyond what they could see. They knew God was using them to accomplish His plan, even though they did not understand it fully. Each one of them recognized that time on earth is short, and God was bringing them to a place beyond the land where they lived. They were not just foreigners in their land; they were foreigners in their world.

As Christ followers, we belong to God's kingdom. We are citizens of heaven who live for the kingdom and not this world (Philippians 3:20). If we care only about this world, we will be consumed by living a legacy for our name. But, if we care about God's kingdom, we will have a zeal to live a legacy for His name. Perhaps the reason so many of us love to read Hebrews 11 is that we are so encouraged by the people's dedication of their lives to God. Their story fuels our endurance. Their faith fuels our faith.

Being a part of the kingdom of God means we join in their legacy of faith! Living a legacy of faith is like running in a relay race, waiting for the person in front of us to go first before handing the baton over to us. Those in Hebrews 11 are the ones who have gone before us. We model their faith, living faithfully for the Lord. As we do, we show those who are coming behind us how to live a life dedicated to the Lord.

"BEING A PART OF THE KINGDOM OF GOD MEANS WE JOIN IN THEIR LEGACY OF FAITH!"

DAY 183
What Can Be Gained From Worry?

Can any of you add one moment to his life span by worrying? If then you're not able to do even a little thing, why worry about the rest?

LUKE 12:25-26

Worry is common to most of us. We do not talk about its underlying sin much at all because we are all so prone to it on a nearly regular basis. Maybe for some of us, worrying lets us feel like we are in control, and if we do not worry, we think others might feel we are irresponsible or lazy. Sometimes we even worry about worrying as it eats away at our time and energy. It causes us to dwell on ourselves rather than the Lord.

Jesus spends a long time teaching His disciples about worry, likely because He knew His followers would struggle with it so much. Jesus's words are the most comforting place we can turn to when the fear and anxiety begin. He points us to eternity, and He shows us the uselessness of worry.

When we worry about our lives, our focus tends to be only on the present. But when we see our worry in light of what Jesus has promised, we begin to understand that the cares and troubles of this world are passing away. Observe the creation around you. God provides for the birds we see flying in the air, and He clothes the wildflowers in the fields. Both the birds and wildflowers will not go on forever. Their lifespans are relatively short compared to ours. Yet, if God provides for them, how much more will He provide for us?

When we recognize that through Christ, we have become God's adopted children, and He loves us fiercely—more than any earthly father could ever fathom—we will begin to trust in God's provision and goodness. Jesus's words in Luke 12:22–34 give us permission to hand our worry and anxiety to the Lord and trust Him, accepting our lack of control. We are to seek the kingdom of God and watch as the Lord provides for His people. Our heart must primarily be where our Father is, not in the world around us.

Worry kills our faith. It makes us fall prey to the lie that we are in control. It robs us of enjoying God's perfect sovereignty, love, and provision for us. Let us surrender our fears. We can gain nothing from worry, but we can experience much peace and freedom as we trust the Lord.

"HE LOVES US FIERCELY."

DAY 184
God's Word Eternal

Heaven and earth will pass away, but my words will never pass away.
MARK 13:31

What is one thing you wished lasted forever? Whether it be a person or possession, most of us have something we wish would stay with us. Yet, the reality is that things on this earth are temporary. When Jesus returns to create the new heavens and earth, the things we see now will pass away. But God's Word will stand forever.

God is eternal. He has always existed and will always exist. Therefore, God's Word is eternal, and because it is eternal, we have something in which we can place our trust. God's eternal Word declares how His words are trustworthy and true. His words will never change. His message will never alter. His truth will never shift. Knowing this encourages us to trust all areas of Scripture. When we read God's Word, we come with confidence, knowing that these words are everlasting.

Because God's Word is eternal, this also means that the good news of our salvation remains steady. The hope of our eternal life with Jesus remains secure. The promise of God's continual forgiveness remains sealed. This should fill us with immense comfort. As believers, we never have to worry that God will change His mind and fail to fulfill a promise. Everything God has said in His Word stands true forever.

Knowing that God's Word stands when all else fades away should remind us not to put our faith and trust in what is temporary. As humans, it is easy for us to place our trust in things apart from God's Word. Yet when those things fail us, we become discouraged and wounded. When something shifts, changes, or dies, our hope collapses along with it. However, we will never be let down when we trust God. Even when the things around us fade away, we have God's Word as an anchor. As long as we cling to Him, we remain steady and secure. And one day, when Jesus comes to make the world new, we will rejoice as we witness God's Word remain. Until then, we can say with confidence that though the grass withers and the flower fades, God's Word will surely stand forever (Isaiah 40:8).

"EVERYTHING GOD HAS SAID IN HIS WORD STANDS TRUE FOREVER."

DAY 185
Freedom in Christ

Jesus responded, "Truly I tell you, everyone who commits sin is a slave of sin. A slave does not remain in the household forever, but a son does remain forever. So if the Son sets you free, you really will be free."

JOHN 8:34–36

What would our lives be like if we could break free from everything holding us back, slowing us down, or entangling us? We would all love to have obstacle-free lives, but God has something better in mind. While Jesus never promises us freedom from life's struggles, He does promise that there is freedom from the power of sin through Him.

Sin's power lies in that it keeps us from a relationship with God as long as we remain in it. Jesus says that when we turn to Him, He sets us free from that sin that separates us from Him. Through the strength and joy we receive from our relationship with Christ, we can overcome the hardships life throws at us.

In this passage, Jesus contrasts the life of a slave with the life of a son. The kind of slavery Jesus references here could be better described as indentured servanthood. Servants would often work for a set number of years to pay back a debt that was owed. For as long as they had a debt, they were a slave to their debtor.

In the same way, our sins result in our owing a debt to God and, therefore, our sin enslaves us (Matthew 6:12). Only it does not matter how long we work to please God, for we could never repay the debt our sins create. Even one seemingly insignificant sin is a glaring imperfection in light of God's perfection and glory.

The only way our debts can be forgiven and we can be released from slavery to sin is through faith in Jesus, who was completely sinless yet was crucified to pay the debts we owe. When we confess our sin, believe in Christ, and receive the salvation offered through Him, we are once and for all set free from the slavery of sin. We are no longer slaves but sons of God, set free from the guilt of sin. In addition to that freedom, we are also now heirs to all of the promises of God (Romans 8:14–17, Galatians 4:7). There exists no greater truth than this: if the Son sets you free, you really will be free.

"THERE EXISTS NO GREATER TRUTH THAN THIS: IF THE SON SETS YOU FREE, YOU REALLY WILL BE FREE."

DAY 186
Encouraging One Another to Heaven

For the Lord himself will descend from heaven with a shout, with the archangel's voice, and with the trumpet of God, and the dead in Christ will rise first. Then we who are still alive, who are left, will be caught up together with them in the clouds to meet the Lord in the air, and so we will always be with the Lord. Therefore encourage one another with these words.

1 THESSALONIANS 4:16–18

There is nothing like reaching the end of a story and seeing all the pieces of the narrative fall into place—characters redeemed, problems solved, all that created tension like a shadow. We sigh in relief as we watch the credits roll or close the book.

As we read God's Word, He takes care to mention the ending of our own story. He will not leave us in this broken world forever but will return and bring us home. In 1 Thessalonians, Paul details what will happen on this wonderful day when the Lord descends from heaven, giving believers new bodies and calling them heavenward with Him to spend eternity, in praise of His glory.

Separation and sorrow will be no more. No longer will there be an opportunity for sin to break our relationship with God, for the Lord will destroy all evil. We will finally have true rest. This is the truth that brings comfort to our weary souls on the days evil and brokenness feel too much to bear. This is the joyful future calling us to persevere. Yet, it is so easy to become caught up in the motions of our days, forgetting the ending of our story. But eternity should be on the minds and hearts of all those who love Christ. Living in light of our heavenly home helps us to live differently.

May we encourage others, reminding them of Christ's return, giving them the only hope that will satisfy. One day our troubles will be no more, and when we finally live in God's eternal city with Him, we will never be separated from Him. Though we cannot see the end of the story quite yet, this day is drawing near. And when it comes, we will stand together as the body of Christ, in awe of the Lord and His great story of redemption. This will be only the beginning of the glorious eternity that awaits.

"LIVING IN LIGHT OF OUR HEAVENLY HOME HELPS US TO LIVE DIFFERENTLY."

DAY 187
Under His Eye

For the eyes of the Lord roam throughout the earth to show himself strong for those who are wholeheartedly devoted to him. You have been foolish in this matter. Therefore, you will have wars from now on.

2 CHRONICLES 16:9

How common it is to rely on our strength instead of the Lord's. This can be especially true when life is going well, and we feel like we do not need God. Yet the reality is that we always need to depend on the Lord's strength, whether or not we feel weak.

This truth is showcased in the story of Asa, king of Judah, in 2 Chronicles 14–16. Asa started strong. The Bible describes Asa as someone who "did what was good and right in the eyes of the Lord his God" (2 Chronicles 14:2). He took away altars to false gods and built fortified cities in which Judah could rest. Because of Asa's actions, God blessed their land, gave them peace, and allowed them to prosper. However, because we live in a broken world, earthly peace cannot endure, and their time of peace was interrupted by an attack from an Ethiopian army. When they attacked, Asa cried out to the Lord for help. As a result, the Lord defeated the Ethiopians and allowed Judah to prosper.

God told Asa that if he sought God, He would reveal Himself to Asa. But if Asa forsook God, then God would forsake him (2 Chronicles 15:2). So Asa took away the remaining idols in the land and made a covenant with God that Judah would seek the Lord (2 Chronicles 15:12). God once again gave them rest.

Unfortunately, we too easily tend to call out to God in difficult times, forgetting Him when times are better. As Judah experienced peace, Asa began to rely on his wisdom and human strength instead of God's. As a result, the time of peace ended for Judah, and Asa died of disease as he refused to seek the Lord's help.

As we see in Asa's story, our reliance on God tends to ebb and flow depending on our emotions or circumstances. However, it is important to remember that God is always watching us, ready to provide His strength for us the moment we ask. If you feel far from the Lord today, remember that He is near. He desires to give you hope and a future (Jeremiah 29:11). Turn to the Lord, for you have not left His watchful eye.

> "WE ALWAYS NEED TO DEPEND ON THE LORD'S STRENGTH, WHETHER OR NOT WE FEEL WEAK."

DAY 188
Our Only Boast is in the Cross

But as for me, I will never boast about anything except the cross of our Lord Jesus Christ. The world has been crucified to me through the cross, and I to the world.

GALATIANS 6:14

What is the root of dissatisfaction? Pride. Maybe you do not struggle with pride when it comes to your possessions as many do. Maybe you are proud of something you have done, like a significant career achievement. Or maybe it is something you have not done, like break the law or make a mistake. Whatever it is that makes you think, *Look at me! I am worthy of love and attention,* is likely where your pride dwells.

In today's verse, Paul explains that no earthly accomplishment is something to boast about to others. Rather, he says the only thing worth boasting about is the cross. What does that mean? It means that Paul is looking at his life through the lens of eternity as we should as well. Jesus's death and resurrection reconcile us with God, giving us eternal peace. In light of that truth, nothing else matters. Paul means that we should not let anything that is temporary puff up our view of ourselves.

Even more than that, Paul says that the world has been crucified to him through the cross. They are as good as dead. Pursuing them does not tempt him, and lacking them does not define him. He boasts not in any earthly thing. Because of Christ's death given on the cross, we have something so much greater to define us, for by His death, He made a way for us to become His children, covered in the righteousness of His Son. And that is eternal.

May we be quick to realize that those things we so easily want to take pride in will never be enough. Those things are not a reason to boast and do not define who we are as Christians. Worldly gains are temporary, and if we choose to cling to them or boast in them, we boast in something that is fleeting. What are you tempted to pursue to find your meaning and value? Is it temporary or eternal? Let us reorder our affections this week and every day so that our boast is found only in the cross of Jesus.

"JESUS'S DEATH AND RESURRECTION RECONCILE US WITH GOD, GIVING US ETERNAL PEACE."

DAY 189
Unashamed for the Gospel

For I am not ashamed of the gospel, because it is the power of God for salvation to everyone who believes, first to the Jew, and also to the Greek.

ROMANS 1:16

What keeps you from sharing the gospel? We often tend to avoid sharing parts of ourselves out of fear of rejection or receiving another negative response. We can withhold the truth from others because we fear that revealing the truth will lead to rejection. We are ashamed to share things, so instead of saying them, we bury them inside. Many times, we do the same thing when it comes to sharing the gospel.

In those moments, we feel embarrassed to share the gospel. We have perhaps forgotten its power. When we hide and withhold the gospel, we prevent others from experiencing God's powerful work of salvation. The Apostle Paul, who wrote the book of Romans, experienced much ridicule for sharing the gospel. He was opposed by others and persecuted many times because of his faith. Even still, Paul never backed down from sharing the gospel. He never let the reactions of others keep him from sharing the good news of Christ. Paul's actions should encourage us in our own evangelism. There is nothing shameful about the gospel message. In fact, the gospel covers people's shame. Though parts of the gospel may offend—that we are sinful and deserving of punishment for our sin—people need to hear about this reality that points to our need for God's grace. His gift of redemption covers our guilt and shame.

If we want to live unashamed for the gospel as Paul did, we must learn to accept any response we receive for sharing the gospel. We need to care more about a person's salvation than our personal reputation. Even if we are rejected for sharing the gospel, may we rejoice that the gospel message is heard. As believers, we have experienced the power of God within us that has wiped our sins clean. There are people around us who need to experience God's powerful work of salvation. God has given us His Spirit to embolden us and empower us to share the message of the gospel with these people. Let us allow the power of the gospel to propel us forward in faith and courage. Let us live unashamed of the good news of Jesus Christ, for we have a message of great hope to share!

"WE NEED TO CARE MORE ABOUT A PERSON'S SALVATION THAN OUR PERSONAL REPUTATION."

DAY 190
The Promised One

For a child will be born for us, a son will be given to us, and the government will be on his shoulders. He will be named Wonderful Counselor, Mighty God, Eternal Father, Prince of Peace.

ISAIAH 9:6

Amid the prophet Isaiah's explanations of the Lord's judgment on the people of Israel, he has countless promises of the coming Messiah. Israel had wandered from the Lord and had become like the other nations around them. God would use the nations of Assyria and Babylon to take the people into exile because of their sin, but He promised that they would one day return to their home. And not only would they return home, but they would also receive the fulfillment of God's promises: a Messiah. And Isaiah tells the people how they will know this Messiah has come.

The Messiah will be born as a child and will be the Son of God. All authority and dominion will be given to Him, and He will go by many names. While the original audience of Isaiah's prophecies did not know who this man would be, we know these verses foreshadow the coming of Jesus. They give us a beautiful description of who He is. Jesus is our Counselor. He understands our neediness because He has experienced our struggles Himself, and He cares for us. Jesus is equal to God the Father. His coming to the earth meant that the Creator walked among us. He is our Prince of Peace because He has covered us in the blood He shed on the cross and given us His righteousness. Jesus is the Promised One to whom all of Scripture points.

We too await His coming, but this time we wait for His final return—when He will end the curse of sin forever and bring His people home. Just like He fulfilled the promise of His first coming, He will fulfill every promise of His second coming. And until that day comes, we can cling to the promises we see in Scripture. We can dwell on the richness of His character, and we can grow to know Him more by reading His Word, spending time throughout the day in prayer, and asking the Holy Spirit to make us more aware of His presence. The Promised One came to give His life for us, and now we wait again for His second coming as His Spirit lives in us, strengthening us in the waiting.

"JESUS IS THE PROMISED ONE TO WHOM ALL OF SCRIPTURE POINTS."

DAY 191
Christ Intercedes

"Simon, Simon, look out. Satan has asked to sift you like wheat. But I have prayed for you that your faith may not fail. And you, when you have turned back, strengthen your brothers." "Lord," he told him, "I'm ready to go with you both to prison and to death." "I tell you, Peter," he said, "the rooster will not crow today until you deny three times that you know me."

LUKE 22:31-34

Before Jesus went to the cross, He predicted how His disciple Peter would deny Him. First, Jesus shares with Peter how Satan desires to bring suffering upon him. The direct translation is that Satan wants to "have" Peter. Yet, Jesus intercedes for Peter by praying that he will be strong in his faith. How gracious of the Lord to intercede in this way, knowing the denial that will take place. Christ shows His love for Peter by actively praying for his protection.

Satan can not do anything without God's permission, and we see him in this passage asking to torment Peter. It may be difficult for us to see how God could allow Satan to inflict suffering, but we cannot miss the power of Jesus's intercession. Satan's desire may have been to shift Simon like wheat, but while Peter will experience suffering and shame because of his denial of Christ, Satan's desire to have Peter will not come about. Even after Peter denies Christ, Peter turns back to Christ. Jesus holds him in His hands and will not let go.

Because of God's power, no scheme of the devil can prevail. Satan may seek to harm us, but Christ's intervention causes the arrows to ricochet. Just as Jesus did for Peter, He prays for our faith to remain strong as well. We can have peace in trial and temptation knowing that Jesus is fighting for us in prayer.

What great comfort we have knowing that Christ's intercession is more powerful than the enemy's schemes. We are not helpless in the fight against sin or in our battles with suffering. Jesus stands at our side, fighting for and strengthening us. May the grace of Jesus cause us to rejoice, even in times of trial. We are in an intimate relationship with One, who interceded for us on the cross and continues to intercede for us in prayer. Our sin, shame, and suffering do not keep Christ from actively caring and fighting for us. We are in His hands, and never will He abandon His children.

"BECAUSE OF GOD'S POWER, NO SCHEME OF THE DEVIL CAN PREVAIL."

DAY 192
New Mercies Every Morning

Yet I call this to mind, and therefore I have hope: Because of the Lord's faithful love we do not perish, for his mercies never end. They are new every morning; great is your faithfulness!

LAMENTATIONS 3:21–23

The rising sun and daily tasks that await completion often seem daunting as we wake each morning. Yesterday's mistakes loom in your mind. Perhaps it is even more discouraging when these mistakes involve a missed Bible reading or lack of prayer. Our shame over our spiritual apathy makes us feel as though we cannot approach the Lord. We keep messing up. He must be disappointed in us.

If we persist in this kind of thinking, we will miss the riches of the gospel that are available to us in Christ. When we have followed Christ as our Savior, we are covered in His righteousness forever. And since His righteousness is perfect and enough to satisfy the Lord, our position before God never changes. Instead of wrath for our mistakes, there is compassion. Instead of perishing because of our sin, we are saved by the Lord's mercy and love. Even on the days when we are faithless, He is faithful to us.

We can walk through any hard day and have hope because the Lord's mercy is new every morning. It never runs out. It is abundant, overflowing, and available to us. Do not let your preconceived ideas of the Lord prevent you from seeing what really is true about Him. He has given you salvation through His Son, and this salvation changes everything for you. When you wake up and feel discouraged, you can speak the truth of His mercy and compassion aloud. You can pull out your Bible and rehearse the gospel to yourself. You are His child. You will spend eternity with Him because He saved you.

So while we never want to take advantage of the Lord's grace for us, we can rest in His sufficiency. Our days do not need to be directed by our feelings of unworthiness or inadequacy. We are nothing without Him, but because of Christ, we are not without Him. The Lord is ours forever. Rejoice in His mercy for you. Let it wash over you each morning as you rise and greet a new day. We will know His faithfulness forever, and that will spur us onward.

"WE CAN WALK THROUGH ANY HARD DAY AND HAVE HOPE BECAUSE THE LORD'S MERCY IS NEW EVERY MORNING."

DAY 193

Faithful Devotion

They devoted themselves to the apostles' teaching, to the fellowship, to the breaking of bread, and to prayer. Everyone was filled with awe, and many wonders and signs were being performed through the apostles. Now all the believers were together and held all things in common. They sold their possessions and property and distributed the proceeds to all, as any had need. Every day they devoted themselves to meeting together in the temple, and broke bread from house to house. They ate their food with joyful and sincere hearts, praising God and enjoying the favor of all the people. Every day the Lord added to their number those who were being saved.

ACTS 2:42-47

God created us to be in meaningful relationships with one another. Life is better when we have a community of people around us. In these verses, the Bible takes it a step further. For the church in Acts, life in community with other believers was not just about being together, but it was about being completely committed to one another. The kind of community these verses describe is nothing short of miraculous.

How was it these believers were able to live such a dedicated and intertwined life? It was because they devoted themselves to learning Scripture through the lens of Jesus's life and death (the teaching of the apostles), consistently gathering together (the fellowship), relaxing and sharing meals together (the breaking of bread), and prayer.

The word "devoted" in verse 42 was the Greek word *proskartereō* in the original text. *Proskartereō* means to persist and keep on with steadfast devotion. Persistence, dedication, and devotion to spiritual disciplines and to one another—that is the secret to experiencing the same kind of dynamic community found in Acts 2.

This passage makes us long for a healthy, vibrant church community. We must be careful, though, that it does not lead us to point fingers in blame at people in our churches who have failed us. What would it look like for you to persevere in a relationship that has hit a rough patch? How could you devote yourself to your church community and people outside your normal social circle? How might you interact with other believers differently if you believed God called you to remain dedicated to their wellbeing? Consider these things, and pray that you would be one who seeks to devote yourself to Christ and His church, glorifying the Lord and those He places in your midst.

DAY 194
The True Vine

I am the vine; you are the branches. The one who remains in me and I in him produces much fruit, because you can do nothing without me.

JOHN 15:5

Can you imagine if there was a branch that broke itself from a tree, bidding it farewell? It was too tired taking in the tree's nutrients and growing through each season. It simply removed itself from the trunk, slid down in joy, and wandered off into the sunset. What a ridiculous notion! No branch can do such a thing, and if a branch does fall or break off from its home, it cannot live without the life-giving nutrients the tree provides.

We tend to live this way ourselves. The Lord saves us from our sin through the gospel, and we accept His gift with joy, but after a while, we believe that we are doing pretty well on our own. And these beliefs slowly take root in our hearts and present themselves through our actions. We may not read our Bible as often. We may think sparingly about prayer. We may forget to think about the Lord at all. Before we realize it, we are just like the branch trying to break from the tree. Within a matter of time, we are spiritually dry and lacking.

Since the beginning of creation, when Adam and Eve committed the first sin in the garden, mankind has attempted to live without God. But He has created us to live in dependency on Him. When we try to do otherwise, we crumble.

Jesus tells us that when we abide in Him, we bear much fruit. Abiding is the act of remaining, and we learn more about what it means to remain in Him the more we spend time with Him each day. Simply put, to remain in Christ means that He is a part of everything we do and is the means by which we can live—out of the overflow of His strength, love, mercy, and kindness. Christ gives us access to Him as He gladly gives of Himself that we may have abundant life in Him.

A life of abiding is better than a life of self-sufficiency, yet we deceive ourselves into thinking it is not. May we diligently fight the temptation to live our days unaware of Him. We are just like a tree branch—unable to do anything apart from our life-giving source.

"CHRIST GIVES US ACCESS TO HIM AS HE GLADLY GIVES OF HIMSELF THAT WE MAY HAVE ABUNDANT LIFE IN HIM."

DAY 195

Seeking the Peace of the City

"Pursue the well-being of the city I have deported you to. Pray to the Lord on its behalf, for when it thrives, you will thrive."

JEREMIAH 29:7

When Jeremiah delivered the news of God's judgment to the people of Judah, he told them that they would go into exile. They refused to repent and turn from their sin, and they had rejected the Lord. Though Jerusalem would fall and life would change drastically for God's people, He would never abandon them or forsake them. He would use their deportation for their good, and eventually, He would allow them to return home.

However, until they came back home, they were to live peacefully in the city of Babylon and care for its well-being. They were to pray to the Lord for the city to thrive. How could this be? The city that destroyed their home, killed their loved ones, and took them as captives? The city that destroyed their temple and place of worship? God was going to use His people's presence for the good of those in Babylon. Their hardship and trial would be for His glory and their good. Throughout the Old Testament, God used the witness of the people of Israel to help other Gentile nations know Him. God's faithful remnant would have the opportunity to demonstrate God's love to the Babylonians, the very people who had caused them immense pain. He did not want them to sulk in despair or sadness.

Since we are not yet in heaven, we are not home. We are in exile in a sense. But while we wait to see Christ face to face, we pray for the peace and well-being of the places around us. We pray for them to thrive, and we actively contribute to loving the people in them. When the communities around us thrive, we can live quietly and at peace, which gives us an amazing opportunity to share the gospel.

God never meant for us to wander aimlessly through this life until we reach heaven. There is work to do here for Christ until we are with Him. That work involves our country, communities, schools, and neighborhoods. May God be glorified as we live out the gospel in the places God has placed us, and may others see how we live and wonder about the God we serve!

"SINCE WE ARE NOT YET IN HEAVEN, WE ARE NOT HOME."

DAY 196
We So Easily Forget

When the people saw that Moses delayed in coming down from the mountain, they gathered around Aaron and said to him, "Come, make gods for us who will go before us because this Moses, the man who brought us up from the land of Egypt—we don't know what has happened to him!"

EXODUS 32:1

When we read the account of Moses, the people, and the golden calf, it is easy for us to lift our noses toward the people of Israel. When God rescued them, and they left the land of their affliction, God guided them in a pillar of cloud by day and a pillar of fire by night. Pharaoh, their greatest enemy, pursued them even after they departed, and God opened the waters of the Red Sea at His command so the Israelites could escape. Once they crossed on dry land, they turned to watch the waters that parted crash down upon the Egyptians who came after them.

The people came to Mount Sinai, and God's presence descended upon the summit of the mountain. Moses went to meet with the Lord and was gone for forty days. The people began to fear and worry when Moses, their visible leader, had not returned after a period of time. They approached Aaron and asked him to make them a god that would go before them into the land promised to them. They had forgotten the Lord's presence at the top of the mountain and who had led them to Mount Sinai.

The Lord had revealed to Moses how the people could enter His land and live His way, but they allowed their fear to overwhelm them. They were quick to turn to plans of their own making rather than trusting Him as their guide.

How easily we do the same thing with the gospel. We see the mighty salvation accomplished by Christ on our behalf, and we are amazed. Still, after a period of time, we often forget the glories of God's grace and chase the gods and idols of the world: beauty, recognition, entertainment, wealth, possessions. We forget where our true identity and salvation are found. May we remember that God is always near, though His presence may seem far in some seasons. He has given us abundant life and provision in the gospel. Nothing we or anyone else can do can compare to what Christ has done and who He is as our loving and gracious Father.

DAY 197
Persecution and Joy

And you yourselves became imitators of us and of the Lord when, in spite of severe persecution, you welcomed the message with joy from the Holy Spirit. As a result, you became an example to all the believers in Macedonia and Achaia.

1 THESSALONIANS 1:6–7

Persecution and joy are not two things we would typically pair. Persecution is difficult. Yet, as believers, we are told that we will endure persecution (John 15:19–20). At the same time, we are commanded to have joy. How can this be?

When the church of Thessalonica heard the gospel message, the people responded with joy, even in their own persecution. The gospel of Jesus Christ was so glorious to them that they did not allow their current opposition to keep them from embracing the gospel. When the gospel is central to our lives, our current circumstances cannot rob our joy.

Scripture tells us that when we are persecuted for our faith, we are blessed (Matthew 5:11; 1 Peter 4:14), for the outworking of our faith brings glory and honor to God. Our unwavering gospel proclamation causes Christ's name to be heard and glorified. This is why Paul and his missionary team continued preaching the gospel, even when they were beaten and imprisoned. Honoring Jesus was their greatest joy. When Christ is our greatest joy, we can maintain that joy, even amid persecution for our faith, because we know the gospel is being heard.

Having joy in persecution also influences those around us. The dedication of Paul to the gospel in times of persecution encouraged the people of Thessalonica to be dedicated themselves. In turn, the Thessalonians were an example to the churches surrounding them. When we stand up for the gospel and stand for the gospel, we encourage other believers in the faith—to persevere and stand firm, no matter the reaction of others.

Joy in the midst of persecution does not deny that persecution is difficult. When Jesus said that we would be blessed in times of persecution, He did not mean that we would not feel the sting of rejection. However, we can experience the hurt and pain without falling into despair. When we cling to Christ amidst persecution, we receive His strength, which fuels our endurance and perseverance through any opposition. When we hold fast to Christ and the gospel, our joy will remain steadfast, we will be blessed, God will be glorified, and the world will hear the name of Jesus Christ.

DAY 198
Loving Jesus More Than Life

The one who loves a father or mother more than me is not worthy of me; the one who loves a son or daughter more than me is not worthy of me. And whoever doesn't take up his cross and follow me is not worthy of me. Anyone who finds his life will lose it, and anyone who loses his life because of me will find it.

MATTHEW 10:37–39

How would you describe a perfect day? What if each day was problem-free and fun, productive and enjoyable, but God was not a part of it? He did not cross your mind nor was He in your thoughts. You did not look to His Word or obey Him or commune with Him in prayer. Would you still define this day as being a great one?

Jesus challenges His followers in regards to their priorities. He says that those who love father and mother more than Him are not worthy of Him. Jesus was not saying that it is wrong to love our fathers and mothers. The Bible commands us to do so. Scripture also teaches that food, family, and hobbies are blessings from the Lord, and it is good to find delight in God's creation. These are gifts from God.

The problem is not that we love these blessings too much. It is that in comparison, we love God too little. When we elevate people or things above God, we love the gifts from God more than God Himself. We are content with a worldly kind of satisfaction when we can find ultimate satisfaction in Christ Himself.

A call to follow Christ means that we put Him first in our lives. For His glory, we eagerly lay down our lives, trusting that His ways are best. For it was He who sent His Son, in love, to die on a cross to save us. In Him, we find greater joy than we have ever known. While we may be given many blessings on this earth, our greatest treasure of all is indeed found in Christ alone. Jesus is of greatest value, and He yearns to be our greatest love.

"A CALL TO FOLLOW CHRIST MEANS THAT WE PUT HIM FIRST IN OUR LIVES. FOR HIS GLORY, WE EAGERLY LAY DOWN OUR LIVES, TRUSTING THAT HIS WAYS ARE BEST."

DAY 199
Treasures of the Heart

Sell your possessions and give to the poor. Make money-bags for yourselves that won't grow old, an inexhaustible treasure in heaven, where no thief comes near and no moth destroys. For where your treasure is, there your heart will be also.

LUKE 12:33–34

Jesus taught His disciples the difference between earthly treasures and heavenly treasures. While earthly treasure is perishable, heavenly treasure is eternal and brings peace. Jesus told the disciples not to be anxious about anything, for life is more than materials. Food and clothing are a part of life, but they are not the source of life itself. He assured them that God would care for them and provide for their needs. The disciples were called to set themselves apart from the world for a greater inheritance and seek the kingdom of God and heavenly treasure. Jesus told the disciples to sell their possessions and give the money to the poor in order to pursue a treasure that will never lose its luster, never be stolen, tainted, or destroyed.

Jesus was certainly not saying to reject all earthly good. Nor was He saying that food and clothing did not have any value. Rather, Jesus is calling us to a life of generosity. By the grace of God, after Jesus's ascension to His heavenly throne, the disciples knew their ultimate treasure was in the Lord. Though this message was directly spoken to the disciples, it is still true for believers today. As sinners, our hearts struggle with resting in God's eternal promises. Our natural desire is to seek created things rather than the Creator of all. We too often do not trust our Savior to provide for our needs, and our affections for the wonders of eternity are forgotten or ignored.

Jesus was the perfect Son whose heart always trusted in His Father. From birth to the cross, Jesus kept His focus on the hope of one day being reunited with God in heaven. And through His death on the cross, He made a way for us to have eternal life with Him. Through our faith in Him, God has given us the same Spirit who empowered the disciples to live with their hearts placed in Jesus and their eternal inheritance. The Holy Spirit enables us to live with generosity as well. May we practice gratitude for the Lord's salvation and blessing. Let us share the earthly gifts God has given us, for they are dim reflections of the greatest treasure that awaits us in Christ.

"JESUS IS CALLING US TO A LIFE OF GENEROSITY."

DAY 200
None like You, Lord

Lord, who is like you among the gods? Who is like you, glorious in holiness, revered with praises, performing wonders?

EXODUS 15:11

The Israelites were stuck. They had quickly abandoned their homes, gathering only what they could carry as they ran from the Egyptians. Just days before, they fled their lives of slavery in Egypt, bravely following the Lord. Now, they were faced with an impassable barrier. Ahead of them was the Red Sea. Behind them were their persecutors, armed and ready to take possession of them once more. We cannot help but picture panic, helplessness, fear.

The Israelites cried out to the Lord, and He made a way for them to be saved, parting the sea so that they could walk through unharmed. Then He closed it over their enemies. He had done the impossible. Through His miraculous work, He freed the Israelites and brought them to safety. In light of this miracle, Moses and the Israelites sang to the Lord (Exodus 15:1–18). Their song boasted of the Lord's victory and strength and worshiped Him for His awesome deeds.

Today there exist many "gods" that fight for our attention and worship. Though we may not bow down to them as statues, we sacrifice our time, money, and attention to the idols of our own choosing. We might worship our image, sacrificing everything to be thin or beautiful. We might worship success, sacrificing time and energy to obtain the next promotion. Or maybe, our idol of choice is money, a boyfriend, or our family. While none of these desires are inherently bad, they become our gods when we set them up on a pedestal. We expect that they will satisfy our deepest desires. We look to them for security and fulfillment in an attempt to make good things fill a void that none but Christ can fill. Only God can satisfy, for He is like no other. He is glorious and holy, worthy of praise. He alone performs marvelous wonders.

When we see Him, nothing else compares. Just like the Israelites, the Lord has delivered us from slavery, too, not from the Egyptians but from our own sin. We were lost, helpless, and hopeless. We were condemned to death. But God made a way through His Son, Jesus. Through Christ, He has parted the waters that separated us from God, and He brings us safely home. He has forgiven us of our sins and covered our shame. He alone is worthy.

DAY 201
A Heart of Belief

If you confess with your mouth, "Jesus is Lord," and believe in your heart that God raised him from the dead, you will be saved.

ROMANS 10:9

If Christian faith could ever be reduced to a formula, Romans 10:9 might offer us that formula. But faith is not formulaic. Faith is a matter of the heart. What Romans 10:9 offers us is an explanation of what happens inwardly and outwardly when we place our faith in Jesus Christ.

This verse contains two hinge points of Christianity: Jesus as Lord and Jesus as the resurrected Lord. Paul wanted to be sure that the Roman Christians he was writing this letter to knew that Jesus was not just any lord, but He was *the Lord*. To drive this point home, he used a Greek word for Lord used to describe God the Father over 6,000 times in Scripture but only used to describe Jesus in this one place. He was making a profound statement—just as the Father is God, Jesus is God.

Even more than that, he was encouraging Roman Christians to declare aloud that, "Jesus is Lord!" This was not an empty or meaningless statement. To declare anyone lord apart from Caesar was a punishable offense. The ones who declared aloud, "Jesus is Lord!" without doubt, did it from a place of unwavering faith and devotion to Jesus, no matter what came.

A statement like this could only flow from a heart of belief. Paul tells us that a heart of belief must believe God raised Jesus from the dead. "Jesus is Lord" is a true statement, but "Jesus is the Lord who paid for my sins with His death then rose again" is a personal and saving statement. This type of belief in Jesus was more than following a formula for faith. It came not from a desire to check faith boxes but from an inward persuasion so strong that the only possible response was to confess and believe.

How is your heart today? Is it a heart of belief? One that reflects on the incalculable riches you have been given in Christ and then bursts forth in a song of faith? Or is it a heart that is just trying to check the boxes and cross faith off your to-do list? If your relationship with the Lord has become more formulaic than faith-filled, pray that He will give you a heart of belief again today.

DAY 202
Our Great Defense Against Sin

I have treasured your word in my heart so that I may not sin against you.
PSALM 119:11

Sanctification is a wonderful gift for believers—what a joy to be sharpened by God to grow in Christlikeness. However, what can often make this process of sanctification difficult is that it is just that—a process. A process takes time. And in sanctification, we must die to sin daily, which means that it can be a struggle to put certain sins to death—to cut them out of our lives. However, God's Word provides comfort as the Lord sanctifies us. He has not left us defenseless in the fight against sin but has gifted us His Word to help us battle temptation. When we stray from Scripture, we are prone to fall into sin, which awaits us at every turn. We need God's Word to help us walk in obedience to Him as we treasure His Word in our hearts.

To treasure God's Word means that your interaction with God's Word does not end when you read it in the morning or in the evening. Instead of skimming through Scripture and closing your Bible, it is helpful and beneficial to meditate on Scripture and carry its words with you through your day. In Ephesians 6:10–18, Paul exhorts believers to put on the armor of God. One of the pieces of armor is the sword of the spirit—God's Word. He instructs us to carry it with us. Without regularly and intentionally being in God's Word, we will not stand equipped to fight sin. God has given us a great defense in the Bible, but we must use it.

Memorizing Scripture is a great way to treasure God's Word. As we memorize verses, we can call to mind words of truth when we are in moments of temptation. Just as Jesus used the Word of God against Satan's temptation in the desert (Matthew 4:1–11), we can use Scripture we have memorized to block his attacks. May we choose to pick up the Bible daily and treasure His Word in our hearts. May we not live as defenseless believers but remain guarded by the truth of God's Word.

> "WITHOUT REGULARLY AND INTENTIONALLY BEING IN GOD'S WORD, WE WILL NOT STAND EQUIPPED TO FIGHT SIN. GOD HAS GIVEN US A GREAT DEFENSE IN THE BIBLE, BUT WE MUST USE IT."

DAY 203
Grounded in Truth and Love

Now the goal of our instruction is love that comes from a pure heart, a good conscience, and a sincere faith.

1 TIMOTHY 1:5

We live in a reactionary world. When opinions are voiced, there is bound to be someone who speaks back in opposition. Sometimes arguments follow, while other times the cold shoulder is given and the end result is a broken friendship. We have all experienced how quickly conversations can heat up and how deeply they scar those who are burned by them.

How should Christians engage with the world? Should we keep the truth of God's Word to ourselves to avoid conflict? Or should we boldly proclaim it, despite the seemingly negative impact it can sometimes have on our relationships? In 1 Timothy, Paul teaches Timothy how to engage with false teachers within the church and how to share Christ with unbelievers.

Paul shows an incredible amount of humility in his teaching. He says, "'Christ Jesus came into the world to save sinners'—and I am the worst of them" (1 Timothy 1:15). We should never enter a corrective conversation with an attitude other than this: I, a sinner, am here to point you, also a sinner, to the Savior we both desperately need.

Paul also gives us a clear goal for confrontational conversations. The goal is love. The goal is not to be right, win, or prove another person wrong. This does not mean we should not speak the truth, but it does mean that it must lead to love when we speak the truth (1 Corinthians 13:4–7). Is what I am saying patient and kind? Or is it said in envy? Is it boastful? Arrogant? Rude? Self-seeking? Irritable? Am I keeping a record of wrongs or finding joy in someone else's unrighteousness? Do I leave this conversation believing, hoping, and enduring through all things?

What a challenge it is to love like this! This kind of love comes from a heart being continually made pure by sanctification in Christ. It comes from a conscience that is clean before the Lord rather than laden with guilt over unconfessed sin. This love comes from a sincere faith rather than a hypocritical faith—one that loves to confront others but never applies to self. The way to be grounded in truth and love is to be humble and honest about our sinfulness and live in close communion with God. Only then can we be ambassadors of the gospel, sharing it in truth and love.

DAY 204
Holy, Holy, Holy

Each of the four living creatures had six wings; they were covered with eyes around and inside. Day and night they never stop, saying, Holy, holy, holy, Lord God, the Almighty, who was, who is, and who is to come.

REVELATION 4:8

God's holiness means that He is set apart, sacred. He is without sin and perfect in every way. He is not like us who stumble, age, and pass away. He is upstanding, righteous, pure, and unchanging. He is exalted, worthy of complete devotion. He is the mighty, one true God. In light of God's holiness, we recognize our own uncleanness.

Before a holy God, we are found incomplete and wanting, dirty and broken, exposed and aware of our sins and failures. But the hope of the gospel is that though we were guilty, God made a way for us to be cleansed through His Son. When Jesus came, He paved the way for our forgiveness through His perfect life, death, and resurrection. All who believe in Him are clothed by His perfection and welcomed eternally into the kingdom of God.

At times, we will be mocked for this belief in a risen Savior. The book of Revelation was written to persecuted churches, real people being killed for their faith. These saints did not need a pep talk or trite encouragement in light of their pending deaths. They needed God Himself. Within this context, John shares the reason for our future hope: God is the victor. He is holy. He is on His throne, surrounded by 24 elders. Before Him are creatures continually crying out His praises. He does not wonder how the future will work out. His Kingdom is securely established, strong, and eternal. He is all-powerful, and from His throne come flashes of lightning and rumblings of thunder. He rules over all and will have judgment over all.

When we are persecuted for our faith, we remember this truth: our King reigns. He is coming again to make all things right, and He is victorious. In light of these truths, we flee our sin today and run to His mercy. We cling to the righteousness of Christ that cleanses us from our sin and makes us acceptable before a Holy God. We press into our discomfort, remembering that Christ endured the worst punishment of all, bearing the weight of our sins on His body. He is the one true God, who was and is and is to come. He is the victor, the Holy One.

"THE REASON FOR OUR FUTURE HOPE: GOD IS THE VICTOR."

DAY 205
His Promise Preserves

> *This is my comfort in my affliction: Your promise has given me life.*
> PSALM 119:50

People often break their promises. When promises are broken, we can feel disappointed and vulnerable, manipulated or abandoned. We, too, can be unfaithful to the promises we make to others and God. However, God's Word never fails, for He is ever faithful. The Bible is a book about God's covenant promise to His people, and the culmination of this promise comes to fulfillment in Jesus Christ.

Psalm 119 is an expression of love for the law of God, and in verse 50, the author praises God for His promise—the agreement to secure a people for Himself and bless them with a place in His presence. God chose the Israelites through whom He would demonstrate His faithfulness. But in order to receive the blessings of this promise, the Israelites had to demonstrate covenant loyalty and love by obeying God's law. The psalmist saw the Law as the pathway to life and security in God. Though God knew the Israelites would disobey, He would not let their corruption break His covenant commitment. He would send a Savior on their behalf so that the blessings of the promise could come to fruition.

Jesus Christ obeyed the Law perfectly in our place and gave His life on the cross to save us. Because of His obedience, He won the covenant blessings. Jesus received the gift of eternal life in the Father's presence and rose from the grave into His heavenly home. Through His saving work, Jesus fulfilled God's promise. Jesus secured a people for the Father and gave them an eternal place in His presence. Through our faith and the indwelling Holy Spirit, we too experience the blessings of God's promise and enjoy the gift of life with God now while we look forward to resting with Him in eternity. We rejoice, for His fulfilled promise gives us life that triumphs over death and erases the darkness. His covenant commitment enables us to obey His Word in gratitude for His salvation as His promise preserves our faith.

> "JESUS CHRIST OBEYED THE LAW PERFECTLY IN OUR PLACE AND GAVE HIS LIFE ON THE CROSS TO SAVE US."

DAY 206
When We Do Not Know Where to Go

Your word is a lamp for my feet and a light on my path.
PSALM 119:105

Without a map on a journey, we may have no idea what way to go. We can be left feeling lost and helpless. Maybe you have also experienced feeling emotionally lost, uncertain about the next big step in life, unsure what you should do. Maybe you have felt as though you have lost your passion or purpose in life. To be lost, whether physically or circumstantially, is a nerve-wracking experience that easily brings with it stress and anxiety.

Thankfully, God has provided a map for our journey in life. He has given us a lamp for our feet and a light for our path. He has not left us alone, searching blindly for the road. He has not expected great things from us and left us to helplessly guess what they are. He has given us His Word.

Sometimes we long to find the hidden will of God through mysterious signs. We look for clues in our lives, coincidences pointing to what He wants for us. But God has told us what He desires from us: that we would love Him with all our hearts, souls, mind, and strength and that we would love our neighbors as ourselves (Luke 10:27). He has given us specific biblical principles that guide us in wisdom of how to choose who to marry (2 Corinthians 6:14), how to resolve conflict (Matthew 18:15–17), and how to parent our children (Ephesians 6:4). He has given us all that we need for life and godliness through His Word. While the Bible does not give the specific name of the college you should attend or the name of your future spouse, He gives us the principles for biblical decision making, and beyond that, the freedom in Christ to choose. In Christ, we can trust that the grace of God covers our mistakes and poor decisions.

God does not sit back, maliciously hiding His will, expecting us to find it on our own. His Word lights our path as we search its truths. He desires what is best for us and has revealed all that we need for life and godliness through Scripture.

"IN CHRIST, WE CAN TRUST THAT THE GRACE OF GOD COVERS OUR MISTAKES AND POOR DECISIONS."

DAY 207

Fully Known

Lord, you have searched me and known me. You know when I sit down and when I stand up; you understand my thoughts from far away. You observe my travels and my rest; you are aware of all my ways. Before a word is on my tongue, you know all about it, Lord. You have encircled me; you have placed your hand on me. This wondrous knowledge is beyond me. It is lofty; I am unable to reach it.

PSALM 139:1–6

God is much greater than we could ever imagine. He knows us so well that Jesus tells us in Luke 12:7, "Indeed, the hairs of your head are all counted." This may be beyond our comprehension. But just as newborn babies do not know how many fingers and toes they have and their parents can easily count them, so is God able to count the hairs on our heads. However, the most amazing thing about God is the depth of His love for us.

Some of us have experienced opening up to someone, only to have them reject us because of what we revealed about ourselves. However, God knows us and loves us completely. He always acts for our good and His glory. God is a safe place for those who know Him. We do not need to be afraid of Him knowing us completely because He will never reject us when we come to Him.

That said, God is also a holy God who cannot be around sin. You may ask, "If God can't be around sin, how can He know us completely and not reject us?" God can do this because Christ came, took on our sin and shame, and died on the cross in our place. In dying on the cross, Christ defeated death and rose from the grave. Because of Jesus's death, He was able to put His righteousness on us. This is why—as long as our faith is in Christ alone—we can rest secure in the knowledge that though we sin, God will never turn us away when we come before Him in repentance and praise of who He is.

If you put on a false self because you are afraid of being known—rest in the truth that God already fully knows you and still loves you. While you were still a sinner, Christ died for you. He takes you as you are—in your mess and weakness—as you trust Him with your life.

"GOD IS A SAFE PLACE FOR THOSE WHO KNOW HIM."

DAY 208

Crowned for Endurance

"This saying is trustworthy: For if we died with him, we will also live with him; if we endure, we will also reign with him; if we deny him, he will also deny us; if we are faithless, he remains faithful, for he cannot deny himself."

2 TIMOTHY 2:11-13

God calls us in His Word to endure the race set before us (Hebrews 12:1). In 2 Timothy, Paul also calls Timothy to endure. Paul writes to Timothy from prison, instructing and encouraging him as he pastors a struggling church in Ephesus. Paul urges him to remember that God has sovereignly placed him in his current position, and so he should not be discouraged by circumstances he faces within the church. He reminds Timothy to remain strong in the Lord as he endures suffering. But why should Timothy choose to endure? Why should we choose to endure in our own trying circumstances?

We can answer both of these questions with the same, resounding answer: Jesus. Jesus endured suffering and was called to endure. He endured mocking, beating, shame, and an agonizing death on the cross so that we could have hope, a reason to endure. In Christ's sacrifice, He made a way for us to be saved and have eternal life with Him. If we have died to ourselves and found life in Him, it is everlasting life, though presently we suffer. This gives us reason to endure, no matter what may come our way.

The Lord will not place circumstances in our lives that He will not also provide for us the strength to remain steadfast. He does not promise Christians an easy life (John 16:33). Neither were Paul and Timothy promised easy lives. They were called to suffer for Christ's sake—for sharing the gospel with others. Paul and Timothy endured great persecution, yet we learn that the hope of Christ and the gospel gave them endurance to the end, their faith anchored in Christ alone.

So as we run our race, let us do so with endurance because of our hope in Him—who He is and what He has done for us. Though our troubles may not cease, neither will our Savior's faithful love or the hope we find in Him. We can look forward to the day that our struggles will be no more. Enduring the race set before us, may we fix our gaze on Christ, who gives us strength. He will remain ever faithful.

"SO AS WE RUN OUR RACE, LET US DO SO WITH ENDURANCE BECAUSE OF OUR HOPE IN HIM."

DAY 209
The Blessing of Reproof

See how happy is the person whom God corrects; so do not reject the discipline of the Almighty. For he wounds but he also bandages; he strikes, but his hands also heal.

JOB 5:17–18

From the moment we can comprehend discipline, we do not like it. We cry, we scream, we stomp our feet, we get angry, we retaliate, and maybe we try to avoid it. Discipline is not fun, correction is not eagerly anticipated, and we do not find our enjoyment in reproof. But as we mature, we find that discipline is necessary for growth and change.

Even if we understand discipline better as we age, we still may struggle to respond well to it. And we may even scratch our heads when we read about Job, who lost every good thing in his life as no consequence to his own doing but sheerly for the testing of his faith. We still witness him saying with confidence, "happy is the person whom God corrects!" After the loss of his children, his wealth and possessions, his wife, his esteem, and almost everything associated with his name, Job's faith in God's purposes is astounding. Though perhaps challenging to comprehend such a response, it is evident that Job trusts in who God is and what He does.

The blessing of God's reproof is that it seeks to correct our course and reorient our gaze toward heaven. God desires better for us, even at the cost of things we wish to hold on to, ever so tightly. Sometimes that means exposing sin, and sometimes that simply means stripping us of our earthly comforts to leave us clinging to Christ. God is determined to sanctify us into the likeness of Jesus Christ, and that means chipping away at the things in our life that stand in the way. Just like a perfect surgeon, He takes a scalpel to the tumor-sized sin in our hearts that threatens to destroy us. He scrapes and wounds us to remove it, but He does so in love to ultimately bind us up and give us new life. When our hearts are chiseled and corrected by God, we can praise and thank Him for His reproof. Even in pain, we can proclaim, just like Job, the blessings of reproof. God cares for us too deeply to leave us unchanged.

"WHEN OUR HEARTS ARE CHISELED AND CORRECTED BY GOD, WE CAN PRAISE AND THANK HIM FOR HIS REPROOF."

DAY 210
Committed to God's Work

So I said to them, "You see the trouble we are in. Jerusalem lies in ruins and its gates have been burned. Come, let's rebuild Jerusalem's wall, so that we will no longer be a disgrace." I told them how the gracious hand of my God had been on me, and what the king had said to me.

NEHEMIAH 2:17–18A

The city of God was in ruins. After the Babylonians invaded Jerusalem, they left the city destroyed. They carried away the gold and silver. Years later, even after many Jews had returned from exile, the people were weary, anxious, and in despair at the state of their nation. After generations of prosperity, the people of Israel were now vulnerable and destitute with no protection, security, or gold.

But while in exile, God raised a man named Nehemiah to rebuild the city of Jerusalem. The Lord put a burden on Nehemiah's heart about the condition of his nation. And in an amazing act of providence, the king of Persia allowed Nehemiah to go and rebuild Jerusalem's walls (Nehemiah 2:8).

God can use whomever He chooses to accomplish His purposes, including a pagan king. And God continued to use Nehemiah too. Nehemiah consistently took the next step of faith placed in front of him, first by asking the king of Persia for permission to go to Jerusalem, then by rallying the people to endure opposition, pray boldly, and restore the city. He led the people to follow the Lord's commands and rebuild the city of Jerusalem, committing himself to God's work and faithfully completing it.

Many years later, Christ became the perfect leader for His people, bravely defying the opposition of sinful man and perfectly obeying the Father. Through His broken body on the cross, Jesus restored our broken temples. He reconciled us to God. And in response to His love, we engage in God's work too.

God uses us to rebuild and restore that which is broken. Because of the fall, we live in a world with constant sickness, despair, and disease. We encounter loss and deceit. And yet, God has placed us here, and He invites us to join His divine mission to tell the world about Him. He calls us to love, serve, and witness to the people in our lives. He ordains our steps and gives us the strength to take them. May we be faithful to accomplish His mission with the energy He so graciously provides (Philippians 2:13).

DAY 211
Our Righteous Judge

It is clear evidence of God's righteous judgment that you will be counted worthy of God's kingdom, for which you also are suffering, since it is just for God to repay with affliction those who afflict you and to give relief to you who are afflicted, along with us. This will take place at the revelation of the Lord Jesus from heaven with his powerful angels, when he takes vengeance with flaming fire on those who don't know God and on those who don't obey the gospel of our Lord Jesus.

2 THESSALONIANS 1:5-8

At times, the world feels heavy. The weight of sin and brokenness presses in, seeking to choke out hope and faith. In this pain and brokenness, we experience anxiety, infertility, disease. The suffering can feel incredibly overwhelming, and when it remains, we can feel as though it will endure forever. However, this brokenness is only temporary; the suffering will not last, for Christ will return to set all things right.

Upon His return, all evil will be destroyed, all affliction will be relieved, all who inflict suffering will be punished. As our righteous judge, God will carry out perfect justice for those who have rejected the gospel. Though it may be difficult to see God as loving in His consequences for sin, He is a good and fair judge and cannot allow sin to go unpunished. Judgment must exist so that sin can be wiped away forever.

God's justice and righteousness should lead us to trust Him. We serve a righteous judge, not one who is impartial or corrupt. Our God cares for the oppressed and vindicates the oppressed. Our God's plan for redemption involves washing away sin forever and restoring the world to everlasting peace.

The reality of God's future judgment should also propel us to share the gospel message. As believers, we have a message that impacts eternity for every person. We should not take for granted our responsibility to share the good news of Christ's salvation. As we await the day of Christ's justice, may we do so with patience and perseverance, using the time we are given to declare the mercy of our great God. And when brokenness and sin press in once again, let us rest in our righteous judge who will one day make all things right and new.

"THE REALITY OF GOD'S FUTURE JUDGMENT SHOULD ALSO PROPEL US TO SHARE THE GOSPEL MESSAGE."

DAY 212
The Wonders of God

Come and see the wonders of God; his acts for humanity are awe-inspiring.

PSALM 66:5

The wonders of God surround you. Sometimes they are hard to see, sometimes we do not stop to look for them, and sometimes we become so busy that we forget they are there at all. Today, let us take time to consider the wonders of our great God.

God has given His Son, Jesus, as a payment for the sins of those who believe. As He died upon the cross, His blood spilled out to set us free. As a result, believers are saved from eternal death and brought into eternal life with Christ! This is a gift, not of our own doing.

We read in Ephesians 2:10 that we are "created in Christ Jesus for good works, which God prepared ahead of time for us to do." We are not purposeless. Believers have been created to do good works and are given the joy of fulfilling them as God's plan for our lives. Let us remember to praise Him for this gift!

Another of God's greatest gifts to mankind is the Word of God that He breathed out and is "profitable for teaching, for rebuking, for correcting, for training in righteousness" (2 Timothy 3:16). God has given Scripture to us as a source of truth and direction for our lives. We are not left aimless in navigating the highs and lows of life but can look to His Word and the truth and wisdom it holds.

The Lord promises that we can have peace in the hard seasons of life. In John 16:33, Jesus says, "I have told you these things so that in me you may have peace. You will have suffering in this world. Be courageous! I have conquered the world." Life will certainly be hard, but we can trust that God will always provide His perfect peace.

God grants us life for all eternity if we have trusted Him as our Lord and Savior. We read in John 5:24, "Truly I tell you, anyone who hears my word and believes him who sent me has eternal life and will not come under judgment but has passed from death to life." The end for a believer is not death but life. We will not be judged based on what we do but rather on what Jesus has done for us. Oh, how wondrous is our God!

"GOD HAS GIVEN SCRIPTURE TO US AS A SOURCE OF TRUTH AND DIRECTION FOR OUR LIVES."

DAY 213
Boast in the Lord

This is what the Lord says: The wise person should not boast in his wisdom; the strong should not boast in his strength; the wealthy should not boast in his wealth. But the one who boasts should boast in this: that he understands and knows me—that I am the Lord, showing faithful love, justice, and righteousness on the earth, for I delight in these things. This is the Lord's declaration.

JEREMIAH 9:23–24

Made in the image of God, humans possess intellect and creativity. Their wisdom equips them in devising plans, making decisions, and building structures. Though a human's physical strength is limited, human beings have an inner strength that endures hardship through the strength of Christ in us. Humans are also wealthy—some adorned in jewels and luxurious fabric. But even the riches of the most decorated woman pale in comparison to the riches of a woman in relationship with Her Creator and others. God is gracious and has given His image-bearers gifts of wisdom, strength, and wealth to reflect His glory.

Humans are fallen creatures too. Often, our gifts are distorted by sin, which has invaded the hearts of all people. Instead of seeing God-given gifts of wisdom, strength, and wealth as reasons to serve the Lord, men and women take pride in themselves. We all likely have an area of work, personal characteristic, or identity in which we take pride and sometimes become boastful.

Through the prophet Jeremiah, the Lord called His people to boast in the knowledge of Him alone. As His creation, we need to be reconciled to our Creator. We need to be freed from sin and come into a relationship with God. But to do so, we need to trust in the Savior's accomplishment on the cross for our sins; through Him, we can overcome pride and put on humility. This Savior, Jesus, possessed true wisdom, strength, and wealth. Jesus was the eternal Son of God, all-seeing, all-powerful, and possessing all the riches as the true King. Through His saving work, we can know God. We can talk to Him as if He was right there with us. We see the Father in the face of Jesus Christ; His faithful love, justice, and righteousness were on display when Jesus died. As redeemed image-bearers, we boast in the cross of Christ (1 Corinthians 1:18–31). We commit our skills, achievements, and talents to honor the Lord and proclaim the gospel until He returns.

DAY 214

Spiritual Habits

When Daniel learned that the document had been signed, he went into his house. The windows in its upstairs room opened toward Jerusalem, and three times a day he got down on his knees, prayed, and gave thanks to his God, just as he had done before.

DANIEL 6:10

What would you do if you knew you would be punished unless you gave up your faith? In Daniel 6, Daniel received word that whoever worshiped anyone other than King Darius would be thrown into the lion's den, and Daniel went immediately to his house to pray. In fact, he continued to pray three times a day, continually thanking the Lord. He knew he could be persecuted for his faith, yet he openly knelt to pray in front of open windows, declaring His worship to God alone.

Daniel's daily prayer routine was a regular rhythm in his life. Could we say the same about our own prayer lives and other spiritual habits? We may not be persecuted for worshiping the Lord, but we should have the same vigilance as Daniel in our own spiritual habits. When we make these habits a priority in our lives, we will find they come naturally in every circumstance.

We grow spiritual habits for the sake of becoming more like Christ as they shape us to be more and more like Him. Their regular rhythm is necessary for our growth as believers. But in order to establish a regular rhythm, we cannot brush them off as unimportant. We long to have a routine of spiritual habits but often fail to make them a priority. When this happens, we likely become discouraged, struggling to follow through with spiritual disciplines of prayer, bible study, and evangelism.

We should consider how we choose to spend our time each day. It can be easy to allow things of this world to shape us more than those of Christ. Prioritizing spiritual habits certainly takes discipline, yet they are worth the work. The more we rely on the Holy Spirit to prompt us toward those habits and intentionally choose to prioritize spiritual disciplines, the more we will find the disciplines as a way of life. Like Daniel, they will be what we practice, not only when joy abounds but when trouble comes.

"WE GROW SPIRITUAL HABITS FOR THE SAKE OF BECOMING MORE LIKE CHRIST AS THEY SHAPE US TO BE MORE AND MORE LIKE HIM."

DAY 215
Remembering His Words

"Remember how he spoke to you when he was still in Galilee, saying, 'It is necessary that the Son of Man be betrayed into the hands of sinful men, be crucified, and rise on the third day'?" And they remembered his words.

LUKE 24:6B–8

Mourning can cause us to forget. In the thick of our grief, sometimes the most we can do is complete the smallest tasks as we try to occupy our minds. We forget details. The days seem hazy, and time almost slips from our fingers. Perhaps Jesus's disciples and the women who followed Him felt this way following His death. Everything must have been a blur.

They had lived and traveled with Jesus for three years. He had instructed them, cared for them, and loved them. The best person and friend they had ever had was now gone. And while, on this side of history, we know what happened three days after His death, they did not. They faced the reality that maybe He was not who He said He was, and maybe Israel was still awaiting a Savior. Maybe they had been wrong.

But when the women made their way to the tomb three days after His death, they saw the stone was rolled away. Jesus's body was nowhere to be found. As they likely looked at each other in wonder, two men appeared to them and told them that Jesus was alive, for He had risen from the grave. These angels said that Jesus had told them this would happen.

And then they remembered. They remembered the words He spoke that tenderly prepared them for what was coming, words they had forgotten as they mourned His loss. And these words made all the difference. If they had remembered these words as Jesus hung upon the cross, they would have known the story did not end there. Jesus told them He would be crucified, but He also said He would rise again. There was hope coming after all of the darkness.

As we wait on Christ's return, it is important that we also remember His Words. Jesus tells us that He is coming soon, and He has given us hope as we wait for His arrival. How easy it is to forget His Words if we do not read them. It is easy to become caught up in our present-day lives if we forget to consider our future home with Christ. We must remember, for His Words change everything about our lives.

"THERE WAS HOPE COMING AFTER ALL OF THE DARKNESS."

DAY 216
Future Grace

Therefore, with your minds ready for action, be sober-minded and set your hope completely on the grace to be brought to you at the revelation of Jesus Christ.

1 PETER 1:13

Our lives are filled with both mountain top and valley experiences. One day we can feel incredible joy, bounding forward in what God has called us to with confidence. Another day we can feel incredibly overwhelmed and discouraged, wondering how to move forward with all our struggles. We can read how we are to be alert and active in Scripture but question how this is possible on the days we can barely keep our head above the water.

God does not call us to action without giving us the ability to abound. By His grace, He has given us a blessed hope that is not only our motivation but our hope as we press on in this life. Our hope is the grace that we will receive when Christ returns. As Christ followers, we have received God's grace. This grace has covered our sins and is transforming us daily into the image of Christ. Though we have not yet received the fullness of God's grace, we will when He returns. He will remove all of our sins from us and transform us into new and glorified people.

We should live with our gaze set on our future hope in Christ. As believers, this future hope helps us abound in the present. Knowing that complete deliverance, joy, and peace await us in heaven with the Lord lifts our spirits on the days we find it hard to stand. And as we await our future grace, we can rest in the present grace Christ gives us, the grace that carries us through this life.

On the good days, when our joy is full, we can be reminded that this is a picture and just a taste of our blessed hope to come. One day, we will know only everlasting joy as we live in bodies and a world free from sin, pain, and brokenness. Until that time comes, may we stand firm in the present, using the time we are given to serve the Lord and make His name known. May we set our hope completely on the grace to come with abounding confidence and perseverance.

"ONE DAY, WE WILL KNOW ONLY EVERLASTING JOY AS WE LIVE IN BODIES AND A WORLD FREE FROM SIN, PAIN, AND BROKENNESS."

DAY 217
A Godly Response

My dear brothers and sisters, understand this: Everyone should be quick to listen, slow to speak, and slow to anger, for human anger does not accomplish God's righteousness.

JAMES 1:19–20

We generally categorize right speech as one that is encouraging, gentle, and loving. We value a tongue that is self-controlled and follows the ear's listening. Why do our consciences recognize what kind of speech is acceptable? We are made in the image of God, whose speech is encouraging, gentle, and loving. Our souls detect ungodly responses and desire words that reflect the Lord's character.

James wrote about a worldview founded on the ultimate truth of God. James was the half-brother of Jesus and a zealous leader in the early church who wrote a letter that was passed around to Christians of Jewish and Gentile descent. James called the readers to live life according to their faith in Christ. He identified that our speech should illuminate knowledge of the gospel and faith in Jesus. Because of our belief in Him, we should produce the fruit of delightful speech—not one that is belligerent, irate, or hasty.

The wisdom literature of James calls us to respond with our words in godly ways. However, the book calls us to a behavior that we do not pursue apart from Christ. We should pattern after Jesus with our godly speech, but His tongue was the only perfect one. Jesus was slow to speak when confronted and wrongly accused by the religious authority. He responded, not in sinful anger but with gracious truth. Jesus was calm and self-controlled so that He did not fall into Satan's trap. Jesus did not defend Himself or cry out for vengeance on the cross. His silence was strength; it was a quiet confidence that His righteousness would accomplish salvation.

Since we are saved by His righteousness, let us continue to walk in Him. We do not need to prove ourselves with aggressive, impulsive, or sarcastic speech. Such words will lead to negative consequences and cause us to miss an opportunity to reflect the gospel. In tense situations, we should listen before we speak, seeking first to understand and empathize. Then, we should examine our hearts and surrender all unbridled passions to Jesus. We can pray that the Holy Spirit would give us godly words. Some of us may wrestle with an angry tongue throughout our journeys, but one day in the new creation, we will perfectly utter words for God's glory.

DAY 218
By Your Words

"For by your words you will be acquitted, and by your words you will be condemned."

MATTHEW 12:37

Our words carry weight. What leaves our mouth has the potential to lift up or tear down, to bring life or to bring death. Often, we do not realize the power or consequences of our words. We speak without thinking about what just left our mouths, and as a result, we can hurt others or harm relationships.

Jesus speaks about the impact of words in Matthew 12 to convict the Pharisees over their speech. The Pharisees were self-proclaimed Christ followers, yet their words did not reflect the God they obeyed. Their words put others down and spoke harshly against Jesus. Their speech revealed that they did not know God and that the condition of their hearts was wicked. We must be careful not to use our words for evil as the Pharisees did, for Jesus warns that each of us will give an account one day for the words we speak.

By God's grace, Jesus has forgiven our past, present, and future sinful words. When we stand before the Lord one day, Christ's grace will acquit our words. However, this does not mean we are free to speak whatever we please. Paul writes in Ephesians 4:29, "No foul language should come from your mouth, but only what is good for building up someone in need, so that it gives grace to those who hear." As believers, we should be careful about what leaves our mouths, for what leaves our mouths is an overflow of our hearts. Words that speak ill of others reveal pride and anger, while words of grumbling and complaining reveal envy and bitterness.

Our words should reflect the God we serve. As gospel witnesses, our words have the potential to point to Jesus or away from Him. The weight of our words should cause us to think critically about the words we speak, examining any sin in our hearts to bring in repentance before the Lord. Spending daily time in God's Word will also shape the words we speak. As we fill our minds with Scripture, we will fill our mouths with words that speak life.

Christ's grace will bring acquittal for our words in the future, but may His grace move us to speak words of compassion, kindness, and love in the present. Our words matter, so let us aim to use our words in a way that honors the Lord.

"OUR WORDS SHOULD REFLECT THE GOD WE SERVE."

DAY 219
Love One Another

I give you a new command: Love one another. Just as I have loved you, you are also to love one another. By this everyone will know that you are my disciples, if you love one another.

JOHN 13:34–35

Most of us can probably relate to lashing out to others at some point or another. If we are honest with ourselves, our gut reaction is often to match rudeness with rudeness. Many of us struggle even to be kind to our families. When our children fray our last nerve, we snap at them. When our husband forgets to close the cupboard doors, we slam them closed ourselves. When our friends forget to invite us somewhere, we decide to ignore them.

It is in our fallen nature to lose our temper, speak harshly, or become upset when we are tired or hurt. On our own, we cannot follow God's laws. God knows this about us. This is why He sent Jesus. Jesus's death on the cross sets us free from that bondage of sin, restores us to Him, and allows us to love others through the power of the Holy Spirit.

Christ's disciples—those who follow Him—are marked by their love because God is love (1 John 4:16). This great love is one of His communicable attributes, meaning it is a character trait He can share with us. And He develops our capacity to love as we spend more time with Him in His Word and in prayer. As we spend time with God, we come to reflect His ways. Just as the people you spend the most time with impact your behavior, it should come as no surprise that spending time with God impacts everything about us—our thoughts, our words, our beliefs, and our actions.

If we ever struggle to show love to someone, we should press into Christ. Spend time in His Word, meditating on the truths of Scripture. Read of His great love for you, and allow that love to overflow through you to those around you. Through your love, may others see the love of their heavenly Father and come to know Him as their own.

> "JESUS'S DEATH ON THE CROSS SETS US FREE FROM THAT BONDAGE OF SIN, RESTORES US TO HIM, AND ALLOWS US TO LOVE OTHERS THROUGH THE POWER OF THE HOLY SPIRIT."

DAY 220
Helping One Another to Heaven

And let us watch out for one another to provoke love and good works, not neglecting to gather together, as some are in the habit of doing, but encouraging each other, and all the more as you see the day approaching.

HEBREWS 10:24–25

The author of Hebrews wrote to persecuted Christians. In chapter 10, we learn these believers were publicly ridiculed and their property destroyed. Because of their troubles, Christians lost confidence in their faith. The biblical author identified their need to persevere in their faith and called them to endure. He encouraged them to resist threats by holding on to their faith.

The people were tempted to shrink back in the face of evil and opposition. However, they could stand victorious because of their salvation. The author reminded them of the joy and compassion of Christ they could show toward their enemies. They could hope in the greater possession given in heaven and have peace that their souls were secure, no matter what happened.

The end of Hebrews exhorts and encourages based on the perfect work of Christ. Earlier in the letter, the author declared Jesus's supremacy. He illuminated Christ, who, by His perfect sacrifice, washed God's people clean so they could enter His presence and be kept safe from evil's torment. Believers can hold fast to Christ since His work never wavers. The writer of Hebrews also moved believers to encourage one another. As a redeemed community, they were to stir up faith in each other when they encountered trials, motivating each other to love and obey. They were not to shrink back from society but continue to meet together, spurring each other onward and focusing on their heavenly hope and the joy of Jesus.

Jesus's supremacy is the foundation on which we hold to our faith and encourage others to do the same. Sin and human frailty cannot take away the gift of salvation. Jesus has encouraged us to endure trials through His Spirit. We may also experience public ridicule or discrimination for our faith, but we can hold fast to our faith as we persevere in Christ. The Holy Spirit urges us onward toward love and obedience and moves us to find strength in community with other believers. If you struggle in your faith, surround yourself with a community of strong believers for encouragement. If you are strong in your faith, exhort a believer who is struggling. Let us all endure together as a picture of the faithful community for whom Jesus will return.

DAY 221
The Safety of Counsel

Without guidance, a people will fall, but with many counselors there is deliverance.

PROVERBS 11:14

We can find comfort and safety by surrounding ourselves with wise counsel, which helps us think objectively and purposefully in times of need. We can be tempted to look for answers within ourselves, only trust our own judgment, or feed our pride by refusing to ask for help. But when we surround ourselves with people who speak truthfully into our lives, we are guarded against making unwise decisions. We see its necessity mentioned continually in Scripture, and the wisdom literature of Proverbs alone is filled with references to the importance of wise counsel.

Wise counsel is guidance and advice shaped with the truth of Scripture. God is the beginning of wisdom, and there is nothing in and of ourselves or anyone else who gives wisdom apart from God (Proverbs 9:10). Though there may seem to be other kinds of worldly wisdom, wise counsel must be rooted in the wisdom of God. When people tell us only what we want to hear, that is not wisdom. When people we seek advice from cannot call out sin in our lives, that is not wisdom. If we ask for help from someone who gives us opinions and counsel based on their own ideas and experiences over what the Bible says, that is not wisdom. Men and women in our lives who faithfully walk with the Lord—using their biblical knowledge and understanding in a useful way that honors God and serves others—are those we can trust for guidance.

The Christian life can be challenging, and we all at some point need help along the way. Wise counsel serves as a guard rail for us in moments of doubt or confusion, trials or hardships. Ultimately, in every circumstance, such counsel should aim to point us back to the central truth of who God is and what He has done. God equips us for these moments with both His Word and His people. Asking for help and wisdom from others encourages a humble heart posture and reminds us of our incapabilities. Because of our sinful nature, it is only by God's good gift of grace that we make any wise decision. God does not leave us to wander when we feel lost, afraid, or helpless. He exhorts His people to be loving and wise reminders of His truth to each other when that truth is forgotten.

"WISE COUNSEL SERVES AS A GUARD RAIL FOR US IN MOMENTS OF DOUBT OR CONFUSION, TRIALS OR HARDSHIPS."

DAY 222
The Curse of Choosing Complacency

On the day you stood aloof, on the day strangers captured his wealth, while foreigners entered his city gate and cast lots for Jerusalem, you were just like one of them.

OBADIAH 1:11

At times, we can neglect the needs of others when we are too focused on ourselves. Instead of moving toward those in need, we stand at a distance, passively allowing them to struggle. In Obadiah, Israel's neighboring nation, Edom, received a prophecy of their punishment for their passivity when Israel was under attack. Though Edom did not belong to Israel, Israel could have intervened, yet they allowed Israel to be seized. While Edom was separate from Israel, the nation shared ties with Israel. The nation of Edom was formed through Esau, brother to Jacob, the father to the nation of Israel. God tells Edom in Obadiah 1:12, "Do not gloat over your brother." In complacency, Edom was gloating over the destruction of their brother instead of helping them. As punishment, God brought destruction upon them.

The book of Obadiah teaches the importance of caring for other image-bearers. Edom did not belong to the nation of Israel, but this did not mean they could not help them. Reversing these roles, Christ's followers should care for everyone, even those who do not know the Lord. Every image-bearer is important to God and, therefore, should be important to us. As followers of Christ, we do not stand at a distance from our brothers but should extend a hand to them. In doing so, we model the love and grace of Christ.

Jesus taught this lesson in the parable of the Good Samaritan. In this parable, Jesus told a story of a Jewish man attacked by robbers. As he lay hurt on the road, he experienced both a priest and a Levite walk past him, yet it was a Samaritan who stopped to help him. Jesus used this lesson to answer the question, "Who is my neighbor?" The Samaritan acted as a neighbor to the hurt man even though Jews and Samaritans did not get along. As believers, we reflect the grace and mercy of Christ by caring for our neighbors. We are to share Christ with all people, no matter who they are. May we move toward others rather than away. May we not resolve to live complacently but actively care for our neighbor.

> "CHRIST'S FOLLOWERS SHOULD CARE FOR EVERYONE, EVEN THOSE WHO DO NOT KNOW THE LORD."

DAY 223
The Purpose of My Life

But I consider my life of no value to myself; my purpose is to finish my course and the ministry I received from the Lord Jesus, to testify to the gospel of God's grace.

ACTS 20:24

We all seek out a purpose in life. We want our lives to matter, to mean something. When we look to the Bible, the Apostle Paul discusses the purpose of his life. Our purpose from a worldly standpoint is to make much of our lives for the sake of ourselves. We strive for success, achievement, and doing something greatly impactful. But for Paul, his purpose was not about him. He did not seek fame, fortune, or a successful career. He did not seek to make a name for himself. His life was about testifying to the gospel of Jesus Christ.

The truth of the gospel transformed Paul's life. He was a sinner, opposing God and walking in disobedience, yet God sought Him out in love and saved his life through salvation in Christ. Apart from God, we are dead in sin and in desperate need of the Savior. Our lives, unfortunately, too often exalt sin and the gratification of our selfish desires. But God desires better for us. He desires to give our lives true purpose and meaning in the way He originally designed them to be.

When we come to know the Lord as our Savior, we die to our old selves. We repent of our sin-exalting ways and turn to put on the righteous ways of Christ. We are raised up from the dead of sin to a new life in Jesus Christ. Because God's grace is displayed through the sacrifice of His Son, we are compelled to live our lives for the glory of His name and not our own. Our purpose, like Paul, becomes God's purpose. God sent Jesus Christ to the world for one reason– to save His people from their sins and restore their relationship with Him. Therefore, our purpose is to testify to the salvation we have received in Christ and share the work that Christ accomplished in us and then commissioned to us as His people. This should remain our greatest aim and purpose in life–to finish this life, having taken every opportunity to testify to the name of Jesus. May we seek to proclaim Him with our lives to a watching world!

"WHEN WE COME TO KNOW THE LORD AS OUR SAVIOR, WE DIE TO OUR OLD SELVES."

DAY 224
Knowing Christ

But everything that was a gain to me, I have considered to be a loss because of Christ. More than that, I also consider everything to be a loss in view of the surpassing value of knowing Christ Jesus my Lord.

PHILIPPIANS 3:7–8A

Paul was a Pharisee, a religious authority who strictly observed Jewish tradition and law. He knew the Word of God inside and out and gave special attention to the extra-biblical standards which Jewish custom imposed. In addition to this influential status, Paul was known for his zeal and righteousness. But his ambition and accolades were stripped away when he encountered the risen Savior, Jesus. In the presence of the Son of God, Paul faced his sin and need for salvation. He dropped his Pharisee title and his good works, viewing them as filth compared to the purity of Jesus's perfection. His redemption spurred him to spread the news of Jesus's death and resurrection. Paul prompted others to exchange their earthly knowledge for the knowledge of Christ, declaring that the blessings of knowing the Savior far outweigh anything else.

While writing a letter to the church in Philippi, Paul was in prison for the gospel mission. This situation was much different than the elite lifestyle he lived as a Pharisee. Paul lost his reputation but gained Christ, who was with him in suffering. Despite his struggles, Paul held to the knowledge of Jesus. To him, the cross was not a failure but a sign of humility and the way to life. He told the Philippians of his desire to know Jesus more and more. Paul denied the ambitious pursuit of earthly knowledge and sought knowledge that lasts for eternity.

Paul's conviction to grow in his knowledge of Christ encourages believers today. As God's redeemed, we too should follow in the way of Christ. Our culture boasts knowledge of many things. However, we must recognize that ambition and accolades do not gain our righteousness. Earthly knowledge is filth if used without the light of Christ. View these achievements as losses compared to our gain in Christ's righteousness. Let us strive toward the goal of knowing God more. The revelation of Jesus is deep and vast; there is so much to discover about the majesty and power displayed in His death and resurrection. Though we are limited in knowing all now, we can look forward to coming into complete understanding when we will fully encounter Him again.

"THE REVELATION OF JESUS IS DEEP AND VAST."

DAY 225
Truthful and Sincere Service

Therefore, fear the Lord and worship him in sincerity and truth. Get rid of the gods your fathers worshiped beyond the Euphrates River and in Egypt, and worship the Lord.

JOSHUA 24:14

In Joshua 24, Joshua gathers the people to renew their covenant relationship with the Lord. These will be the last recorded words Joshua speaks to Israel as their leader before his death. Joshua reminds the people of their history and the faithfulness of God. As he tells event after event, a theme repeats itself. The Lord has gone before the people, and He has always delivered them. Though the people had rejected the Lord and turned to foreign gods, He remained the same—steadfast and committed to His covenant with Israel.

Joshua reminds the people of who God is and what He has done so they will remember to properly fear Him and worship Him. The Lord did not want the people to worship Him only for show or because it was what they "had to do." He wanted their whole hearts. He wanted them to be committed to their covenant relationship like He was. And in order for their whole hearts to be His, there could be no other god or idol stealing their worship.

It is easy for us to judge the Israelites and wonder how they could ever look to a man-made god to save them when they had witnessed the miraculous and saving power of the Lord, but we struggle in the same way. The glorious grace of the gospel has saved us and given us abundant life in Christ, yet we look to other things and people for comfort and hope. We often give our primary adoration to our families, friends, and even ourselves. The gods we worship today may not be carven images like the gods in the days of the Israelites, but these false gods have not gone away. They have only taken different forms. We see them in the desire for earthly wealth, social status, beauty, comfort, and acceptance.

In order for us to observe our worship and put off idols, we must ask the Lord for help. He is the One who changes us to become more like Himself, and He will reveal where our worship may be wrongly directed. Let us also remember the faithfulness of God, and let us ask the Lord to remove our own idols so that we can worship Him rightly and give Him the glory due to His name.

DAY 226

Eyes on Glory

So we do not focus on what is seen, but on what is unseen. For what is seen is temporary, but what is unseen is eternal.

2 CORINTHIANS 4:18

The objects of our gaze can reveal the vitality of our spiritual health. Scripture calls us to gaze on the eternal truths of God so that we can have life in Him. Paul emphasized the importance of gazing at the unseen. In his second letter to the Corinthians, he wrote about the suffering he encountered for preaching the gospel, losing his prestige, physical strength, and former colleagues because of his faith. His eyes once focused on these visible things when he was a Pharisee. But, after his conversion, Paul traded his former life of earthly significance for the eternal value of Christ's salvation. Paul's eternal perspective helped him through his suffering as well. He knew the sorrows and the imperfections he saw in his flesh would not last. The affliction was temporary and would prepare him to enter into Christ's glorious presence.

Jesus was surrounded by many things that could have grabbed His attention. However, He was never distracted. Jesus looked to His Father, who would supply Him with the strength and satisfaction needed to accomplish His redemptive mission. Jesus kept His eyes on the plan of salvation through the cross. He focused on the glory and victory that awaited Him. Yet Jesus did not condemn earthly things, for He purposed all to reflect His beauty and creativity. The ultimate disposition of His heart found treasure in the Lord's unseen activity: the establishment of His kingdom and the restoration of His people.

We must seek to see our world with the eyes of Jesus. He will direct our gaze to His unfailing truth. However, because we live in a fallen world, we will continue to wrestle with wandering eyes. When we notice our eyes fixate on the visible, we should examine our hearts. We should consider what our eyes are revealing: could it be an inner need for rest, pleasure, or peace? Whatever the need, we know Jesus will supply. Let us keep our eyes fixed on glory and His glorious return that awaits.

"JESUS DID NOT CONDEMN EARTHLY THINGS, FOR HE PURPOSED ALL TO REFLECT HIS BEAUTY AND CREATIVITY."

DAY 227
We Look to You

Our God, will you not judge them? For we are powerless before this vast number that comes to fight against us. We do not know what to do, but we look to you.

2 CHRONICLES 20:12

Do you remember a time you found yourself in a seemingly impossible situation? Maybe you questioned what to do and where to go? We might experience this feeling after losing a job, experiencing heartbreak, or hearing challenging medical news. These moments remind us how little we control, leaving us in the uncomfortable reality of the unknown.

Jehoshaphat likely experienced similar feelings as a king who grew anxious with his surroundings. During Jehoshaphat's reign, he strengthened and established Judah, and his kingdom knew peace, prosperity, and protection. He ruled over his people with a fear of the Lord, and he instructed his people to be strong in the Lord (2 Chronicles 19:11). At the time he delivered this exhortation, Jehoshaphat suddenly faced an impending battle against the enemies. The troops were many and coming with little time for him to prepare his own army for defense. He must have been afraid. But King Jehoshaphat used his fear as an opportunity to go before the Lord in prayer. He likely had many questions and concerns, but he knew he could not answer and resolve them himself, so he allowed his anxious thoughts and fears to lead him to God.

When we find ourselves in desperate need, we find our greatest help and comfort in the Lord. We can posture ourselves like Jehoshaphat, calling out to the Lord with the simple truth of our reality that we do not know what to do, but He does and can provide us with wisdom along the way. Our prayer displays a relinquishing of control and receiving of God's ultimate sovereignty and care.

Jehosaphat's prayer encompassed many elements. He acknowledged who God is. He recounted God's faithfulness. He affirmed God's promise to always hear and deliver. And He concluded with a petition and plea for help. Jehoshaphat found his strength, not in his defenses or in his strategic mind or his own confidence when trouble was at hand, but he did just as he had instructed his people—he found strength in the Lord through prayer. Prayer positions us under the mighty hand of God. It postures our hearts toward His purposes. In moments when we cannot find words, may we take our troubled hearts before the Lord and trust in His perfect care.

DAY 228
Two Ways to Live

The path of the righteous is like the light of dawn, shining brighter and brighter until midday. But the way of the wicked is like the darkest gloom; they don't know what makes them stumble.

PROVERBS 4:18–19

Many children are allowed to play outside as long as the sun is out, but as soon as the sun starts to go down, they are often called back inside. Consider children, though, who refuse to listen to their parents. Instead of going back inside when the sun goes down, they trek out into the woods. As they walk further and further, the sun begins to dip below the trees, causing the light to fade, and the children are left in complete darkness, lost in the woods. The way of the wicked, or those without Christ, is like those children lost at night. Without the light of the gospel, they are lost in the darkness of sin, stumbling around in the dark with no understanding of what is causing them to stumble.

The way of the righteous, those who know Jesus and have a relationship with Him, is different. This path is lit by the light of the Son, Jesus Christ. Unlike the path of unrighteousness, the knowledge of the gospel allows us to see everything clearly. We can recognize sin and temptation and can avoid sin through the help of the Spirit. The path of the righteous also leads to eternal life, whereas the path of the wicked leads to eternal destruction. Every person has a choice to make: to pursue the path of righteousness or the path of unrighteousness. Even those of us who are believers can benefit from remembering to stay on the path of righteousness.

As believers, the grace of Jesus has secured our eternal destination, but the temptation of sin can cause us to wander into the dark. We can chase after sinful desires and pleasures, which only lead us further and further into the darkness of sin. To combat these desires, we must follow the light of Christ. It is Jesus who set us on the path of righteousness, and it is Jesus who we follow on that path. As long as we pursue Him, we will continue to walk in the light. So may we walk on, allowing Jesus to guide our way.

"IT IS JESUS WHO SET US ON THE PATH OF RIGHTEOUSNESS, AND IT IS JESUS WHO WE FOLLOW ON THAT PATH."

DAY 229

Deeply Rooted

So then, just as you have received Christ Jesus as Lord, continue to live in him, being rooted and built up in him and established in the faith, just as you were taught, and overflowing with gratitude.

COLOSSIANS 2:6–7

You may have heard the phrase, "being fired up for Jesus." Many times, after a church retreat or conference, there can be an exuberance and passion reignited in our hearts from being with the body of Christ and taking intentional time to spend time with the Lord. We are left encouraged to persevere in our faith.

But what tends to often happen after these events is that we try to walk from them in our own power and strength instead of realizing what Christ has done on our behalf. We may know that we can do nothing without Christ, but our day-to-day lives display something different. We hardly acknowledge Jesus as we go from task to task. We talk about Him in our Bible studies and church events, but when they have ended, we just keep going with our own lives, giving little thought to the truths we should have taken away from that time. Each day becomes another display of ourselves and our abilities, desires, frustrations, and failures. And all the while, Christ waits for us to realize that He is all we need.

After we have received Jesus as our Savior, we are to continue walking in Him. This means we are to walk in union with Him. Because we have received salvation in Christ, we are automatically united with Him, covered in His righteousness. But though union with Christ is our reality, many of us live as though we have no union with Him. We try to please Him and worry when we sin that He is disappointed in us. We forget that we always have access to Him through the Holy Spirit, and it is through His power and strength that we can live for Him at all. We are rooted and built up in Christ, and this establishes us in our faith forever. The rest of our lives are our sanctification—the everyday process of becoming more like Him.

As we realize the blessings and joy that come from being united in Christ, we will think more of Him and less of ourselves. We will trust in His strength rather than our own. Our Savior offers Himself to us in every moment as we are rooted in Him.

"WE ARE ROOTED AND BUILT UP IN CHRIST, AND THIS ESTABLISHES US IN OUR FAITH FOREVER."

DAY 230

Ready in Every Season

I solemnly charge you before God and Christ Jesus, who is going to judge the living and the dead, and because of his appearing and his kingdom. Preach the word; be ready in season and out of season; rebuke, correct, and encourage with great patience and teaching.

2 TIMOTHY 4:1-2

It was not supposed to be this way. This truth rests in the heart of nearly every human. We intrinsically know that there was an Eden, perfection, and constant communion with our Creator. And we somehow know that there was a fall from perfection. As humans, we long to return to the garden. And sadly, many lament the brokenness of the world without the hope of reconciling with their Creator. Yet, as believers, we know the end of the story. We know that there is a return to the garden.

All of our greatest longings are satisfied in Christ. At the end of days, Christ will return to set everything right. All the pain and heartache will be gone. Someday, God will restore heaven and earth, and all will be right once again with the world. We have this hope that makes this life bearable as we wait for Christ's return. Yet, we often keep this hope to ourselves. Maybe we get busy or tired or are in a difficult season ourselves. Yet God wants us to share our hope—preach the Word—in and out of season, whether we feel like it or not.

More than that, we are called to rebuke, correct, and encourage—all with patience and by teaching. This means that we need to know God and His Word well enough to align our teachings with the truth. It also means that we will have to have hard conversations and maybe call sin out in one another's lives so that we can encourage each other to continue to walk in His righteousness. This can be an overwhelming call, and it is one that we can only be obedient to if we are spending time in prayer and God's Word, as only God can equip us to fulfill this command.

God's restoration plan is in the works. Even as you sit reading this devotional, God moves to restore His people to Himself. We know that the aching and heartache of this life will not last forever. So in every season, in heartache, happiness, anxiety, and contentment, we must be prepared to preach His Word and remind others of the great hope they have in Him.

"WE NEED TO KNOW GOD AND HIS WORD WELL ENOUGH TO ALIGN OUR TEACHINGS WITH THE TRUTH."

DAY 231

Spirit of Power

For God has not given us a spirit of fear, but one of power, love, and sound judgment.

2 TIMOTHY 1:7

We can feel anything but powerful in our human flesh. Our bodies are weak, and we often struggle with insecurity, fear, and fatigue. However, even though we live in broken bodies, God has given us strength through Christ. As Christ followers, we are equipped with the Holy Spirit who empowers us, fuels our love, and gives us wisdom.

But sometimes, we can forget that God has not given us a spirit of fear and be overcome with doubts, worries, and fears that make us feel hopeless and powerless. As believers, we do not have to live in fear because of Christ's victory on the cross. There is nothing for us to fear. We have the promise of life after death, perseverance in affliction, and the gift of God's constant presence. The Christian life is one of courage. Therefore, we can walk in boldness, knowing that nothing can defeat us, even death itself.

Life without Christ is a life of fear, for without Jesus, there is no certainty or hope to cling to. Because of the grace of Jesus, we are given a life of security, hope, and confidence through Christ. We are to walk in this new spirit we have been given, resting in the power of the Holy Spirit in moments we feel weak. We are to love others without hesitation or timidity. We are to use the wisdom we have been given to make wise decisions that help us pursue righteousness. As we walk in God's power, love, and sound judgment, we will walk in the life of freedom Christ has given us.

In moments we feel afraid, let us remember the spirit we have been given, our spirit of fear forever removed. Let us remember that the spirit of power is ours because of Christ. May we walk in the spirit we have received, full of courage and confidence in the One who created us.

"AS WE WALK IN GOD'S POWER, LOVE, AND SOUND JUDGMENT, WE WILL WALK IN THE LIFE OF FREEDOM CHRIST HAS GIVEN US."

DAY 232
Crafted for His Work

Yet Lord, you are our Father; we are the clay, and you are our potter; we all are the work of your hands.

ISAIAH 64:8

If you have ever watched potters work, you know how mesmerizing it is to see their art take form. The potter places clay onto his wheel and molds the clay into the shape of his design. The clay needs the steady hands of the potter to come alive. Without the hands of the potter, the clay would spin into an utter mess. In this picture, God is the potter, and we are the clay. As God's creation, we are the work of His hands. As our potter, God molds and shapes us how He so wills.

In Isaiah 64:8, the people of Israel were receiving consequences because of their disobedience to the Lord. In this passage, the prophet Isaiah grieves Israel's sins and is pained by how wicked the nation has become. In this dire situation, Isaiah recognizes that Israel is in the hands of God. To be shaped as His people, Israel must surrender to the Lord's actions, even in these painful consequences. After all, the nation of Israel was hand-picked by God to be a holy people, set apart to declare His glory. Through hard circumstances, the Lord was reshaping them into the people He chose them to be.

We can learn from Isaiah by being open-handed to how the Lord shapes us. Just as clay is at the disposal of the potter, so are we at the disposal of the Lord. We need His guidance and intentional hands to form and shape us into the people He created us to be. As God's workmanship, we are created to proclaim the good news of the gospel. It should be our life's joy to point others to Christ.

As God's workmanship, we must be content with the ways He molds us. God will use hard and painful circumstances and the pruning work of sanctification to shape us. We must see how God is forming us to be a greater gospel witness to those around us in these moments. He uses all things to shape us into the image of His Son. The more we surrender to His hands, the more we will grow, the gospel will spread, and God will be glorified. May we be moldable clay in the hands of our Potter—willing to be crafted for His great purposes.

"IT SHOULD BE OUR LIFE'S JOY TO POINT OTHERS TO CHRIST."

DAY 233
Devoted to the Lord

Now Ezra had determined in his heart to study the law of the Lord, obey it, and teach its statutes and ordinances in Israel.
EZRA 7:10

What does it mean to be wholly devoted to the Lord? Is it more than reading our Bibles or praying each night as we lay down to sleep? More than attending church? Or more than serving others on as many committees as our schedules will fit? While these things are undoubtedly good and beneficial as believers, we must ask ourselves, *"What is it exactly to which our hearts are truly devoted?"* Is it our to-do lists? People's thoughts and opinions of us? Our fear of missing out? How easy it can be to devote ourselves to family or friends. Or maybe you find yourself devoted to your work or your favorite hobby.

So often, we give endlessly of our time, emotions, and thoughts to the people and activities around us, without much consideration as to why we do them in the first place. How quickly we can forget to look to God—genuinely devoting ourselves to His call on our lives: to seek and obey Him, sharing the truth of the gospel with those around us and glorifying Him in all that we say, do, and think.

Our devotion to the Lord stems from our love for the Lord and His commandments. We read in Ezra 7:10 that Ezra "determined in his heart to study the law of the Lord." He took time to learn what it said—not simply to glaze over the words in an effort to mark it off a list but because He desired to know God more. He took the Scriptures to heart and learned its instruction and what the Lord desired of Him. In knowing God's Word, Ezra could obey its valuable instruction in his life. And in obeying the Lord, the Lord was able to use Ezra to teach its instruction. Jesus calls us to go and make disciples of all nations, teaching God's commands.

May we follow Ezra's wise example—devoting ourselves to time in God's Word and in prayer, offering all of ourselves to Him. As we commit our lives to the Lord in this way, we will find joy in obeying the Lord and teaching others of the great joy it brings!

"OUR DEVOTION TO THE LORD STEMS FROM OUR LOVE FOR THE LORD AND HIS COMMANDMENTS."

DAY 234
True Faith and Repentance

Two men went up to the temple to pray, one a Pharisee and the other a tax collector. The Pharisee was standing and praying like this about himself: "God, I thank you that I'm not like other people—greedy, unrighteous, adulterers, or even like this tax collector. I fast twice a week; I give a tenth of everything I get." But the tax collector, standing far off, would not even raise his eyes to heaven but kept striking his chest and saying, "God, have mercy on me, a sinner!" I tell you, this one went down to his house justified rather than the other; because everyone who exalts himself will be humbled, but the one who humbles himself will be exalted.

LUKE 18:10–14

When Jesus shared this parable, He knew there were many, namely the Pharisees, who outwardly claimed obedience to God but inwardly were filled with pride and self-glorification. The example Jesus presents makes a distinction between a Pharisee and a tax collector. It was not the words or the actions that made the two so different, but it was the posture of their hearts. The Pharisee was puffed up and presented his righteous acts to God, even to the point of belittling another to make himself look better. But the other man, the tax collector, humbled himself before the Lord and acknowledged His great need for mercy and forgiveness.

Only the tax collector truly understood his need to repent and receive God's grace. The Pharisee lacked a humble and genuine desire to seek forgiveness and an understanding of his great need for God's grace. Jesus reminds us through this parable that faith is not about our outward presentation of obedience but the humble posture of our hearts. Only with humble hearts are we able to truly repent and seek forgiveness. Our repentance is disingenuous when disguised with comparison and a checklist of righteous deeds. God is not impressed with our deeds because they will never be enough. Only through salvation and genuine faith in Jesus Christ do we find our true sufficiency in Him.

When we humbly come before the Lord, a Holy God, we rightly see our need for His mercy and forgiveness. Our standard of perfection is not our neighbor, and even the worst of neighbors cannot make us look good. We are far more sinful than we know, and God is more gracious than we could ever fathom to those who display true faith and repentance.

DAY 235
A Tree and its Fruit

Either make the tree good and its fruit will be good, or make the tree bad and its fruit will be bad; for a tree is known by its fruit.

MATTHEW 12:33

When a tree's fruit is in season, it is obvious what kind of tree it is. In Matthew 12:33, Jesus uses imagery to describe how our actions reflect who we are. Just like the fruit a tree produces reflects what kind of tree it is, so do the words and actions we produce reflect the kind of people we are. An apple tree cannot make itself into a lemon tree, for a tree cannot force itself to produce fruit it was not meant to produce. Jesus described this reality in Matthew 7:18 when He said, "A good tree can't produce bad fruit; neither can a bad tree produce good fruit."

Before coming to know Christ, we all were like bad trees. Our sinful actions reflected our sinful nature, and no amount of good deeds could make us into "good" people. But when Jesus saved us through His death on the cross, we were transformed. By His grace, Jesus forgave our sins and cleansed our iniquities, declaring us holy and blameless in the eyes of the Lord. His righteousness has covered our unrighteousness, trading His good for our bad. Through Christ, we are made new.

While Christ has made us new, we should still consider what kind of fruit we are producing. As Christ followers, we should reflect Jesus through our words and actions. When others look at us, they should know we are believers by the way we speak and act. But how often do our actions reflect something different than the gospel?

As believers, we are to be gospel witnesses in a dark and broken world. When our fruit looks more like who we once were, instead of looking like who we are as believers, we do nothing to advance the gospel. However, there is good news for our struggle to produce good fruit. Because of Christ, we can produce good fruit. While our sinful nature may tempt us to sin, through Jesus and the power of the Spirit, we are equipped to fight the sin that produces bad fruit. And as we obey God's Word and rely on Christ, we will continue to produce good fruit. As a result, the world around us will know who we are—disciples of the Lord Jesus Christ.

"HIS RIGHTEOUSNESS HAS COVERED OUR UNRIGHTEOUSNESS, TRADING HIS GOOD FOR OUR BAD."

DAY 236
God Cannot Lie

God is not a man, that he might lie, or a son of man, that he might change his mind. Does he speak and not act, or promise and not fulfill?

NUMBERS 23:19

Humans have a tendency to withhold the truth at times. We are sinful people, and our tongue reflects this. We bend the truth, lie to protect ourselves, and make commitments without the follow-through. But God is different. God is a holy and perfect God. As a holy and perfect God, it is impossible for Him to lie. If He did, He would cease to be God. God wants us to trust Him, but we can sometimes act like He is untrustworthy or doubt His words instead of believing Him. We question His promises, unsure if He will do what He says He will do.

Living with a mistrust of God leads us further away from Him. The enemy wants this to happen. If we think back to the garden of Eden, it was the serpent who persuaded Eve to question the Lord's truthfulness, asking, "Did God really say, 'You can't eat from any tree in the garden'?" (Genesis 3:1). The enemy tricks us by causing us to doubt the words of God. Doubting God's words led to Adam and Eve's downfall, and we must be careful not to do the same. When we reject the Lord and His commands, we grow in bitterness toward Him. We begin growing calloused against His Word. As we turn away from Him to go our own way, we fall into sin or into a place of anxiety and hopelessness.

Every word that God speaks, promise He makes, and action He takes is trustworthy. We hold His truth in our hands when we open the Bible. We never have to worry that God is saying something untrue or will say something only to change His mind. We never have to worry that God promises something He never means to fulfill. The truthfulness of the Lord washes over our doubting hearts. If we still question the faithfulness of the Lord, all we must do is look at Christ. He is truth incarnated. He is the Word of God in the flesh. He is the fulfillment of everything God has promised. In the moments you find yourself tempted to mistrust the Lord, remember who He is and what He has done for you on the cross. Indeed, He is our faithful God.

> "IN THE MOMENTS YOU FIND YOURSELF TEMPTED TO MISTRUST THE LORD, REMEMBER WHO HE IS AND WHAT HE HAS DONE FOR YOU ON THE CROSS."

DAY 237
Satisfaction in God's Hand

You open your hand and satisfy the desire of every living thing.
PSALM 145:16

God is our Provider. He scans every creature, from human to small insect, and addresses the needs of His creation. As indicated in the verse, the Lord supplies our desires as well. Unlike needs, desires reveal the wants of the heart. A need is necessary, but a desire is something that brings pleasure. Desire expresses the longings of the soul. We have great needs and desires. The solution for them is found in the Lord and the saving work of Jesus.

Man's desires were innocent initially. In the garden of Eden, Adam and Eve were pleased in the presence of God. However, when the serpent enticed them, their desires shifted to crave autonomy. Sin corrupted their desires. We also experience the impact of the fall and place our desire in the wrong things. What do you desire most? Is it a beautiful home, a stable career, or lasting friendships? Do you pursue these things? When you attain them, are you left desiring more? Earthly pursuits are not meant to satisfy. A home can be destroyed in a fire. A career can plummet in an economic crisis. Friends can move away. These are temporary gifts but not God's all-satisfying grace.

Our greatest desire is to experience total well-being in the presence of God. We can only obtain this desire through Christ. Jesus accomplished the plan of redemption, and by His life, death, and resurrection, we can enter into a relationship with the Lord. Jesus freely gives salvation from His open hand. We do not have to pry it from His tight fist. We do not have to bribe Him with our imperfect obedience. Jesus willingly blesses us with satisfaction in Him because of His love and faithfulness.

We can go to the Lord with our needs and desires. *Oh, we want to be full in You and You alone, Jesus! Help us to seek your goodness and find our satisfaction in You. Help us to remember that You desire our well-being and will fulfill it in Your return.*

"OUR GREATEST DESIRE IS TO EXPERIENCE TOTAL WELL-BEING IN THE PRESENCE OF GOD."

DAY 238
Undivided Trust

Trust in the Lord with all your heart, and do not rely on your own understanding; in all your ways know him, and he will make your paths straight.

PROVERBS 3:5–6

Would you say you trust God with all your heart? If a sense of frenzy or fear marks our lives, we most likely are not trusting the Lord. James describes a doubting heart when he says, "For the doubter is like the surging sea, driven and tossed by the wind. That person should not expect to receive anything from the Lord, being double-minded and unstable in all his ways" (James 1:6–8). We become unstable when we try to trust God while holding on to our own understanding. We end up bouncing back and forth between trusting God to doubting Him, following His plans to following our plans. This divided trust keeps us from being grounded and centered and leads to anxiety and overwhelm.

Peter experienced this reality in Matthew 14 when he chose to walk to Jesus on the water. One minute he trusted the Lord as he walked out on the water, but then looking at the storm around him, his trust in Jesus wavered. Peter's doubt made him unstable amidst the surging sea, and he began to sink. Like Peter, our trust wavers when we take our eyes off of Jesus, doubting that He is capable of helping us. We cling instead to our own strength and understanding.

Without trust in the Lord, we find ourselves tossed by waves of fear when storms arise. However, we do not have to remain tossed to and fro by doubt. We do not have to rely on our own understanding. Just like Jesus reached out and took hold of Peter, He takes hold of us. We can surrender our understanding because we serve a God who knows all things. We can trust God because He knows what we need before we ask. The more we remind ourselves of who God is, the more we will learn to trust Him. In times of doubt, we must learn to keep our eyes fixed on Christ. Even when we fail to trust God wholeheartedly, God does not look down at us in anger but in grace. He invites us to trust Him once again. With Christ as our sure foundation, our feet remain grounded, our lives fully secure in the Lord.

"WE CAN SURRENDER OUR UNDERSTANDING BECAUSE WE SERVE A GOD WHO KNOWS ALL THINGS."

DAY 239
Man Shall Not Live By Bread Alone

He humbled you by letting you go hungry; then he gave you manna to eat, which you and your fathers had not known, so that you might learn that man does not live on bread alone but on every word that comes from the mouth of the Lord.

DEUTERONOMY 8:3

When God's people wandered in the wilderness, He allowed them to experience hunger. The Israelites began their journey to the Promised Land and immediately began grumbling about their hunger and thirst. They had just witnessed God miraculously part the Red Sea on their behalf as they escaped Egypt, and Pharaoh's army drowned in the waters that crashed back down. The people went so far as to say they wished they were still in Egypt as slaves. The Lord freed them, but the first moment of hardship revealed their hearts. They desired comfort and full stomachs more than what the Lord had for them at that moment. This hunger would give them a sense of desperation for their physical needs to be met to show them they needed to be desperate for God. He was their provider and sustainer, and what He offered them was far better than anything they could find in Egypt.

While the Lord may not ask us to endure hunger in that way, we have likely endured other trials that seemed unbearable at the moment. We may have pleaded and cried for the Lord to take the struggle away. Through Jesus's death and resurrection, He ultimately made a way to fill us with Himself so we could be wholly satisfied in Him. In our trials, may we be driven to the Lord, for when we realize our need for Him, we come to the end of ourselves. Our self-sufficiency dies, and we are driven to His Word, which is the anchor of our souls.

When Jesus faces hunger pains in the Judaean wilderness while being tempted by the devil, He uses Scripture to destroy Satan's affront. Jesus uses His trial as a way to honor God and show His need for the Words of the Lord rather than bread alone. Though our struggles may be difficult, what blessing that the Lord can use the hardship we feel, the hunger we feel, to draw us to Himself—to reveal to us our dependence on Him that is all too easily forgotten. He uses our hunger for other things to help us remember that He alone—the Bread of Life—fully satisfies our every need.

"WE ARE DRIVEN TO HIS WORD, WHICH IS THE ANCHOR OF OUR SOULS."

DAY 240
A Clean Slate

Therefore, if anyone is in Christ, he is a new creation; the old has passed away, and see, the new has come!

2 CORINTHIANS 5:17

How easy for us to remember the sins and mistakes of others, tainting how we interact with them and causing us to hesitate in trusting them. Imagine then how we might view ourselves if we could see our every sin against God. We could not stand beneath the weight of it all, knowing the extent to which we have wronged our Creator and deserve to be eternally separated from Him.

But God, our gracious and compassionate Father, who is perfectly holy and righteous, sees all of our sins and chooses to extend forgiveness. How incredible! The One who made us for His glory and our good to then watch us reject Him and chase our own desires gladly welcomes us back into His arms. And unlike us, He does not hold grudges or hesitate with His love toward those who once wronged Him. He restores us completely, no questions asked. He has made a way through the cross of His Son that all of our sins can be washed away, making us new creations.

It is hard to fathom this reality, which is likely why many of us also wrestle with living in our new identity as fully forgiven sons and daughters of God. But we miss out if we wallow in who we once were before the gospel changed us. We have been saved from spiritual death, and now we have been given abundant life. Each day is an opportunity to thank the Lord for what He has done. He has made us new.

Our transformation also hints at another transformation to come in heaven for all believers. One day, our bodies will be redeemed, and we will be forever free from the presence of sin. The old earth will pass away, and the new heavens and earth will begin. And the abundant joy in Christ we experienced on earth will seem to be just a shadow of what we will experience then.

If you are tempted to dwell on your sin or the sin of another before the gospel changed your heart and theirs, choose to remember instead that God has made all believers completely new. He does not hold grudges against you, and He offers you complete forgiveness. As we extend this same forgiveness to ourselves and others, may we walk in His abundance.

"ONE DAY, OUR BODIES WILL BE REDEEMED, AND WE WILL BE FOREVER FREE FROM THE PRESENCE OF SIN."

DAY 241
It Wasn't You, It Was God

I rescued you from the power of Egypt and the power of all who oppressed you. I drove them out before you and gave you their land.

JUDGES 6:9

Many books and movies are known for their depiction of princesses, kingdoms, and the defeat of evil. Though these stories show the triumph of goodness over evil, some also show moral victory as a result of human effort. Within, the character finds the answer to overcome his or her flaws and the inner strength to defeat the villain. While it is not necessarily wrong to read these books or watch these movies, it is important to recognize how this belief can deny the impact of sin on the human condition. In the Bible, we see a different narrative.

Scripture tells us that we all have a sinful nature inherited from our first parents, Adam and Eve. It is one that pulls us away from God. Dead in our sins and captive to its power, we cannot choose goodness on our own. Only through God's grace and mercy do we do good. Through His plan of redemption, God saves us from sin's oppression. Through Christ's life, death, and resurrection, Jesus defeated evil and was raised in victory. He established God's kingdom and gave us the Holy Spirit, who helps us live in Christ's goodness.

We often forget our salvation comes from the Lord. In the book of Judges, we see how God's chosen people forgot the Lord's protective hand over their lives. God appointed judges to serve as military leaders who would lead the Israelites in a battle to secure their place in the Promised Land. Scripture tells us that they were victorious. God ultimately defeated their enemies and made them a great nation, but with their accomplishments, the Israelites and the judges grew proud and did not depend on God. They turned to idolatry and committed evil before the Lord. So, God removed His hand from them, and their enemies overcame them. Even still, our faithful and patient God reminded the Israelites of His working in their lives and preserved their trust in Him.

Like the Israelites, when we look at our accomplishments and growth, we may want to attribute the success to our own efforts. We forget our sin, moral inability, and need for a Savior. But, through prayer, studying Scripture, and journaling, we can remind ourselves that our successes are not because of us. These successes happened through God's grace alone.

DAY 242
The Story of His Glory

And most certainly, the mystery of godliness is great: He was manifested in the flesh, vindicated in the Spirit, seen by angels, preached among the nations, believed on in the world, taken up in glory.

I TIMOTHY 3:16

Timothy was a young believer in Lystra. He accepted Jesus as his Savior and was committed to serving the gospel mission. Timothy became Paul's protégé, so to speak, and represented him at different churches. While they were separated, Paul wrote his first letter to Timothy to guide him in leadership. Paul concluded his letter with a poetic confession of faith in Jesus Christ, reminding Timothy that the bedrock of ministry was the story of Jesus.

First Timothy 3:16 contains a brief summary of Jesus's life. It begins with His entering the world as a baby. The eternal Son of God took on flesh and did not comprise His divinity. The verse then highlights Jesus's resurrection. Though death and injustice stung Him, Christ overcame and proved Himself righteous when He rose from the grave and ascended into heaven. Though God's physical presence was no longer on the earth, the Holy Spirit came to dwell inside His people, empowering them to believe and declare Christ's greatness in the world.

This plan existed before time began, for eternity, fixed in the mind of God. When He divided the waters and created nature, God had a plan to restore them from the corruption of sin. When He formed man from the dust of the earth, God knew He would send the Son of Man to save His people from their fallenness. Wickedness spread through the nations and penetrated human hearts, perverting God's established order and distorting truth. And when all hope seemed lost, the Savior came in the person of Jesus Christ, who showed us the way to true religion and taught us that all of our efforts should be founded in Christ alone.

In the same way, Christ's body, the Church, should illustrate God's story. His glory should radiate through our songs, sermons, and programs. This Christ-centered framework can help us avoid sinful disorder as we glorify the Lord with every part of ministry. And, as we stand, may we keep our eyes focused ahead as we await Christ's return to call us home to eternal glory.

"AS WE STAND, MAY WE KEEP OUR EYES FOCUSED AHEAD AS WE AWAIT CHRIST'S RETURN TO CALL US HOME TO ETERNAL GLORY."

DAY 243

Fishers of People

As he passed alongside the Sea of Galilee, he saw Simon and Andrew, Simon's brother, casting a net into the sea—for they were fishermen. "Follow me," Jesus told them, "and I will make you fish for people." Immediately they left their nets and followed him. Going on a little farther, he saw James the son of Zebedee and his brother John in a boat putting their nets in order. Immediately he called them, and they left their father Zebedee in the boat with the hired men and followed him.

MARK 1:16–20

If you heard someone say to you, "Follow me," how would you respond? In Mark 1, Jesus's disciples followed Him immediately, though they did not know Him. When He performed a miracle by filling their nets with so many fish their boats began to sink, the men were likely astounded and in awe of this great man. This stranger's invitation was intriguing, and they followed Him in light of His miracle.

Jesus's miracle in the abundance of fish gave the men a visual representation of their call. Simon, Andrew, James, and John would be fishers of men, which is a phrase that refers to all people. By changing their role from fishermen to fishers of men, Jesus appointed them as His disciple-makers, creating disciples as numerous as the fish they caught. As Christ followers, we too are fishers of people. By faithfully sharing the gospel, we partner with the Holy Spirit, who opens the eyes of sinners to the truth of Jesus Christ.

Yet, following Jesus is costly. The disciples had to leave their livelihood to follow Jesus, and the text is clear that they left their nets and boat behind. Even still, the call to follow Jesus was greater to them than their livelihood. Just as the disciples laid down their nets, we too must lay down our lives for Christ. Whether it be a job, relationship, or something else, we may have to lay these things down to pursue Jesus whole-heartedly, for following Him leads to abundance that no earthly thing or sinful desire can give.

How comforting it is to know that Jesus calls ordinary people, with weakness and sin, to be fishers of people, to be disciple-makers. We can find encouragement in this truth when we feel unworthy of sharing the gospel. God has chosen you purposefully to share His good news. May we joyfully accept the task of being fishers of people as we invite others to follow Jesus.

DAY 244

The Only Way

Jesus told him, "I am the way, the truth, and the life. No one comes to the Father except through me."

JOHN 14:6

When Jesus went to celebrate Passover in Jerusalem with His disciples, He knew that His hour had come. It was time for Him to fulfill the purpose He came to complete. Jesus was going to die and then be raised again so that all of those who love Him may live forever. But before He did this, He spent time encouraging His disciples. John records all of these precious words in the last few chapters of his gospel. These are passages believers cling to as we longingly await Christ's return.

As Christ speaks of returning to the Father, He explains that He will prepare a place for all who love Him. The disciples are anxious about getting there and are worried that their teacher and friend, the One they know is the Messiah, is speaking of leaving them. But Jesus tenderly comforts the disciples and explains that they gain eternal life only through Him. The way to heaven is not something they can figure out on their own. Jesus Himself is the way.

John 14:6 reveals the truth that Christ is the only way to eternal life. But the verse also shows us that no one can approach God without Jesus, which is why we must be united to Him through the Holy Spirit inside us to approach the Father. When the Lord sees us, He sees the righteousness of Jesus, and we are welcomed into His kingdom.

Jesus is the way to eternal life, and if we have trusted in Him as our Savior, we do not need to be anxious over how we will arrive in eternity. Jesus will be our guide. Every worry ceases at the mention of His name. Every desire or longing we have is satisfied in Christ. Every answer is found in Him. He will be with us every moment of our lives, and He will bring us into eternity with Him. Jesus is all we need.

"JESUS IS THE WAY TO ETERNAL LIFE, AND IF WE HAVE TRUSTED IN HIM AS OUR SAVIOR, WE DO NOT NEED TO BE ANXIOUS OVER HOW WE WILL ARRIVE IN ETERNITY."

DAY 245
The Well of Salvation

On that day you will say: "I will give thanks to you, Lord, although you were angry with me. Your anger has turned away, and you have comforted me. Indeed, God is my salvation; I will trust him and not be afraid, for the Lord, the Lord himself, is my strength and my song. He has become my salvation." You will joyfully draw water from the springs of salvation, and on that day you will say, "Give thanks to the Lord; proclaim his name! Make his works known among the peoples. Declare that his name is exalted."

ISAIAH 12:1-4

If you have been a Christian for a while, perhaps the gospel story has become dull to you. Maybe you prayed a prayer when you were little and are reading this devotional in hopes of reigniting the passion you once had. Or maybe you have recently come to know the Lord and are evaluating the Christian faith with fresh eyes today. Regardless of your background, let us remember the God of salvation today. Christ secured our salvation through His own sacrifice.

The truth is that we were all broken, dirty, and separated from God. We were His enemies, stuck in our guilt and shame. But while we were blinded in the darkness of our own making, God revealed His great light to us. He sent His Son, Jesus, into the world to perfectly fulfill the Law's commands. Not only this, Jesus paid the penalty that we deserve and died a gruesome death on a cross. In His sacrifice and resurrection, Jesus destroyed the penalty of sin and death and set us free from its bondage, restoring us to God.

If you have never trusted Christ with your life, spend some time today evaluating your heart. What is keeping you from following God today? Or, if you are in Christ, spend time giving thanks to the Lord for your salvation. Thank Him for His steadfast and eternal love. Then, consider those in your life who do not yet know the Lord. Pray that God would open their eyes and that they would be saved.

God is worthy of worship from every person, tribe, and nation. He is set apart, the Holy One. As His followers, we are to make His name known to all, for He has done marvelous things. We praise His name, rejoicing that He has given us faith to believe!

"WHILE WE WERE BLINDED IN THE DARKNESS OF OUR OWN MAKING, GOD REVEALED HIS GREAT LIGHT TO US."

DAY 246
Give Me Life

Give me life in accordance with your faithful love, and I will obey the decree you have spoken.

PSALM 119:88

Psalm 119 is an acrostic poem with eight verses of poetic prose for each of the twenty-two letters of the Hebrew alphabet. Its language is artistic and beautiful, sometimes somber and other times joyful but always exuding awe for God's glory. What could be the topic of such a carefully crafted work of words? What provoked the author to speak so impassioned and with such length? The answer is rules. Yes, rules.

But, not just any rules, God's rules. Over the entire ten-page poem, only seven verses do not mention God's law. Rarely do you hear someone gushing over the excruciatingly detailed Levitical laws, but this psalmist does just that. The writer thoroughly delights in the statutes, commands, precepts, and testimonies of God, for true life only comes from Him. God has given His rules as a guide to joyful, abundant life.

The psalmist desperately wants to experience the happiness that comes from living in the ways of God but also knows God's ways are impossible to perfectly keep. Knowing this, the author of the book voiced much inner wrestling with God throughout this psalm. The psalmist commits to following in God's ways and begs God for strength to follow through on this commitment.

We can all relate to this tendency. We desire to do what God asks. We want to be committed, wholehearted, unwavering in our adherence to Him. Yet, we also know that we are weak and imperfect. Rather than allowing this conundrum to discourage us, we can follow in the steps of the psalmist and cry, "Give me life! Strengthen me! Put the desires of your heart in mine!" And God will delight to do so.

We have hope in knowing that our position with God does not depend on our keeping the rules. Living according to God's set standards decreases the brokenness and pain in our lives, but in Christ, we stand before God perfectly forgiven on our best days and on our worst. While we seek to grow continually in righteousness and Christlikeness, we know God unconditionally accepts us when we trust in Him!

Do you love God's laws and desire to keep them? Or do you struggle to follow through in those desires? Ask God to strengthen you, and thank Him for His forgiveness in the times we fall short.

DAY 247
We Love Because He Loved

God's love was revealed among us in this way: God sent his one and only Son into the world so that we might live through him. Love consists in this: not that we loved God, but that he loved us and sent his Son to be the atoning sacrifice for our sins. Dear friends, if God loved us in this way, we also must love one another.

1 JOHN 4:9-11

While earthly love can sometimes feel out of our grasp, God's love is always accessible for us, no matter the circumstances in which we find ourselves. We need only to look at the life and death of Jesus to see the love of God perfectly displayed. From teaching to healing to rebuking, all of Jesus's days on the earth were spent demonstrating the love of the Father. However, His love was shown ultimately through His death. Although it was not deserved, He bore the punishment of death on the cross willingly so that we could be saved from our sins.

God's love for us cost Him everything. He withheld nothing. And what a deeply challenging truth this is, considering that verse 11 tells us that just as God loved us in this way, we are to love one another in the same way. We are to withhold nothing selfishly and be willing to love at all costs. This challenge likely feels beyond the scope of what we are capable of most days. While this passage is not telling us to submit to or excuse abuse or harm, it tells us to love like Jesus by forgiving others, often extending grace in a way that does not come easily.

We have the example of Christ to follow as we learn to love in this sacrificial way. His example teaches us to be the first to love others because He was the first to love us. He did not wait for us to clean up our act or seek Him. First, He sent Jesus, who submitted Himself to death in our place. Then, He invited us into His love and forgiveness. Even if we reject Him, His love remains steadfast.

Remember God's gracious love toward you—how He loved you before you loved Him. Consider people in your own life who may need your love right now. Is there someone you can forgive, even if you do not feel they deserve it? You can forgive because God has forgiven you. You can love because God loves you.

"GOD'S LOVE FOR US COST HIM EVERYTHING.
HE WITHHELD NOTHING."

DAY 248

Your Possessions Can't Save You

Looking at him, Jesus loved him and said to him, "You lack one thing: Go, sell all you have and give to the poor, and you will have treasure in heaven. Then come, follow me."

MARK 10:21

Though some tried to catch Jesus in His words, there were always those who genuinely sought Him out for wisdom. But at times, people would ask Jesus a question from the wrong perspective or attitude. The story in Mark of the rich, young ruler gives an example of such a person. This man was wealthy, well-liked, powerful, and lived a fairly righteous life. In his mind, he had accomplished much, and when he spoke to Jesus, he was trying to complete the most important task of all—making sure he was going to heaven. He wanted eternal life and thought he could gain it by doing the right things, just like he had done with everything else.

The ruler was so caught up in himself that he was blind to the salvation before him. Jesus, His Savior, looked on this man in love. He was all the ruler needed, but Jesus knew the ruler needed to realize his inadequacy before he could ever live devoted to the gospel. Jesus tells him to give everything he owns to the poor, which would mean a loss of wealth, status, and importance. Everything he placed his identity in would be gone.

The young man could not complete the task. He walked away from salvation and joy in despair over things that could never save him. This story teaches us not to believe that we can achieve our own salvation, but it also warns us of misplacing our affections in the things of the earth. Our earthly possessions will not last forever. They are passing away and returning to dust. All that is eternal is what counts, and it has already been given to us through the gospel. When our treasure is found in Christ and our future home with Him in heaven, we will enjoy this earth so much more. Our focus will not be on what we lack here because we know that at the end of the day, these things are a shadow compared to the joy that is to come. Our treasure must be in Jesus. He has provided everything we need for this life, and He will continue to provide for us until we meet Him face to face.

"ALL THAT IS ETERNAL IS WHAT COUNTS, AND IT HAS ALREADY BEEN GIVEN TO US THROUGH THE GOSPEL."

DAY 249
Living to Serve

For even the Son of Man did not come to be served, but to serve, and to give his life as a ransom for many.

MARK 10:45

As Jesus and His disciples walked on a road toward Jerusalem, Jesus predicted His arrest and death. He would be mocked, beaten, and killed, but He would rise from the grave on the third day. Two of Jesus's disciples, James and John, seemed to hear only the ending of His prediction. They did not listen to the part about suffering and were drawn to Jesus's promised resurrection. They knew the Messiah would be risen in glory and ascend to His heavenly throne at God the Father's right hand. James and John asked to sit with Jesus there. However, though they sought this place of importance, they ignored the necessary humiliation.

Jesus, the perfect Son of God, would die on the cross as the punishment for our sin. He would drink the cup of judgment and would bear God's wrath until justice was satisfied, surrendering to the Father's will, not in pursuit of prestige but in humble obedience to the Lord's plan of redemption. Jesus admitted that though James and John would not suffer as He did, they too would suffer for their faith.

James's and John's question stirred the other disciples. Jesus warned them not to let power divide the group. They were instead to pursue servanthood, for service was Jesus's mission. The eternal Son of God took on flesh and became our perfect representative. He left His heavenly home for the fallen world and surrounded Himself with the poor, diseased, and oppressed. He healed them from their affliction while urging faith in Him as the promised Savior. He bore the weight of sin and became lowly and dejected. Jesus endured the hardship to the cross where He gave up His life to pay for our sins. Because He served us, we escape judgment and are forgiven for our sins.

What does Jesus's service say about our identity in Christ? We too were meant to be servants. When we focus our care on others, we receive the greatest fulfillment, but our service should not be vain. As we strive to overcome sin, we might be tempted to use our service as merit for our good works and become prideful. But let us be servants like Jesus, the One who did not seek greatness but humbled Himself to lift us up from sin. In Christ, we can place the good of others above our ambitious pursuits.

"BECAUSE HE SERVED US, WE ESCAPE JUDGMENT AND ARE FORGIVEN FOR OUR SINS."

DAY 250
The Things of This World

For everything in the world – the lust of the flesh, the lust of the eyes, and the pride in one's possessions – is not from the Father, but is from the world. And the world with its lust is passing away, but the one who does the will of God remains forever.

1 JOHN 2:16–17

How easily we lust for the pleasures this world has to offer. God's Word makes it clear that this lust is not from the Father. The world fills us with desires for earthly pleasures, but God fills us with godly desires. While it is not wrong to enjoy the things of this world, our ultimate joy should not be found in the things of this earth. When we cling to what the world offers, we cling to things that are temporary rather than eternal. They are all passing away and can never satisfy our deepest longings. Social status is temporary, material wealth and possessions are temporary, pleasure and appearances are temporary. But our God is eternal.

The Lord wants us to cling to the things of the kingdom rather than the things of this world. When we live with an eternal perspective, we realize that the things of this world pale in comparison to the riches of God's kingdom. When we live for Christ, when we remember what He did for us on the cross and what He calls us to as disciples, we find what matters most. We seek first and foremost to glorify His name in all that we say and do as we make His great name known in this world.

Sometimes still, our minds will wander, our focus will become misaligned. When we find ourselves in these moments, we can come to God and lay aside our desires for temporary satisfaction in pleasures outside of Christ. We can ask the Lord for His help to set our eyes on what matters to Him and His kingdom. We can ask for the Spirit to reveal to us where we are holding on too tightly to this world and what we need to lay down. Each day, we have a choice of how to live this life and for whom we will live. May we choose to live every day for the eternal kingdom of God that holds all that we need.

"WHEN WE LIVE FOR CHRIST, WHEN WE REMEMBER WHAT HE DID FOR US ON THE CROSS AND WHAT HE CALLS US TO AS DISCIPLES, WE FIND WHAT MATTERS MOST."

DAY 251
The Throne of Grace

Therefore, since we have a great high priest who has passed through the heavens—Jesus the Son of God—let us hold fast to our confession. For we do not have a high priest who is unable to sympathize with our weaknesses, but one who has been tempted in every way as we are, yet without sin. Therefore, let us approach the throne of grace with boldness, so that we may receive mercy and find grace to help us in time of need.

HEBREWS 4:14–16

When we sin, we may find ourselves cowering in shame, frustrated that we have disappointed God. In our pride, we may even think that we know better than God, that His commands are outdated. We withdraw from Him with our thoughts, attitudes, and prayers.

Yet, we can boldly run to Christ and receive forgiveness because He sympathizes with us in our weakness. He is the perfect One who was tempted in every way but never sinned and wants to help us live lives that honor Him in purity and love, enabling us through His Spirit to walk in faith. He is our Savior and helps us in our day-to-day battles against sin.

Jesus helps us in our weakness, and He makes us clean. He made it possible for us to approach God's throne by becoming the Great High Priest. In the Old Testament, priests played an important role by offering sin sacrifices on behalf of the people. But when Jesus died on the cross for our sins, He was the once and for all perfect sacrifice. We no longer need to cower in shame or offer animal sacrifices, for Jesus has already paid for our sins.

We can come to the throne of God boldly, then, with confidence and without fear of judgment because of the blood of Christ. We can come to Him even when we sin because we know that He is merciful. God is the holy King, the One who is perfect and righteous. He is the only way to be forgiven. We can rejoice and press near to God even in our weakness because Jesus secured our path to victory through His death for our sins on the cross. We can pray boldly, knowing that we will receive mercy and find grace in our times of need. So, in your moments of weakness or trials, draw near to your sympathetic Savior. He offers you mercy and grace.

"JESUS HELPS US IN OUR WEAKNESS, AND HE MAKES US CLEAN."

DAY 252

Like Jewels in a Crown

The Lord their God will save them on that day as the flock of his people; for they are like jewels in a crown, sparkling over his land.

ZECHARIAH 9:16

The Imperial State Crown worn by the Queen of England contains 2,868 diamonds, 17 sapphires, 11 emeralds, 269 pearls, and 4 rubies. If you go to the Tower of London in England, you can see the crown up close. Behind the glass, you can watch the jewels catch the light as they sparkle and shine. The crown is a magnificent sight. In Zechariah 9, God's people are described like jewels in a crown, sparkling over God's earth.

We are precious to the Lord, and He looks upon us with delight. Zechariah 9 is a prophecy describing the restoration of Israel and ultimately speaks to our restoration through Christ. The picture of a King riding on a donkey foretells Jesus's triumphial entry through Jerusalem. The language of war and victory describes Jesus's triumph over sin and death. The salvation and restoration of God's people speaks to the salvation and restoration made possible through Christ.

It is Christ who makes believers like jewels. As sinners, we are tarnished and broken. But when we come to Christ, Christ's forgiveness washes away our sins, restoring our brokenness and making us new. Because of His sacrifice, we are transformed into precious jewels. It is His mercy and grace that makes us worthy and innocent before the Father. It is His blood that makes us sparkle and shine.

This picture of perfection is a glimpse of eternity for believers. When Christ returns, He will fully restore the earth to its original design. The world will be free from sin, and there will be lasting peace and prosperity. We will be fully glorified, completely sinless, and entirely righteous. We will sparkle as we fill the new heavens and earth, delighting in and worshiping our Lord and Savior.

A crown symbolizes majesty and sovereignty. Like jewels in a crown, we reflect the majesty and sovereignty of our Lord. Our redeemed and restored selves point to His glory. For all our days, our great King of kings is worthy of being praised for His work of salvation. And as we wait to be fully glorified in the future, in the present, we can shine in the world as testimonies to Christ's forgiveness, pointing others to our Savior who rescued and restored us. Like jewels in a crown, we reflect the glory of our great King.

"WE REFLECT THE MAJESTY AND SOVEREIGNTY OF OUR LORD."

DAY 253
The Song of Salvation

Sing for joy, Daughter Zion; shout loudly, Israel! Be glad and celebrate with all your heart, Daughter of Jerusalem! The Lord has removed your punishment; he has turned back your enemy. The King of Israel, the Lord, is among you; you need no longer fear harm.

ZEPHANIAH 3:14-15

Seasons of suffering can be long and hard. Days and nights seem to run together. Though you may be vaguely aware of the rising sun, the dawn never seems to come. You feel a gnawing sense of loss, usually beginning in the pit of your stomach as a dull ache, growing until it spills over, turning into groans and tears. You long for life to be pieced back together.

You do not know when the end of the season will come, but it will. Someday, the beating drum of your suffering will stop. The dull ache will slowly, yet surely, be replaced with a sense of joy that rises out of you in the same way your sorrow once did. But instead of groans, you will laugh. Instead of tears of sorrow, you will experience tears of joy. You may never find complete healing on this side of heaven—perhaps there will always be a dull ache—but one day soon, God will redeem it all.

We see this truth play out in the Old Testament when Zephaniah wrote to Judah to warn them of God's wrath if they did not turn from their evil ways. Most of this book is filled with images of how Judah will suffer if they fail to return to God. However, the last chapter is a beautiful song about how God will redeem and restore the people of Judah after their time of suffering. God also reminds Judah that He is with them and will save them.

Your own suffering may not be because you turned away from God. We live in a broken world, and we will endure hardships because of it. Still, this truth found in Zephaniah still applies to you. God is with you, and He will save you if you place your hope in Him. So if you are experiencing darkness right now, if your suffering seems to beat on without end, trust in the promises of God. The night will not last forever. Keep your eyes peeled for the dawn. Hope is here.

> "GOD IS WITH YOU, AND HE WILL SAVE YOU IF YOU PLACE YOUR HOPE IN HIM."

DAY 254
Taming the Tongue

So too, though the tongue is a small part of the body, it boasts great things. Consider how a small fire sets ablaze a large forest.

JAMES 3:5

A harsh word to our neighbors or friends. A quick slip of the tongue in frustration to our parents or co-workers. An impatient remark to our children or the cars in front of us. We have all said words we wish we never uttered aloud. And we know the possible devastating consequences of those words. Like James says in James 3:5, the tiny tongue boasts great power. Though the tongue is small, its spark can set ablaze an entire forest. Our words, though they sometimes feel meaningless, are not. They are powerful indeed and can greatly impact the world around us.

Just two verses earlier in James 3:3, we are given a contrasting example of the power of the tongue. It can be used for good! Like a bit guides a wild animal, so our tongue can guide our lives in the right direction. And as the rudder of a ship is small yet controls the destiny of the giant vessel, so our words can set our course in the right direction. The Bible has plenty to say on using our speech for good and not harm. Taming the tongue is living in a way that is glorifying to the Lord as Scripture instructs us, with the guidance of the Holy Spirit. James 1:19–21 encourages us to be quick to listen and slow to speak. We can catch our imperfect words before they travel from head to mouth. Proverbs teaches us that fewer words mean fewer opportunities to sin (Proverbs 10:19). We do well to restrain our words and filter them by God's Word before we speak them, for our words hold power.

Words can so easily slip out before we have time to consider their effect. As we remember this, may we seek to use the power of our words for good, to build up, to encourage. May we use our words to praise our heavenly Father, who loves us so. And may we use our words to spread the truth of the gospel so that others will know what Jesus has done for us on the cross. Jesus calls us to be disciples of His good news, so let us go! Let us go and share with those around us, that they may know the truth of Christ and the joy of salvation.

"MAY WE USE OUR WORDS TO PRAISE OUR HEAVENLY FATHER, WHO LOVES US SO."

DAY 255

A People for His Own Possession

For the grace of God has appeared, bringing salvation for all people, instructing us to deny godlessness and worldly lusts and to live in a sensible, righteous, and godly way in the present age, while we wait for the blessed hope, the appearing of the glory of our great God and Savior, Jesus Christ. He gave himself for us to redeem us from all lawlessness and to cleanse for himself a people for his own possession, eager to do good works.

TITUS 2:11–14

The gospel. The good news. It is the means through which all Christians enter into a relationship with God. It is our present salvation and future hope. This sounds simple enough, but the gospel is actually quite complex. Many of us have some sort of general understanding of it, but we might struggle to explain it in detail. We can better understand the gospel from the clear and concise definition found in Titus 2:11–14.

The gospel begins with Jesus. He brought the grace of God from heaven to earth in the most tangible way possible, and through Him, salvation is available to all who choose to believe. The gospel provokes us to turn away from ungodliness, move toward righteousness, and look toward the hope of glory.

Visualize walking along an uneven and rocky path. Looking ahead to where the path leads, we see a treacherous pit and look around for another path to take. A gracious guide appears and says that if we follow him, we will find a safe path. He seems trustworthy, so we follow. The guide's path is narrow, rocky, uneven, yet we have a faithful leader in whose footsteps we can follow. The glorious destination shines in the distance, and we hear stories of how free, whole, and joyful it is. The guide should know, for it is His home he leads us to, after all. And so, filled with hope, we continue to our destination.

Jesus is our gracious guide, who offers us the grace of following Him instead of marching on toward emptiness and death. He gave His life on the cross so that we could do just that, so that we would have the chance to turn to Him as our Savior, receiving forgiveness though we have sinned greatly and deserve death. This is the work of the gospel. May we strive to follow in the Lord's steps and travel with the hope of heaven in view.

"MAY WE STRIVE TO FOLLOW IN THE LORD'S STEPS AND TRAVEL WITH THE HOPE OF HEAVEN IN VIEW."

DAY 256
Faithful Prayers

I said, Lord, the God of the heavens, the great and awe-inspiring God who keeps his gracious covenant with those who love him and keep his commands, let your eyes be open and your ears be attentive to hear your servant's prayer that I now pray to you day and night for your servants, the Israelites.

NEHEMIAH 1:5-6A

Prayer is hard for many believers. Sometimes we are not sure what to say, or it feels like our prayers are hitting the ceiling. In today's verse, the prophet Nehemiah just received word that the people of Israel, who survived the exile in Babylon, were in trouble. Even worse, the walls and gate of the glorious city of Jerusalem had been destroyed. Nehemiah's response is one of deep grief. However, his choice of words to God demonstrates great faith. He does not lash out at God or question Him. Instead, He declares His faithfulness.

What we believe about God impacts our prayers. In times of suffering, we may view God as unfair or cruel, weakening our prayer lives. Our hearts may become bitter toward God, and we can refuse to pray altogether. What shapes faithful prayers is remembering we pray to a faithful God. In this moment of despair, Nehemiah calls to mind the Lord's faithfulness. He declares that God is a God who keeps His covenants and commands. Even in light of the tragedy, Nehemiah believes that God is good and faithful. We must do the same.

When we struggle to believe God's promises, the words we speak in prayer help strengthen our faith. In times of hardship, we should declare what is true about God. Declaring His faithfulness causes our hearts to trust in who God is. We can recognize the reality of our sufferings while still recognizing our faithful and loving God, who has always kept His promises. Throughout the Old Testament, the Lord kept the covenant of salvation Nehemiah speaks of, which was fulfilled in Jesus Christ through His life, death, and resurrection. If we struggle to believe who God says He is, all we must do is look at the empty grave. Times of difficulty do not alter God's promises. He is always working and moving in ways that we cannot see. Allow who God is to shape your prayers. Declare His faithfulness, even in your place of pain. You serve a faithful God who hears you and loves you deeply.

DAY 257
But God Intercedes

He saw that there was no man—he was amazed that there was no one interceding; so his own arm brought salvation, and his own righteousness supported him.

ISAIAH 59:16

Isaiah was an Old Testament prophet who relayed God's word to the kingdoms of Israel and Judah. Isaiah warned them of the coming downfall, which was just punishment for their sin. He confronted their kings who fell to the lure of other gods and did not uphold justice. Unfortunately, the rest of the nation followed in their ways. All of Israel lived in darkness. God's face, which shined on them, was now hidden. It is not that God could not hear their cries or could not see their suffering and injustice. But, there was a separation between God and His people. Because of their sin, God gave them over to the desires of their hearts and withdrew His mercy. But God would still act to deliver them. There was the hope of restoration because of God's faithfulness. He promised to intercede, which means "to act on behalf of another." Jesus would be the righteous Redeemer to stand in the gap between God and man.

No man, not even one, is obedient to the Lord. Men and women were the special creatures, set apart to reflect God's glory and honor. God commissioned Adam, the first human, to live as a righteous king adhering to the Lord's commands. But, Adam failed, and we, who are the descendants of Adam and Eve, have failed as well. Steeped in rebellion, we cannot be the worshipers whom God originally intended. We are separated from our loving Creator. The gap between Him and us is wide. Our sin sends us into darkness. But, fulfilling His promise in the book of Isaiah, God interceded by sending Jesus, who entered the darkness, to rescue us. God took on flesh and became human. He interceded by coming down from His throne and doing the work that we failed to do.

The God-Man was faithful, just, and obedient. His righteousness surpassed all men. His record was blameless, and in His death, He took the punishment we deserved so that we could have life in Him. In His resurrection, He filled the chasm between God and us, and now, we can enter the Lord's presence. Jesus is our Redeemer. And, because He interceded for us, we are made whole in Him. Through the strength Jesus gives, may we intercede in prayer for others so that they too may come to know Jesus.

DAY 258
God's Power through Christ

> *He exercised this power in Christ by raising him from the dead and seating him at his right hand in the heavens—far above every ruler and authority, power and dominion, and every title given, not only in this age but also in the one to come. And he subjected everything under his feet and appointed him as head over everything for the church, which is his body, the fullness of the one who fills all things in every way.*
>
> EPHESIANS 1:20–23

Have you ever experienced complete weakness? Perhaps you have experienced physical weakness, where you were so sick that getting out of bed seemed impossible. Or maybe you have experienced emotional weakness, where no matter how hard you tried to keep it together, it felt as though you might break apart at any moment. Maybe it was spiritual weakness, where you kept falling into sin and temptation.

Though we are weak, our God is not. He is all-powerful and in control of everything. God displayed His power in many ways. In the Old Testament, He displayed His power by parting the Red Sea (Exodus 14:21), bringing dry bones to life (Ezekiel 37:1–14), and saving Daniel from the lions' den (Daniel 6). However, God's greatest display of power was in raising Christ from the dead, defeating death and Satan forever. In the gospels, we see how God offered His one and only Son to live a perfect life that we could never live and take our place on the cross where we belonged. But He would rise from the grave on the third day, making a way for us to have a relationship with Him through His Spirit.

It was there on the cross that God dealt the final blow to Satan. It was there God fulfilled the promise made in Genesis 3:15 to provide someone to crush the head of the deceiver. It was here that God displayed the fullness of His power and strength. There is no darkness, no evil, no dominion that is over our God.

So, if you are experiencing weakness, if you are overwhelmed by your lack of energy or fallen nature, remember to fall on Christ. It is through your weakness that His power is made perfect (2 Corinthians 12:9–10). It is in His unrelenting love and perfect power that you can rest. It is a power God displayed through Christ on the cross, and it is a power that you have access to today through Christ.

> "THERE IS NO DARKNESS, NO EVIL, NO DOMINION THAT IS OVER OUR GOD."

DAY 259
Immeasurably More

Now to him who is able to do above and beyond all that we ask or think according to the power that works in us—to him be glory in the church and in Christ Jesus to all generations, forever and ever. Amen.

EPHESIANS 3:20–21

God's grace and power are immeasurably more than we can imagine. They exceed what we can think or dream. They are above and beyond, generous and extravagant. They are expressed in mundane moments, working body organs, and the thousands of breaths we take for granted. His grace and power are displayed as He blesses us with community and conviction. They are seen in answered prayers and in unanswered ones. But, ultimately, His grace and power are seen in the gospel message as Jesus fulfilled the Law's demands through His perfect life, death, and resurrection.

Through Christ's sacrifice on the cross, He made a way for us to be right with God. While we were still sinners, He gave His life for us. He poured out His grace on us in His suffering, and He suffered because of us. But in His power, He rose again, and He adopts us into His family when we accept Him as our Savior. Our heavenly Father cares for us as His children when what we deserve is death. But, because in grace God sent His Son to die, His power gives us life.

God's blessing comes to us in every moment for His glory so that we can know Him in new ways and experience His deep love and care for us. He provides mercy in our pain and companionship through the local church. He loves us even when we sin. He equips us and secures our identity in Himself. He shows us who we are and gives us peace and purpose. He calls us to join Him in His eternal mission of spreading His glory to the ends of the earth.

These blessings we could never earn by our own merit. The Lord chooses to shower them over us according to His grace that is immeasurable more than we deserve. So then, in response to our blessings in Christ, let us worship Him today. God is powerful and able. He can do more than we could ever ask or imagine. To God be the glory forever and ever!

"GOD'S GRACE AND POWER ARE IMMEASURABLY MORE THAN WE CAN IMAGINE."

DAY 260
Who Can Be Against Us?

What, then, are we to say about these things? If God is for us, who is against us? He did not even spare his own Son but offered him up for us all. How will he not also with him grant us everything?

ROMANS 8:31–32

How extravagant and trustworthy is God's gift of grace. In the passage immediately preceding today's verses, Paul describes God's astounding goodness toward us. He explains that God has proven His love for us through the gospel by sending His Son to die for our sins. He took care of our biggest need, saving us at great cost to Himself as He gave up His life for our sins, blameless though He was in every way. He found us when we were still dirty and full of shame, and He clothed us in the righteousness of His Son. He cared for us, called us, and predestined us from the beginning of time to be His children. He gave us a new name and a great calling. He justified us before His holy throne and united us with Him. He has shown steadfast love and care for His children and proven over and over again that His love is stable and sufficient. He has provided all we need—we cannot be wholly satisfied apart from Him.

In light of this, Paul concludes this: if God is for us, who can be against us? Even as he asks this rhetorical question, Paul implies the answer, "No one." If God is for us, no one can be against us. If we have Christ, we have all we need. This does not mean that we will never suffer. Remember that this verse was written by a man who was beaten, imprisoned, and killed for the name of Jesus. Paul did not say lightly that we have victory as God's children. He knew firsthand that we would face sorrows and persecution for our beliefs on this side of eternity. Today's verse reveals a greater truth, reminding us of God's ultimate, spiritual victory over every kind of evil.

God has destroyed the power of sin and death, saving us eternally with Him. And one day, He will come again to make all things new. But until then, we wait, and we believe in His goodness. If God gave up His own Son, sending Him to suffer and die for us, we can trust that He will take care of everything we need today.

> "IF GOD GAVE UP HIS OWN SON, SENDING HIM TO SUFFER AND DIE FOR US, WE CAN TRUST THAT HE WILL TAKE CARE OF EVERYTHING WE NEED TODAY."

DAY 261
Loving the Law

How I love your instruction! It is my meditation all day long.
PSALM 119:97

No matter what age we are or where we live, we are often bothered by limitations. We want to regulate ourselves, but rules prove we have an authority to whom we answer. We complain or rebel when a law is imposed on us, and we try to define our own ways instead. Our most severe rebellion is against the Lord of the universe. As our ultimate authority, God has brought us into a relationship with Him through Jesus Christ, and He has given us His law to show how to live as His redeemed people. Defying God's Word is called sin. We have a nature rooted in sin, making us unable to follow God on our own. Without Christ, we do not love God's law and are unwilling to submit our lives to its wisdom. But, in Jesus Christ, we can become lovers of the Law like He was.

Though saved, there will be times in our spiritual journeys when we will not want to heed biblical instruction. We will wrestle with our earthly nature. Persistent sins will try to challenge our new identity in Jesus. We might become discouraged by shame. We might be distracted by the false promises of this world. Or we might become lazy in pursuing our spiritual progress toward Christlikeness. Then, we might find ourselves drifting from the Lord's law again, quietly rebelling against His good Word. In these moments, we can pray that the Holy Spirit will change our perspective. As God's beloved children, we can come before His throne without fear of judgment. Our Father will cover our weaknesses with the blood of Christ.

Let us trust that the Holy Spirit will free us from sin and help us to delight in the law like the writer of Psalm 119 conveyed. As God works inside us, we can reflect on the fact that the Law is an extension of the Lord's grace. God's Word keeps us from spiritual harm and guides our souls down the path of abundant living. The greatest commandments to love God and our neighbors are laws that give believers much freedom. Oh, the beauty that can come from a life of love toward God and man! The law of God is not burdensome but a blessing. Let us lean on it day by day as an act of gratitude for our salvation and worship unto the Lord.

"OUR FATHER WILL COVER OUR WEAKNESSES WITH THE BLOOD OF CHRIST."

DAY 262
Meditations of the Heart

This book of instruction must not depart from your mouth; you are to meditate on it day and night so that you may carefully observe everything written in it. For then you will prosper and succeed in whatever you do.

JOSHUA 1:8

These words of Joshua 1:8 were part of the Lord's instructions to Joshua after Moses's death. Moses was the man who led Israel out of Egypt and, in many ways, represented God's deliverance to the people. He stood in the Lord's presence on Mount Sinai and received the Law, and the Lord Himself had many conversations with Moses. He was a spiritual giant. And now Moses was gone, and Joshua was left.

However, Moses was not the hero of the people, though they might regard him as such. The Lord was the hero. The reason Moses was able to lead the people was because the Lord was with him. The Lord also promised to be with Joshua as He promises to be with us today. The Lord did not leave Joshua empty-handed or guessing about how to lead the people. He gave Him specific instructions. Joshua and the people of Israel were to meditate on the Lord's Word day and night and obey it. If they did so, they would prosper. If they ignored God's Word, they would not. God wanted His people to love Him and to know Him. The more they knew God through the study of His Word and remembered how He delivered and provided for them, the more they would desire to obey His commands.

The call to meditate on the Word was not just for the people of Israel. It is also for His people today. We are to let God's Word dwell in us richly, and it should affect everything we do (Colossians 3:16–17). His Word allows us to know who He is—to know God and His Son Jesus, whom He sent to the earth to save us. And while we may not receive what the world would define as "success" from obeying His Word, we will prosper in our spiritual growth and joy in Christ. As we know His Word, it becomes a part of us, and we will realize that our earthly happiness is because of the Lord and our future hope in Him. We will not be shaken by the unknown. Our hearts will be planted in God's Word and His unchanging character.

"THE CALL TO MEDITATE ON THE WORD WAS NOT JUST FOR THE PEOPLE OF ISRAEL. IT IS ALSO FOR HIS PEOPLE TODAY."

DAY 263
Christ Honored Through Me

My eager expectation and hope is that I will not be ashamed about anything, but that now as always, with all courage, Christ will be highly honored in my body, whether by life or by death.

PHILIPPIANS 1:20

What is your greatest goal in life? The Apostle Paul had one goal in his life: to live for Christ. Throughout his life as a believer, Paul was fully committed to serving and glorifying Christ. Even when he faced imprisonment and execution, his greatest goal was for Christ to be honored in him and through him. Can we say the same about ourselves?

We should not wait until death looms near to evaluate our lives. Right here and now, we can think critically about how we are using the life we have been given through Jesus. We live for the One who saved us by seeking to serve, worship, and obey Jesus. This is not always easy, as we can find ourselves living for our glory rather than Christ's. Our sinful flesh beckons us to live for our wants, desires, and needs. As a result, we end up focusing on what matters to us rather than what matters to Christ.

We were made to worship and serve the Lord, and as we do, we walk in freedom and joy. But our motivation to honor Jesus should not be the blessings we receive but the glory we give to Christ for the sacrifice He made for us. May we live our lives in constant gratitude for the mercy and grace we have received. We are to joyfully take up the worthy calling of glorifying Christ in all things.

It takes courage to live for Christ. It takes courage to follow Jesus, even if it means we are persecuted. It takes courage to speak the gospel amongst people who despise the truth. Yet it is when we boldly live out the gospel that Christ is honored. Although we may fail at times, let us pursue the goal of honoring Jesus. Let us wake up each day with the intention of using our words and actions to glorify Him.

"WE WERE MADE TO WORSHIP AND SERVE THE LORD, AND AS WE DO, WE WALK IN FREEDOM AND JOY."

DAY 264
The Word of Life Revealed

What was from the beginning, what we have heard, what we have seen with our eyes, what we have observed and have touched with our hands, concerning the word of life—that life was revealed, and we have seen it and we testify and declare to you the eternal life that was with the Father and was revealed to us.

1 JOHN 1:1–2

John wrote a letter to Christians after reflecting on the nature and work of Jesus. This letter testified about the revelation of Jesus as the Word of God who came to give life and show us the Father. Through the Holy Spirit, John understood who Jesus was and brought the Lord's message of hope to the dying world. He warned against false doctrine, and John tells us some people rejected the fact that Christ became man.

John explained that the Word was incarnate. He and the other disciples heard Jesus speak; they saw Him eat and touched the scars on His body. Jesus was with them in human form during His life and after His resurrection. Jesus's incarnation was essential to accomplishing a way of salvation for us. We needed a perfect human representative to stand in our place of punishment and earn for us the gift of eternal life. The eternal Word, who was with the Father before the beginning, left His throne and came to the earth. He took on flesh in the form of a baby and dwelt among us. Jesus experienced every stage of life without sin. His sacrifice was a pure offering before the Lord. Jesus's blood cleansed us from unrighteousness and opened the doors of heaven for us to enter.

Like John, we must meditate on God's Word to defend the nature and work of our Savior. Though false doctrine grew in his culture, John remained resolute in what he witnessed in Christ. Similarly, our culture has many false doctrines, some claiming that Jesus was only a man. However, if Jesus were just a man, He would not have remained sinless and obedient. He would not have sacrificed Himself for our behalf. He would not have shown us unfailing love and faithfulness. Let us draw toward the deep truths of God. Let us hear, see, and touch Jesus as we reflect on Scripture. We can trust that the Holy Spirit will bring us into the life Jesus offers and grant us the opportunity to bear witness to His glory.

"WE MUST MEDITATE ON GOD'S WORD TO DEFEND THE NATURE AND WORK OF OUR SAVIOR."

DAY 265
Judgment Meets Compassion

"Have you seen how Ahab has humbled himself before me? I will not bring the disaster during his lifetime, because he has humbled himself before me. I will bring the disaster on his house during his son's lifetime."

1 KINGS 21:29

How does God handle evil? With judgment and compassion. Ahab was one of the evilest kings in the nation of Israel's history (1 Kings 21:25–26). Ahab, who should have been leading the people to live in reverent submission to the Lord, instead bowed his knee to idols. He persecuted servants of the Lord. Repeatedly, he called the prophet Elijah his enemy because Elijah spoke God's judgment on him.

Although Ahab severely lacked in character, God did not hesitate to respond to his moment of repentance. But he would return to his wicked ways only one chapter later. That one moment of true repentance, overcome with despair from Elijah's words, was enough for God to relent. God promised an ugly demise for Ahab, but in His compassion, He postponed it to befall his son instead. Ahab, however, went back on his word and abandoned the Lord once again. As a result, he died a horrible death a short time later. Ahab's son, Ahaziah, was also a wicked man and died as a young king.

These passages may seem harsh or not make much sense to us. But, we can rest assured of three things. First, God knows the hearts of men (1 Kings 8:39, Romans 8:27). He knows every sin, every righteous act, and every intention behind every deed, good and bad. He knew the hearts of Ahab and Ahaziah.

Second, God is just (Psalm 146:7–9). He never acts wrongly toward someone. Even when we do not understand His actions, we can trust that He is acting in accordance with His perfect justice.

And third, God has given us reprieve in Jesus from receiving His justice for our sins. Those who believe in Jesus are saved by grace through faith from the eternal consequences of their sin. If God showed such great compassion for the horribly evil Ahab in one brief moment of repentance, how much more does He show compassion on those who live repentant lives and are covered by the atoning work of Christ? Immeasurably more!

Today, let us revel in our God, who is just in the face of evil and compassionate to those who repent. We can surely trust Him to establish justice and peace on the earth!

DAY 266
Overlooking Offenses

A person's insight gives him patience, and his virtue is to overlook an offense.

PROVERBS 19:11

To offend means that we sin against, upset, or go against someone. We have all likely felt the pain of an offense and the hurt and frustration that follow. Often, our gut reaction is to make someone pay for the ways they have offended us. But at the heart of such a response, we are missing the message of the gospel. We are the greatest offenders, yet we did not get what we deserved.

In God's perfect holiness, He set a standard of righteousness for us so that we might have a right relationship with Him. However, instead of walking in obedience, we are inclined to gratify the desires of our flesh, choosing our own ways, and disobeying God. Because of this, we have offended the Lord and broken our relationship with Him. Rather than making us pay the penalty for offending Him, in His great love and rich mercy, He offered Christ to stand in our place, to forgive our offenses against Him.

What we see at the cross of Christ is profound. Jesus Christ, who walked in perfect holiness, willingly and lovingly chose to stand in our place. He chose to pay the penalty of our sin and bear the wrath of God so that we could be clothed in His righteousness and united with God. How humbling is this truth!. We are the greatest offenders, yet Christ has set us free; He has paid our debt. He has made a way for us to have an eternal relationship with Christ!

It is only by God's grace that we see our offenses through a gospel lens. Overlooking an offense does not negate justice. It does not mean we turn a blind eye or pretend that sin does not exist. We fix our eyes not on the offense but on the grace offered to us in Christ.

Just as we have been given the gift of grace in Christ Jesus, how much more should we desire to offer that grace to others? May we aim to walk as those who have been rescued from our debts and freely forgive as we God has forgiven us. May those around us see the gospel of grace in the way we live our lives, and may it draw them to know Christ in the same way.

"WE FIX OUR EYES NOT ON THE OFFENSE BUT ON THE GRACE OFFERED TO US IN CHRIST."

DAY 267
Longing for Better

If they were thinking about where they came from, they would have had an opportunity to return. But they now desire a better place—a heavenly one. Therefore, God is not ashamed to be called their God, for he has prepared a city for them.

HEBREWS 11:15–16

When God called Abraham to leave his home, Abraham did not know where he was going. Nonetheless, Abraham picked up his things and left with his family to become a sojourner. He trusted the Lord by leaving the land he knew to walk with God toward a new place. Abraham knew that God was unfolding a plan of great blessing and joy.

By walking with God, Abraham began to understand the ultimate destination of the journey. While God was bringing Abraham and his descendants to a new land, this land was not the end but a shadow of the ultimate land, a heavenly land where God's people would dwell forever. Through their experiences, they understood that they were not just sojourners in a new land but also on this earth. They desired and awaited a heavenly place that would be unlike the world in which they were currently living. This faith would not be in vain, for God's redemptive plan included entrance to a heavenly city granted by God's great grace.

As Christ followers, we live in this world but do not belong to this world. Like the people in Hebrews 11, we are sojourners on this earth. Living in a broken world leaves us with longings—ones of restoration and renewal, hope for our true home. Like those of faith who trusted in God through the wilderness journey, our desires and longings too will be satisfied in eternity one day. Christ will return and mend the brokenness of this world. He will transform the earth and restore it to a place of everlasting peace and joy.

Heaven will meet earth permanently, and we will spend eternity with our great God. As we await this day, we are to joyfully take up our identity as sojourners. We should refrain from adopting the sinful practices of this world and walk in holiness. We use the time we are given to spread and live out the gospel so others can join God's kingdom. We can persevere in hope and faith when the world feels dark and heavy, knowing that this is not the end. There is a place far better than where we are now, and this future place will be our forever home.

"AS CHRIST FOLLOWERS, WE LIVE IN THIS WORLD BUT DO NOT BELONG TO THIS WORLD."

DAY 268
The Side of Truth

"You are a king then?" Pilate asked. "You say that I'm a king," Jesus replied. "I was born for this, and I have come into the world for this: to testify to the truth. Everyone who is of the truth listens to my voice."

JOHN 18:37

Culturally, when divisive topics arise, people often comment that one should get on the right side of history. This claim exhorts people to consider all of the topics and issues humanity was wrong about in the past and avoid making that same mistake. When thinking this way, it can leave us in limbo. How can we possibly know what side is the right side until time passes and history tells us so?

In asking these questions, we must determine what serves as our gauge and guide. For the Christian, the right side is the side of God's Truth. We determine what is true by looking to the Word of God as our guide. We are shaped and informed by Scripture to help us to determine what is truly right and good and will not always align with what the world thinks is right and good. In fact, we may even be rejected because of our firm grounding in God's truth. Jesus came to testify to the truth of God, and the world rejected Him. He was not only cast out, ridiculed, and mocked, but He was put to death on a cross. He endured such persecution because God's truth mattered to him more than anything else. Jesus held fast to the words and purposes of God.

We are daily faced with opportunities to stand firm on the side of truth. We may be tempted to agree with the majority in such a way that compromises what we believe to be true. We may be tempted to withhold the truth in fear of others rejecting us. But there is only one truth that will stand the test of time, and that is God's truth revealed through His Word. When questions and doubts arise, and we feel unsure about what is true, may we run and cling to God's Word for guidance that we may reflect Jesus and serve as living vessels for God's truth.

"THERE IS ONLY ONE TRUTH THAT WILL STAND THE TEST OF TIME, AND THAT IS GOD'S TRUTH REVEALED THROUGH HIS WORD."

DAY 269
Heirs of Hope

But when the kindness of God our Savior and his love for mankind appeared, he saved us—not by works of righteousness that we had done, but according to his mercy—through the washing of regeneration and renewal by the Holy Spirit. He poured out his Spirit on us abundantly through Jesus Christ our Savior so that, having been justified by his grace, we may become heirs with the hope of eternal life.

TITUS 3:4-7

Every follower of Christ is an heir. We may not always consider this special identity, but the implications of being an heir are great. You cannot be an heir without the entitlement to receive something. A prince is entitled to the throne when the king or queen passes. As followers of Jesus, we are entitled to receive the kingdom of God and everlasting life with Christ. Yet this entitlement is not based on something we have done or earned. A prince is an heir because he has the privilege of being a part of the royal family, yet we do not naturally share this privilege. Before coming to Christ, we were paupers, not princes. Nothing special or unique about us qualified us as heirs. We were destitute, with no ability to provide redemption or restoration for ourselves.

But then the King appeared. When Christ came, He saved us according to His steadfast love and mercy. He washed away our sins and renewed us by the power of His Spirit. He set His robes of righteousness upon us and declared us children of the King for those who would trust Him as their Lord and Savior. He took our lowly position and set us high on the throne at the right hand of the Father. Because of God and His abounding grace, we have a royal status in the kingdom of God forever.

While we await the fullness of God's kingdom, God does not leave us without hope. The inheritance of eternity in God's kingdom is our hope. We can persevere in this life knowing that a glorious future awaits us. One day, we will be reunited with the King of kings and spend eternity in His kingdom. We are heirs to a kingdom that will never end, so let us rejoice and rest in the hope of our inheritance.

"BECAUSE OF GOD AND HIS ABOUNDING GRACE, WE HAVE A ROYAL STATUS IN THE KINGDOM OF GOD FOREVER."

DAY 270
Sealed with the Spirit

In him you also were sealed with the promised Holy Spirit when you heard the word of truth, the gospel of your salvation, and when you believed. The Holy Spirit is the down payment of our inheritance, until the redemption of the possession, to the praise of his glory.

EPHESIANS 1:13-14

When you imagine a seal, what comes to mind? One of the most common types of seals can be found on an envelope. The seal protects the contents of that envelope and keeps it closed, but it can also reveal the letter's author, often with specific etchings or designs. If a letter bears a famous seal, the recipient knows the message inside is of great importance.

When Paul describes us as being sealed with the Holy Spirit, He means that we have been marked by the Lord as His own. He has placed His own Spirit within us. From the moment we heard the truth and believed, He gave this seal to us, and once we are sealed with the Spirit, it can never be unbroken. The Holy Spirit is our guarantee of the salvation we have received in Christ, and it is a salvation that can never be taken from us.

What is even better is that the Holy Spirit is only a down payment of the inheritance we have in Christ! The presence of the Holy Spirit inside us is far more than we deserve. Paul says that there is much more blessing on the horizon—that the riches of the gospel will be experienced fully in God's physical presence one day when we see Him face to face.

The Lord has sealed you for His own possession, and He did so by giving you His Spirit. His Spirit guides you into all understanding and wisdom. He reveals the beautiful truth of the gospel to you. He instructs you as you read the Word of God. And He is evidence that you are a child of God. One day, you will stand before the Lord and receive the inheritance He has promised you as His child. He has so much to give us on the day we are finally united with Him forever. Until then, may we lift up praises that He has sealed us as His own!

"ONE DAY, YOU WILL STAND BEFORE THE LORD AND RECEIVE THE INHERITANCE HE HAS PROMISED YOU AS HIS CHILD."

DAY 271
Careful Stewards of Creation

The Lord God took the man and placed him in the garden of Eden to work it and watch over it.

GENESIS 2:15

There is something deeply satisfying about caring for a garden. But for anyone who has grown a garden, you know the work is slow and continual. To keep plants flourishing, you must keep up the tending, watering, feeding, and weeding. Like caring for a garden, caring for creation takes work and does not necessarily come naturally to the way we live. As Christians, we are not called to coast through life the easy way but to be careful stewards of God's creation. How often do we pause to consider what that means for the way we live?

In Genesis, we see God create the world with intention and order. With each step of creation, He declares the goodness of all He has made. He appoints Adam and Eve to be stewards and caretakers over His good work as a privileged responsibility. Because everything He made is good, everything holds value as a means to display His glory to the world. We cannot simply view creation as something intended to serve us but something to cultivate and steward what God has provided.

While there can be great debate about the specifics of how to care for God's creation, we can all agree that we should do our personal best to take care of His creation. In our role as careful stewards of God's creation, we may be tempted to think small personal changes will have little impact on the world. But, God has given His people instructions to steward our possessions well, and we must recognize our personal responsibility. However, it is also important to recognize that God is ultimately in control over all. We can work to honor Him, but our work will never earn our salvation. Jesus's death on the cross already accomplished that work. So, may we posture our hearts to care for God's creation with gracious and selfless care, knowing that His care and protection ultimately triumph all.

> "GOD HAS GIVEN HIS PEOPLE INSTRUCTIONS TO STEWARD OUR POSSESSIONS WELL, AND WE MUST RECOGNIZE OUR PERSONAL RESPONSIBILITY."

DAY 272
Draw from the True Well

Jesus said, "Everyone who drinks from this water will get thirsty again. But whoever drinks from the water that I will give him will never get thirsty again. In fact, the water I will give him will become a well of water springing up in him for eternal life."

JOHN 4:13–14

When we do not drink enough water, we get dehydrated. And if we go without water for long enough, we cannot survive. The water Jesus offers in John 4:13–14 is of even greater value than the water we drink out of a glass. He is our living water. Without the water of eternal life, we would die not only a physical death but a spiritual one, condemned in our guilt and shame without hope of joy, comfort, or peace.

But with Jesus, there is hope. He offers eternal life freely to all. He offers healing and forgiveness, the promise of eternal life with Him. He promises to be our satisfaction, hope, and peace. He has paid for our sins upon the cross, which secured our redemption through His resurrection. To receive His gift of grace, all we must do is repent and believe, trusting in Him as our Savior.

When Jesus described this water in John 4, He was speaking to a Samaritan woman. Contextually, Jews and Samaritans did not associate with one another. They were enemies. On top of this, she was a woman, which would have made it culturally unacceptable for her to talk to Jesus. It is to this culturally marginalized woman who Jesus promised eternal life. Jesus does not limit His grace based on societal rankings or popularity. He does not play favorites. He offers forgiveness to all who come to Him.

Each one of us may sometimes find ourselves searching for satisfaction and life apart from Christ. We seek salvation and happiness in our careers, our families, our wealth, all of which will disappoint us when we place our hope in them. In His grace, God offers the water of eternal life to all who believe in Him, and in Him, our living water, we can place our hope. Yet, while this grace is offered freely, it came at a cost. The costly blood of Christ paid for our eternal salvation. In response to this extravagant gift, let us now draw from the true well—Christ our Savior—with thanksgiving and worship. Let us drink deeply and offer our praises to God, who provides eternal water that never runs dry.

"THE COSTLY BLOOD OF CHRIST PAID FOR OUR ETERNAL SALVATION."

DAY 273
Loving Your Enemies

You have heard that it was said, Love your neighbor and hate your enemy. But I tell you, love your enemies and pray for those who persecute you, so that you may be children of your Father in heaven.

MATTHEW 5:43–45A

Because of the curse of sin, we each reject God and choose our own way. We are born into sin as enemies of God. We desire things that are opposed to the Lord's will for us. We worship ourselves instead of Him. But God in His mercy calls us to Himself—we have despised Him, rejected Him, ignored His commands, but He beckons us still. He changes our hearts, allowing us to see the truth of His Word and accept Him as our Lord and Savior. This sort of love is incomprehensible. And it has been given to us.

When God saves us and makes us His children, He calls us to imitate Him and how He has loved us. On our own, we are not capable of showing this love to Him or others, but through salvation, He gives us His love that it may overflow to those we interact with from day to day.

We are not only to love those who are kind to us but our enemies too. This does not mean we should ignore wrongs done to us or have feelings of love toward those who have hurt us. But God is the righteous judge, and He will hold them accountable on judgment day. Loving our enemies means that until the day of judgment comes, we do not lash out in anger or seek retaliation. Rather, we display the gospel to all who are watching as we show grace and forgiveness through our actions and the way we live as believers. When others wonder the reason for our love and ask how it is possible, we can tell them of Christ and what He has first done for us. We lead them to our Savior.

The gospel changes everything. It is revolutionary to the ways and norms of the world, and it allows us to experience love for those who have no love for us at all. But this is only because we know Jesus first loved us—so much that He died for us—and how unworthy we are of receiving His love. Now, we represent His love to others. May they stand in marvelous wonder as they realize the love and grace our Savior has for His children.

"THE GOSPEL CHANGES EVERYTHING."

DAY 274
Searching the Scriptures

As soon as it was night, the brothers and sisters sent Paul and Silas away to Berea. Upon arrival, they went into the synagogue of the Jews. The people here were of more noble character than those in Thessalonica, since they received the word with eagerness and examined the Scriptures daily to see if these things were so. Consequently, many of them believed, including a number of the prominent Greek women as well as men.

ACTS 17:10–12

Christian teaching is more available now than ever. Countless sermons and soundbites are just a click away. Unfortunately, a lesson's availability or even popularity does not always mean that it is biblically accurate. So how can we tell if the content we are consuming is sound?

Paul and Silas's trip to Berea took place approximately twenty years after Jesus's death. At this time, the apostles were spreading the gospel message wherever God opened doors for them to go, but there were many areas of the ancient world that had not yet heard of Jesus. The New Testament was still being written during this time, so the Jews in Berea had Scriptures that contained only the Old Testament books. When they heard Paul and Silas teach of Jesus's death and resurrection, they wondered if it could be true. Could the promised Messiah of the Old Testament really be this Jesus?

To discover the answers to their questions, the Bereans received the apostles' teaching with eagerness and examined the Scriptures to confirm its genuineness. Today's verse commends this approach, and therefore, this passage also teaches us how to handle our own questions regarding biblical accuracy of the teachings we encounter. We should receive Christian teaching with eagerness, without being hyper-skeptical. However, simply because we eagerly listen to a lesson does not mean we should accept it without question. We should examine its truths to be sure they align with Scripture.

God's Word is cohesive. We can trust the Bible's every word. Studying its pages only leads us into a deeper, more committed relationship with God. Through it, we gain a deeper understanding of the gospel message—of God's great love for us and Jesus's coming to make a way for sinners to be saved. As we grow in knowledge of Scripture, we can better recognize true biblical teaching. May we find great joy in this as we seek to know Him more!

"WE CAN TRUST THE BIBLE'S EVERY WORD."

DAY 275
His Purposes Cannot Be Thwarted

...my word that comes from my mouth will not return to me empty, but it will accomplish what I please and will prosper in what I send it to do.

ISAIAH 55:11

Through the book of Isaiah, the Lord spoke of His sovereignty, His control over everything. Whatever the Lord decrees will come to pass. God's plans are not like ours. We forget, fail, and change our plans. But, the Lord never forgets, and His divine purposes never fail nor change. Isaiah relayed this truth within a section speaking on the Lord's compassion. At the beginning of chapter 55, God invited the thirsty, poor, and unsatisfied to come to Him and partake in His feast. There, His people would delight themselves in milk, wine, and rich food. Their ears would hear of the Lord's blessings over them. Their hearts would lift at promises to redeem and restore them. God proclaimed that His people would not receive shame but forgiveness and care. Like the rain that nourishes seeds and sprouts crops, the words of the Lord will produce good for His people.

We can trust that the Lord's compassion is a sure thing. Furthermore, it is effective. Good will result because God has decreed it for us. We might be tempted to perceive that His compassion will produce material good. However, though God delights in giving us earthly gifts, material good is not our greatest treasure. Isaiah's use of language like "milk," "wine," and "rich food" were images that pointed to the spiritual satisfaction of salvation and the fruits of sanctification, the day-by-day process of becoming more like Christ. The Holy Spirit works to shed our impurities and helps us glorify God in all that we are. The Lord's compassion leads to our becoming better worshipers, lovers, and servants.

This divine purpose was achieved through the saving work of Jesus Christ. In Him, we see the compassion of the Lord on full display. Jesus died on the cross for the just penalty we deserved. And, like rain that transforms the seed into a crop, the Lord's compassion transforms us as well. Through faith in Jesus, our sins are forgiven, and we receive His perfect record. His righteousness equips us to pursue righteousness. We are able to delight in the eternal gift of the Lord's presence and become like our Savior. We can give up our inferior plans and trust in the divine purposes Jesus accomplished.

"THE LORD'S COMPASSION LEADS TO OUR BECOMING BETTER WORSHIPERS, LOVERS, AND SERVANTS."

DAY 276
The Problem with Envy

Do not covet your neighbor's house. Do not covet your neighbor's wife, his male or female servant, his ox or donkey, or anything that belongs to your neighbor.

EXODUS 20:17

On any given day, many of us might find ourselves tempted to covet or envy something that someone else has. Envy is ravenous. James 3:16 tells us that where there is jealousy, there is disorder. Simply speaking, envy never leads to anything good. It ruins or hurts our relationships with others and the Lord. The problem with envy is that it stirs up dissatisfaction and bitterness within our hearts. We revile others for the things they have. Instead of celebrating others, we compare ourselves to them. Instead of being grateful for what we do have, we shake our fists at God for what we do not have. Envy is both divisive and destructive.

God did not tell us not to covet because He does not want good things for us. God desires us to be joyful and wants to give us good gifts. Yet, He does not want us to desire good gifts outside of Him. When good gifts become the basis of our satisfaction, they become idols. God's commanding us not to covet is meant to keep our hearts content in Him alone. We were not made to be satisfied by anything other than the Lord. When we chase after other things for fulfillment, we run away from the only One who truly satisfies. Even if we receive what we think we desire, we will still find ourselves unsatisfied.

God has not withheld what we need but has graciously given it to us through Christ. The greatest gift we could ever receive is salvation through Him. With Christ, we have all that we need. We do not need to envy what others have, for we have already received what we truly need—Jesus. The cure for an envious heart is contentment in Christ. As we remain content in Christ, we will not grow envious of what other people have. We will learn to appreciate what other people have without feeling the need to have it ourselves. We will turn to God in gratitude for our many blessings without demanding more. Let us ask the Lord for His help in trading our envy for delight in Him. May we seek contentment in Christ rather than in the things of this world. What wonderful contentment we will find in Christ as we experience the true joy He gives.

"GOD HAS NOT WITHHELD WHAT WE NEED BUT HAS GRACIOUSLY GIVEN IT TO US THROUGH CHRIST."

DAY 277
A Great Exchange

For while we were still helpless, at the right time, Christ died for the ungodly. For rarely will someone die for a just person—though for a good person perhaps someone might even dare to die. But God proves his own love for us in that while we were still sinners, Christ died for us.

ROMANS 5:6-8

Our sinful nature makes us broken and helpless beings. Without God, we cannot function as we should. We are broken. There is a deficiency in us that we cannot fix ourselves. Yet there is hope for our brokenness, and it is the gospel. The gospel declares the greatest exchange ever known. By dying on the cross, Jesus took the punishment that we all deserve for our sins. He put Himself in our place. This was an unlikely exchange because it is rare for someone to die for another. It is even rarer for a perfect person to put himself in the place of an imperfect person. But this is exactly what Christ did. He looked at our helpless and broken state and gave us Himself. Out of His great love for us, God in the flesh sacrificed Himself for our sake. What makes our exchange with Christ so impactful is that we do not deserve this exchange. We do not deserve to be given forgiveness and freedom through Christ, but He gives it freely by His grace.

On the cross, another exchange took place that transforms those who believe in Christ. Our unrighteousness was traded for Christ's perfect righteousness. Theologians call this the "great exchange." Christ's righteousness covers our sin, and we are considered innocent, set free from the punishment of our sin. We become new creations. Our restoration to God restores us to who we were created to be. We no longer are faulty and broken people, for the grace of Christ has made us new.

It is a comfort to know that Christ's grace is not dependent on our sufficiency. Jesus did not ask for us to clean ourselves up before making the exchange. He did not ask for us to make ourselves "good" before He would die for us. Out of His great love, Jesus took our place, despite our sin and brokenness. In the moments we find ourselves taking the gospel lightly, let us remember Christ's exchange. He took our place so we could be free. He gave us His righteousness so we could be made new. Praise be to Him forevermore!

"IT IS A COMFORT TO KNOW THAT CHRIST'S GRACE IS NOT DEPENDENT ON OUR SUFFICIENCY."

DAY 278
Loving Discipline

The Israelites again did what was evil in the Lord's sight, so the Lord handed them over to the Philistines forty years.

JUDGES 13:1

Have you found yourself caught in a cycle of sin? You may suffer the consequences then find yourself falling back into the same traps and consequences again and again. Sin is evil and detestable in the sight of the Lord. It will lure us in repeatedly if we let it. When we look at the history of Israel, we see people who fell into the same sin cycle over and over again. At one point in their history, Israel did evil in the sight of the Lord, and God used the Philistines as a means of discipline. The Philistines seized the land and attached their name to it. They were oppressive and held Isreal in slavery for a long time.

It can be tempting to question God's punishment at times. We might downplay our sin and see His means of discipline as too harsh. We might view corrections as a means of keeping us from doing what we want when actually the correction is an act of love. Our sin makes us deserving of death, for it is a blatant rejection of God. The Lord is too holy to disregard the necessary discipline that sin requires. But He is also too kind to leave us in it. His discipline reminds us of sin's true harm and its ultimate promise of death.

Israel continually turned away from God, yet He continued His pursuit of drawing them back to Himself by whatever means necessary. As a parent faithfully redirects a child's actions through discipline, so does God do the same for us as His children. God loves us too deeply to leave us where we are. God longs for us to delight in obedience and to walk faithfully in His ways. God grieves our sin, and He sent His only Son, Jesus, to rescue us from its grip. When we find ourselves in a place similar to the Israelites, may God humble us to receive His loving discipline. May it remind us of His ultimate grace and kindness toward us by redirecting our hearts back to the freedom found in Him.

"AS A PARENT FAITHFULLY REDIRECTS A CHILD'S ACTIONS THROUGH DISCIPLINE, SO DOES GOD DO THE SAME FOR US AS HIS CHILDREN. GOD LOVES US TOO DEEPLY TO LEAVE US WHERE WE ARE."

DAY 279
Know Who You Are

My sons, don't be negligent now, for the Lord has chosen you to stand in his presence, to serve him, and to be his ministers and burners of incense.

2 CHRONICLES 29:11

The four books of Kings and Chronicles detail the lineage of the kings of Israel. Some kings were just and faithful to the Lord, and some were evil worshipers of idols. Ahaz was a king who forsook the Lord and idolized the gods of other nations. During his rule, the temple was abandoned, offerings were not made to the Lord, and the Levites shirked their responsibilities as the temple priests. Ahaz led the entire nation away from God.

When Ahaz died, his son, Hezekiah, became king. Hezekiah did not follow in his father's footsteps but instead rededicated the nation and the temple to the Lord and urged all of the people to consecrate themselves to God. Verse 11 was his encouragement to the Levites who needed to return to their duties at the reopened temple. They were being called upon to fulfill the holy work for which they had been specially chosen—to stand in His presence, to serve Him, and to be His ministers and burners of incense.

What significance this is for us still today! Christians have been invited to become a holy priesthood who also make sacrifices before the Lord (1 Peter 2:4–6). Only, these sacrifices are not slain animals but spiritual sacrifices. No longer must we sacrifice animals in atonement for our sins, for when Jesus came to die for us, He made a way for us to live under grace instead of under the Law. As Christ sacrificed His only Son to make a way of salvation for us, so we offer our bodies to Christ as living sacrifices, willing and ready to do His will, sharing the good news of the gospel with everyone we meet.

Romans 12:1 says, "Therefore, brothers and sisters, in view of the mercies of God, I urge you to present your bodies as a living sacrifice, holy and pleasing to God; this is your true worship." Christians should regard their role as a holy priesthood with great value as the Levites did. May we be vigilant when it comes to offering our time, gifts, and resources as an offering to the Lord. Let us remember who we are as the children of God and eagerly stand in His glorious presence, ready to do the work we have been called to do.

"MAY WE BE VIGILANT WHEN IT COMES TO OFFERING OUR TIME, GIFTS, AND RESOURCES AS AN OFFERING TO THE LORD."

DAY 280
Children of God

See what great love the Father has given us that we should be called God's children—and we are! The reason the world does not know us is that it didn't know him.

1 JOHN 3:1

To be a Christian is to be transformed. Once we were slaves to sin, but now we are slaves to Christ. Once we were blind, but now we see. Once we were children of darkness, but now we are children of God. We may be familiar with these transformations, but when was the last time we stopped to consider them, stand in awe of them? When the author was writing this letter, this is exactly what he was doing. He was trying to convey the sheer bliss and astonishment he experienced as a result of being brought into the family of God.

First, the author says, "See what great love the Father has given us." He does not say, "glance toward" or "take a peek at what great love the Father has given us." He uses the word "see." Some scholars even believe that "behold" could be a more accurate translation. Let us behold the love of God together for a moment.

We could begin as the author of these verses did, by considering what immense love it took for us to become children of God. A child's entrance into a family is always initiated by the parents. Whether through birth or adoption, the child has little choice or authority over which family he or she enters and when. The same is true of our adoption into God's family. We have never been clever or kind enough to earn the title of a child of God. No, adoption into God's family always begins with His love and desire for us.

Romans 5:6 says, "For while we were still helpless, at the right time, Christ died for the ungodly." God's love comes to the helpless and makes them heirs. In no earthly context does this make any sense. This love is astonishing, breathtaking, nothing short of miraculous. Yet, it is real, and those who believe in Jesus have experienced it first hand. What would it look like for you to behold the extravagant love of God today—not just give it a passing thought but actually sit and consider in detail how God's love has brought you near to Him? Consider these things, and rejoice that Jesus made a way for our salvation and that we can become His own.

"GOD'S LOVE COMES TO THE HELPLESS AND MAKES THEM HEIRS."

DAY 281

How Great is Our God

For the Lord is great and highly praised; he is feared above all gods. For all the gods of the peoples are idols, but the Lord made the heavens.

1 CHRONICLES 16:25-26

Have you ever had a moment that makes your soul sing? Perhaps you have looked in awe at the grandness of God's creation or the unexpected recovery of someone who has been sick for a long time. God's greatness is often magnified in these moments. But while it can be easy to see God's greatness in moments like these, it can be equally difficult to see His greatness in the mundaneness of life. It might feel as though we are stumbling through our days, and for some reason, life feels really hard. Nothing is particularly wrong, but nothing is awe-inspiring either. And we long for another mountain-top moment that leaves us in awe of our mighty God.

This type of mountain-top moment is where we find David in 1 Chronicles 16. After years of trial, exile, and war, David finally becomes king. He is victorious in battle and able to bring the ark of the covenant, where God dwells, back to Israel after the Philistines stole it many years before. The difficulty in getting the ark back to Israel highlights David's need for God. After the ark returns, David writes a Psalm of thanksgiving to the Lord. This is a pinnacle moment for David, and he stands in awe of God's greatness.

However, it is important to note that though we see David praising God in a good moment here, he also praises God in life's difficulties. Psalms is full of poems in which David praises God for His powerful hand in troublesome times. It is common to forget to praise God when circumstances are hard or just lack excitement. But even in these mundane moments, our God is great. As you focus on praising Him for His greatness—even in the valleys—you learn to operate in His strength instead of your own. So whatever season you may be in today, may you praise His holy name, trusting that He is good and He is your strength in every moment.

"AS YOU FOCUS ON PRAISING HIM FOR HIS GREATNESS—EVEN IN THE VALLEYS—YOU LEARN TO OPERATE IN HIS STRENGTH INSTEAD OF YOUR OWN."

DAY 282
Peace in Suffering

I have told you these things so that in me you may have peace. You will have suffering in this world. Be courageous! I have conquered the world.

JOHN 16:33

What comes to your mind when you hear the word "peace"? A tranquil sunset? A steaming, fresh cup of coffee sipped in the quiet morning hours? A lazy weekend with no impending to-do list? All of these things sound lovely, but they fall short of the kind of peace Jesus promises in this passage.

Biblical peace is different from worldly, temporal peace. It does not require you to be in a certain location, it is not dependent on circumstances, and it cannot be interrupted by the unforeseen. Biblical peace is called *shalom*. *Shalom* is more than just the feeling of being at ease. It is both the absence of harm and also the presence of good. And *shalom* is not circumstantial but is based on our relationship with God. Through Christ, those who believe have peace with God now (Romans 5:1) and the promise of eternal peace in His presence (Romans 5:21).

Because God is our maker, creator, sustainer, sanctifier, eternal hope, and glorious inheritance, the fact that we are at peace with Him means we have true, lasting peace despite anything unpeaceful happening in our lives. Jesus explains plainly in today's verse that we will have suffering, and in Him, we will have peace. Jesus's peace, *shalom*, is not the absence of suffering but the presence of God in the midst of suffering. His peace is the promise that the suffering we experience now will not last forever and cannot overtake the God who sustains us.

Paul says in Romans 8:18, "For I consider that the sufferings of this present time are not worth comparing with the glory that is going to be revealed to us." And 2 Corinthians 4:17–18 reads, "For our momentary light affliction is producing for us an absolutely incomparable eternal weight of glory. So we do not focus on what is seen, but on what is unseen. For what is seen is temporary, but what is unseen is eternal." Suffering is real. The weight of suffering is heavy, sometimes overwhelmingly so. Jesus never discredits the impact of suffering. But He also reminds us that suffering ends while God's eternal purpose does not. Jesus promises full and complete redemption and restoration in Him one day. And because of that, we can have peace in the suffering that we face today.

"SHALOM IS NOT CIRCUMSTANTIAL BUT IS BASED ON OUR RELATIONSHIP WITH GOD."

DAY 283
Thanking God for Faithful Saints

I always thank my God when I mention you in my prayers, because I hear of your love for all the saints and the faith that you have in the Lord Jesus. I pray that your participation in the faith may become effective through knowing every good thing that is in us for the glory of Christ. For I have great joy and encouragement from your love, because the hearts of the saints have been refreshed through you, brother.

PHILEMON 4–7

Paul's prayer in Philemon captures the heart of what our prayers should sound like for others in Christ. Each time Paul mentions his brother in Christ in prayer, he thanks God for him. At times, we may not have the love for other believers displayed here by Paul. We can grow frustrated with other believers, which leads us to grumble rather than pray for them. Paul's prayer presents us with a convincing question: Do we spend more time complaining about other believers or thanking God for them?

What makes Paul's prayer powerful is that he spends time commending his brother before challenging him. The book of Philemon is a letter written by Paul to confront Philemon and plead for him to reconcile with his slave, Onesimus. Paul begins his letter by thanking God for Philemon and speaking words of encouragement to him. Paul knew his brother in the faith was a source of love to the saints, and because of this, knew that Philemon would heed his confrontation.

Fellow believers may not always make the right decisions, but this does not mean they are not worth our gratitude. It is a blessing to be a part of the family of God, committed and faithful to the Lord. God graciously uses other Christians to spur us on in our faith, care for us, and speak truth and encouragement to us. Every saint is a gift, and we should thank God for the gift they are. In the moments we find ourselves tempted to grumble about our brothers or sisters in Christ, we should stop and say a prayer of thanks for them.

Paul's prayers encourage us to thank God and pray for other believers daily. As we continue to lift them up with prayers of petition and thanksgiving, our hearts will remain warm toward them. Our hearts will be refreshed as we dwell on the faithfulness of other saints and the impact they are having on the kingdom. Every believer is a gift, so let us thank God for them.

DAY 284
Your Labor is Not in Vain

Therefore, my dear brothers and sisters, be steadfast, immovable, always excelling in the Lord's work, because you know that your labor is not in vain.

1 CORINTHIANS 15:58

Have you ever tried to share Jesus with someone, only to feel as though your message fell on deaf ears? How disheartening it can be to proclaim the gospel, only to have it rejected. You may even wonder whether it is worth it to share the gospel in the face of such rejection. If you feel this way, know that you are not alone. Consider the missionary William Carey. William Carey served in India for seven years without seeing one person come to faith in Jesus Christ. Even the Apostle Paul in the New Testament experienced rejection when telling others about the gospel (Acts 13:44–48).

However, both William Carey and the Apostle Paul persevered, and eventually, both saw fruit from their labor. Carey saw over 700 people come to faith in Jesus. And as you likely know, Paul is responsible for giving us much of the New Testament and starting many early churches. That said, even if they never saw anyone come to faith, their labor would still not have been in vain because they were obedient to Christ's call. After all, God uses our daily obedience and time spent with Him to sanctify us, which is the process of becoming Christlike. Our sanctification will lead to our glorification—the final removal of all our sin in heaven—because of the life Jesus gave for us on the cross.

If you are feeling discouraged today from proclaiming the gospel, take heart. Let nothing shake you from dedicating yourself to studying His Word, praying, and growing close to Him. Proclaim the good news to as many people as you can, knowing that it is ultimately God who draws people to Himself. And, at the end of all things, you will experience "What no eye has seen, no ear has heard, and no human heart has conceived" (1 Corinthians 2:9)—an eternal life spent with God the Father, experiencing things that we cannot even imagine.

So, one day at a time, continue the good work of growing in Christ, knowing Him more, and worshiping Him for all He has done. Continue proclaiming Him and "warning and teaching everyone with all wisdom" (Colossians 1:28), for the work you do is not in vain.

DAY 285
God's Word at Work

This is why we constantly thank God, because when you received the word of God that you heard from us, you welcomed it not as a human message, but as it truly is, the word of God, which also works effectively in you who believe.

1 THESSALONIANS 2:13

Ministry brings communal celebration, whether through baptism, missions, testimonies, or worship. This shared praise is the result of God's Word at work through relational evangelism. Relational evangelism means that relationships are integral to someone receiving the message of Jesus. For instance, a mature believer lovingly points a nonbeliever to the cross through years of faithful friendship and sacrificial love. Through evangelism, the mature believer trusts that the Holy Spirit will soften the nonbeliever's heart and the Word of God will penetrate. In the Lord's sovereign time, the person will turn to Jesus. Through this relational process, God's Word will produce an effect.

We see God's Word at work through relational evangelism in Paul's letter to the church in Thessalonica. Through Paul's ministry, the gospel message came to the Thessalonians. Those who heard this message knew the story of Jesus's death and resurrection was true. They knew the message was from God Himself and inclined their ears to listen. The Thessalonians turned from their idols to the Lord, desiring to follow the ways of Christ, and became an example to all believers. They were a testimony to the power of God's Word in the lives of sinners. Paul encouraged and urged them to receive the gospel and walk in the new life guaranteed through salvation in Christ. Preaching the gospel through relational ministry brought a harvest in Thessalonica, and Paul thanked God for His effective Word.

Was there someone in your life who lovingly led you to Christ through preaching the gospel? Even if you came to God in silence, a community of angels rejoiced at your repentance (Luke 15:10). There is a celebration when God's Word works in us to produce faith. But, His Word does not stop there; Scripture continues to shape us into the image of Christ. His Word equips us to walk in His ways as we persevere in this life, and it will bring us to our destination. Let us participate in this work by reading Scripture and recalling the gospel message every day. We can trust that Jesus will wash us in His Word as He rejoices over the sanctification taking place in our hearts that will find its completion when He calls us home.

DAY 286
Seek God's Wisdom

"So give your servant a receptive heart to judge your people and to discern between good and evil. For who is able to judge this great people of yours?" Now it pleased the Lord that Solomon had requested this. So God said to him, "Because you have requested this and did not ask for long life or riches for yourself, or the death of your enemies, but you asked discernment for yourself to administer justice, I will therefore do what you have asked. I will give you a wise and understanding heart, so that there has never been anyone like you before and never will be again."

1 KINGS 3:9-12

Solomon, the son of King David and Bathsheba, succeeded his father as the next king of Israel. Keep in mind that when he became king, there had been a mere handful of rulers in Israel's history. And while some of them tried to please God, they had all failed to obey the Lord in one way or another. The legacy of Israel's kings was not as glorious as what the people had expected it to be. Solomon's father, David, was the closest example Israel had of a righteous king.

As Solomon began his reign, instead of trusting in himself or flaunting his famous lineage, he humbly came before the Lord and asked for wisdom. He recognized his inability before God and knew he could not judge God's people without divine intervention. The plea of Solomon was the plea the Lord desired from all of His people—to seek Him and realize their need for Him. Solomon asked for what truly mattered. God was well pleased and blessed Solomon abundantly. Though Solomon would fail in many ways as others who came before him, he would forever be known as the wisest king of Israel.

How often do we try to accomplish everything in our own power and strength, forgetting we can do nothing without the Lord? We forget that the Lord desires to grant us His wisdom if we would only ask and seek Him (James 1:5). Every situation and moment of our days must be lived through the power of God's wisdom. As we come before the Lord in prayer each day, asking Him for help, we demonstrate our belief that He is God and we are not. In these moments of humility and dependence on Him, we find all we need. The Lord will freely give His wisdom to the humble heart who seeks Him.

"THE PLEA OF SOLOMON WAS THE PLEA THE LORD DESIRED FROM ALL OF HIS PEOPLE—TO SEEK HIM AND REALIZE THEIR NEED FOR HIM."

DAY 287

The Joy of Restoration

But many of the older priests, Levites, and family heads, who had seen the first temple, wept loudly when they saw the foundation of this temple, but many others shouted joyfully. The people could not distinguish the sound of the joyful shouting from that of the weeping, because the people were shouting so loudly. And the sound was heard far away.

EZRA 3:12–13

When Israel was restored back to their land, it was time for the Israelites to rebuild the temple after it was destroyed during a siege. However, this new temple was not as glorious as the one before. Those in Israel who beheld the grandeur of the previous temple wept at the sight of this new one, for they failed to appreciate God's restoration.

We may judge this group of Israelites for their reaction, but we can often fall into the same mentality. Most of us have experienced moments when something has been taken away from us only to be replaced by something else. Maybe this looks like a different living situation, job, or material possession. But this new thing makes us yearn for what we had before. If we dwell in this disappointment long enough, our hearts can grow bitter. Like the Israelites, we can despair. However, when we grumble over what we have received, we miss God's gift of grace. When we experience change and struggle to accept what we receive, may we be moved to joy rather than grief, for in every circumstance, God is working to restore, though we will not experience perfect restoration until we enter eternity with Christ.

The most joyful restoration will be our restoration to God. For those of us in Christ, our broken relationship with God has been mended and restored. Even more than this, our old sinful selves are gone, and we have received new selves—sanctified daily by the Lord. If we grieve our old selves, we take for granted the grace of Christ in our lives. His work of restoration by His grace has made us new! Let us not grieve past joys while missing God's present work of restoration in our lives, for each work is a gift of God's grace.

"IN EVERY CIRCUMSTANCE, GOD IS WORKING TO RESTORE, THOUGH WE WILL NOT EXPERIENCE PERFECT RESTORATION UNTIL WE ENTER ETERNITY WITH CHRIST."

DAY 288
If the Lord Wills

Come now, you who say, "Today or tomorrow we will travel to such and such a city and spend a year there and do business and make a profit." Yet you do not know what tomorrow will bring—what your life will be! For you are like vapor that appears for a little while, then vanishes. Instead, you should say, "If the Lord wills, we will live and do this or that."

JAMES 4:13–15

It is natural to dream and make plans for the future. However, today's verse cautions us to dream and plan in the right way—in humility, submission to the will of God, and with an eternal perspective. In James 4:13–15, James is confronting Christian businessmen who set their strategies apart from God. They considered only their desires and the possible profit when planning their ventures. They were ruled by their own arrogance and greed, not by the Spirit.

James reminds them that life cannot be lived in service to money and self, for both will fade away. Psalm 39:5–6 says, "In fact, you have made my days just inches long, and my life span is as nothing to you. Yes, every human being stands as only a vapor. Yes, a person goes about like a mere shadow. Indeed, they rush around in vain, gathering possessions without knowing who will get them." Slaving to amass wealth serves the self but not God. The true sin of these men was their unbelief in God. They lived as if He did not exist.

When we make plans for the future, we should make them humbly, knowing that any good thing we receive comes from the Father's hands and not our own wisdom and works. We should also make plans in submission to the will of God. The Bible is clear that we cannot serve two masters. We can either choose to serve God or serve money (Matthew 6:24). Our plans should reflect that our end goal is to glorify God above all else.

Finally, we should make plans with eternity in mind, for no earthly thing will go with us to heaven. In heaven, we will receive eternal rewards based not on our possessions but our good works for God. God's economy has a currency of Christlikeness (Matthew 6:19–21). Let us humbly submit our plans to the Lord, looking forward with great joy to the day God brings us home to true and eternal riches in Christ.

DAY 289
Be Alert

Be sober-minded, be alert. Your adversary the devil is prowling around like a roaring lion, looking for anyone he can devour. Resist him, firm in the faith, knowing that the same kind of sufferings are being experienced by your fellow believers throughout the world.

1 PETER 5:8-9

As we walk through each season of our lives, we should heed Peter's warning to remain sober-minded and alert. For our enemy, Satan, roams the earth looking for those whom he can destroy. He would stop at nothing to bring us to a place where we are far from God, resisting His work in our lives and refusing to trust Him as our Savior. Satan seeks to tempt us, feed us lies, make us believe we are above weakness that would lead to sin, cause us to feel so hopeless that we give up the fight. His attacks against us come when we feel helpless and hurting and when we are happy, full of life. Playing on our weakness, he tempts us to forsake trust in the Lord as we forget that He is sovereign and good. Or he attacks when we feel unbreakable—as though we could never fall to any great sin—so we place trust in ourselves instead of Christ, who is our true strength.

Our faith in Christ must be the rock upon which we stand. When we are hurting or angry or weary from our present circumstances, we must rest in God's grace to carry us. When we are full of joy and feel as though blessing rests upon us, we cannot forget that even as we walk with Christ, we too are susceptible to temptation and sin. But what mercy that when we do mess up—and we will, for we are sinners in a broken world—may we know that we stand forgiven and redeemed through the cross of Christ.

While we should not live life in fear of Satan's attacks, we should remain on guard against Him. We must remind ourselves of the truth of God's Word, meditating on it day and night, and use it—the sword of the Spirit—to fight sin. When we are at our weakest, may we remember that Christ is our strength, and He fights for us. Jesus has already won the victory over temptation and sin. May we keep our eyes ever focused on Him and His great love for us.

"MAY WE KNOW THAT WE STAND FORGIVEN AND REDEEMED THROUGH THE CROSS OF CHRIST."

DAY 290
Genuine Repentance

Furthermore, both people and animals must be covered with sackcloth, and everyone must call out earnestly to God. Each must turn from his evil ways and from his wrongdoing.

JONAH 3:8

There may be times when we confuse repentance over our sin with remorse over our sin. Most of us feel guilty but can often excuse sin instead of repent from sin. Often, we can say we are sorry to God about a certain sin we have committed, only to go right back and repeat that same sin. Genuine repentance involves turning away from sin, not just being sorry for sin or sorry that we were caught. Repentance involves an understanding that our sin offends God and that continuing to sin hinders our walk with the Lord. As followers of Christ, we are to daily turn away from our sin, putting it to death. For us to be conformed to the image of Christ, we must pursue godliness instead.

Putting sin to death is a battle, and we will not win this battle by allowing ourselves to continue sinful habits. Because God sent His Son to die, He made a way for His presence to be with us always. By God's grace, He has equipped us with the Holy Spirit, who not only encourages our repentance but empowers our repentance. Without God's help, we would struggle to turn from our sin. His Spirit inside us helps us recognize our sin and need for repentance. But He also gives us the strength we need to turn from our sinful ways and pursue Christlikeness above all else. When we find ourselves struggling to put sin to death, we can call out to the Lord and rely on the Spirit's strength to fight the sin that seeks to entangle us.

Daily we should examine our hearts for unrepentant sin, praying that the Lord would reveal areas in our lives where we are excusing sin instead of repenting from it. As the Spirit illuminates these areas, we do not need to be scared to come in repentance before God. We can embrace God's great love and grace that beckons us to come to Him. May we not turn toward sin but fix our eyes on Christ, pursuing obedience to Him.

"WITHOUT GOD'S HELP, WE WOULD STRUGGLE TO TURN FROM OUR SIN. HIS SPIRIT INSIDE US HELPS US RECOGNIZE OUR SIN AND NEED FOR REPENTANCE."

DAY 291
A Reflection of God's Love

Then the Lord said to me, "Go again; show love to a woman who is loved by another man and is an adulteress, just as the Lord loves the Israelites though they turn to other gods and love raisin cakes."

HOSEA 3:1

The story of Hosea is a beautiful but sad account in the Bible. God called the prophet Hosea to love a woman who was a prostitute and have children with her. But after they were married and Hosea brought his wife, Gomer, into his home, she was unfaithful to him. The penalty at that time for such unfaithfulness was death, but instead of accusing his wife, God calls Hosea to love and redeem her. He buys her out of prostitution and brings her back home. Though Gomer was unfaithful, Hosea was faithful to his wife.

The Lord's love for Israel despite their covenant unfaithfulness to Him is reflected through this story. The Lord entered into a marriage covenant with His people, yet they continued to run after other gods. Time and time again, He pursued them and took them back. He was faithful, even when they were unfaithful. The Lord would never abandon His people.

And so it is the same with us. Even after we are saved, we will always struggle with sinful desires. But God's love for us is not dependent upon our actions. It is sealed with the blood of Christ. He offers us forgiveness and restoration in Him. He is faithful when we are anything but. God's love for us causes us to worship Him in awe. Who is this God who created humanity and wanted fellowship with them, was rejected by them, and still chose to pursue them? Why does He love us? It is because He is glorified through His love for His people, and they are finally satisfied when they find their joy and purpose in Him.

Let His love draw you to Him, even when you feel you are undeserving. You will never fully comprehend the heights and depths of God's love, and what joy that believers have the immense gift of learning that love for the rest of our days. While we may be tempted to wallow in shame because of our unfaithfulness, we are never too far that we cannot experience His love and forgiveness. He desires fellowship with you and waits with open arms to welcome you when you come to Him.

"GOD'S LOVE FOR US CAUSES US TO WORSHIP HIM IN AWE."

DAY 292
Nothing New Under the Sun

What has been is what will be, and what has been done is what will be done; there is nothing new under the sun.

ECCLESIASTES 1:9

Solomon was one of the wisest, richest, and most powerful men who ever lived. And while we observe his life and may wonder if he lacked anything at all, reading Ecclesiastes shows us that Solomon struggled with knowing the ultimate purpose of life. Since Solomon was given much wisdom, he saw the futility in the passions and pursuits of the people around him. He described life—its joys and struggles—as a constant cycle that never stops. And to some extent, he is right. The same things happen all around us again and again: the sun rises, the sun sets, seasons pass, and new seasons begin. The earth goes on and on, but human beings grow older and die. Sins repeat themselves in each new chapter of history.

And it really would be depressing if this life was all we were living for because each of our stories has the same ending. Eventually, each one of us will breathe our last, but this is not our end. When we leave this life, we will be with the Lord for all of eternity. Solomon gives us one final piece of advice at the end of his musings in Ecclesiastes: "When all has been heard, the conclusion of the matter is this: fear God and keep his commands..." (Ecclesiastes 12:13). In the familiar patterns of the world today, where everything seems to repeat itself, there is nothing new on earth—nothing new under the sun—that will ever offer us more satisfaction and pleasure than following Christ.

People have pursued every worldly pleasure, but none can fill the need inside the human heart apart from Christ. When we recognize Him as our Savior and follow His ways, we experience meaning in our lives. Our lives may be quickly passing, but there is much more ahead that will rival all we know here, for we will be reunited with Him. As believers, our hearts have been satisfied in God, and because we know Him, we can enjoy our lives to His glory in each moment, in every passing day and every season.

"OUR HEARTS HAVE BEEN SATISFIED IN GOD, AND BECAUSE WE KNOW HIM, WE CAN ENJOY OUR LIVES TO HIS GLORY IN EACH MOMENT, IN EVERY PASSING DAY AND EVERY SEASON."

DAY 293
The Light of His Glory

Night will be no more; people will not need the light of a lamp or the light of the sun, because the Lord God will give them light, and they will reign forever and ever.

REVELATION 22:5

After years of life in pools of dark caves, fish grow blind. With no light to illuminate their surroundings and put their eyes to work, they lose their sight. Consider how necessary it is to have physical light in your own life. Think of the many things you would stumble over in the middle of the night without lights. Imagine how different our days would be and how little of the world we would know if there was no rising sun. We need the light.

Scripture tells us there will be no need for lamps and sunshine in heaven. We should marvel at such a thought! The book of Revelation reveals that in the heavenly city, the Lamb of God will be our light. We are blind to the truth of God, and on our own, we fall victim to the lies of this world (2 Corinthians 4:4). Sin veils our eyes and leaves us wandering in darkness. But, Jesus is the true light who came to shine light in a dark world (John 1:9). His light brings our sin out of the shadows when we confess and turn from our sin. Jesus pierces through the darkness of our sin and shines the glory of God into our hearts. The truth of the gospel unveils our blinded eyes and shines in our hearts the knowledge and truth of who God is and what He has done for us.

Jesus, our true light, will shine forever in heaven. Until that day, we will live in the darkness of the world and experience the effects of sin. But Christ lights our hearts with hope. We will see Jesus face to face, and the light we see dimly now will shine in full glory then. The light will leave no shadow untouched, everything exposed. But there will be no shame, for we will be transformed into the likeness of Jesus Christ. All will fade away, but the glory of God will never grow dim. May we never hide the work that Christ has done in our hearts. Instead, may we let our light shine before others so that they may see the knowledge of God at work in us and desire to know Him too.

"CHRIST LIGHTS OUR HEARTS WITH HOPE. WE WILL SEE JESUS FACE TO FACE, AND THE LIGHT WE SEE DIMLY NOW WILL SHINE IN FULL GLORY THEN."

DAY 294
Imperishable Inheritance

Blessed be the God and Father of our Lord Jesus Christ. Because of his great mercy he has given us new birth into a living hope through the resurrection of Jesus Christ from the dead and into an inheritance that is imperishable, undefiled, and unfading, kept in heaven for you.

1 PETER 1:3-4

One of the greatest blessings God gave Israel was the Promised Land. God spoke of this inheritance to Abraham and continued to retell its promise as Israel walked with God. However, the first generation of Israelites rebelled against God, and as a punishment, they were banned from entering the Promised Land. The second generation also rebelled against God, and while they were able to acquire the Promised Land, they lost the privileges of their inheritance when God sent them into exile.

As we journey through Scripture, we learn how the inheritance of the Promised Land is but a shadow of the ultimate Promised Land that is heaven. God's plan of redemption ends with the restoration of our world, a world free from sin in which we will dwell with God forever. As Christ followers, eternity with God is our inheritance. A home with Him is a living hope that we cling to on this side of eternity. Unlike the Promised Land in the Old Testament, our inheritance cannot be taken away, for it is kept in heaven with Christ.

By His great grace, our inheritance is locked tight within His grip, and nothing can loosen His hold. Because our unchanging, eternal, and holy God holds our inheritance, we can be confident that our inheritance is imperishable, undefiled, and unfading. Knowing that our inheritance can never fade or be taken away gives us security when the world around us is shaken and heavy, for we have a hope that remains.

Our inheritance of eternal life with God is a promised and imperishable hope. Therefore, we can have full confidence as we walk in this world, knowing that we will arrive at the true Promised Land. We can endure hardship and suffering with hope knowing that this is not the end, and a glorious future awaits us. One day, God will fulfill in whole His promise to us. We will receive the blessing of our inheritance and experience the wonder of heaven, granted to us because of the great mercy of Jesus Christ. May we respond with gratitude to our Savior who purchased our inheritance and guards our inheritance until we arrive.

"OUR INHERITANCE IS LOCKED TIGHT WITHIN HIS GRIP."

DAY 295
The Gift of Understanding

Counsel in a person's heart is deep water; but a person of understanding draws it out.

PROVERBS 20:5

There is something sweet about a friend who asks great questions or a counselor who helps us identify our true thoughts and feelings. Our hearts are deep chambers. We were created to be fully known by God and open our hearts to His worship-filled knowledge and understanding. However, sin brought disorder, and our hearts have grown hardened. We are prone to suppress and withhold our true thoughts and feelings.

Though we remain fully known and understood by God, we do not truly understand ourselves, much less one another. The ability to consider others and seek to understand them is a Spirit-led gift. Most people feel misunderstood to some degree, for the only One who fully understands the thoughts and intentions of our hearts is God. But God imparts wisdom and discernment to His people to grow us in understanding toward others.

The Bible paints a picture of one who is humble and thoughtful, with gracious words. Humility allows us to posture ourselves with a heart of grace and compassion and considers others before ourselves (Philippians 2:3–4). A humble heart leaves no room for quick judgments or unfair assumptions but seeks to serve. Throughout Jesus's ministry, he asked thoughtful questions. He did so intending to uncover the true motives of the heart, and when we ask questions, we encourage the same self-reflection. Those who are gracious with their words are slow to speak and quick to listen, desiring to understand before speaking. Let us seek to reveal the gospel to others through our conversation, that they may come to know Jesus Christ, the One who came to save them.

The gift of understanding is a great need for the church today. We need faithful men and women of understanding. God equips us through His Word to grow in understanding and discernment. The hope in doing so is to help one another avoid the shallow and surface-level relationships and go deeper with God and with one another. It helps us to draw out deep sin, hidden fears, and growing disbelief. Our hearts are deceitful and need to be exposed. There are great depths to uncover in our own hearts and the hearts of one another, but out of love for one another, we must be willing to dive deep. In doing so, we know that no matter what we uncover, God's love and grace can meet us there.

DAY 296
But God Intended It for Good

You planned evil against me; God planned it for good to bring about the present result—the survival of many people.

GENESIS 50:20

The glory of Jesus Christ and His plan of redemption in the midst of our suffering is a theme present throughout Scripture. Joseph, one of the sons of the Israelite patriarch, Jacob, embodied this theme in his story. The favored son, Joseph, was hated by his brothers. They devised a plot to sell Jacob into slavery. As a result, Jacob was taken to Egypt to serve in Pharaoh's court. For his God-given dream interpretation skills, Jacob became a respected figure in Egypt, and through his godly wisdom, Jacob saved Egypt and the nation of Israel from famine. As a result, the Israelites, God's chosen people to bring about the Promised Savior, continued to live as the symbol of hope to the world.

In Genesis 50:20, Joseph tells his brothers, "You planned evil against me; God planned it for good to bring about the present result—the survival of many people." God is sovereign, which means He is in control over everything that happens. Nothing can come to pass without God ordaining or decreeing it. But does this mean that God even ordains suffering? God is not the author of evil. Bad things occur because of sin, spiritual evil, and the fallen condition of the world. But the workings of sin and evil do not occur outside of the hand of God. So, God, in His sovereignty, has an active control over the suffering we experience. But, because He is good, God directly uses it for His redemptive purposes. Through Joseph's suffering, his brothers exercised hatred and wanted to dehumanize him by making him a slave. But, praise to God, through Joseph's suffering, God put him in a place of influence in Egypt and saved the Israelites from famine, continuing His redemptive mission.

From Scripture, we can know that God is in control, even when we are amid hardship and working everything for good. This good involves God's glory and our becoming more like Jesus. God does not want us to suppress our grief. Rather, He wants to walk with us and carry our burdens so that, in grief, His love will sustain us. While overwhelmed with tears and aches, we will still experience the true joy of being saved by Christ, for it is His salvation that will soon overcome all evil and bring eternal good.

"WE CAN KNOW THAT GOD IS IN CONTROL, EVEN WHEN WE ARE AMID HARDSHIP AND WORKING EVERYTHING FOR GOOD."

DAY 297

First Things First

But seek first the kingdom of God and his righteousness, and all these things will be provided for you.

MATTHEW 6:33

What we dwell on shapes our actions and emotions. Often, worry and anxiety are present in our lives because fears of safety and provision consume us. In Matthew 6, Jesus encourages us not to worry but trust the God who takes care of us. Part of this trust involves focusing our minds on what matters. When life gets heavy or hectic, it is easy for our thoughts to dwell on our circumstances, and while it is not wrong to feel grieved by life's circumstances, our circumstances should not control our lives. We should instead focus our attention on Christ and His kingdom.

As believers, though we live on the earth now, we are citizens of heaven. Yet, too often, we can focus on what is temporal rather than what is eternal. Being part of God's kingdom means that we live for Him and not the temporal things of this earth. Jesus taught us to pray, "Your kingdom come. Your will be done on earth as it is in heaven" (Matthew 6:10). By God's grace, we take part in bringing the kingdom of God to earth through the way we live our lives—as a reflection of the gospel and Christ in us. We live our lives in such a way to make the gospel known so that others might see what Christ has done for them.

We must fix our attention on what matters to the Lord. As we focus on the kingdom of God, we will not be consumed with earthly matters. Our security does not have to be in our own provision but in the God who provides for us. He has always taken care of us and always will. Shifting our thoughts from worry to trust frees us to dwell on what matters most. As we leave our lives in God's hands, we can remain dedicated to the task of kingdom building. In the moments we find ourselves falling back into worry or doubt, let us ask for God's help to set our minds on Him and His kingdom that will never be shaken. May we live out our citizenship by seeking Christ above all things.

"BY GOD'S GRACE, WE TAKE PART IN BRINGING THE KINGDOM OF GOD TO EARTH THROUGH THE WAY WE LIVE OUR LIVES—AS A REFLECTION OF THE GOSPEL AND CHRIST IN US."

DAY 298
You Will Not Be Overwhelmed

A person's steps are established by the Lord, and he takes pleasure in his way. Though he falls, he will not be overwhelmed, because the Lord supports him with his hand.

PSALM 37:23–24

The Christian life often feels like walking and falling and stumbling forward. We know the way to walk, yet life is filled with roadblocks along the way. Maybe the roadblocks come as the result of our own sin, the sin of others, or simply Satan's orchestration of evil in this world. Sometimes it feels like we get knocked down so many times that we do not know how to get back up. Maybe we feel stuck in our sin and do not know how to change. Maybe we feel hurt by relationships or exhausted from challenging circumstances. We feel confident that the next hard thing that comes our way will overtake us. We feel weak, weary, burdened.

The Bible shows that many experience this. David committed adultery with Bathsheba and had her husband, Uriah, killed to cover his sin. His sin led him in a downward spiral until he cried out to the Lord in deep repentance. He is referred to in Scripture as "a man after God's own heart." Job lost everything in his life—his family, his possessions, his health—and questioned why God would allow such things to happen to him. But God used his circumstances to strengthen his faith. Peter constantly succumbed to the thoughts and opinions of others, even to the point of verbally denying God. But God used his shortcomings to equip him to teach the saints what true obedience and faithfulness to the Lord look like. Each of these men fell, but through faith and trust in the Lord, they were not overwhelmed.

God reminds us through His Word that when our steps are established and supported by the Lord, we will never be overwhelmed or overtaken by the challenges and difficulties of this life. Not only does the Lord uphold us, but His way brings great pleasure and joy. When the path ahead does not look like we might have imagined, we can rest assured that our steps are ordained and established by our perfectly sovereign God. He anticipates our every move, and He upholds us with His right hand. Though we may find ourselves in hard places, bracing ourselves for the fall, God's people will never be overwhelmed but kept safe in His supportive embrace.

DAY 299
God is Working in All Things

We know that all things work together for the good of those who love God, who are called according to his purpose.

ROMANS 8:28

How often do we find ourselves in seasons where we cannot see God at work? Maybe you have fought through years of infertility, hoping for the news of a positive pregnancy test. Maybe you find yourself walking through a season of unspeakable grief. Maybe you fight anxiety and depression, wishing for a day when you will see and feel life differently. Perhaps you are walking through a season that feels as though it is taking everything from you. No matter what our circumstances are, we can remain confident that God is actively at work in the lives of His people. When no answers present themselves, no outcomes arise, and no fruit seems to come from your circumstances, there is One who sees all, knows all, and is in all, giving us greater hope for what He is doing behind the scenes.

The Bible tells us that "all things work together for the good of those who love God, who are called according to His purpose" (Romans 8:28). This verse has, at times, been misinterpreted to mean that if we love God, He will give us every good thing we desire. However, this is not the message of the passage. The importance of this passage is that God is working all things. He is not a distant God on the sidelines who watches our lives unfold and intervenes only when He deems fit. God is working, creating, moving, and redeeming. Whether good and gracious gifts or unwelcome trials, God uses them all. He uses each part of our lives according to His purposes, according to His greater story. Even as we walk through circumstances that leave us wondering how the story will end, we can trust wholeheartedly in the author and Creator of our story.

We stand as witnesses to God at work in the midst of every season. What is He teaching us about Himself? What are we learning about ourselves that only this season could have allowed us to see? What truths do we cling to as reminders of God's continual work in our waiting? Whether our seasons and circumstances are full of joy, triumph, doubt, or pain, may we seek out every opportunity to lean in and learn, truly searching for a way to witness God working all things together for our good and His glory.

"GOD IS WORKING, CREATING, MOVING, AND REDEEMING."

DAY 300
Refinement Through Fire

I will put this third through the fire; I will refine them as silver is refined and test them as gold is tested. They will call on my name, and I will answer them. I will say: They are my people, and they will say: The Lord is our God.

ZECHARIAH 13:9

The gold jewelry is made of does not begin by looking beautiful. The gold was once part of the earth, mixed with other elements. But when gold is placed in a fire, it is purified and can be formed into the metal we see on our hands and around our necks. Without fire, it cannot become the desired metal it is.

In Zechariah 13:9, the prophet Zechariah prophesies how God will bring judgment upon Israel. He will remove all who are wicked and unrepentant but promises to save a portion, sinful as they may be. This portion will be faithful to Him and will have an intimate relationship with Him. They will be His people, and He will be their God. Yet this joyous relationship is paired with the promise of refinement by fire. As God's chosen and holy people, Israel must undergo trial and suffering, for they need such refinement to be shaped into an obedient and holy nation.

In the same way, believers today experience the same promise. Jesus has saved us from the punishment of our sin, though we did not deserve His grace. Because of Christ's sacrifice and forgiveness, we are brought into an intimate relationship with God. We are God's chosen people and a royal priesthood, called to be set apart to proclaim the great grace of the God who saved us (1 Peter 2:9). As a set-apart people, we are to grow in the image of Christ, and we do so as we put sin to death and walk in Christlikeness, even through our struggles. God is not malicious but kind to allow trials and sufferings to grow us more and more into His image. Refining work is sanctifying work.

We can press on through our trials, withstanding the fire they bring, knowing that God is using these circumstances to sanctify us. The refining fire of trials is worth it because it is a joy and honor to be made into the One who saved us. May we embrace the fire trials bring and allow God to form us into His likeness, the likeness of Christ.

"REFINING WORK IS SANCTIFYING WORK."

DAY 301
The Sharpening of a Friend

Iron sharpens iron, and one person sharpens another.

PROVERBS 27:17

One of the best things about being in a Christian community in our churches is growing with other believers. When you begin to plug into small groups or Bible studies, these connections can grow, as do the depth of your conversations. And as you talk to each other about the Lord and what He has done in your lives, you spur one another on to persevere in the faith and love Jesus more. We need these kinds of relationships, and the Lord has given us the church body in order to have them.

We all need each other, but friendship in the gospel involves sharpening from both sides. A relationship needs mutual encouragement, not just one person speaking into the life of another. In order to be a friend who sharpens, you must first be sharpened by the sword of the Spirit, the Word of God (Ephesians 6:17). When you invest yourself in God's Word and allow it to change you, it will transform your mind, words, and actions. Your entire life will change, and you will see everything through the lens of the truth of Scripture. Because of this, all of your conversations with others will be marked by it, even if you are not directly quoting from it each time you talk to a friend.

God's Word will direct you, encourage you, and guard you. And all that the Lord does in your life through His Word will naturally flow into your relationships. Look for people who are captivated by Scripture, and you will find a friend who sharpens you. Aim to be that kind of sharpening friend in return.

Also, remember that sharpening is not always an easy or painless process. Sharpening sometimes involves gentle correction. Do not be surprised if your brother or sister in Christ gently confronts you with sin they have seen in your life. They want you to live and experience freedom in Christ. This kind of confrontation, while hard, is the best kind you can have, especially with someone who loves the Lord and His Word. Do not be afraid also to offer gentle corrections to friends, yet may it never be done out of a heart that is proud. Rather, may it be done from a desire to see your friends flourish in their walks with Christ.

"FRIENDSHIP IN THE GOSPEL INVOLVES
SHARPENING FROM BOTH SIDES."

DAY 302
Courageous for God's Glory

Blessed be the Lord, the God of our ancestors, who has put it into the king's mind to glorify the house of the Lord in Jerusalem, and who has shown favor to me before the king, his counselors, and all his powerful officers. So I took courage because I was strengthened by the hand of the Lord my God, and I gathered Israelite leaders to return with me.

EZRA 7:27–28

The Israelites, expelled from their land because of the Babylonian invasion, longed to return from exile. They ached for the restoration, and years later, God responded to His people by raising up faithful men who would lead them back home. One of these men, a priest named Ezra, was burdened with restoring God's temple and received a letter from the king providing treasures to rebuild it. Ezra praised the Lord who had given him favor through His power to move the hearts of kings (Proverbs 21:1). Ezra then pressed on to fulfill his mission as He trusted in God's sovereign protection and faithfulness, spurring him to action.

In the same way, our courage to follow God is by faith in Him and His promises. On our own, we can do nothing. Yet, we can be courageous for God's glory because we have faith in His Word. We pour out our lives to those around us, knowing that every act of service to the Lord is not in vain. We obey the Lord by living honest lives. We read the Word each day, trusting in the promises of Scripture. We defend our faith in a hostile world. And we gather with other believers, sharing our burdens. We are reminded of His power as He changes the hearts of those around us and us as well. Filled with good courage and confident hope, we press on in faith (2 Corinthians 5:6–7).

However, at times our faith will fail. Our courage will be weak, and we will stumble. Praise God, we have a Great High Priest who never fails. Jesus, who was perfectly courageous, followed the Father's will to the point of death. Only by His blood are we cleaned. We can be courageous for God's glory because He has gone before us, securing victory. Because of the cross, we are not abandoned. Though we face opposition around us and fear from within, our King leads our every step. In light of the cross, we can have courage because we are strengthened by God's hand (Ezra 7:28).

> "WE POUR OUT OUR LIVES TO THOSE AROUND US, KNOWING THAT EVERY ACT OF SERVICE TO THE LORD IS NOT IN VAIN."

DAY 303

Drawing Strength from the Only Source

The person who trusts in the Lord, whose confidence indeed is the Lord, is blessed. He will be like a tree planted by water: it sends its roots out toward a stream, it doesn't fear when heat comes, and its foliage remains green. It will not worry in a year of drought or cease producing fruit.

JEREMIAH 17:7-8

We will experience countless things that leave us searching for deeper and more lasting strength. Whether bouts of depression, grief and loss, unmet expectations, sin struggles, or disappointment, the challenges of this broken world bring us to our knees. When we face hardship again and again, eventually, we will find ourselves exhausted and depleted by our own efforts.

Jeremiah reminds us that when we put hope in ourselves and our own strength, we will be like "a Juniper in the Arabah; he cannot see when good comes, but dwells in the parched places in the wilderness, in a salt land where no one lives" (Jeremiah 17:6). A juniper tree in the desert is likely dry and stunted in growth due to lack of good soil and little rainfall, remaining weak and barely alive. Looking to ourselves for motivation and endurance will produce a similar life to the juniper tree—weak and searching for strength. Yet, on our own, we will always be left without enough sustenance. We will be tossed to and fro by the wind and waves of life, with no security in our roots to help us remain steadfast through our circumstances.

However, those who put their hope in the Lord will have strength, just as the tree by the water is nourished and sustained by the stream. No matter what life brings its way, its roots are secured and prepared to face any conditions. When we look to the Lord for hope and trust, He empowers and sustains us to walk in faithfulness and obedience as we remain firmly planted, rooted in Him.

God gives us abounding grace in His Spirit and truth. He gives us confident reassurance that He is greater than our best efforts. Finding our ultimate strength in God, we can confidently depend on Him to lead us in His ways, no matter what life may bring.

"THOSE WHO PUT THEIR HOPE IN THE LORD
WILL HAVE STRENGTH."

DAY 304
Seek and You Will Find

But from there, you will search for the Lord your God, and you will find him when you seek him with all your heart and all your soul.

DEUTERONOMY 4:29

Even when God feels far, He is always near, always present, and always available. Moses gave the Israelites this reminder in Deuteronomy 4:29. Moses encouraged the Israelites by saying that even if the Israelites sinned and disobeyed God, they could find Him and return to Him. Even though they did not have to go far to seek God, they needed to have their hearts in the right place. By worshiping other idols, Israel sought earthly things and abandoned their love for the Lord, turned from Him, and chased after meaningless idols of wood and stone. When Israel repented, they had the promise of God's presence. However, their hearts needed to turn back to the Lord.

Like the Israelites, we can often chase after the things of this world for satisfaction. We run to relationships, money, and social status to make us feel happy and loved. We turn away from God to seek after our own desires. Yet, when those things fail us, we do not have to despair. Though we turn from God, God will never turn from us. When we sin and fail in our obedience, God remains near. God will never abandon us or hide from us.

Through Jesus, we have permanent access to our heavenly Father. Jesus spoke of this availability through prayer in Matthew 7:7 when He said, "Ask, and it will be given to you. Seek, and you will find. Knock, and the door will be opened to you." As God's children, we are not left wandering and searching for our God, knocking on the door of His heart with no answer. Because of Jesus Christ and His sacrifice on the cross, we have unhindered access to the Lord.

Though the Lord is ever-present, we need to seek Him. May we seek Him with all that is in us. Let us seek God when we go to His Word and come before Him in prayer. Let us seek Him as we turn away from idols to worship Him alone. And in the times we fail, let us remember the sure promise that when we turn to the Lord, He is there.

"WHEN WE SIN AND FAIL IN OUR OBEDIENCE, GOD REMAINS NEAR. GOD WILL NEVER ABANDON US OR HIDE FROM US."

DAY 305
Unobstructed Eyes on Jesus

Therefore, since we also have such a large cloud of witnesses surrounding us, let us lay aside every hindrance and the sin that so easily ensnares us. Let us run with endurance the race that lies before us, keeping our eyes on Jesus, the source and perfecter of our faith. For the joy that lay before him, he endured the cross, despising the shame, and sat down at the right hand of the throne of God.

HEBREWS 12:1–2

Hebrews 12:1–2 addresses the race in the Christian life. The author begins his exhortation with an image of being surrounded by a large crowd. From the earlier chapter, we know these individuals are the saints of the Old Testament, people who persevered in faith through their trials. Like them, we must practice spiritual disciplines like prayer and reading Scripture to overcome Satan's schemes, endure suffering, and fight sin.

The author of Hebrews calls us to put off hindrances that would prevent us from growing in Christ—things like temporary pleasures, anger, unforgiveness, apathy, cynicism, and shame. We can pray that God will break us free from those struggles and areas of sin so that we can run by His might. We do not have to become hung up on our past. Rather, let us focus on what lies ahead. We keep our eyes on Christ, for He is the only One who can bring us through to the end. In ourselves, we are weak and need the Savior's strength to run and carry us to the finish line.

Jesus ran the race of righteousness. As the God-Man, He alone possessed the supernatural strength to endure testing and endured pain on the cross, separation from the Father, and utmost sorrow. He stayed focused on accomplishing God's plan of redemption, for there was joy before Him. He looked to the end and saw our redemption and restoration from sin. He saw His world taken back from its fallen state to reflect the glory of God. And, when He crossed the finish line, His reward was great. For in Jesus's death and resurrection, conquering the grave, He gave us the hope of eternal life with Him. In our Savior, we exchange rags for riches and are given the gold medal of righteousness. This righteousness is not our own but Christ's. We can look forward to forever standing in His glory before His throne.

"WE KEEP OUR EYES ON CHRIST, FOR HE IS THE ONLY ONE WHO CAN BRING US THROUGH TO THE END."

DAY 306
The Reach of God's Grace

Yet the number of the Israelites will be like the sand of the sea, which cannot be measured or counted. And in the place where they were told: You are not my people, they will be called: Sons of the living God.

HOSEA 1:10

The Israelites, God's people, rebelled and turned from God and their covenant with Him. It was heartbreaking, and God had every reason to cast them out of His presence forever. But God, even despite their unfaithfulness, would remain faithful to His promise for them to be His people and Him their God. Though God did promise judgment for their sin, His judgment would not last forever. He would eventually redeem and restore the relationship that had been broken. Even in our sin and rebellion, God does not reject His people forever. God was certainly angry with the nation of Israel, but He never stopped loving them. He points out Israel's rejection of Him, but He meets it with His everlasting love.

Hosea was an illustration of God's love and forgiveness toward Israel. Gomer, Hosea's wife, did not honor their marriage covenant. She was promiscuous and broke the covenant promises they made to each other. But instead of Hosea breaking his promise, too, and leaving her forever, Hosea forgave her. He remained faithful, even in her unfaithfulness. This does not diminish the grief and consequences caused by her sin, for breaking such a promise is painful. But because her sin cut so deeply and Hosea still forgave her, we see the beauty of grace magnified through forgiveness.

God continues to draw near to His people, even when we try to pull away. There is no place too far that His grace cannot reach. Even when we feel we have strayed too far, His grace meets us there. The wickedness of Gomer, Israel, and even our own sin is so unlovely and heartbreaking, yet God still loves with an everlasting love, one so great that He gave up His life for us on the cross to give us eternal life. His love is beyond what our human minds can fathom and beyond what our human hearts can offer in return. Through repentance and faith, we become recipients of God's abundant grace and love. Regardless of our shortcomings and sin, God will remain faithful to His promises to the end. What love, what grace!

"GOD CONTINUES TO DRAW NEAR TO HIS PEOPLE, EVEN WHEN WE TRY TO PULL AWAY."

DAY 307
In Highs and Lows, Praise the Lord

Hallelujah! Praise God in his sanctuary. Praise him in his mighty expanse. Praise him for his powerful acts; praise him for his abundant greatness.

PSALM 150:1–2

The book of Psalms is full of some of the highest highs and lowest lows. While some are psalms of great joy, others are psalms of greatest despair and longing. Verses like Psalm 59:16 ring with joy: "But I will sing of your strength and will joyfully proclaim your faithful love in the morning." However, others like Psalm 69:1 show us the depths of sorrow: "Save me, God, for the water has risen to my neck." The writers of the psalms were normal people like us who lived normal lives full of hardships and hope, trials and joys. Through their circumstances, they poured out their hearts to God through psalms. How would this book of raw emotions and real heartache end? In Psalm 150, the book closes with praise to the Lord, for He has been faithful and true in every high and every low.

The psalmist writes, "Hallelujah! Praise God in His sanctuary," which is where He resides in the heavenly realm, where He sits at the right hand of the Father. We cannot see God's sanctuary, but we can imagine how it must be filled with His unending glory and splendor. When the psalmist goes on to say, "Praise Him in His mighty expanse," he refers to the mighty expanse as the space between God's heavenly dwelling and the earth. And as we continue reading in verse 2, we see that God is praised for His powerful acts and abundant greatness. These last phrases refer to God's perfect work on the earth, for nothing He does falls short of glorious.

This psalm traces the work of God from His heavenly throne to the earth below. Although God could choose to be distant, He chooses to be near. His Spirit dwells within us when we come to know Him, and He works in powerful and abundant ways within each of our own lives. He has chosen to draw near to mankind. And His nearness has been shown most fully through Jesus Christ. Jesus came to earth to be God with us. Even more, God gave His life to pay the price for our sins so that we could one day be united with God in heaven. No matter the highs or lows we face, we look ahead to eternity with Christ. And we sing together, "Hallelujah! Praise God!"

"ALTHOUGH GOD COULD CHOOSE TO BE DISTANT, HE CHOOSES TO BE NEAR."

DAY 308

Bought to Belong

At that time you were without Christ, excluded from the citizenship of Israel, and foreigners to the covenants of promise, without hope and without God in the world. But now in Christ Jesus, you who were far away have been brought near by the blood of Christ.

EPHESIANS 2:12–13

There is a desire in every human heart to be a part of a family—to belong and to be loved. And this is not a coincidence. It is God's own handiwork in His creation. We are all born lost, for we are all born without Christ. We do not belong to the Lord but rather, to the sin of the world. We are foreigners and outsiders to the promises of God without caring to be a part of them. We have no hope because we do not have God, but our hearts grow frustrated and tired without Him, for only He gives true strength and offers true life. No human heart could ever be satisfied without His love.

In Christ, we can find belonging. The Lord saw us far off from Him and decided in the riches of His kindness, grace, and mercy to bring us near. He had compassion on us and wanted us for Himself. And to do this, He sacrificed His only Son, Jesus, upon the cross so that we might be His sons and daughters. It would have been more than enough for the Lord to simply forgive us of our sins, but His grace extends further. We not only have His forgiveness, but He brings us into His family. God fills the desires of our hearts, and He saves us from being lost or abandoned.

What incredible news this is for us. Though we wanted to belong, we did not first look to find this need satisfied in Christ. Instead, we chased other people and things. But God gave His only Son for us still, and Jesus's life, death, and resurrection pardoned us from sin and gave us eternal life. Because we have been bought through Christ's sacrifice, we are brought near to our heavenly Father. We are no longer outsiders. We belong to the Creator of the world, and we will experience the blessing of being His now and forever.

"IN CHRIST, WE CAN FIND BELONGING. THE LORD SAW US FAR OFF FROM HIM AND DECIDED IN THE RICHES OF HIS KINDNESS, GRACE, AND MERCY TO BRING US NEAR."

DAY 309
Carried to Completion

I am sure of this, that he who started a good work in you will carry it on to completion until the day of Christ Jesus.

PHILIPPIANS 1:6

While people often fail to complete their tasks, God never does. His intent is clear for those He calls to Himself. God always completes the good work He begins in our hearts. Romans 8:29–30 explains this good work: "For those he foreknew he also predestined to be conformed to the image of his Son, so that he would be the firstborn among many brothers and sisters. And those he predestined, he also called; and those he called, he also justified; and those he justified, he also glorified."

God's good work is to predestine, call, justify, and glorify those He foreknew. In other words, we become like Christ. Bound up in Romans 8 is a complicated puzzle surrounding the words "foreknew" and "predestined," which bring up questions and fears. Does God choose some and not others in whom to do His good work? We may never know the perfect answer to that question on this side of Heaven. But, we do know that God allows us the freedom to choose if we will love and serve Him and, at the same time, sovereignly presides over our choosing. God's foreknowing and predestining will perfectly hold these two truths together as only God can. Of this we can be assured—God does His good work to the fullest extent in those He calls.

The spiritual lives of Christians are set in unstoppable motion for all of their days, on this side of eternity and the next. Some have understood this to mean that God will give good things and answer good prayers of believers while on earth. While God does do these things when we are in accordance with His will (1 John 5:14), the culmination of God's good work in a believer is even greater than that. The culmination is that we will someday be perfectly united with God through Jesus in eternal glory and joy, free from sorrow and pain, free from lack, free from sin.

The good work God promises to carry to completion is the one we should most desire—to live close to God, free from sin, and in a world where God's righteousness reigns and evil is overcome. Glory awaits believers in Christ. Of this, you can be sure, for God will never stop working until that glorious day comes!

"GOD ALWAYS COMPLETES THE GOOD WORK HE BEGINS IN OUR HEARTS."

DAY 310

Casting Your Cares

Humble yourselves, therefore, under the mighty hand of God, so that he may exalt you at the proper time, casting all your cares on him, because he cares about you.

1 PETER 5:6–7

How often do you feel as if your capacity is full? To-do lists pile up. You are overcommitted and overworked. You find yourself in a spiritual drought, hoping to see the light at the end of the tunnel. Maybe you are burdened by grief or a friend's suffering. Hopes and dreams are deferred. Finances close in, and fears of the future creep into your thoughts.

A natural response to overwhelm and overload is anxiety. When we feel stressed and anxious, we can grip our burdens tightly, trying to manage and push through, trying to take care of everything on our own. But holding tightly to our cares is the opposite of what God's Word commands. When we look to God's Word, we see a message of God's necessary involvement in our worries and concerns. Psalm 55:22 says, "Cast your burden on the Lord, and He will sustain you; he will never allow the righteous to be shaken." We can give our cares to the Lord to carry. He is secure, and He will keep us safe and steady.

In order to trust God when we are anxious and overwhelmed, we need humble hearts. Humility cultivates a heart posture bent toward God's sovereignty. When we try to take matters into our own hands, we assume we are more sovereign and efficient than God. Without a humble posture toward God's sovereignty, we, in turn, exalt ourselves, and self-exaltation is not a safe place to be.

When we remember God's true capabilities, we crumble in our own strength. He brought His people out of slavery, and He parted the Red Sea to bring His people through it. He carried His people through the wilderness. He brought His people to the Promised Land. He conquered sin and death through sending His one and only Son and raising Him from the grave. He is more than capable of bearing the weight of our cares. He delights in doing so. Peter reminds us to cast our cares on God because He cares for us (1 Peter 5:6–7). God's care is extensive, and He knows everything about us. God knows our needs before we do, and He can care for them better than we ever could.

"WE CAN GIVE OUR CARES TO THE LORD TO CARRY."

DAY 311
He Knows Our Needs

So don't worry, saying, "What will we eat?" or "What will we drink?" or "What will we wear?" For the Gentiles eagerly seek all these things, and your heavenly Father knows that you need them.

MATTHEW 6:31–32

How much is your worry rooted in what you need? The more we dwell on our needs, the more anxiety can grow in our hearts. As humans, we want to know that we will be okay. We like to feel secure and comfortable, so we can feel overwhelmed when something robs our security. In moments of worry, we tend to forget the Lord's faithfulness. But, up to this very point in your life, God has taken care of you. Why would He not take care of you now?

We can still doubt God's daily provision. Too easily, we seize control of our lives and become frazzled trying to hold the pieces of our lives together. However, no matter how much we try, we cannot hold everything together in our own strength. Instead of crumbling in despair, we need to lift our eyes to the God who takes care of us. He does not see us in need and stand idly by, watching our anxiety grow. God is actively involved in every part of our lives. He knows our needs and provides for them. But this also means that God will provide for us in ways we did not expect. Sometimes God will provide in a timing that is not ideal to us or in a way that is not quite the way we had in mind. Let these moments move us to gratitude instead of frustration. Let us lift our hands in praise for the giver of good gifts.

God takes care of every part of His creation—from the birds of the sky to the lilies of the field. Because He holds all things in His hands, He holds you in His hands. Every day, we can wake up in peace knowing that our heavenly Father will take care of us each day. When worry begins to set in, we must surrender our control and trust that God will give us what we need. May the daily provision of our heavenly Father soothe our anxious hearts. May His great faithfulness quiet our worried thoughts. Faithful He has been, and faithful He will forever be.

"GOD IS ACTIVELY INVOLVED IN EVERY PART OF OUR LIVES."

DAY 312

Only What We Need

Keep falsehood and deceitful words far from me. Give me neither poverty nor wealth; feed me with the food I need. Otherwise, I might have too much and deny you, saying, "Who is the Lord?" or I might have nothing and steal, profaning the name of my God.

PROVERBS 30:8–9

We may see those who seem to live in luxury and believe they have no cares or worries. We envy their "stability." We want their peace of mind. But we also observe those who have nothing at all—people who do not know where their next meal will come from—and perhaps we become afraid that we will one day face the same circumstances. While people's socioeconomic status is different throughout the world and luxury in some countries would be considered poverty in others, most of us will never live in these extremes. Proverbs tells us that this is how it should be, and while neither being rich nor poor is wrong, both circumstances provide unique challenges to those who love the Lord.

If we live in luxury and money is no object, it can become easy to rely on wealth instead of the Lord. It is all too easy to depend on ourselves and our income instead of viewing all earthly riches as coming from the Lord's hand. And in light of eternity, these earthly riches are all passing away. Riches are false security that tempt us from placing our ultimate trust in God and His provision.

Believers might also struggle with the circumstance of poverty. When you have to deal with hunger or homelessness, desperation can drive you to do something unwise. It can tempt you not to trust in the Lord and take matters into your own hands. While this is more than understandable from a human perspective, we can also trust that God is bigger than our circumstances, and He will provide for us.

Proverbs 30:8–9 is a helpful reminder of what a beautiful thing it is to have just exactly what we need. This allows us not to get so caught up in this life on earth but rather to look forward to the life to come. What if we lived like God was all we needed? No matter what side of wealth or poverty you live on, look for ways to practice gratitude throughout your day and thank God for His provision in your life. In the end, we can all trust God that He will supply us with exactly what we need and that it is all serving the same purpose to make us more like Christ. So, if you are tempted to wish you had more or worry that you will not have enough, thank the Lord that He has provided what you need for today. And when you wake up tomorrow, watch for His provision again!

DAY 313
Anchor for Our Souls

We have this hope as an anchor for the soul, firm and secure. It enters the inner sanctuary behind the curtain.

HEBREWS 6:19

A lone boat sits at sea as waters rage around it. A storm approaches with winds and rain that wash over the tiny ship in sweeping, violent gusts and torrents, tossing it from side to side. Waves crash against the boat, beating at the seams. Yet, the boat is not lost, for its anchor is sound. We cannot see the anchor, for it is veiled beneath the sea. But it is there, holding the tiny boat—grounding it—so that through the storm, it rests secure. This anchor is the vessel's only hope.

The author of Hebrews refers to the Lord when he writes, "we have this hope as an anchor for the soul," and he describes this anchor as "firm and secure." As Christians, we find our anchor in Christ alone. With no anchor, the vessel would have little chance of weathering the storm. And it is not just in possessing the anchor but proper use of the anchor—throwing it into the deep where it cannot be seen—that the anchor can serve its purpose. If the ship's captain kept the anchor on board and in his sight, it could not stabilize the boat. So too it is with Christ—though we cannot see Him, He is ever-present in times of trouble. Our heavenly Father holds us secure, though the waters rage.

God promises in Deuteronomy 31:6 that He will never leave us or forsake us. Though we face trials, He will hold onto us. The currents of events that could sweep us away with no anchor cannot pull us from Christ, who gave His very life for us, and neither can they pull us from His mighty hand that raised Him from the grave. May we not place our hope in temporal things of this earth, for those things cannot hold us secure as He does.

When chaos seems to erupt in our world broken by sin, we can remember our true anchor is Jesus. We cannot run to temporary fixes that the world promises will make us better. Worldly pleasures may create feelings of security for a short time, but true peace in the storm is found in Christ alone—He is our anchor and our only hope.

"OUR HEAVENLY FATHER HOLDS US SECURE, THOUGH THE WATERS RAGE."

DAY 314
Can These Dry Bones Live?

He said to me, "Prophesy concerning these bones and say to them: Dry bones, hear the word of the Lord! This is what the Lord God says to these bones: I will cause breath to enter you, and you will live. I will put tendons on you, make flesh grow on you, and cover you with skin. I will put breath in you so that you come to life. Then you will know that I am the Lord."

EZEKIEL 37:4-6

Ezekiel's vision of the valley of dry bones came to him after prophesying Israel's rebirth. God spoke through the prophet of the restoration and blessings to come, likely sounding impossible considering Israel's present condition. They had lost everything and were a divided and scattered nation.

In the valley full of dry bones, God asked Ezekiel if the bones could live. But bones cannot live, for they are missing the parts necessary for life. But Ezekiel answered differently. He knew God's power, and He knew that God could bring dry bones back to life. And indeed, God instructed Ezekiel to prophesy to the dry bones and tell them God would give them flesh, tendons, and skin, and He would breathe life into the bones, just as He breathed life into Adam (Genesis 2:7). When Ezekiel did as God commanded, the bones came to life and became a vast army. All of this brought hope for Israel. God had plans for Israel's restoration and reminded them who He is and why they could turn to Him.

Before we came to know Christ as our Savior, we were dead in our sin like dry and lifeless bones (Ephesians 2). We walked in the ways of this world, rebelling like Israel and carrying out selfish inclinations of our flesh. It would take a miraculous act of God to bring us back to life. And because of God's great love for us, He miraculously brings us to life through salvation. We are rescued from our sins so that God may display the riches of His grace to us.

Compelled by God's love, we get to speak the truth of His grace to all who will listen. We get to speak life into a dying world. Even to those we may cast off as an impossible convert, may we carry the gospel forth with knowledge of God's power and grace. God can bring the dead to life. May this truth lead us to live in light of His resurrection power.

"COMPELLED BY GOD'S LOVE, WE GET TO SPEAK THE TRUTH OF HIS GRACE TO ALL WHO WILL LISTEN."

DAY 315
Beware the Life of Ease

Woe to those who are at ease in Zion and to those who feel secure on the hill of Samaria — the notable people in this first of the nations, those the house of Israel comes to.

AMOS 6:1

The Roaring Twenties was a period of opulence, prosperity, and comfort in American history. After World War 1, stock prices boomed, and industry production increased. Americans celebrated the victory of the war and ushered in a culture of artistic rebirth, lavish parties, and consumerism. However, underneath the glitter and gold, there was much corruption. Organized crime ran amok in the cities. Lust permeated the nightlife. The wealth gap pushed the poor more into poverty. Though it was a period of riches and ease, the overindulgence, injustice, and perversion brought the Roaring Twenties to a somber conclusion with the Great Depression. The glitter and gold faded to reveal the sin of man and the world's fallenness.

The Roaring Twenties mirrored a period in biblical history. Under King Jeroboam II, the kingdom of Israel experienced economic, military, and cultural prosperity. The Lord gave the Israelites peace from their surrounding enemies. With this blessing of rest, the people of God flourished. The Israelites were God's chosen people to represent His plan of redemption, but the Israelites did not live up to being God's faithful people. The Israelites grew complacent in prosperous living. They no longer saw their need for God, as they trusted in their wealth and influence for security. They disregarded the Lord's authority and word, exposing their sinful hearts. The prophet Amos called out their wrongdoing. He urged the Israelites to repent and prophesied that the kingdom of Israel would fall if they refused. All its lavish palaces and holy places would be destroyed. Exiled from the Promised Land, the Israelites would be stripped of their ornate clothing and given sackcloth.

The Lord ordains periods of blessing and peace. But God also ordains periods of loss and instability. We must not put our trust in earthly gifts, for they are not the source of our peace; instead, they are only dim reflections of the life accomplished through Jesus Christ's redemption. In our earthly gifts, we must avoid complacency. We must actively fight the sin in our hearts through the transforming power of the Holy Spirit. Let us lean on Jesus to help us prioritize heavenly rest and riches above the world's glitter and gold.

DAY 316
A Harvest of Righteousness

No discipline seems enjoyable at the time, but painful. Later on, however, it yields the peaceful fruit of righteousness to those who have been trained by it.

HEBREWS 12:11

The original audience of Hebrews encountered hardship from religious persecution, but they also met hardship from their own sin. In chapter 12, we read that the people grew weary and discouraged from their fight against sin. Nevertheless, the author of Hebrews urged them to lay off their shortcomings. On the other side of the cross, the audience of Hebrews could look at the accomplished work of Christ as proof that He would bring them into His righteousness.

The author wrote that endurance in the fight against sin was to submit to the Father's correction. Though there would be grief when believers violated the Lord's commands, they should not become weary or discouraged. The sting of conviction was evidence of the Lord's gracious reproof. The author encouraged the people to see God's discipline as an extension of His love and desire to be with them. He compared the Lord to an earthly father who disciplines his children in love so that they do not go astray. How much more does God the Father display His love when He corrects His children? The audience of Hebrews could overcome persistent sin and the heartbreak it brings because Jesus would one day make them perfect.

Though Jesus was sinless, He still endured testing and took the punishment for unrighteousness. He embodied the curse of disobedience and was led to the cross. He encountered unbearable pain, humiliation, and rejection. As He was crucified, Jesus felt utmost grief from fighting sin. However, through the agony, He looked to the joy before Him. He knew His death was not final as He would rise again and ascend into glory. He knew He was making a way for His people to stand redeemed in God's presence.

Jesus Christ endured the fight against sin so that we would not remain weary in our faith. From Scripture, we can learn that conviction over persistent sins is discipline, and discipline brings us closer to Jesus. Let your conviction drive you to God, not away from Him. See how your grief of sin is discipline from the Father's loving hand; discover how He uses it to mature you in Christ. Our fight against sin is a training ground. In the end, our efforts will produce for us a harvest of righteousness, as we share in Jesus's victory.

DAY 317
Don't Give Up

Let us not get tired of doing good, for we will reap at the proper time if we don't give up.

GALATIANS 6:9

When our alarms go off in the morning, our desire to sleep often seems to set in all the more if we have not rested well. It sometimes feels impossible to pull ourselves out of bed, daunted by all the tasks of the day. Many days, we may want to just pull the covers up and hide. The same can be said about our spiritual lives. Each day we wake up is another day away from the physical presence of Christ. And though He offers us abundant life now with His Spirit inside us, the weight of being in the world is often heavy.

The world around us does not celebrate Jesus or His goodness. It chases the dark, and it rejoices in evil. Living here can be wearisome, especially as we see others reject the truth that has given us peace, joy, and salvation. But Paul encourages us in Galatians 6:9. Though we feel tired, we must persist in doing good. We are not saved by these good works but by Christ's blood alone, yet these good works are the fruit of our love for Him. They are our offering of worship and adoration for our Savior, and they produce the fruit of the Spirit within us.

As we as believers produce this fruit, the time for the harvest is nearing. This means that as we grow in godliness and persist in working unto the Lord, we are preparing ourselves for the day of His return. One day, we will stand before the Lord and see how the work we did for Him was not meaningless. It had eternal value. So as you experience the weariness of this world, remember that your hope is not here. Your hope is in heaven with Christ. And one day, when you stand before your Savior, with all Christians throughout history, you will not experience tiredness any longer. You will not have the temptation to give up. You will be free from sin, and you will experience the joy of being in the physical presence of the One who saved you. Eternity will be your home, and you will rejoice and celebrate with God's people forever.

"WE ARE NOT SAVED BY THESE GOOD WORKS BUT BY CHRIST'S BLOOD ALONE, YET THESE GOOD WORKS ARE THE FRUIT OF OUR LOVE FOR HIM."

DAY 318
He Before Me

He must increase, but I must decrease.
JOHN 3:30

John the Baptist caused quite a stir. All of Judea was coming to see him, and people were being baptized left and right after hearing his messages of repentance. The religious leaders too came to ask him questions, wondering who he was and why he was baptizing. But everything changed when Jesus arrived. Many of John's followers left him to pursue Christ, and Jesus began to baptize like John. Some of John's disciples were aggravated over this. Everyone had at one point been talking about their Rabbi, but now the people's interest had shifted to Jesus. All of their statuses were beginning to dissipate.

John quickly helps his disciples understand that this was exactly how it was supposed to be. John was called to prepare the way for the Son of God. He had done so, and Jesus, God in flesh, had arrived. The people did not need to stick close to John. They needed to hear from the Savior of the world.

The frustration of John's disciples is a circumstance that might sound familiar to some of us. When we become believers, we try to live like Christ, and sometimes this brings us attention. It could be that people admire us, or we may be placed in positions of authority or leadership. And while this has nothing to do with us and is only through the power of Christ's Spirit at work in us, we can begin to wrongly take pride in what we have accomplished for the Lord. We forget to worship the Lord for what He has done and rightly attribute the praise to Him. How quickly our sin can twist our service and work for God.

And so John's reminder to his disciples is also for us. We must decrease, and He must increase. Our work for the Lord should not point to our own glory but the Lord's—more of Christ and less of us. We should aim to let our service to others cause them to love the Lord more as we seek to make His gospel known—that He gave His life on the cross for us so that we could have eternal life with Him. The world needs Christ, so as we live our days, may our greatest desire be to make much of who He is, pointing to His marvelous glory and might.

"THE WORLD NEEDS CHRIST."

DAY 319
The Son of Righteousness

But for you who fear my name, the sun of righteousness will rise with healing in its wings, and you will go out and playfully jump like calves from the stall.

MALACHI 4:2

In the Old Testament, the day of the Lord was prominent for the nation of Israel. Israel understood this day as a time when God would bring judgment on their enemies but restoration and salvation to Israel. This day of the Lord points to the ultimate day of the Lord when Christ returns to bring salvation to believers and judgment to non-believers. Malachi describes the impending judgment as a fierce fire that will consume the wicked. God spares those who trust and believe in Jesus from this wrath. When Christ returns, we will not respond in fear but in joy over our Savior coming to deliver us.

Jesus will rise like the sun, coming in blazing glory to bring lasting restoration to those who belong to Him. We will rejoice in the presence of our great God and the deliverance He brings. While we await this day, we have anticipation and hope. As believers, the day of the Lord is a day of delight, for it means the brokenness we experience now will be mended. The darkness of this world will be removed. The sin we fight will be defeated forever. And most of all, we will dwell for eternity with the Son of righteousness, our great Savior who died for us and gave us new life.

The seriousness of this day should also motivate our evangelism. While we are spared from God's punishment, there are many today who will face this punishment because of their unrepentance. May we share the gospel by engaging our neighbors and those around us with the message of Christ. Our world is broken and in desperate need of healing, but our Son of righteousness, Jesus Christ, is the answer. He provides us healing in the present as His grace and forgiveness cleanse us from sin, and He restores our brokenness. But He will also provide us healing in the future by permanently removing our sin and brokenness and restoring the world to a place where sin will never reside. May this glorious truth motivate us to share the good news of the gospel and the healing Jesus Christ provides. One day we will all sing for joy at the sight of our Savior, but in the here and now, we rejoic, knowing that restoration is a promised reality.

> "JESUS WILL RISE LIKE THE SUN, COMING IN BLAZING GLORY TO BRING LASTING RESTORATION TO THOSE WHO BELONG TO HIM."

DAY 320
A Call for Kindness and Mercy

The Lord of Armies says this: "Make fair decisions. Show faithful love and compassion to one another. Do not oppress the widow or the fatherless, the resident alien or the poor, and do not plot evil in your hearts against one another."

ZECHARIAH 7:9-10

The book of Zechariah records prophecies and instructions given to the exiles who returned from Babylon to Jerusalem. The people who returned were survivors of destruction. Either they were taken from their homes at a very young age when the Babylonians attacked and overruled Judah, or they had been born into captivity. Regardless, exile was all they had known. We might assume that being in such difficult circumstances would have prompted them to realize their sin, or their return home would have inspired long-lasting devotion to the Lord, yet this was not the case for God's people.

When they returned home, everything that was once glorious was gone. Their people were entirely uprooted and disheveled. Many of them had lost loved ones. The temple was destroyed. They had to start all over again. How daunting! So while they were frustrated with God and their situation, their frustrations also began to affect each other. They did not take God seriously and wandered from Him, so they also wandered from His instruction. Instead of acting like His family and letting His love guide them in all they did, they oppressed one another, specifically those who were the least—the widows, the fatherless, the immigrants, and the poor. They acted like the world and forgot the value system of God.

What is more heartbreaking is that God's people had been saved from destruction and oppression because God had chosen them, and yet they did not mirror the love He had given them. They treated others with the same contempt they received in captivity. Do we not do the same? We have been shown immense grace, but we are quick to keep it from the ones with whom God has called us to share. And by doing so, we are not properly able to display Christ's love to the world, and the people around us do not witness how His salvation changes our hearts to serve whoever is in our path. The Lord has saved us with His extraordinary love. May we carry God's love into the world, letting it bless those He has placed in our paths.

"THE LORD HAS SAVED US WITH HIS EXTRAORDINARY LOVE."

DAY 321
The Voice of Grief

I have been deprived of peace; I have forgotten what prosperity is. Then I thought, "My future is lost, as well as my hope from the Lord."

LAMENTATIONS 3:17–18

Have you ever experienced a deep sorrow of the soul? You cannot remember happier days. Deprived of peace and filled with darkness, there seems to be no hope for tomorrow. You are not sure how to go on with a smile on your face. Heaviness follows you like a weary shadow. Darkness feels like your closest friend. You cannot escape your pain, even in sleep. Grief is deep suffering, usually resulting from loss. Perhaps you recently lost a loved one, or maybe yours is the loss of a dream. Maybe you grieve the loss of a season or a job. Whenever we lose something we love, we mourn and grieve. We often do not understand why. We rage against the brokenness of this world, first in shock, and then typically in anger or despair.

Often in our reeling emotions, we respond by pulling away from the Lord, assuming God has abandoned us or that He cannot help in our pain. We see no reason to pray or read the Word. But in truth, the story of the gospel is one full of suffering. Notice that the hero of this story Himself was called the Suffering Servant. Jesus, who is fully God, left the splendors of heaven to come and live among us. He was hungry, hurt, and harmed. He was abandoned and neglected. He befriended sinners who betrayed Him by putting Him to death on a cross. He had friends who died. He was alone, misunderstood, and mistreated. He is a man who was acquainted with sorrow and familiar with grief (Isaiah 53:3), yet He trusted His Father through it all—He knew the victory that was coming.

God not only understands our grief but is with us in it. He mourns with us, cries with us, and comforts us. He is not a stoic Father, wanting us to suppress our emotions or robotically claim happiness as our tune. He is with us in our sadness. He is with the brokenhearted and binds up our wounds (Psalm 147:3). And one day, He will wipe away every tear and bring us home to a kingdom where every sad thing will be no more. We will live restored and redeemed forevermore.

"JESUS, WHO IS FULLY GOD, LEFT THE SPLENDORS OF HEAVEN TO COME AND LIVE AMONG US."

DAY 322

His Spirit Poured Out

After this I will pour out my Spirit on all humanity; then your sons and your daughters will prophesy, your old men will have dreams, and your young men will see visions.

JOEL 2:28

The prophet Joel delivered a message of repentance and hope to the people of Judah after a plague of locusts devastated Judah, foreshadowing the impending doom of God's judgment. Like the plague, no one could escape the day of the Lord when God would rightly judge wickedness. He pointed the people to repentance to escape this judgment, urging them to leave their sin and return to their compassionate God with faithful hearts. The Lord would be merciful and restore them if they turned to Him for salvation. Joel gave images of flourishing crops and animals as symbols of new life that would come after God's restoration. With this new life, the Spirit of God would descend on all of the Lord's people and quicken them to bear witness to their Savior.

The message of repentance and hope continued through the prophets after Joel and culminated in the prophet, John the Baptist. John called people to repent and put their faith in Jesus, who was God's Son and Anointed Savior and foreshadowed the Holy Spirit's coming. Jesus Himself would pour out the Spirit on the hearts of God's people to redeem them. Jesus accomplished this plan of redemption. He was the embodiment of God's compassion and love. When He died on the cross, He took on judgment and extended God's grace and mercy. After He rose from the grave and ascended to heaven, Jesus sent the Holy Spirit to dwell in those who would believe in Him. Many pronounced the truth of Jesus's saving work, the indwelling Holy Spirit replacing their sinful hearts with faithful ones and applying Jesus's redemptive work to their lives.

The Spirit of God gives people new life in Christ and empowers them to speak of Jesus. Those dead in sin come alive in Christ by the power of the Holy Spirit. With the Holy Spirit inside us, we can engage the world in a way that glorifies Him. Let us remain faithful by repenting and holding on to our hope in Christ. Rather than fear the day of the Lord, we look forward to Jesus's second coming when He will fully manifest His good kingdom, and the Spirit will apply Christ's redemptive work to all of the earth, and all will be made new—restored.

"THE SPIRIT OF GOD GIVES PEOPLE NEW LIFE IN CHRIST AND EMPOWERS THEM TO SPEAK OF JESUS."

DAY 323
Better is One Day

Better a day in your courts than a thousand anywhere else. I would rather stand at the threshold of the house of my God than live in the tents of wicked people.

PSALM 84:10

The psalmist wrote Psalm 84 to celebrate the temple of God in Jerusalem, God's dwelling place among the people. The psalmist described the temple as God's lovely dwelling place, which he longed with joy to enter. His experience in the temple, the courts of God, was incomparable to his experiences elsewhere. As we read this psalm today, we clearly see the psalmist's love of the temple. But how does this psalm speak to us today? The beauty of this psalm reminds us of the joy we find in the presence of God, whether in our personal devotions, prayer, or even as we gather together to worship with other Christians. Because God has made Himself near and known to us through salvation in Jesus Christ and because the Holy Spirit lives and dwells in us, we can experience the presence of God wherever we are. We do not experience His physical presence here, but He has given us His Spirit to live inside those who know Him as their Lord and Savior.

The "courts of God" can also indicate worshiping alongside other Christians. The New Testament affirms that God's people serve as a dwelling place for God and no longer a building (Ephesians 2:19–22). We find encouragement and joy by celebrating the presence of God as we gather together with God's people for worship and fellowship. God is with us there, for His Spirit is inside us.

Jesus Christ was the Word of God made flesh. Through Him, we receive forgiveness of our sins through salvation. His death and resurrection paved the way for us to enter into a relationship with God. The only way we gain access to God's presence is through the finished work of Jesus Christ. In His presence, we find a fullness we could never find elsewhere. Even the best days on this earth, the grandest adventures, and the most glorious experiences cannot compare to the joy found in the presence of God. God is preparing us now for a day when we will know the joy of His presence as we have never known, for we will see Him face to face. What a hope this offers. Thousands of the best days in this lifetime cannot compare to even one day with God in His eternal kingdom!

"WE CAN EXPERIENCE THE PRESENCE OF GOD WHEREVER WE ARE."

DAY 324
Not For People

Whatever you do, do it from the heart, as something done for the Lord and not for people, knowing that you will receive the reward of an inheritance from the Lord. You serve the Lord Christ.

COLOSSIANS 3:23-24

It can be easy to live in service to the Lord when others are watching. But what happens when no one is around? What happens when no one sees? Do we slip into old habits, sin issues, or selfish ways? This simple passage reminds us that we are called to work heartily as unto the Lord and not to men. God sees all things, and what He thinks of our service should not contend with what man thinks. It is the Lord who purchased our redemption through the death of His Son on the cross, not man. Our working and serving should hold the highest regard to honoring Christ as a response to His sacrificial display of love.

The thoughts and perceptions of others can so often preoccupy us that we give little concern to how God sees us. But Christians are called to live in service to Jesus Christ. How do servants of Christ live? They live with pure intentions of the heart that honor the Lord without just living for show. We delight in the Lord and use every opportunity to honor Him. That means using our office hours to work diligently and efficiently. It means using our time wisely when there may be other things we would like to do. It means being honest with others when it would be easier to keep the truth to ourselves. It means spending time with the Lord because we genuinely desire to know Him and not because we want to appear righteous.

There are numerous ways our actions can genuinely reflect hearts of service to the Lord, but we must constantly evaluate who we are aiming to please. When we work as unto the Lord, we become less and less concerned with the watching eyes of others. We seek to please God and God alone. And our God-honoring actions actually end in serving and honoring people in ways that please God. The Lord will use our service when done for Him alone. He will bless it and use it to the glory of His name. And when we reach heaven one day, what a glorious inheritance awaits those who have given their lives to sharing Christ's name and the beautiful truth of the gospel.

"CHRISTIANS ARE CALLED TO LIVE IN SERVICE TO JESUS CHRIST."

DAY 325
Is God Enough for You?

Then Job stood up, tore his robe, and shaved his head. He fell to the ground and worshiped, saying: Naked I came from my mother's womb, and naked I will leave this life. The Lord gives, and the Lord takes away. Blessed be the name of the Lord.

JOB 1:20-21

Job was a man of "perfect integrity," according to the Lord (Job 1:8). He feared God and did no evil, and yet God allowed him to be tested by Satan. The Lord had given Job everything, and Satan believed that if Job lost it all, he would turn away from the Lord and curse Him. God permitted Satan to have a hand on everything Job owned, but Satan was not to touch Job himself. So Satan destroyed everything Job owned and loved. His oxen, donkey, sheep, camels, servants, and children were taken from him in a single day in a devastating loss. Job grieved deeply, tearing his robe, shaving his head, and falling to the ground. But then, he did the unthinkable. He worshiped God.

When it would have been easy for Job to curse God for allowing everything to be taken from him, he turned to the Lord in worship. Job realized how small He was in comparison to the greatness of God. He credited God with giving Him his animals, servants, and family. Job realized that since they all belonged to the Lord, the Lord could do what He pleased with them, even if that meant taking them away. But Job trusted in the sovereignty of God, and he blessed His name still. Though Job had everything taken from him, the Lord was enough.

If everything was taken from us, would we respond as Job did in humility and worship? For many of us, the answer would be no. Our response might look different, and we may be tempted to reject God, refusing to turn to Him in prayer or worship. But when we come to the end of ourselves, when we lose everything, we can be confident that God will come close to us, even in the midst of our pain. His nearness to us is not based on our right response in our pain. God changes our hearts in our grief and shows us that He is enough. Christ will always be enough for us, and as we draw near to Him, we can trust Him no matter what our lives may bring.

"GOD CHANGES OUR HEARTS IN OUR GRIEF AND SHOWS US THAT HE IS ENOUGH."

DAY 326
Keep in the Love of God

But you, dear friends, as you build yourselves up in your most holy faith, praying in the Holy Spirit, keep yourselves in the love of God, waiting expectantly for the mercy of our Lord Jesus Christ for eternal life.

JUDE 20–21

The Christian life is one of perseverance. Believers should not be idle in their walks with the Lord but should be active, growing daily in relationship with the Lord. But growing in our faith takes perseverance as our broken world will cause us to walk through difficulty. With the help of the Holy Spirit, we can move forward and have the strength to endure whatever hardship we may experience.

As we walk with Christ, we are to keep ourselves in the love of God. This does not mean we might fall away from God's love. It was the love of God that saved us while we were sinners, and it is God's love that daily surrounds and keeps us, despite our mistakes. As believers, we sometimes pursue our sinful desires instead of living in obedience to God. However, that is not loving God. Jesus calls us to abide in His love, and if we love Him, we are to keep His commandments (John 15:9–10). To abide in Christ's love is to draw close to Him and remain obedient to Him. We keep ourselves in the love of God as we delight in God and seek to obey Him.

It is a gift of grace to always have God's love with us, but we are to respond to this gift of grace by our love for Him. If we truly love the Lord, we will desire to follow what His Word says. While our sinful flesh will cause us to struggle in our obedience, we can pray to the Spirit for help. If we are to build ourselves up in the faith, we do so as we read God's Word and remain committed to God's Word. Daily dependence on the Lord and obedience to His commands shape us into the image of Christ. Therefore, remaining in the love of God is what enables our sanctification. As we wait expectantly for Christ's return in the future, we remain active in our walks with Christ in the present. Christ has saved us with His great love, so let us respond to that love by remaining close and obedient to Him. May we keep in the love of God that ever surrounds us.

> "CHRIST HAS SAVED US WITH HIS GREAT LOVE, SO LET US RESPOND TO THAT LOVE BY REMAINING CLOSE AND OBEDIENT TO HIM."

DAY 327
Every Tribe and Tongue

After this I looked, and there was a vast multitude from every nation, tribe, people, and language, which no one could number, standing before the throne and before the Lamb. They were clothed in white robes with palm branches in their hands. And they cried out in a loud voice: Salvation belongs to our God, who is seated on the throne, and to the Lamb!

REVELATION 7:9–10

God made mankind in His image, and together we all reflect a better image of Him. If everyone around us looked the same, shared a similar cultural upbringing, thought similarly on every issue, and shared no real differences, we would have quite a limited picture of God. When we put God into a narrow image, we limit ourselves and misunderstand God's good design. God does not reflect His nature through one ethnicity or nationality, and neither does He reflect Himself through one personality type or language. We see this similarly in God's disbursement of spiritual gifts. If we all shared the same gift, we would miss out on God's full and creative design. We need each other. We are limited in our personal experiences and perspectives.

Therefore, let us celebrate our cultural and racial differences. We see them celebrated in heaven when Revelation paints the picture of worship around God's throne as "a vast multitude from every nation, tribe, people, and language, which no one could number, standing before the throne and before the Lamb." This description is found in Scripture because it is important. These details encourage us to take notice! There will not be people just like each other gathered together in worship but people from every tribe, tongue, and nation. We will all come together from all places, united under the banner of Jesus as we give Him all the glory, honor, and praise due His name.

Because we know heaven will be filled with diverse people, we should strive toward knowing a diverse group of people now. Everything we do today is in preparation for heaven. Getting to know people who have differences across cultural, ethnic, political, and economic lines prepares us for heaven. When living with this intention, our lives communicate who God is to a watching world—a God who transcends racial, cultural, even blood lines and a God who, through salvation in Jesus, invites every kind of person from every kind of place to be a part of His family and to belong in His kingdom.

"EVERYTHING WE DO TODAY IS IN PREPARATION FOR HEAVEN."

DAY 328

Gracious Father

So he got up and went to his father. But while the son was still a long way off, his father saw him and was filled with compassion. He ran, threw his arms around his neck, and kissed him.

LUKE 15:20

There is something to be gathered from each one of Jesus's parables. The parable of the prodigal son centers around a father and his two sons. The younger son asked the father to go ahead and distribute the assets of his estate to himself and his brother, one of the most dishonorable requests one could make. Each took his inheritance but handled it differently. The older stayed home working for his father, doing what seemed most honorable. However, the younger son took all he had and left home, wasting his money on foolish things.

When the young son found himself in the most desperate place, the young son decided to return home and seek forgiveness. His father saw him in the distance and was filled with compassion, running to his son and embracing him. His love exemplified a father who was willing to lay down his son's transgressions against him and open his arms to receive him. Not only did the father welcome him back, but he threw a celebration for his son's return!

This story illuminates our tendency to misunderstand the gospel of grace. We cannot run too far from God, nor can we earn our way into His presence. God displays the greatest act of grace by offering the gift of salvation through the sacrifice of His Son, Jesus, and by it, we are welcomed into God's family as His children. It knows no bounds and exceeds the depth of our brokenness and heights of our best efforts. The hope offered through this parable is not that if we work hard enough to please God, we will receive His grace. It is not that if we run too far away from Him, His grace is lost. The hope offered through this parable is that Jesus made a way for us to receive grace, a gift that has nothing to do with us but everything to do with Him.

"WE CANNOT RUN TOO FAR FROM GOD, NOR CAN WE EARN OUR WAY INTO HIS PRESENCE."

DAY 329
Give Thanks to the Lord

Give thanks to the Lord, for he is good. 'His faithful love endures forever.'
PSALM 136:1

There are countless reasons we should thank God, but Psalm 136 tells us specifically to thank God for His goodness and enduring, faithful love. How often do you thank God for these things? At times, we can become consumed with our to-do lists or the circumstances of our day and fail to stop and give thanks to God. But thanksgiving impacts us more than we realize.

Thanksgiving reminds us of God's character and the good things that He has done. In fact, the rest of Psalm 136 gives an account of God's miraculous works for the Israelites. This psalm teaches us that the proper response to God's character and works is to have and express gratitude.

Having gratitude for what God has done in the past encourages us to trust God with the future. It can be easy to forget all of God's past works and grow worried about the future. Recalling what God has done for us reminds us that we can trust Him to take care of us just as He has done before. Because God's faithful love endures forever, we can be confident that the faithful love He has demonstrated in the past will remain strong and steady all of our days and into eternity.

One of God's greatest works that warrants our praise is giving us Jesus. Though we were dead in our sin and rebellious to God, God sent us Jesus to save us and bring us new life. The kindness and goodness of our God to die for us should motivate our thanksgiving to Him. We did not deserve Christ's grace and forgiveness; therefore, we should be moved to gratitude for Jesus's sacrifice. As Colossians 2:6-7 tells us, "So then, just as you have received Christ Jesus as Lord, continue to walk in him, rooted and built up in him and established in the faith, just as you were taught, and overflowing with gratitude." The good news of the gospel fosters our gratitude, and the more we reflect on the gospel, the more our hearts will be lifted up in thanksgiving to God.

Every day is a day to give thanks to the Lord. It may take intentionality to incorporate gratitude into the everyday moments of our lives, but the result will be a joyful heart and renewed trust in the Lord. So today, let us give God thanks and praise Him for who He is and what He has done.

DAY 330
Choose Life

I call heaven and earth as witnesses against you today that I have set before you life and death, blessing and curse. Choose life so that you and your descendants may live, love the Lord your God, obey him, and remain faithful to him.

DEUTERONOMY 30:19–20A

Throughout the book of Deuteronomy, God clearly outlined the rules for approaching His throne, as well as what it meant to live a holy life. He told the people about the blessings that would follow obedience and the curses that would follow disobedience. He renewed His covenant with the people, knowing that they would rebel against Him and quickly break His laws. But unlike normal parents, God knew what the future held. He knew exactly how the Israelites would rebel against Him. He knew that they would want to do things their own way and would soon disregard His commands. Even so, God was merciful and made a way for them to return to Him. Not wanting His people to feel stuck in their disobedience, He reminded them that when blessings and curses have come upon them, and they return to Him, God will restore them (Deuteronomy 30:1–4).

Each day, God sets before us the choice to follow Him or to disobey His commands. And every day, we have the opportunity to choose life or death. Some days, we may live more victoriously, resisting temptation and resisting sin. Other days, we may fail miserably, going back to our sins like a dog to its vomit (Proverbs 26:11). But even on our best days, we are not perfect. We might covet our friend's cute shoes or car. Maybe we treat food in an unhealthy manner or snap at our children. Even on our best days, we are not enough—we are not sinless.

Praise be to God because He knew this ahead of time. He knew we could never obey Him perfectly, and He provided a way for us to be right with Him again. When Jesus came, He perfectly fulfilled the Law's demands, obeying them with pure and holy motivation. He honored His Father without envy, sinful anger, or impatience. Indeed it is only through Christ's righteousness that we are made holy. Through belief in Jesus, we can have life, blessing, and victory over death. Even as we seek to honor Him and "choose life" day-by-day, we rejoice because we know that our life is secure through Christ. Jesus secured our victory, and He is enough.

DAY 331

But if Not, He is Still God

Shadrach, Meshach, and Abednego replied to the king, "Nebuchadnezzar, we don't need to give you an answer to this question. If the God we serve exists, then he can rescue us from the furnace of blazing fire, and he can rescue us from the power of you, the king. But even if he does not rescue us, we want you as king to know that we will not serve your gods or worship the gold statue you set up."

DANIEL 3:16–18

Our God can do all things. But what of the times it seems our requests, cries, and pleas fall on deaf ears. What of the times we thought He heard our prayers yet answered by leading us down roads we would never choose. Though He may answer our prayers in ways we had not planned for ourselves or may not seem to answer those prayers at all as we walk through difficult circumstances, He is still God, He still loves us, and He is still good. We read of Shadrach, Meshach, and Abednego, who refused to bow down to a false god and proclaimed to King Nebuchadnezzar when he threw them into a blazing furnace that their God was powerful to save them. They also believed that if He chose not to save them, He was still God, and His plans for them were perfect.

God is sovereign, true, unchanging. If all we know to be steady in this world comes crashing down around us—even there, His hand will lead and hold us (Psalm 139:10). This world is broken by sin, but what joy we find in knowing that the Lord redeems and restores, regardless of the trials we experience. When He calls us home to heaven, there will be no more tears, sickness, or pain. Because of Jesus's death on the cross, we can one day experience that full redemption and restoration if we have placed our faith in Him.

We rejoice in prayers answered the way we hoped as Shadrach, Meshach, and Abednego rejoiced in the Lord's saving them from the fire. There will also be tears of sorrow, but let us remember that our God is still good. God has not forgotten His children and walks closely with us through suffering. He longs with us for the day when we reach heaven and know only the joy of His presence forevermore.

"GOD IS SOVEREIGN, TRUE, UNCHANGING."

DAY 332

Repentance and Restoration

Take words of repentance with you and return to the Lord. Say to him: "Forgive all our iniquity and accept what is good, so that we may repay you with praise from our lips... I will heal their apostasy; I will freely love them, for my anger will have turned from him.

HOSEA 14:2, 4

In Hosea 14, God is the kingly benefactor who offered extravagant forgiveness to His people. He offered a gift that seemed too good to be true. And still, for many years, the people withdrew from Him. The Israelites tried finding satisfaction apart from God. They tried paying their bills on their own but came up short. They turned to other saviors, who could not deliver (Hosea 14:3). They forgot the kindness of their King. But, although the people strayed from God, He urged them to return. He promised to heal the Israelites' apostasy and unfaithfulness. He offered to pay the price for all of their sins and to love them. He vowed to turn His anger from them and love them. He promised to do good to them when they returned with confession in their mouths and repentance in their hearts. To those who had rebelled against Him, God offered healing, love, forgiveness, and blessing.

Jesus offers the same to us today. He will forgive us of every sin we confess, including the sins we are too embarrassed or ashamed to say aloud. He is waiting with open arms, yearning to cover us with His forgiveness and righteousness. Often, we withdraw from the Lord in our sin, too ashamed even to come before Him in prayer. But God is a loving Father, who bids us to come. He does not want us to stay in our poor decisions or destructive sin patterns. He wants to redeem and restore what has been broken, lost, hurt. God wants us to repent and return to Him.

Like the Israelites in Hosea 14, we are all sinners, which is precisely what qualifies us for His grace. We deserve death, condemnation, destruction, and hell. But God is willing and able to forgive us. Because of the perfect work of Christ on the cross and because He rose again from the grave, He has made a way for our sins to be paid. In Christ, the hurting find healing, the fatherless are adopted, we as sinners are forgiven—no strings attached, no hidden catch, just extravagant grace.

"GOD WANTS US TO REPENT AND RETURN TO HIM."

DAY 333
But We Do See Jesus

For in subjecting everything to him, he left nothing that is not subject to him. As it is, we do not yet see everything subjected to him. But we do see Jesus—made lower than the angels for a short time so that by God's grace he might taste death for everyone—crowned with glory and honor because he suffered death.

HEBREWS 2:8B–9

Mankind was given the earth to rule, subdue, cultivate, and populate. We were supposed to do so according to the will and ways of God. Had we done this, we would have a perfectly ordered and beautified planet on which to live. But we did not do this as we should. Instead, we let sin order our actions and define the type of beauty we pursue. Even when followers of Christ work tirelessly to spread the presence and light of God throughout the world, there are parts and people left untouched. As a result, the world is far more godless than it should be.

But we do see Jesus. Because of Jesus's arrival, God will redeem the earth from eternal darkness and depravity. Jesus was both fully God and fully man. He did what the first man, Adam, failed to do. He lived wholly and completely according to the ways and will of God. He healed what was broken, forgave what was evil, clarified what was misunderstood, and brought order to the chaos man had made in the world. The world subjected to Jesus is the world as God desires it to be. Yet He went beyond only righting the world during His short life and ministry. He also chose to make a way for us all to live in eternal perfection with Him. He tasted death for everyone, suffering the ultimate end—physical and spiritual death, separated from Christ. But because He is not just man but also God, Jesus defeated death and the grave and lives!

God invites us into this story where we are not sentenced to death but to eternal glory if we believe in Christ. We are already joined with Christ but are not yet glorified with Him. Some days we feel the weight of "not yet" heavier than others. We long for the end of sickness, death, torment, evil, and injustice. And it is on these days that we can say, "We do not yet see everything subjected to him. But we do see Jesus."

"JESUS DEFEATED DEATH AND THE GRAVE AND LIVES!"

Who is My Neighbor?

"Which of these three do you think proved to be a neighbor to the man who fell into the hands of the robbers?" "The one who showed mercy to him," [the law expert] said. Then Jesus told him, "Go and do the same."

LUKE 10:36–37

While trying to trap Jesus, a religious law expert asked what he must do to gain eternal life. Jesus pointed him to God's commands—that one must love God and one's neighbor. The Jewish authority of the time had only considered fellow Jewish people or the elite class as their neighbors. But, Jesus told the expert of the Law a parable that highlighted that one's neighbor is anyone near. Regardless of class, race, or gender, if two people are in proximity, they are neighbors.

In Jesus's parable, a story told to teach a biblical moral or lesson, a priest and a Levite, in their callousness and false piety, passed up a man who was injured and left unconscious by robbers. However, a Samaritan, who was considered the most unlikely person to show mercy, stopped to give aid. Jesus's use of this character must have stunned the religious leader. The Samaritan treated and helped the man as though he were his neighbor and expressed love toward him. Though the religious leader thought he had been keeping the Law, Jesus exposed his pride and shortcomings.

Many of us are guilty of failing to love our neighbors as we ought. Maybe we are unsympathetic or distracted or consider ourselves greater than others. But, Jesus kept His Law perfectly. Jesus was our good neighbor, perfect in every way, saw us distressed by sin, cared for us, and made us clean by dying on the cross to cleanse us from our sins. Like the Samaritan in His parable, Jesus gave us life and paid our debts. When we place our faith in Jesus, He is always near to us through the Holy Spirit, who comes to live inside us when we trust the Lord as our Savior. Because Jesus rescued us from spiritual poverty when we deserved no such thing, we can exhibit neighborly love in gratitude for His work. While sacrificing our comfort, time, and space, we can serve those God puts in our paths, no matter who they are. As we do, we display the stunning grace of the gospel of Christ.

"JESUS WAS OUR GOOD NEIGHBOR, PERFECT IN EVERY WAY."

DAY 335
Vain Pursuits

Unless the Lord builds a house, its builders labor over it in vain; unless the Lord watches over a city, the watchman stays alert in vain.
PSALM 127:1

Have you ever come to the end of your day and realized you had not thought about the Lord? You hurried through your to-do list, accomplished more than you thought you would, maybe had a few frustrating things happen along the way, but you made it through the day without speaking once to your heavenly Father. When you go to jump in bed at night, pull the covers around you, and begin to say a prayer, you realize it is the first time you have talked to God all day.

These thoughts should produce a godly grief within us. We are so easily fooled into believing that we can accomplish great things without the Lord. We imitate Adam and Eve in the very first sin when they forgot about the treasured fellowship they had with God and rebelled against Him. And we do our work in vain because unless the Lord is with us, our labor is for nothing.

When we become followers of Christ, our faith is not just limited to the time we spend reading our Bibles or in prayer. Our pursuit of Christ influences every aspect of our lives. We are united with Him through the gospel, and He has given us His Spirit. Jesus is with us always and desires to be a part of our every moment. He does not want us to labor in our own strength but to rely on Him.

This is a beautiful aspect of the Christian life. Everything we do is done through the power and strength of Christ. This does not mean life will suddenly become easy. We live in a broken world that is still full of the presence of sin, and we feel its effects every day. But it does mean that when we become exhausted and weary, we can cry out to Jesus and remember that He is the One who enables us to push through the challenges of life.

So whether you are building a home or watching over your children or cleaning the kitchen, know that you are working in the Lord's strength and under His loving care. We no longer labor in vain. Rather, we labor with an eternal perspective. Jesus has become a part of everything we do. His presence fills our days. And God alone deserves the glory!

DAY 336

Brought Out of Exile

"For I know the plans I have for you ... plans for your well-being, not for disaster, to give you a future and a hope ... You will seek me and find me when you search for me with all your heart. I will be found by you ... and I will restore your fortunes and gather you from all the nations and places where I banished you"—this is the Lord's declaration. "I will restore you to the place from which I deported you."

JEREMIAH 29:11–14

The hopeful words of Jeremiah 29:11 are nestled between words declaring exile for the people of Israel. However, this current context does not change the impact of Jeremiah 29:11. In fact, it may even create a greater impact. The Israelites experienced seventy years of exile from Babylon. But God did not allow His people to be in exile without giving them hope. Though they would experience the turmoil of exile, there was deliverance on the other side. God promised to restore what they had lost and repair their broken relationship. God had plans to restore them and give them a future full of abundance.

When God allows hardship and suffering, we often question what God is doing and may wonder if His plans are really for our well-being. But God is a God who restores and does not allow us to experience suffering without the promise of deliverance. God's plans are for our good. His plans for us may involve walking through trying circumstances, but there is restoration on the other side. In times of hardship or seasons with lots of unknowns, we can trust in God's plans.

For the Israelites, they could trust God in the present because He had shown them what was ahead. In the same way, as believers in Christ, we know what is ahead. The pages of Scripture open our eyes to this future that awaits every believer — that Jesus is making a place for us and will one day return to bring us with Him to His everlasting kingdom. God's promise of the future should encourage our perseverance in the present, even if we do not know step by step what life will look like. God has a plan to lead us to a glorious future in eternity. So we have confidence and trust God in every season.

"GOD HAS A PLAN TO LEAD US TO A GLORIOUS FUTURE IN ETERNITY."

DAY 337
Unity in Christ

For those of you who were baptized into Christ have been clothed with Christ. There is no Jew or Greek, slave or free, male and female; since you are all one in Christ Jesus. And if you belong to Christ, then you are Abraham's seed, heirs according to the promise.

GALATIANS 3:27–29

We live in a world utterly divided because of sin. But the gospel of Jesus smashes every barrier and social construct the world creates. The gospel brings us into God's unshakable kingdom. His kingdom is not like earthly kingdoms, consumed with power and prestige. His kingdom puts every member in equal standing, for we are all equally sinful and equally covered in the righteousness of Christ.

None are clothed more in His righteousness or less in His righteousness when they are saved. Their identity is the same in the Savior. This means that the division the world loves to make is deemed meaningless, and we are free to experience the joy and peace of unity with our brothers and sisters in Christ. Our race or ethnicity should not keep us from that unity. Our economic status should not keep us from that unity. Our gender should not keep us from that unity. Paul even mentions in Galatians that slaves and free men and women are unified in the gospel. At the time he wrote this letter, that would have been a dramatic upset in their culture.

All followers of Christ are grafted into God's family, and we are now heirs to the promises God made to Israel long ago. We are part of the family that brings blessing to the world, because we are messengers of the Savior, Jesus. We are equal in standing before the Lord and are all a part of His family. There is no reason for division and hostility toward one another. While we may have different roles and gifts within the body of Christ, these serve to remind us of the Lord's provision for His people. God gives us salvation, makes us His own, and shows us how to live. Our differences need not divide us. Instead, they should push us further to unity for His mission—telling more and more people about the salvation we have received so they also can become a part of the family of God.

> "WE ARE NOW HEIRS TO THE PROMISES GOD MADE TO ISRAEL LONG AGO."

DAY 338
God Does Not Change

Because I, the Lord, have not changed, you descendants of Jacob have not been destroyed.

MALACHI 3:6

God is perfect and unchanging. In Genesis 15, God made a covenant with Abraham. He promised to give him a son, make his offspring as numerous as the stars, give them land as their own, and bless the world through his family line. In response, God asked Abraham to trust Him and live according to the rules that He put forth. Abraham and all of his descendants struggled to keep their word to God. They feared, doubted, disobeyed, and clung to their idols. But God never changed, even as the Israelites messed up over and over again. God never wavered in His commitment to the covenant.

At times, He doled out well-deserved consequences for sin. At other times, He mercifully held back His judgment. Sometimes, He hid his presence from the sinful, and other times appeared in glory despite the unworthiness of the Israelite people. In all of this, He never changed His mind or His commitment to the covenant He established.

This promise is beautifully reiterated in Isaiah 46:4: "I will be the same until your old age, and I will bear you up when you turn gray. I have made you, and I will carry you; I will bear and rescue you." God's promises endure in the lives of His people from their first days to their last. He will be ever faithful to those who have accepted Him as their Lord and Savior. The beauty of this promise grows more stunning when we see God's covenant-keeping culminate in the life, death, and resurrection of Jesus Christ. Through Him, the covenant is no longer only for those in the direct family line of Abraham but for all who believe. The Lord is unchanging. He is "the same yesterday, today and forever" (Hebrews 13:8). Therefore, everyone who believes in Jesus and receives His grace and forgiveness is brought into this beautiful covenant with an unchanging God!

Today, remember that even when your heart is fickle, God is faithful. Even when you are wayward, God is resolute in His relationship with you. Even when you give in to sin, God remains merciful toward you, extending forgiveness. What joy we can have that we serve an unchanging God—we can place full confidence in His enduring character and Word.

DAY 339
Necessity of Prayer

Very early in the morning, while it was still dark, he got up, went out, and made his way to a deserted place; and there he was praying.

MARK 1:35

Throughout the gospel accounts, Scripture highlights many moments when Jesus took time to spend with God the Father. But Mark 1:35 expresses His urgency in prayer. First, there is a phrase that indicates time. Our minds are taken to a setting in the early morning hours. Mark's emphasis on time conveys that prayer was the priority for Jesus, for the sun had not yet risen. However, Jesus was awake and longing to converse with His Father. The looming judgment and wrath Jesus was about to face for our sin could have been troubling Him, and Jesus sought the source of His help and peace.

Mark writes that Jesus "got up" and "went out." With no mention of hesitancy or drowsiness, perhaps His steps were clear and ordered in the path the Holy Spirit led to a "deserted place." We can imagine the stillness of the area. Prior to this moment, Mark writes how Jesus healed so many people. There were so many people that Scripture describes the whole town of Capernaum gathered at Jesus's door. The sick and lowly looked to Jesus for freedom, and by His Word, He proved He was the Son of God and would give them freedom from sin. During Jesus's healing ministry, crowds surrounded Him and yelled out His name. The scene was loud and stimulating. But, now, in the dark hours of the morning, in the deserted place, it was quiet and calm.

Through His actions, Jesus showed us the necessity of prayer. His prayer life, or His continual communication with God, was instrumental in accomplishing the plan of redemption. Because Jesus's work saves us, let us consider how our actions demonstrate the necessity of prayer. In Christ, we can cultivate intentional prayer lives by dedicating time and space for it. Ultimately, these structures should reflect our gratitude and love for Jesus and a longing to commune with Him.

"IN CHRIST, WE CAN CULTIVATE INTENTIONAL PRAYER LIVES BY DEDICATING TIME AND SPACE FOR IT."

DAY 340
The Cost of Discipleship

"Then Jesus said to his disciples, "If anyone wants to follow after me, let him deny himself, take up his cross, and follow me. For whoever wants to save his life will lose it, but whoever loses his life because of me will find it. For what will it benefit someone if he gains the whole world but loses his life? Or what will anyone give in exchange for his life?"

MATTHEW 16:24–26

The Bible is a beautiful story of how God relentlessly sought to redeem and restore us to Himself. However, the cost of our redemption was high. Because God is holy and just, someone needed to pay for our redemption. In the Old Testament, this was done through priests who made sacrifices on the Israelites' behalf. However, this part of God's plan was only temporary. In the New Testament, God reveals His complete plan for our redemption in Jesus.

God sent His Son to pay the price of our sins. To do this, Jesus left heaven and took on human flesh, along with all the pain and strife humans experience. Then, He served as the ultimate sacrifice by dying on the cross in our place (Matthew 27:46). This was the cost of our redemption. However, His death was not eternal. Instead, Jesus rose three days after His death. He did this so that we could be presented as righteous and restored to God (2 Corinthians 5:21).

Jesus's sacrifice on the cross was for us. However, it still requires something of us. Just like we need to accept earthly gifts to experience them, so we need to accept the gift of God's mercy. And to accept this gift, we need to deny ourselves and follow Christ. This may feel like a costly gift to us, and in some ways, it is. As we follow Christ, we will experience persecution. However, this cost is nothing in light of eternity as it saves us from eternal separation from God.

If we look at the price Jesus paid to redeem and restore us, we realize that God is not asking too much when He asks that we give up the world to gain our life (Matthew 16:26). The Bible is truly a beautiful story of how God relentlessly pursued us to restore us to Himself. And as we lay down our lives, we can experience the fullness of the life God intended for us. This is the gift and the cost of discipleship.

"JESUS'S SACRIFICE ON THE CROSS WAS FOR US."

DAY 341
True Beauty

Charm is deceptive and beauty is fleeting, but a woman who fears the Lord will be praised.

PROVERBS 31:30

The end of the book of Proverbs contains a very familiar passage of Scripture for many women. It is one of the few places in the Bible that specifically gives us a vision of what it means to be a biblical woman. These 22 verses about a "wife of noble character" are written as an acrostic poem. Each stanza begins with a different letter of the Hebrew alphabet. Using acrostics in wisdom literature was very common for Hebrew authors, and it would have made memorizing what was said much easier.

This last chapter of Proverbs is a passage that was written by a king's mother. The mother's goal was to give advice on how to find a godly woman. However, this passage also serves as the perfect bookend to summarize much of what Solomon has said. Throughout the book of Proverbs, wisdom and folly are personified in women. Folly is described as a woman who is an adulteress or a prostitute. She deceives those she meets with smooth and charming words, but all that she promises leads only to death. And then there is Lady Wisdom, and she is a treasure to be desired and cherished. She leads to life.

Yet, here at the end of Proverbs, the king's mother makes the connection that wisdom is not only personified as a woman, but it can be found in godly women as well. In fact, it is the most desirable quality a wife can possess, for wisdom leads to fear of the Lord. The charm and beauty that the world sees as desirable is deceptive and fleeting. At the end of the day, charming words fall flat against what is true, and worldly beauty cannot overcome the toll of each passing year. But a woman who fears the Lord possesses something that can never be taken from her.

Fear of the Lord will not fall flat as everything to be known about God is true and good. And as a woman ages, her hair may gray, and her face may wrinkle, but her fear for the Lord will become all the more beautiful as she seeks Him—to grow in knowledge and understanding of Him and His perfect Word. When we place our identities in Christ rather than in our wisdom, outward appearance, or possessions, we invest in a kind of beauty that never fades. Proverbs 31 speaks of a beauty that is eternal. And that true and lasting beauty is found wholly in knowing and serving Christ alone.

DAY 342
Our Blessed Hope

...we wait for the blessed hope, the appearing of the glory of our great God and Savior, Jesus Christ. He gave himself for us to redeem us from all lawlessness and to cleanse for himself a people for his own possession, eager to do good works.

TITUS 2:13–14

What makes you feel hopeless? Maybe it is when something you were excited about does not happen. Or maybe it is feeling as if you are never going to win the battle with fear or sin. When troubling circumstances arise, it can feel as though there is no hope. But when life feels grim, every believer has the blessed hope of Christ's future return. While life can be difficult, we have a glorious future in which Christ will return and set all things right, redeeming and restoring all that is broken.

Christ's return is a blessed hope because it will be the culmination of everything for which we are waiting. The redemption we have received from our salvation and the process of sanctification we are undergoing will be complete. The world and our bodies will be cleansed from sin. No more will we struggle with the evil of this world. No more will we struggle with fear. No more will we struggle with brokenness. Everything will be as it should be.

The best part is that we will get to spend eternity with the One who saved us. We will see our God and our Savior face to face and live forever in His presence. Right now, we wait for this blessed hope, but we do not wait in vain. In Revelation 22:20, Jesus promised the hope of Christ's second coming when He said, "I am coming soon." As we wait for the day to come, we do not wait idly. Out of a response to our future hope and our salvation through Christ, we are to eagerly do good for the Lord. We can value the time we are given as an opportunity to bring glory to God in the way we act and speak. When we walk through difficult times, we can see those moments as opportunities to glorify God in the way we persevere and hope in Him. In the moments you feel hopeless, remember that you have a blessed hope. Instead of fixing your eyes on your circumstances, set your eyes on what is to come. Set your eyes now on the glorious hope of Jesus Christ!

"CHRIST'S RETURN IS A BLESSED HOPE BECAUSE IT WILL BE THE CULMINATION OF EVERYTHING FOR WHICH WE ARE WAITING."

DAY 343
Compelled to Love

For the love of Christ compels us, since we have reached this conclusion: If one died for all, then all died. And he died for all so that those who live should no longer live for themselves, but for the one who died for them and was raised.

2 CORINTHIANS 5:14–15

Scripture tells us that the love of Christ compels us. This compulsion is one not of obligation but delight. When we move toward something naturally, it is because we have a desire for that object. As believers, the love of Christ compels us because we have received the love of Christ. The great love that Christ has shown us motivates us to move toward others and show His love to them. Christ's love is so great that we cannot help but love others in response.

Yet, sometimes, it feels like a struggle to love others. People can be difficult to love, especially those who have hurt us. When we find ourselves struggling to love others, we must delight in the love of Christ. We must open up God's Word and remind ourselves of the great love we have received, even while we were still sinners. We must ask God to remind us of the love that flows in us because of our union with Christ. The more we delight in Christ's love, the more we will share His love. In order to do this, we must daily spend time in prayer and in God's Word, going to the very source that reveals God's love to us so that we can continue to be fueled by God's love.

Not only this, but the Holy Spirit aids us in our love for others. In times when we struggle to show the love of Christ, the Holy Spirit ignites the fire of Christ's love within us. As we delight in the love of Christ, may we be filled with gratitude for the salvation Christ has given us. For out of that deep gratitude will grow an overflow of desire to tell others about the gospel's good news. If you find your heart is cold today, go to God's Word, and warm your heart with the reminder of Christ's love. And as it begins to warm, press into the Holy Spirit, and share the love of Christ that overflows from within you.

"AS WE DELIGHT IN THE LOVE OF CHRIST, MAY WE BE FILLED WITH GRATITUDE FOR THE SALVATION CHRIST HAS GIVEN US."

DAY 344

Worship Creates Soft Hearts

Come, let's worship and bow down; let us kneel before the Lord our Maker. For he is our God, and we are the people of his pasture, the sheep under his care.

PSALM 95:6-7

Our tendency as humans is to do what we want and to think we know what is best. When we turn our eyes from God to ourselves, we no longer seek obedience to the Lord but what we desire instead. In pride, we chase after our own glory and satisfaction instead of praising God for His glory and finding our satisfaction in Him. Our hearts grow cold toward God and His Word.

When pride seeks to harden our hearts, we must warm our hearts with worship. In humility, we must lay down our glory to fix our eyes on the glory of the Lord and what He did on the cross. In submission, we must kneel before the Lord, who is our Maker, lifting our praises high. Continual worship of the Lord keeps our hearts soft and humble, orienting our hearts to God rather than to ourselves. As we worship the Lord, we declare that He is the One who deserves all honor and glory. The more we remain worshipful, the more we elevate God to the highest place in our lives.

The best way to encourage our worship of God is to remind ourselves of the gospel. When we take our eyes off the gospel, we can forget the price Jesus paid to save us. We can forget the grace given to us, though we did not deserve it. With no way for us to be saved from the punishment from our sin apart from Christ, the great mercy and grace of God to save us should move us to our knees.

Every day, we should seek to have the gospel at the forefront of our minds. And on the days we find the significance of the gospel fading into the background of our minds, we can pick up God's Word and read. We can go to God in prayer, asking Him to warm our hearts again to the wonder of the gospel. As we are reminded of the grace that has been given to us, let us take the time to worship. Let us lift our hands in praise to our Savior. Let us worship and bow down before our great God. Let us kneel evermore before the Lord our Maker.

"AS WE WORSHIP THE LORD, WE DECLARE THAT HE IS THE ONE WHO DESERVES ALL HONOR AND GLORY."

DAY 345
Broken Cisterns

For my people have committed a double evil: They have abandoned me, the fountain of living water, and dug cisterns for themselves—cracked cisterns that cannot hold water.

JEREMIAH 2:13

In John 4, Jesus approached a lonely woman in the heat of the day and asked her for a sip of water. As they talked, the woman quickly realized that this man was different from all the others. He knew the secrets she had hidden in her past. He knew what she tried to hide. And then, He offered her something strange—water that leads to eternal life. Though this woman remains unnamed in the book of John, she was known by Jesus. Jesus knew that she was looking for satisfaction apart from the Lord and would never be truly satisfied by anything but God. She needed the living water that only He could offer.

God is and has always been what we need. He is our life, our joy, and our fulfillment. But in the book of Jeremiah, the people had forgotten this. Although God had faithfully protected His people, they turned from Him. Though He had saved them from the Egyptians and brought them to the Promised Land, they wanted to go their own way. God's people, the Israelites, who had seen Him work in marvelous ways, should have trusted in His provision. But instead, they abandoned Him. They looked for water, which symbolized life and security, apart from God. In an attempt to secure their independence from Him, they dug wells, but these cisterns were broken and cracked. And as the people sought a life apart from God, ironically, they rejected the giver of life Himself.

We often do the same. We commit the double evil of abandoning God and trying to find life outside of Him. We look to our jobs to make us feel successful. We depend on the success of our children or the amount in our bank accounts to give us security. We abandon God, His people, and the Bible in order to "find ourselves." But when we try to find these things apart from God, we abandon the true source of stability, security, and life. We forget that He is what we needed all along. God is the source of living water, contentment, fulfillment, and joy. God is what we need, and He is to be treasured above everything else. Let us look to Him today to bring us lasting satisfaction, salvation, security, and peace.

"GOD IS THE SOURCE OF LIVING WATER, CONTENTMENT, FULFILLMENT, AND JOY."

DAY 346

Hungry for God's Word

Look, the days are coming—this is the declaration of the Lord God—when I will send a famine through the land: not a famine of bread or a thirst for water, but of hearing the words of the Lord.

AMOS 8:11

The prophet Amos delivered a message of judgment to the northern kingdom of Israel before the Assyrians destroyed them. God used Amos to warn the people from continuing to practice evil. They had not only rejected God, but they had also rejected and mistreated the poor and helpless among them, the very people God instructed them to care for the most. Amos was a shepherd before the Lord called him to speak to His people. But when God did call, Amos obeyed, though the message was heavy and not easy to hear.

One of the worst judgments God gave the people through Amos is found in today's verse. Because the people rejected God, they would experience a famine of hearing His Word. The people had Scripture that had already been recorded at that time; they also had the words God gave to them through the prophets. They had no desire for either, and soon, they would hear nothing of His Word.

When we speak about famines today, we know that, for the most part, they are circumstances that we cannot control. But this famine in Amos was a result of the people's disobedience. They had turned away from God, so there would be an absence of the Word of God. How terrible this was, for as Deuteronomy 32:47 says that God's words are our very life.

An absence of the Word of God meant a spiritual desert for God's people. He would leave them to their disobedience. If we lost the Word of God and had no access to Scripture, would we be devastated? Would we hunger for its truth? We must evaluate our attitude toward God's Word and treat it as a lifeline, for it truly is the sustenance we need the most in this life. A loss of food or water may lead to physical death, but the spiritual death that follows a lack of taking in God's Word is worse. May we see our need for the truth of Scripture and not be like the people of Israel, who rejected God and His Word and then lost it altogether. May we have a hunger that cannot be satisfied and a thirst that cannot be quenched for the life-giving words of the Lord.

"WE MUST EVALUATE OUR ATTITUDE TOWARD GOD'S WORD AND TREAT IT AS A LIFELINE."

DAY 347
The Beauty of Bearing Another's Burden

Carry one another's burdens; in this way you will fulfill the law of Christ.

GALATIANS 6:2

Bearing burdens is one of the greatest ways we can care for one another as Christians. Showing hospitality, offering comforting words, praying thoughtful prayers, gathering together in the local church all provide a means for us to enjoy, learn, and share in the life of another. Needs will arise, and we cannot simply enjoy the good without acknowledging the hard. How easy it is to rejoice with someone over life's many blessings, but how difficult it can be to take on someone else's pain, helping them walk through struggles that come in different seasons of life. The Christian life is hard, and we all need help along the way. We could likely name numerous times when the load in our lives felt too heavy to bear alone. What a relief we can find in sharing our burdens with a faithful friend.

The beauty of bearing burdens is that we get to share in the work of Jesus Christ. When we look to the cross, we see One who carried our heaviest load. The greatest burden to bear, Jesus Christ bore. He carried our sin to the cross on our behalf and suffered the wrath of God that we deserved. Jesus held the weight of our greatest transgressions, our heaviest loads, so that we would never have to carry them. And He did this not out of duty with grumbling but with a heart full of love, mercy, and grace for His children and desire to see them come to a true faith in Him. It is a testimony to others as they watch us walk through trials beside them, giving of ourselves so their loads might be lighter. Indeed they will see a reflection of Christ in us.

As we bear one another's burdens, we reflect the beautiful work of the gospel. And we lift up His people in encouragement and by walking alongside them in suffering so that they can do the same. Because Christ carried our burdens, we are free to share in the burdens of another and to care for God's family. It is easy to stay concerned with ourselves, avoid someone else's challenging circumstances, or pass off the load to someone else, but Christians are called to more. May we take advantage of every opportunity to encourage, build up, strengthen, and share in the sufferings of all who belong to the household of faith (Galatians 6:10).

> "JESUS HELD THE WEIGHT OF OUR GREATEST TRANSGRESSIONS, OUR HEAVIEST LOADS SO THAT WE WOULD NEVER HAVE TO CARRY THEM."

DAY 348
The Power of Our Thoughts

Finally brothers and sisters, whatever is true, whatever is honorable, whatever is just, whatever is pure, whatever is lovely, whatever is commendable—if there is any moral excellence and if there is anything praiseworthy—dwell on these things.

PHILIPPIANS 4:8

Paul sat in a Roman prison, writing a letter of joy to the Philippian church. A leading figure in the spread of the gospel, Paul began his career as a Pharisee, the Jewish religious authority of the time. In this role, Paul persecuted believers for their faith in Christ. But after an encounter with the risen Jesus, Paul repented and gave his life to following the Lord. One of the churches planted due to Paul's evangelism was the congregation in Philippi. However, the Philippian church struggled with disunity and rivalry. Paul identified two people who were in conflict: Euodia and Syntyche (Philippians 4:2). We do not know their disagreement, but we can infer from the letter that it was affecting the ministry.

Conflict begins with disapproving thoughts, which can be critical or demeaning views of oneself, other people, or situations. Thinking in these ways can cause relational friction. Paul's response to Eudoia and Syntyche's conflict was a call for them to rejoice, set aside anxieties, and reflect on things pleasing to the Lord. Paul asked them to establish peace in the church. He listed qualities on which one should reflect. One should think about whatever is true, honorable, just, pure, lovely, and commendable. They should seek to dwell on the excellent and praiseworthy things. These characteristics are attributes of God, fully displayed in the person of Jesus Christ. Paul's exhortation was a call to meditate on the gospel so that unity and joy would abound.

We can be distracted from the work God calls us to do because of false, unjust, impure, judgmental, and condescending thoughts we entertain in our minds. But, these thoughts do not reflect Christ's humility nor the joy we have in Him. Though He was God, Jesus was a servant and cared for others. Because of our rebellion, we were in utmost relational conflict with God, but Jesus reconciled us in love. Jesus looked on us, and though we were sinners, He died so that we could have life everlasting in Him. And by the Holy Spirit, we can reflect His glorious image. May we strive to obtain the humble mind of Jesus. Rejoicing In Him, let us focus on the good news accomplished in Christ so that unity can be restored and relationships healed.

DAY 349
Our Stronghold

The Lord is good, a stronghold in a day of distress; he cares for those who take refuge in him.

NAHUM 1:7

Imagine you are in the middle of a storm on the sea. The sky is dark, lightning strikes, and rain pours down. Your boat cannot keep steady amidst the waves beating against its sides. In your distress, you look around for something, anything that could be a source of security from the storm. In the distance, you see the beam of a lighthouse shine across the water. At last! There is a place to find refuge. We may not know what it is like to be tossed about in a storm at sea, but we most likely know what it is like to feel tossed to and fro in the waves of suffering. Our broken world washes suffering into our lives in the form of anxiety, infertility, depression, and hardships of many kinds. Moments of suffering come and often make us feel as though we stand in the middle of a storm, our afflictions causing us to feel insecure, distressed, and unstable.

As Christ followers, we are not left without refuge in storms of suffering. Just as a lighthouse offers refuge and direction, God is our refuge and the most secure stronghold we can have in moments of pain and distress. The Lord is powerful and unchanging, which means He will never falter or shift. Unlike the strongholds of this world, God will never weaken. The things of this earth cannot withstand the weight of our need, but God can. In moments of distress, we have a refuge to whom we can run. The reconciliation Jesus made possible for us on the cross allows us unhindered access to God in any and every affliction. Not only this, but our union with Christ also means that we have continual access to Christ's strength, peace, and rest.

When we experience suffering, we do not have to be overwhelmed by our distress but can come to the Lord and seek refuge in Him. The Lord will keep us from drowning under the weight of our pain and will keep us secure and steady in His hands. As we come to the Lord, we will receive His loving care and perfect peace. Though our circumstances may rain heavily upon us, we can rest in the security of the Lord, our great stronghold, whose walls of comfort surround us.

"OUR UNION WITH CHRIST ALSO MEANS THAT WE HAVE CONTINUAL ACCESS TO CHRIST'S STRENGTH, PEACE, AND REST."

DAY 350
An Invitation to the Weary

Come to me, all of you who are weary and burdened, and I will give you rest.

MATTHEW 11:28

In Matthew 11:28, Jesus calls us to come to Him, and He will give us rest. This promise to come and find rest in Him would be untrue for anyone else to say, except God, for He is the only One who can deliver on claims of eternal peace. He is the answer to all of life's problems; He is our Sabbath rest. Jesus invites us to come to Him today and be satisfied. All are welcome before the foot of the cross. Lest you think your past sins or shame disqualify you from grace, He invites you today to come and find rest for your soul. He is quick to forgive and does not want any to perish but all to come to repentance (2 Peter 3:9). No sin or past mistakes can disqualify you from grace.

We are often tired and weary in life. We carry self-inflicted loads and place expectations upon ourselves that we simply cannot fulfill. On top of this, we face disappointments, internal struggles, and fatigue. We all can become tired and weary. If this describes you today, you are not alone (Isaiah 40:30–31). The word "burden" in today's verse is thought to imply the loads that are given by others. In Matthew 23:4, Jesus tells the religious leaders that they gave people "heavy loads that are hard to carry, and put them on people's shoulders, but they themselves aren't willing to lift a finger to move them." Sometimes, we can be deeply burdened by all of life's to-do lists. We feel constrained by all the rules of society and feel deeply burdened to please everyone by taking on more and more.

Rest, peace, refreshment, calm, the place where strivings cease—are these not things for which we search and yearn? An invitation to come to Jesus is one to find deep rest for our souls. As Jesus promised, all who are weary can come to Him and find rest. If you are heavy-ladened today, burdened and exhausted, come to Jesus. If you hunger and thirst for righteousness, come. If you are looking for more in life, disappointed and weighted down by the burdens of life, come. Do not withdraw in your pain and your sorrow. Come to Jesus, and discover the One who welcomes you into His care and loves you with an everlasting love. He will give you rest.

"IF YOU ARE HEAVY-LADENED TODAY, BURDENED AND EXHAUSTED, COME TO JESUS."

DAY 351
He Has Not Left You

The women said to Naomi, "Blessed be the Lord, who has not left you without a family redeemer today. May his name become well known in Israel. He will renew your life and sustain you in your old age. Indeed, your daughter-in-law, who loves you and is better to you than seven sons, has given birth to him."

RUTH 4:14–15

At the beginning of the book of Ruth, we read of Naomi and her husband, Elimelech. They had two sons and moved from Judah to Moab due to famine. Tragically, Elimelech died, and Naomi is grieved. Her two sons married wives of their own, but soon her sons too would also die, leaving Naomi devastated and alone with her two daughters-in-law, Orpah and Ruth. She moved back to Judah, and upon her return said, "I went away full, but the Lord has brought me back empty" (Ruth 1:21). She was a suffering widow without a way to provide for her daily needs. But the Lord was with her.

Naomi's daughter-in-law, Orpah, left, but despite all odds, Ruth stayed beside her. Through divine circumstances, Ruth met Boaz, one of the few people who could lawfully marry Ruth, buy the family property, and become caretaker for Naomi. This was a hopeful discovery amid a bleak story. But would Boaz want to marry an outsider, a Moabite woman like Ruth? Would he willingly take on the extra burden of caring for the bitter Naomi as well?

Although Ruth never bore a child in her previous marriage, she became pregnant and had a son soon after her marriage to Boaz. Not only would Boaz care for the widows now, but this son would care for them in the future. Upon the realization that her emptiness had been filled with the goodness and provision of the Lord, Naomi's friends say, "Blessed be the Lord who has not left you without a redeemer!"

This story carries real hope for those who are grieving, but it also carries gospel hope for all who need a spiritual redeemer, which is all of us. God has not left us without a redeemer but has sent us Jesus, who gave His life as payment for our sins so that He could redeem us from death and grant us eternal life. Like Naomi, we are not alone in our pain, for God is with us and has a plan for our redemption. He has in His divine providence given us our Redeemer—Jesus!

"GOD HAS NOT LEFT US WITHOUT A REDEEMER BUT HAS SENT US JESUS."

DAY 352
A Quiet Life

In fact, you are doing this toward all the brothers and sisters in the entire region of Macedonia. But we encourage you, brothers and sisters, to do this even more, to seek to lead a quiet life, to mind your own business, and to work with your own hands, as we commanded you, so that you may behave properly in the presence of outsiders and not be dependent on anyone.

1 THESSALONIANS 4:10–12

We see the idea of a "quiet life" referenced in 1 Thessalonians 4:11 as an encouragement written by Paul to the Thessalonians. Paul charges the saints of Thessalonica to seek the quiet life, mind their own business, and work diligently. He knows the value of this because it is so contrary to the way people in their city behaved. Similarly, in our world today, we rarely hear encouragement from the surrounding culture to live quietly. "Quietness" is often equated with passivity or indifference. However, this is not a reference to the volume of our voices but the soundness of our spirit.

Displayed through God's Word, we find that the quiet life is one of humility, contentment, and faithfulness, all hidden in the finished work of Jesus. Humility is living with a quiet peace for the life God has gifted you. It is not envious. Humility does not scream for attention. Contentment quiets the desire to do more, have more, and see more. A life of contentment rests securely, knowing that if nothing else is given to us on earth, the gift of Jesus was already more than enough. The flashing lights of earthly ambition will dim with our lives, but the eternal hope of Jesus will always shine, even beyond this life. A quiet heart of contentment is not restlessly stirring for something else but rests securely in the greatest gift ever given—salvation in Christ. In the quietness of humility and contentment, we are free to live faithfully in the work we are called to as ambassadors of Christ. God's hand is threading every act of faithfulness into the tapestry of His kingdom work.

A quiet life may not seem grand or attractive in the world's eyes. However, in God's eyes, a quiet life hidden in Christ is worthy of praise. So may our aim be a life of spiritual quietness—a powerful quietness piercing into the noise of this fallen world and speaking only to the good of God's glory and praise.

> "CONTENTMENT QUIETS THE DESIRE TO DO MORE, HAVE MORE, AND SEE MORE."

DAY 353
God Gives the Growth

So then neither the one who plants nor the one who waters is anything, but only God who gives the growth.

1 CORINTHIANS 3:7

How often do we serve another and speak to them about the gospel, only to see them walk away and seem to care less about it than they did before? We can feel defeated and may become nervous to talk to others again about what God has done for us in our lives. We may assume that we did not say the right things, or we could have made our presentation more exciting. Our critiques can be endless, but when we look at Scripture, we realize these worries are in vain. We can only receive Christ and grow spiritually if the Lord has softened our hearts to the truth of His Word. He is the One who works and develops fruit in the lives of others, not us. We are responsible only for planting seeds of truth and bringing the life-giving water these seeds need. But we do not control when or how others grow, so we relinquish those things into the Lord's hands.

When we meditate on this truth and how it applies to our lives, it offers great comfort and rest. What a beautiful thing that the Lord chooses to work through the words and actions of His people. We do not have to be skilled speakers or trained pastors to share the truth of the gospel—that Christ died so that we might be free and have eternal life with Christ, glorifying Him as long as we live on this earth and then forevermore. So as you faithfully present the message of Christ or encourage other believers, the Lord takes your words and actions and uses them to soften and change the hearts of those to whom you speak. You do not give growth, but the Lord may use you to care in a way that leads to growth.

Wherever you are and whatever season you are in, look to serve the Lord through your words and actions to others. Watch as God uses the simplest interactions to spark growth in the life of another, and praise Him for any victory you see. He is a good God—loving and kind—who is all-powerful and all-knowing. How glorious that we have the privilege of witnessing His handiwork and redemptive plan for all of our days and in eternity to come.

"THE LORD TAKES YOUR WORDS AND ACTIONS AND USES THEM TO SOFTEN AND CHANGE THE HEARTS OF THOSE TO WHOM YOU SPEAK."

DAY 354

Godly Sorrow

Grieve like a young woman dressed in sackcloth, mourning for the husband of her youth.

JOEL 1:8

Joel, a prophet, speaks to the people of Judah about how their sin has brought devastating consequences to themselves and the land in which they live. Joel uses descriptive language in the first chapter to describe a storm of locusts tearing apart the people's fields and destroying anything in its path. The way he describes these locusts should remind us of the plague of locusts God sent to Egypt as judgment. God used the plagues to try and wake Egypt up to the knowledge that there was no other God besides Him, and the plagues also encouraged the Egyptians to let God's people be free from their bondage of slavery.

But now, God was sending the same sort of plague to His people, the ones who should have known Him best. They had fallen asleep to who God was and what He commanded them to do, and because of this, they faced His wrath for their disobedience. Joel tells Judah to mourn over their sin like a young woman mourns when the husband of her youth dies. It is a picture of how the relationship between God and Judah has been broken. They have forsaken their covenant relationship with the Lord, and they need to grieve over what their sin has done.

Sometimes, when we sin against the Lord, we too quickly jump over the necessary steps of repentance and grief. Even though we have received grace from Christ and our sin no longer separates us from God, we still need to repent to the Lord and mourn the consequences of our sin. Sin hurts our fellowship with God, but it also hurts our fellowship with others. Godly sorrow is a good thing for the believer. This period of grief over sin helps us to hate sin all the more. When we are tempted to repeat a mistake, we think about the period of sorrow the sin caused us before, and it helps us see the sin as not worth the pain it produces. May we remember that we are not to stay sorrowful forever. Sorrow over sin leads to joy for God's grace and forgiveness. While we should not ignore a period of grief, we should also not ignore the joy that comes when the Lord forgives us!

"SORROW OVER SIN LEADS TO JOY FOR GOD'S GRACE AND FORGIVENESS."

DAY 355

Consider Your Soil

The sower sows the word. Some are like the word sown on the path... And others are like seed sown on rocky ground... Others are like seeds sown among thorns; these are the ones who hear the word, but the worries of this age, the deceitfulness of wealth, and the desires for other things enter in and choke the word, and it becomes unfruitful. And those like seeds sown on good ground hear the word, welcome it, and produce fruit thirty, sixty, and a hundred times what was sown.

MARK 4:14–20

The foundation of our faith is of vital importance for growth and flourishing. How we hear and receive the gospel's truth can establish our understanding of what it means to live in light of that truth. The parable of the sower provides a rich example of this reality. A seed is planted in various types of soil. The foundation of the soil depicts how well-positioned we are to grow.

Those whose faith is planted on the surface level never truly plant roots, and therefore, Satan can easily tempt them out of the truth they have come to know. That may look like using the Christian faith to gain approval, experience blessing, or using it as a means to temporarily serve our own purposes. Those whose faith is planted in the rocky ground can only establish its roots to an extent, and their faith and zeal are only short-lived. Those whose faith is planted among thorns get choked out by the cares, concerns, and desires of this world. That may look like someone gaining wealth and fortune and letting their love of money replace their love for God. It may even look like being surrounded by people who encourage you to indulge in sin instead of walking faithfully with God.

But those whose faith is planted in the good soil hear the truth of the gospel and let it permeate every part of their hearts, minds, and souls. Their faith plants roots deep into the hope of Jesus Christ, our Savior, and they find themselves anchored in Him through hardship. Whether drought, storm, or seasons of fruitlessness, the roots remain secure, and the soil surrounding them provides opportunities to flourish. Life in the good soil looks like continually preaching the gospel to ourselves, surrounding ourselves with people who will help us walk faithfully, clinging to God's Word, and hoping in the fruit God will bring from our faithfulness.

DAY 356

What Are You Looking For?

The two disciples heard him say this and followed Jesus. When Jesus turned and noticed them following him, he asked them, "What are you looking for?" They said to him, "Rabbi" (which means "Teacher"), "where are you staying?"

JOHN 1:37-38

Throughout His ministry, Jesus asked intentional questions. Often when addressed by someone, he would respond with a question to invoke a moment of self-reflection. Instead of simply providing answers, He was getting to the heart of the people. In John 1:38, we see the first recorded question in the gospels where Jesus asks, "What are you looking for?" The magnitude and weight of this question deserve our attention.

Jesus was beginning His ministry on earth. He was gathering His disciples and teaching the gospel to all who would hear it. But the call to follow Him was costly. He made it clear from the beginning that whoever followed after him must deny themselves, take up their cross, and follow Him (Matthew 16:24). It was not a short-lived movement; following Jesus was and still is a life-altering choice. It requires sacrifice and change, transformation and sanctification. The cost is worth the reward, but Jesus does not sugar-coat the necessary means to follow Him.

John the Baptist was preparing the way for Jesus's ministry, sharing the truth of who Jesus was to those closest to him. One day, while standing with two of his disciples, Jesus passed by John, who said, "Look! The Lamb of God!" (John 1:36). The two disciples were intrigued and followed Jesus. When Jesus noticed, He asked them, "What are you looking for?" This question gets to the heart of all of humanity. What are we truly looking for? What are we truly searching for in this life?

Our answer to this question can be met with the hope of Jesus every single time. If we are looking for hope, purpose, security, fulfillment, or anything else, these things can only be found in Christ. We can try to fill the void with other things, but those things will never truly give us what we desire. We find our greatest need for Jesus when we uncover what we are really searching for and realize that it can only truly be found in Him. The greatest thing we could ever seek is a relationship with Jesus. And when we seek Jesus with all of our heart, He promises we will find Him.

DAY 357
The Gift of Genealogies

So all the generations from Abraham to David were fourteen generations; and from David until the exile to Babylon, fourteen generations; and from the exile to Babylon until the Christ, fourteen generations.

MATTHEW 1:17

For many, the story of redemption in the Bible sounds too good to be true. This is one of the reasons why the secular world often views the Bible as a great mythology. However, the Bible is more than a great myth. It is an inerrant, God-inspired book we can trust to tell us the truth about God's character and Jesus Christ. One of the ways we know this is that we can trace the people of the Bible with genealogies. Two of the purposes of the Bible's genealogies are to affirm its historical reliability and show God's faithfulness. In essence, biblical genealogies are a gift to us because they confirm that biblical characters are not fictional. Instead, they are real people who walked the earth.

Furthermore, the purpose of the genealogy in Matthew is to tell the story of how God worked through real people to be faithful to His promise to restore us to Himself. We can trust this is true for a couple of reasons. First, secular culture widely accepts that Jesus was a historical figure. The majority of historians acknowledge that a person named Jesus lived and walked on the earth. We also know that Matthew did not pull this genealogy out of thin air. Instead, it was documented in the Old Testament for hundreds of years by different authors. This should strengthen our faith because it tangibly shows that God fulfills His promise to Abraham in Genesis 12 in Jesus Christ. In Genesis 12:3, God says to Abraham that "all peoples on earth will be blessed through you." And through this genealogy, we know that Jesus fulfills this promise by coming to earth, dying on the cross, and resurrecting on the third day so that God could restore us to Himself.

When we examine this genealogy today, we see what a gift it is. We can see how God fulfilled His promises to Abraham, Jacob, and David. How incredible that God offers so much evidence of His faithfulness throughout Scripture. And this evidence is not abstract. Through genealogies, we see concrete proof that Jesus was a real person who came to earth through Abraham's lineage. May we be filled with hope as we read genealogies and see how the Lord is faithful to fulfill all of His promises.

DAY 358
Jesus is the Fulfillment

He told them, "These are my words that I spoke to you while I was still with you—that everything written about me in the Law of Moses, the Prophets, and the Psalms must be fulfilled."

LUKE 24:44

Throughout Jesus's ministry, He answered many of His disciples' questions. They were confused and in amazement of their teacher, and though they would affirm who He was, they would also reveal that they did not understand how Jesus was the fulfillment of everything God had promised. However, Jesus knew that eventually, they would understand and take His message to the ends of the earth.

After Jesus died on the cross for our sins, He was buried. For three days, the disciples hid in fear from the religious rulers who sentenced Jesus to death, and they mourned His loss. But on the third day, Jesus rose from the dead, defeating the power of sin and death. The disciples knew He had risen, for when the women who followed Jesus went to His tomb, the stone in front was rolled away, and Jesus's body was gone. Two men in dazzling clothes appeared to the women, telling them that Jesus had risen just as He said He would. The women reported this message to the disciples, and Peter ran to the tomb to see what the women had seen—an empty tomb with no body.

When Jesus appeared to the disciples physically, He was in their very midst. They must have been in both awe and disbelief. They knew Jesus died, though many of them had fled the scene of His arrest. Could this really be Him? Jesus let them see His scars and touch them. He had accomplished what He said He would. And, while they sat in disbelief and joy in His presence, He opened their minds to understand Scripture and see how He was at the center of it all. Jesus had spoken many of these things while He was with them before His crucifixion, but now they finally understood. Jesus is the Savior God promised from the very beginning (Genesis 3:15).

As we read Scripture, we have an incredible opportunity to see how Jesus fulfills His promises from cover to cover. He stands as the centerpiece to the story of redemption—His Word—and as we read it, we discover more of Him. Each piece of God's Word is anchored in who He is and what He did upon the cross to save the ones He loved.

"JESUS IS THE SAVIOR GOD PROMISED FROM THE VERY BEGINNING."

DAY 359
The Glory of Christmas

Then an angel of the Lord stood before them, and the glory of the Lord shone around them, and they were terrified. But the angel said to them, "Don't be afraid, for look, I proclaim to you good news of great joy that will be for all the people: Today in the city of David a Savior was born for you, who is the Messiah, the Lord."

LUKE 2:9–11

So much joy and wonder fill the Christmas season. Children count down the days until Christmas Day and cannot wait to wake up that morning. As we grow older, the wonder of Christmas can sometimes fade. We forget what Christmas is about as the holidays throw us into a busy season of preparation. But what if we would see Christmas as an opportunity to be like a child again—wide-eyed and in awe of its glorious nature?

When the shepherds saw the display of angels before them, they were moved to terror. Yet, it was not the angels who overwhelmed them but the glory of God shining. The angels did not want the shepherds to be afraid, for they had come to share a message with them that would change everything. A baby was born who was the Messiah, the One for whom they had been waiting for so long. This good news was followed with an encore of praise, giving glory to the Lord. Through the angels' worship, we learn what Christmas is all about—the good news of Jesus Christ.

Hearing the good news from the angels and seeing the display of glory propelled the shepherds to find Jesus. They wanted to find this child, this King. But the good news of Jesus also led the shepherds to share about Jesus (Luke 2:17–18). Do you find yourself amazed by Jesus during the Christmas season? Do you stop and revel over the glory of God that was revealed through a baby boy in a manger?

Do not let the busyness of the holidays distract you from the glory of Christmas. Step into the shoes of the shepherds, and become overwhelmed in joy over the Messiah's birth. The baby born in Bethlehem grew up to offer Himself as a sacrifice on our behalf. His triumph over death would bring about peace on earth by reconciling sinners to their God. May the gospel be at the center of the Christmas season. But may the glory of Christmas also move us to proclaim the good news for all to hear.

"WHAT IF WE WOULD SEE CHRISTMAS AS AN OPPORTUNITY TO BE LIKE A CHILD AGAIN—WIDE-EYED AND IN AWE OF ITS GLORIOUS NATURE?"

DAY 360
Where the Weary Find Strength

Do you not know? Have you not heard? The Lord is the everlasting God, the Creator of the whole earth. He never becomes faint or weary; there is no limit to his understanding. He gives strength to the faint and strengthens the powerless. Youths may become faint and weary, and young men stumble and fall, but those who trust in the Lord will renew their strength; they will soar on wings like eagles; they will run and not become weary; they will walk and not faint.

ISAIAH 40:28-31

Life can be taxing, and every day it can feel as though rest is out of reach. Our daily responsibilities can quickly drain our strength, and we can sometimes think that we must be the ones to re-fuel that strength. It is not surprising that we feel this way as we see the world praising independence and self-sufficiency, which only perpetuates weariness. Soon we discover that we do not have enough strength in ourselves to maintain rest. We need something greater to give us strength.

There is good news for the weary soul: you do not have to find strength in yourself. Isaiah 40 teaches us how we gain strength from a God who never grows weary. We may be limited in our strength, but God's strength is unlimited. In His kindness, God does not keep His strength to Himself but freely distributes it to His people. Those who trust God find their strength renewed. We must turn from our own self-sufficiency and place our trust in a God who is all-sufficient. However, this takes humility as we must lay down our belief that we can be strong on our own. As we come to the Lord for strength, we surrender our self-sufficiency, celebrating that we have a God who stands ready to help us.

As we lean on the Lord's strength, we will find our own strength renewed. We need the Lord every day, which means we must come to the Lord for strength every day. Jesus tells us in John 15 that apart from Him, we cannot do anything. This could not be any more true! Our union with the Lord means that we are eternally connected to a source of strength. The more we abide in Christ and rely on Him, the more we will find rest. May we trust in Him and experience the renewal He so graciously provides.

"AS WE COME TO THE LORD FOR STRENGTH, WE SURRENDER OUR SELF-SUFFICIENCY, CELEBRATING THAT WE HAVE A GOD WHO STANDS READY TO HELP US."

DAY 361
Why the Resurrection Matters

And if Christ has not been raised, your faith is worthless; you are still in your sins.

1 CORINTHIANS 15:17

Though we know the resurrection is true, we sometimes go through our days without acknowledging the importance of the resurrection in our lives. However, the validity and significance of the resurrection should matter to us every day. Without the continual reminder of Christ's overcoming the grave, we can quickly forget vital gospel truths that encourage us as followers of Christ. And what vital truths they are in the Christian faith. In 1 Corinthians 15, the Apostle Paul explains that if the gospel message is not true, if Christ has not truly risen from the grave, then our faith is meaningless.

Without Christ's resurrection, forgiveness is unattainable. If Jesus did not rise from the dead, there would be no salvation from sin. We would still be in our sinful state, with no hope of forgiveness or redemption. But we know from God's Word that Jesus did rise from the grave. And through Christ's resurrection, Jesus declared victory over sin and death, offering those who trust in Him salvation and eternal life with Him. This truth of the resurrection allows us to live each day with confident assurance in our God.

Without the truth of the resurrection, our faith would, in fact, be futile. There would be no grounds for our faith and nothing rooting our faith in the truth. Yet, because Jesus did rise from the dead, we can be encouraged in our faith. The gospel message that we believe and declare is a message of truth, for Christ indeed conquered the grave. We do not have blind faith but faith that is rooted in the risen King. The resurrection confirms that our faith is not worthless. What we believe is real and grounded in unshakable truth, and we read of that truth over and over again in God's Word.

May we take time to daily consider and meditate on the resurrection of Christ. Through the resurrection, we have security, assurance, and comfort. We can press on as followers of Christ with boldness, knowing that our faith is not in vain. We can look to our future with hope and at our sins with triumph, knowing that God forgives us completely. Christ's resurrection matters, so let us cling to the great truth it declares.

> "MAY WE TAKE TIME TO DAILY CONSIDER AND MEDITATE ON THE RESURRECTION OF CHRIST. THROUGH THE RESURRECTION, WE HAVE SECURITY, ASSURANCE, AND COMFORT."

DAY 362
Sin Over-promises and Under-delivers

"No! You will certainly not die," the serpent said to the woman. "In fact, God knows that when you eat it your eyes will be opened and you will be like God, knowing good and evil." — Genesis 3:4–5

The Lord God said, "Since the man has become like one of us, knowing good and evil, he must not reach out, take from the tree of life, eat, and live forever." So the Lord God sent him away from the garden of Eden to work the ground from which he was taken. — Genesis 3:22–23

This world is filled with things that seem enticing. In a similar way, Satan uses advertising tactics to direct our eyes toward sin. Often he does so by filling our minds with false promises of what sin can offer us. Maybe we gossip because we believe a subconscious idea that we will make ourselves look better. Maybe we idolize materialism because we believe earthly treasures will make us happy. Maybe we engage in sexual sin because we believe it is the only way to feel loved. There are a myriad of promises sins offer us. And because we are all sinners and live in a fallen world, we know those promises can never hold true. Even if they temporarily give us what we want, they will all eventually fail us.

Sin over-promises and under-delivers. It cannot hold the weight of the fulfillment we are really searching for and will always lead us away from the only One who offers us what we need. Adam and Eve fell victim to Satan's false promise that if they disobeyed God and ate from the Tree of Knowledge of Good and Evil, they would be like God. But instead, they received death and were cast out of God's presence into a world broken by sin for every generation that would follow.

Praise be to God that He does not leave us to forever chase after the empty promises of sin. He fulfilled the most astounding promise when He sent a Savior to rescue us from sin. God saves believers from sin and seals them with the hope-filled promise of eternal union with God. Sin could never offer anything comparable. When sin tempts us to believe lies, may our affections and desires be ruled and shaped by an ultimate hope in Christ—the only One who perfectly promises and perfectly delivers in every way.

"SIN OVER-PROMISES AND UNDER-DELIVERS."

DAY 363
Standing Firm in the Truth

So then, brothers and sisters, stand firm and hold to the traditions you were taught, whether by what we said or what we wrote.

2 THESSALONIANS 2:15

Paul makes it clear in his second letter to the Christians at Thessalonica that Christianity is not a passive religion. There was confusion among the Thessalonians about Christ's second coming. Some believed He had already come, while others thought He was coming soon. Paul used the confusion among the Thessalonians to teach a timeless lesson—that if Christians do not actively hold fast to the Word of God, we will be swept off our feet and swept away into confusion, chaos, and untruth.

"Stand" and "hold" are both action words. "Stand" as a verb means "to take up or maintain a specified position or posture," while "hold" as a verb means "to have or maintain in the grasp." Both words include the word "maintain" in their definition. As Christians, we must maintain our stance and hold on to the truth. It takes daily care and attention to maintain something. A garden cannot be maintained without being watered and weeded. A car cannot be maintained without fuel and frequent tune-ups. A Christian cannot maintain a pure and vibrant faith without dedication to the study and application of Scripture. Of course, the Thessalonians did not yet have the entire Bible as it was still being written. But they did have the spoken and written words of Paul. He urged them to stand firm in what he had taught them. And we are urged to stand firm in the whole counsel of Scripture. What might change if you awoke each morning with the intent to actively maintain your understanding of and application of Scripture? What would you do if you really believed that standing firm in and holding fast to God's Word would prevent chaos and confusion from shipwrecking your faith? How can you actively stand firm in the truth today?

The next two verses are a great encouragement to us in our pursuit of lives firmly planted in the truth. 2 Thessalonians 2:16–17 read, "May our Lord Jesus Christ himself and God our Father, who has loved us and given us eternal encouragement and good hope by grace, encourage your hearts and strengthen you in every good work and word." Jesus loves us and is eternally encouraging us toward every good work and word. We do not persist in the faith alone, for He is with us every step of the way!

"A CHRISTIAN CANNOT MAINTAIN A PURE AND VIBRANT FAITH WITHOUT DEDICATION TO THE STUDY AND APPLICATION OF SCRIPTURE."

DAY 364
Sin Grows Best in the Dark

The one who conceals his sins will not prosper, but whoever confesses and renounces them will find mercy.

PROVERBS 28:13

There is a common experiment where one slice of bread is placed in a dark place, and one slice is placed in a well-lit area. The goal is to document which slice of bread begins to mold more quickly. In comparing the two slices, we would find that mold grows faster in the dark than in the light. The same is true for our sin; it grows faster when hidden in the dark. If our sins are left unexposed, they will only fester over time.

As Christians, we can be tempted to keep our sin in the dark due to fear of the consequences that come with exposing it. Maybe we fear what others will think of us. Maybe we fear humiliation. We may even fear losing our "perfect" appearance. But where does hiding leave us? Is it really better than being exposed? Hiding can only last for so long if we desire a deep and meaningful relationship with others and an honest relationship with God. Sin invades, entices, dilutes, distorts, and devours. When we fear our sin coming to light, we never truly deal with it, which leaves no room for repentance and change. We should never minimize or overlook the temptations of sin or ignore Satan's crafty schemes. And we should certainly not ignore the consequences of covering up our sin. Doing so will only grow and entangle us more over time, eventually enslaving us to it.

If we do succeed in hiding our sin from others, our sin is never hidden from God. God knows every facet of our being—our thoughts, intentions, and actions. Therefore, God, in His sovereignty, had a plan of redemption, a plan to send His Son to die on our behalf, to bear the weight of all the sin that pushes us into the shadows. He rose from the grave three days later so that all who repent of their sin and seek forgiveness in Jesus are raised up to walk in the light with Him. God knows the most detestable parts of our hearts and still chose to send His Son to rescue us. He sanctifies us into His likeness. He carries our sin to the cross and clothes us with radiant faces (Psalm 34:5). As we confess and repent of our sins, bringing them to light, Christ promises to meet us with mercy and forgiveness.

"GOD KNOWS EVERY FACET OF OUR BEING—OUR THOUGHTS, INTENTIONS, AND ACTIONS."

DAY 365
Come, Lord Jesus

He who testifies about these things says, "Yes, I am coming soon." Amen! Come, Lord Jesus!

REVELATION 22:20

Having something to look forward to has that way of filling us with delight in the present. Whether it be a much-needed vacation or a visit from a friend we have not seen in a while, knowing that something good is coming soon brings us joy. Yet when life grows somewhat monotonous and mundane, our delight and excitement can diminish. If there is nothing to look forward to, our days can feel long. What joy that, as believers in Christ, we do not have to live without hope or delight for the future. We have a sure promise from the lips of Jesus Himself: Jesus is coming back, and He is coming soon.

We should be filled with great anticipation, knowing that Jesus is returning soon. God is not leaving us to remain in a broken world forever. In fact, He came into the world so that through His sacrifice, we could be made whole again one day. Jesus is coming back, and He is going to make all things new—He will come to redeem and restore the brokenness of this life. In the moments the present seems mundane, difficult, or painful, may we set our eyes on Christ. When the brokenness of the world feels too heavy, we can whisper in hope, "Come Lord Jesus." Our surest hope in the sufferings of life is that Jesus is coming soon. Even when it feels as though our wait is long, Jesus is closer than we realize.

May the reminder that Jesus is coming soon bring us patience and perseverance in the present. On the days when His new and glorious kingdom feels so far away, let us rest in our coming Christ. As we wait for Jesus, let us also use our time intentionally in the present. Just as we prepare and make ready for a visit from a friend, let us prepare and make ready for our coming Christ (Matthew 24:46). Let us remain active in our call as disciple-makers. We have an important role in sharing the gospel with others, and knowing Jesus is coming soon should fuel our evangelism. May we not sit on the sidelines but work diligently until the day Christ returns. When the journey feels long, allow these words to wash over your weariness and your doubts: He is coming soon! Come, Lord Jesus!

"AS WE WAIT FOR JESUS, LET US ALSO USE OUR TIME INTENTIONALLY IN THE PRESENT."

Jesus is coming back, and He is coming soon.

May the *security of our salvation* move us in gratitude for the grace of God.

> Day 105
> THE GOSPEL CHANGES EVERYTHING

*Thank you for studying
God's Word with us!*

CONNECT WITH US
@thedailygraceco
@dailygracepodcast

CONTACT US
info@thedailygraceco.com

SHARE
#thedailygraceco

VISIT US ONLINE
www.thedailygraceco.com

MORE DAILY GRACE
The Daily Grace App
Daily Grace Podcast